Is This The Real Life?

THE UNTOLD STORY OF

QUEEN

MARK BLAKE

First published 2010 by
Aurum Press Limited
7 Greenland Street
London NW1 0ND
www.aurumpress.co.uk

This paperback edition published in 2011

A catalogue record for this book is available from the British Library.

ISBN 978 1 84513 713 7
E-book ISBN 978 1 84513 659 8

10 9 8 7 6 5 4 3 2 1
2015 2014 2013 2012 2011

Typeset by SX Composing DTP, Rayleigh, Essex

Printed and bound by CPI Group (UK) Ltd, Croydon, CR0 4YY

Contents

CHAPTER ONE

You Beautiful People

'Tell the old faggot it's gonna be the biggest thing that
ever happened.'
Bob Geldof persuading Queen to play Live Aid

'Hello World!'
Audience banner at Live Aid, Wembley Stadium

'I have to win people over. That's part of my duty. It's
all to do with feeling in control.'
Freddie Mercury, 1985

It is 13 July 1985, and for rock stars of a certain vintage, it's a difficult time. Many who came of age in the sixties and seventies are
living off past glories and the blind goodwill of fans. The world
has yet to invent the pensioner rock star, and Pete Townshend's
adolescent mission statement 'Hope I die before I get old' has never
seemed more ill-judged.

Today's Live Aid concerts in Philadelphia and London will unite
musicians of every age. The common cause is to raise funds for
Ethiopian famine relief, but there is another agenda. There
are over eighty thousand people in the audience at London's
Wembley Stadium alone, and a satellite TV link-up means that a
further 400 million people in over fifty countries will witness the
action, both good and bad. Reputations will be made and lost,
while those watching donate a total of £150 million to aid the
starving people of Africa.

Over the next few hours, this global audience will see an under-rehearsed Bob Dylan, an underwhelming Led Zeppelin, and pop peacocks Mick Jagger and David Bowie shaking their tail feathers in each other's faces. Live Aid will prove a pivotal moment in the careers of the still-novice U2 and Madonna, but will do nothing for the longevity of Adam Ant, Howard Jones or the Thompson Twins. For Dire Straits and Phil Collins, the ubiquitous multi-platinum-sellers of the day, it will never get any bigger than this.

Into this disparate mix comes a rock group with 14 long years on the clock. This multi-millionaire band (listed in the 1982 *Guinness Book of Records* as Britain's highest-paid company directors) have notched up a daunting run of hit singles and albums, with a restless musical style encompassing rock, pop, funk, heavy metal, even gospel. While their reputation as a supreme live act precedes them, even their most loyal supporters couldn't have predicted what would happen today.

At 6.44 p.m., the group's appearance is heralded by the arrival of TV comedians Mel Smith and Griff Rhys Jones. Smith is dressed as an officious police sergeant, Jones as his hapless constable. The gag is simple: authority versus 'the kids', and the pair's jokes – 'there have been complaints about the noise . . . from a woman in Belgium' – help whip up the crowd but are almost drowned out by the sound of the road crew behind them making last-minute adjustments. Finally, Smith removes his copper's helmet, jams it under his armpit, and stands to attention for 'Her Majesty . . . Queen!'

Interviewed later, Live Aid's organiser Bob Geldof will try to describe the inherent oddness of these four individuals. Bounding onstage at Live Aid, they look, as Geldof says, 'like the most unlikely rock band you could imagine'.

John Deacon (Geldof: 'the reserved bass guitarist') takes up his position at the back, close to the drum riser. Despite a pop star's shaggy perm, he most resembles the electronics engineer he'd have become had a career in music not panned out. Earlier in the day, when the band had been summoned to line up and meet Live Aid's royal guests, the Prince and Princess of Wales, thousands of Queen fans watching on TV wondered why a man that looked suspiciously like a roadie had taken John Deacon's place. 'I was too shy to go and meet Princess Diana. I thought I'd make a fool of myself,' he said later, admitting he'd sent his roadie, Spider, instead.

Brian May, of the praying-mantis physique and busby of dark curls ('the hippy guitarist', says Geldof), looks almost unchanged since the group began. May undercut his guitar-hero posings with a naturally studious manner. For the Bachelor of Science and former schoolteacher, guitar playing is a serious business. In the early days, May would mutter under his breath like a tennis player psyching himself for an important point.

Meanwhile, you wonder if Roger Taylor isn't frustrated at spending his working life hidden behind a drum kit. With his blond coiffure and dainty features (he once grew a beard to stop people mistaking him for a girl) and offstage passion for sports cars and model girlfriends, Taylor is the band's most obvious pop star. In recent years, his bass drum skin has been decorated with a close-up picture of his face, visible from even the cheapest seats. While Taylor remains largely unseen, he will not go unheard; his distinct, cracked backing vocals are an essential part of Queen's sound.

Whatever Freddie Mercury's bandmates do over the next twenty-two minutes, they rarely divert attention from, as Geldof calls him, 'that outrageous lead singer'. At the very beginning, Mercury was a glam-rock pimpernel. Not now. The hair is short and greased back; the satin Zandra Rhodes creations of old replaced by a gym vest and snug pale jeans.

When it comes to his sexuality, Mercury has been playing cat-and-mouse with the press for years, but his image is clearly modelled on the 'Castro Clone' look popular in US gay circles. The finishing touches include a studded bracelet circling his right bicep, and a dense moustache – Freddie's trademark – almost, though not quite, covering his oversized teeth. When Mercury jogs on stage, his exaggerated gait suggests a ballet dancer running for a bus.

It's difficult to imagine any twenty-first-century music business Svengali or reality TV judge buying into the notion of the 38-year-old Mercury as a global pop star. And yet, in years to come, Mercury will have more in common with today's wannabes than history currently allows. Years before Live Aid, as an art student with musical ambitions, the man born Farrokh Bulsara told anyone who would listen that he would 'be a star one day'. Few believed him.

Despite their usually unshakeable self-belief, the band are keenly aware that this not just their crowd. Not for them, then, the sloppy approach taken by some of their peers. This band have drilled themselves with four days of intensive rehearsals, timing their twenty-minute set to the very last second, and selecting their songs for maximum impact. After a quick lap of the stage, Freddie Mercury seats himself at a piano stage left. The audience erupts as he picks out the opening figure to 'Bohemian Rhapsody' – how else to start? – crossing his hands with a camp flourish to play the high notes. As he delivers the opening line, the crowd responds again. The song's sense of melodrama is undiminished, despite the piano being adorned not with candelabra, but Pepsi-branded cups and plastic glasses of lager. Undaunted and already in the moment, Freddie manages to sing as if he's conveying a message of world-shattering importance. Today, Live Aid will belong to Queen.

■ ■ ■

The rest of the band joins in, with May weaving in his baroque guitar solo, and then, without warning, Mercury jumps to his feet, 'Bohemian Rhapsody' cut off at its first big crescendo and before it overstays its welcome.

Freddie's roadie Peter Hince hoves into view, passing the singer his instantly recognisable prop – a sawn-off mic stand. Mercury prowls the lip of the stage, punching the air, cocking his head and pouting. Behind him, Taylor beats out the introduction to 'Radio Ga Ga', Queen's number 2 hit from the year before. With its modish synthesiser and electronic rhythm it is the antithesis of 'Bohemian Rhapsody'.

The song's lyrics are an indignant commentary on the state of modern radio, sweetened by a singsong chorus. But its promo video, with scenes lifted from the 1920s sci-fi movie *Metropolis*, which helped to sell the song. Today, on the first chorus, the audience mimics a scene in the video, with thousands of hands above heads clapping as one. 'I'd never seen anything like that in my life,' admitted Brian May later.

From here on, the group appears invincible. Mercury teases the audience, flexing his vocal cords with some call-and-response banter, before launching into 'Hammer to Fall'. A modest hit, its comic-book heavy metal is still made for stadiums such as these. A visibly more relaxed Brian May whips out the riff, while Mercury joshes with the onstage cameraman, mugging into his lens, before prancing around the guitarist like a matador goading a bull. Then, while May scrubs away, Mercury fixes the crowd with a mischievous smile and starts tugging the end of the microphone, now pointing out at crotch level.

Less lusty rock star, more naughty schoolboy, the twinkle in Freddie's eye suggests that he takes none of this, including himself, seriously. Live Aid's worthy cause and the disposition of many pop stars has resulted in plenty of furrowed brows on the Wembley stage today. Not, it seems, on Queen's watch. 'They understood the idea that Live Aid was a global jukebox,' said Geldof. 'And that Freddie could ponce about in front of the whole world.'

Onstage, Queen may have already tasted victory, but behind the scenes it was a different story. In November 1984 they had been absent from the recording of the Band Aid single, in which pop's great and good (and less good) had collaborated on a charity record to aid Ethiopia. 'We were all in separate parts of the globe at the time,' Mercury said later. In reality, having just completed shows in South Africa's Sun City for which they'd been lambasted, Queen had been licking their wounds before resuming a world tour.

Tension between the band members had often led to creativity in the studio, but by 1985 Queen were, as Roger Taylor, put it 'feeling jaded'. The drummer's frank assessment that the band had 'outlasted some of our marriages' didn't exclude that same marriage from now being on the rocks. Years of touring, making music and generally accommodating each other's egos had taken its toll.

Queen's most recent album, *The Works*, had restored some of the momentum lost when 1982's *Hot Space*, with its dance grooves and noticeable lack of guitar, proved an experiment too far. Queen's star had waned, especially in the US. There had been numerous problems: wrangles with the American record label; a lack of airplay; divisive influences within the Freddie camp; and the promo video for the single 'I Want To Break Free', in which Queen dragged up in women's clothes (much loved in the UK, but less so in the US).

May, Taylor and Mercury had all made solo albums, with Freddie's debut released just two months before Live Aid. None had yet succeeded in forging a separate identity as a solo artist away from what Brian May called 'The Mothership'. The plan after Live Aid was for Queen to take time off, and not to tour again for at least five years, if at all.

Later, Live Aid promoter Harvey Goldsmith will applaud the band for not fighting for a later, more prestigious slot on the bill. But it was all part of the plan. Years before, while waiting for Queen to get their big break, Brian May had watched David Bowie unveil his Ziggy Stardust alter ego onstage and been struck with jealousy, wondering when it would be Queen's turn to make their mark. Later, Queen had shared management with Elton John, and fought for attention. Tonight, Bowie and Elton will follow Queen, giving the band the perfect opportunity to upstage both of them. Meanwhile, Queen's early evening slot means their performance will also be screened on American TV.

After 'Hammer to Fall', Mercury takes his first pause for breath. Slipping a guitar over his shoulders, he addresses the crowd. 'This song . . . ah . . . is dedicated to you beautiful people here tonight,' he tells them. 'Ah . . . that means all of you . . . thank you for coming along and making this a great occasion.'

The musical mood flips again. Having already delivered what Brian May calls 'mock-opera', synth-pop and heavy metal, it's time for the cod-rockabilly of Queen's 1979 hit 'Crazy Little Thing Called Love'. Mercury claimed he wrote while sitting it in the bath. By the song's last lap, Freddie has stopped strumming the guitar altogether, slung it over his back and trotted to the front to tease the crowd, as if he can't quite stand to leave them alone even for a few seconds.

On the home run now, Roger Taylor hammers away at the familiar tattoo to 'We Will Rock You' while the audience takes over from Mercury on the first chorus. An hour and a half before

Queen, U2 had delivered an arresting performance, but a fan's U2 banner seems out of place now. May's distorted guitar solo hurries 'We Will Rock You' to its conclusion, before Mercury returns to the piano.

'We Are the Champions' is the Queen song that has always worked the band's fiercest detractors into a lather. In 1977, the song's shameless sentiment – bigger, better, more, and damn the losers – was at odds with the prevailing musical mood of the time. Back then, a generation of younger punk bands singing about real-life issues was supposed to depose the likes of Queen. Live Aid's audience, some of whom may never have counted themselves as fans before today, care not one iota. 'We Are the Champions' is a Hollywood blockbuster of a song, a piece of escapist tosh, just like last year's *Terminator* or next year's *Top Gun* movies. There could be no other way to end the show.

Bowie, Elton John and Paul McCartney will all follow in Queen's wake, but to no avail. In just 20 minutes the consummate stadium rock band have run the gamut from rock opera to electro-pop to heavy metal to rockabilly and power ballads: every song a hive, every song instantly recognisable and infectiously memorable. It is an unforgettable performance that will have a lasting impact on the band itself. 'Live Aid was a shot in the arm for us,' said Roger Taylor. All plans for rest and recuperation are put on hold. The rocky marriage is, it seems, back on course. But then as Freddie Mercury admits, 'When you've tasted success as beautifully as I have, you don't want to let it go in a hurry.'

CHAPTER TWO

Are You Experienced?

'Freddie Mercury was very much his own creation. He made himself.'

Roger Taylor

'Never in my wildest dreams would I have imagined someone like Brian May would be a rock 'n' roller.'

Freddie Mercury

'Roger Taylor is the Peter Pan of rock.'

Brian May

It is Christmas 1964, and at Isleworth Polytechnic – just six miles from the noisy sprawl of Heathrow Airport – the drama group is staging its end-of-term production. Arnold Wesker's social drama *The Kitchen* is the story of a thwarted love affair between a young chef and a married waitress.

The part of the porter, Dimitri, a Cypriot frustrated by his menial job, is played by an eighteen-year-old art foundation course student named Farrokh Bulsara, known to all as 'Fred'. Eager to fit in, and to be involved with any of the college's social activities, Bulsara is popular with his peers and instantly recognisable for his trademark jacket: a maroon-coloured blazer slightly too small for him that he brought with him from his previous home on the island of Zanzibar. In *The Kitchen*, Fred Bulsara has traded the blazer for a white porter's jacket. His stage prop is a broom.

Ten years later, the front page headline of the 28 December 1974 edition of *Melody Maker* is 'QUEEN'S CHRISTMAS MESSAGE'. Beneath it is a photograph of Queen's lead singer Freddie Mercury, looking illustrious in fur waistcoat, flanked by seasonal tinsel and proffering a glass of champagne. Alongside his head is a speech bubble with the word 'Cheers!' Queen have ended the year on a high. After an earlier number 2 album, *Sheer Heart Attack*, the final date of their latest tour at a 6,000-seat venue in Barcelona has sold out in twenty-four hours.

Inside the paper is an interview with Queen, but for one ex-Isleworth Polytechnic student, there is something oddly familiar about the photographs of Freddie Mercury. The photographer has captured Freddie's popular habit of sucking his lower lip to conceal his top front teeth. Despite the rock-star hair and clothes, it is an immediate giveaway. 'That was when it clicked that it was Fred Bulsara,' remembers his old college friend. 'That nervous tic was even more of a distinct trademark than the maroon blazer.'

Just a few months before Freddie made his UK stage debut in *The Kitchen*, his family had arrived in England for the first time. Farrokh Bulsara was born on 5 September 1946 in Zanzibar City on Unguja, the largest of Zanzibar's two islands. A protectorate of the British Empire since the late nineteenth century, Zanzibar was once the epicentre of the African slave trade; its prime industry had since become the export of spices.

Freddie's father Bomi worked as a High Court cashier for the British governor. His wife Jer had joined him in Zanzibar from Gujarat, Western India. Both were Parsee Indians, followers of Zoroastrianism, one of the world's oldest religions. Many Parsees had fled to the Indian subcontinent centuries before to escape persecution in their original home of Persia. A thriving Parsee community had grown up on Zanzibar. Bulsara's birth date fell on the Parsee New Year's Day, and the name Farrokh was especially fashionable in the religious community. As a young boy, the future Freddie Mercury was initiated into the faith with the traditional Naojote ceremony involving the recitation of ancient prayers and a bathing ritual.

As the family of a senior civil servant the Bulsaras enjoyed a comfortable standard of living in Zanzibar City's ancient Stone

Town district. They employed domestic staff, including an *ayah* (nanny) for their young son and his baby sister Kashmira, who was born in 1952. 'By Zanzibar standards, they were upper middle-class,' recalls a family friend. 'It was a common thing for folks in that income group to have some additional help. They weren't rich, but Bomi had the income of a civil servant working for the colonial government, which meant he could afford an Austin Mini as his family car.'

Freddie himself would claim to have had what he called a 'sheltered' upbringing, recalling the splendour of his uncle's villa in Dar es Salaam in neighbouring Tanganyika: 'I'd be woken by the servant. Clutching an orange juice, I'd literally step out on to the beach.' In truth, Freddie's paternal uncle, Manchershaw Bulsara, worked for the Zanzibar Electrical and Telegraph Company, also in Stone Town. Interviewed in 1974, Mercury would also scotch the notion that he'd enjoyed a privileged childhood, deploying the smoke-and-mirrors approach he liked to use when asked about his personal life: 'It wasn't as affluent as people think. But I suppose I give the appearance of being affluent. I love that.'

At the age of five Freddie began attending the local missionary school, and showed the first glimmer of interest in music, singing for his family and guests at social functions. In early 1955, his life would undergo its first upheaval. Believing that his education on Zanzibar was limited, the Bulsaras enrolled their eight-year-old son at a boarding school in India. 'I was a precocious child,' said Mercury. 'My parents thought boarding school would do me good.'

Later, when asked by one interviewer why he was 'so sensitively defensive of his Persian roots and the family ties he has in India', Mercury snapped, 'Oh, you sod. Don't ask me about it. Oh, it's so mundane.' During his lifetime then, the finer details of his upbringing remained vague. Contrary to earlier claims, the Bulsaras did not move as a family to India. Instead, Freddie alone made the voyage to Bombay (now Mumbai), where his maternal and paternal aunts lived.

Once in India, Freddie travelled by train 168 miles north to his new school in the Maharashtrian province. According to its records, Bulsara began his new life at St Peter's Boys School in Panchgani in 1955. St Peter's was founded in 1902. It ran on traditional disciplinarian lines, with a school motto of 'Ut Prosim' ('I may profit'), and had an outstanding academic record, priding itself on educating its pupils to English university standard. While welcoming pupils of many faiths, including Parsees, St Peter's was essentially a Church of England school. It also adopted many of the traits of the English public school system. Boys roomed together in dormitories, and Freddie became part of Ashlin House, one of four schoolhouses. In a letter from 1958, Bulsara wrote: 'My friends at the Ashlin House are like a second family.' It was a fortunate arrangement, given his physical distance from the real thing.

Another pupil, in the year above Freddie, remembered him as 'a shy, timid boy, who had to wear a very painful brace on his teeth', and who could sometimes be the victim of cruel comments from his schoolmates. 'Of course there were feelings of being sent away from my parents and sister − feelings of loneliness, feelings of rejection − but you had to do what you told,' Mercury said later. 'So the sensible thing was to make the most of it. One thing boarding school taught me was to fend for myself.'

At St Peter's, Fred became friends with Subash Shah, the school's only other pupil from Zanzibar. 'We were born on the same day and in the same year, my parents knew his father, but we had never seen each other in Stone Town,' says Shah now. During some school holidays, the two would make the long trip back home together. 'We were together on that ship twice. It would stop in the Seychelles, Mombassa, Zanzibar and then on to South Africa.' To pass the time, the boys played endless games of table tennis, at which Freddie became an expert. 'On one trip the captain realised that there were a few of us from the same school travelling together,' says Shah. It was here that the future Freddie Mercury experienced his first upgrade. 'Most of us were travelling third class, but the captain made an exception and let us join the second- and first-class customers, which meant we had special privileges and much better games.'

During other school holidays, when he couldn't take the ship, Freddie would remain at St Peter's or stay at his maternal grandmother and aunt's house in Bombay or with friends from school. It was his Aunt Sheroo who noticed he was becoming a good artist, and she bought him a set of oil paints. She also spotted his growing interest in music and suggested to his parents that they sign him up for piano lessons at the school. With the encouragement of his teachers, Freddie studied with an elderly Irish pianist, who, according to one former pupil, 'absolutely doted on him'.

During his first few terms, Freddie became close friends with four other pupils in Ashlin House: Bruce Murray, Farang Irani, Derrick Branche and Victory Rana. 'We used to listen to the pop charts on the radio,' recalls Bruce Murray now. 'It was a programme sponsored by a toothpaste company. We'd hear these songs, and then Freddie would go to the piano and play them note-perfect, only after hearing them once. His passion was for Little Richard, Fats Domino, Cliff Richard . . .' Subash Shah adds, 'His knowledge of Hindi was limited but he could also listen to Indian songs and somehow capture the same rhythm on the piano. When he wanted to, he could be incredibly focused.' Freddie joined most of his friends in the school choir, which gave them a rare opportunity to mix with pupils from the affiliated girls' school. 'Hindu, Muslim, Christian . . . if you could sing you were in the choir,' says Murray.

Although shy, the future Freddie Mercury's flair for drama showed itself at St Peter's, in more ways than one. He played a doctor in the school's production of the nineteenth-century farce *Cure for the Fidgets*, and, during one performance, was accidentally jabbed in the backside by another actor's sword. Outraged, he slapped the guilty pupil across the face and stormed off the stage. 'There was a side to him which was somewhat frenzied,' recalled Derrick Branche, who likened the teenage Freddie's demeanour to that of Dean Martin's goofball comedy partner Jerry Lewis: 'Hands flapping and legs going every which way.'

In Panchgani, the boys were surrounded by classical and Indian music, but Western pop was the soundtrack of choice. As Bruce Murray explains, 'We all wanted to be Elvis.' Three years into their time at school, Freddie, Bruce, Farang, Derrick and Victory formed their own group, The Hectics. The band commandeered the art room close to their new dormitory, and drove their art teacher to distraction with their primitive twanging and thumping. Murray sang, Branche played guitar, Rana the drums, while Farang Irani copied the popular English skiffle groups of the time by fashioning a makeshift one-string bass out of a tea chest, a stick of wood and a piece of wire. Freddie played the school's upright piano.

In an environment starved of the real thing, The Hectics became the star attraction at any school function, playing to a mixed audience that included a highly enthusiastic contingent from the neighbouring girls' school. 'They would stand at the front and scream,' recalled Derrick Branche, 'just like they'd heard girls the world over were beginning to do when faced with current idols.' Yet Freddie was happy to let Bruce Murray hog the limelight. 'Freddie didn't seem a natural frontman at all,' said Branche. 'He was quite content to stay well in the background.'

'I was the singer as I was the best-looking one,' laughs Murray. 'We played The Coasters' "Yakety Yak", lots of Elvis, Dion, maybe some Ricky Nelson stuff. Fred sang backing vocals, but his thing was still the piano. He also had this quirky way of moving onstage, which you could see a little of later with Queen. We never played outside the school, except one time when I was visiting my aunt in Bombay and I saw Freddie on the street. He came into the house and he played the piano while I sang. For years after, my aunt would ask about "the boy with the buck teeth that played the piano".'

A photograph of The Hectics onstage shows a typical teenage school group of the early sixties. In the standard dress of white shirts, black ties, pleated trousers and identically greased hair, they pose self-consciously with their instruments; Farang Irani preparing to leap from the top of his cumbersome tea chest, onto which the band's name has been wonkily stencilled. Bulsara looks even less like a future pop star than his bandmates, still a gawky schoolboy, grinning and showing the protruding front teeth, caused by the presence of four extra teeth at the back of his mouth.

Bruce Murray insists that nobody called Freddie 'Bucky' to his face ('or they would have had us to contend with'). But others maintain that he was widely known by this nickname or, as Subash Shah remembers it, 'Buckwee'. Similarly, while Bruce Murray says that Freddie was always known by his adopted English name, Subash Shah remembers him only being known by his birth name of Farrokh while at Panchgani.

At the age of twelve, Freddie won the school's annual Junior All-Rounder prize for combined academic and sporting achievement. As the years passed, he became a capable cricketer (though he later claimed to loathe the game), field hockey player and bantam-weight boxer. It was in the boxing ring that his friends saw further evidence of their classmate's strength of character and focus. 'I never fought him as I was a different weight,' remembers Shah. 'But those who did fight him had to go for a technical knockout. Because of his teeth, his mouth would bleed very badly. So to protect himself, he used to really give it to his opponent.'

Bruce Murray witnessed a particularly vicious bout. 'Freddie's mouth was bleeding; he had blood all over his face. I was his second in the corner of the ring, holding the towel. I kept saying, "Look, Freddie, give up. You're getting hurt." But he would not stop. He had this steely look in his eye, as if he was looking at you but straight through you. I saw him again later when we met in England. This attitude of "Fuck them, I will do this" . . .'

By his final year at St Peter's his results were slipping. Perhaps distracted by music and art, he had become an average student. While he was alive, the official party line was that he had acquired 'several O-Levels, including English Literature, Art and History'. In truth, he failed to pass any at Panchgani. Another possibility is that teenage hormones proved a distraction. While having female friends at the neighbouring girl's school, Freddie was never romantically linked to any of them. One ex-pupil, Gita Bharucha (later Choksi) supposedly became the object of his first schoolboy crush. 'If he liked me, he didn't tell me,' said Gita, interviewed in 2000. 'But it was a very simple, uncomplicated life. Boy meets girl. Boy holds hand with girl.'

Shockingly for the time, some teachers recall that Freddie had also begun using the term 'darling' to address other males, giving him the rarefied air for which he'd become known in Queen. According to some, he was teased about his effeminate behaviour, but more often that not it was ignored simply because, as one friend explained, 'it was just Freddie'. While some of his St Peter's contemporaries maintain that he was obviously gay, others contend he wasn't. 'I saw no sign of it,' insists Bruce Murray. But Derrick Branche took a different view. 'St Peter's was no different to all the other public schools of the boarding variety,' he said. 'Pupils there, including Freddie, went through their own fair share of confusion as puberty overtook them and their bodies began giving their minds conflicting signals.'

Various conflicting rumours surfaced about Freddie Mercury's schooldays, particularly in the years following his death. One story claimed that he had a relationship with another older male pupil at school; another that he was romantically involved with a boy in Bombay. Interviewed in the *Hindustan Times* in 2008, a former teacher from Panchgani claimed that one of Freddie's homosexual relationships had been discovered, with drastic consequences: 'His father would have been informed and I'm sure very disappointed. The family has a very rigid background going back generations, and Zoroastrians completely forbid homosexuality.' The closest Mercury came to revealing more was in an interview with *NME* in 1974: 'All the things they say about them [boarding schools] are true . . . I've had the odd schoolmaster chasing me. It didn't shock me. I had a crush on a master and would have done anything for him.' When asked if he was the 'pretty boy that everyone wanted to lay', Mercury replied, 'Funnily enough, yes . . . I was considered the arch poof.' When asked, in the parlance of the mid-seventies, if he was 'bent', Freddie answered, 'Let's put it this way, there were times when I was young and green. It's a thing schoolboys go through, and I had my share of schoolboy pranks, but I'm not going to elaborate any further.'

In 1962, Freddie left St Peter's and returned to the family home in Zanzibar. One of the last photographs of him at the school shows a louche sixteen-year-old reclining on a bench outside one of the dormitories. In it, Freddie sports large sunglasses and a perfectly sculpted quiff. A parting message written in a friend's autograph book that year reads: 'Modern paintings are like women, you can't enjoy them if you try to understand them – your pal always, F. Bulsara.'

In 1979, his mother Jer donated photographs of her son and other memorabilia to St Peter's, but it would be the closest Freddie came to revisiting his old school. In the years following his death in 1991, St Peter's opened its doors to TV crews and journalists seeking to uncover more about Freddie's Mercury's childhood. Much of the school's premises remain unchanged; the school hall in which The Hectics performed almost the same as it was in the fifties. Even the piano on which he performed remained intact, until partly destroyed by a fire in 2002.

Of his bandmates in The Hectics, Farang Irani opened a restaurant in Mumbai, where he still shares stories with those stopping off for lunch as part of the Freddie Mercury Indian School Experience tour, Derrick Branche and Bruce Murray moved to England – Branche became an actor in countless seventies and eighties TV programmes and 1985's Oscar-nominated film *My Beautiful Launderette*, while Murray went into music management. Victory Rana, The Hectics' drummer, later graduated from the United States Army War College, and became Inspector-General of the Nepalese army, before being appointed by Kofi Annan as Commander of the United Nations peacekeeping force in Cyprus in 1999. Branche and Murray both came back into Freddie's life later. But as another of his contemporaries recalled, 'I think Freddie was keen to forget India and get on with the next stage in his life.'

That next stage would be a year with his family, trying to finish his education in Stone Town. Here, he again met up with Subash Shah, whose parents had decided to take him out of Panchgani after he had failed one of his exams: 'Freddie walked into my class, and I was shocked as I had presumed he was already halfway across the Indian Ocean going back to Panchgani. But he never told me why his parents had brought him back from India, and I never asked.'

There would be no Hectics II in Zanzibar. Instead, Freddie gleaned any scraps of information about pop culture from the English magazines that arrived weeks, sometimes months after publication. For his birthday, he received a tape recorder and would record pop music broadcast late at night on British programmes. At school, Freddie, Subash and the other male pupils would sit in strictly delegated lines behind the female pupils. 'All the African Arab girls would wear a traditional headdress called the *bui-bui*,' says Shah. 'One time we all went to the beach as a class. At this time the dance craze the Twist was very big on the island. It was the first time any of us had seen the girls without their *bui-buis*. There they were, twisting their butts off, with Freddie in the middle doing the same.'

By now, Cliff Richard, Fats Domino and Little Richard, who had fired up The Hectics barely a year before, were about to be usurped. By the close of 1963 in England, The Beatles had arrived and were busily revolutionising pop music, with the Rolling Stones about to follow suit. In Zanzibar, too, everything was about to change, with a political upheaval that would change the Bulsara family's lives for ever.

By the early 1960s, British colonial rule of the island was weakening. Following an election in December 1963, the British handed power to the Arab-dominated Zanzibar and Pemba People's Coalition Party. The opposition, the mainly African Afro-Shirazi party, believed the election had been rigged. To maintain order, the new government banned some opposition parties and expelled African policemen from the island, fanning the dissent. On 12 January 1964, several hundred party opponents including many of the expelled policemen, took to the streets amid violent protests. Under the stewardship of 'Field Marshall' John Okello and a hardcore of some forty leading rebels, they seized control of government buildings in Zanzibar City, and had all but taken control of the island within nine hours.

'After the revolution, things went crazy,' recalls Shah. 'But we had a routine where I would go over to Freddie's house at around five-thirty for tea, and then we would go for a walk around town before making sure we were back home for seven-thirty. There had been so much death on the island that I asked him, "Buckwee, how long do you think you are going to live?" And he said, "For some reason, the number forty-five comes into my head." Then he asked me how long I thought I was going to live, and I said, "Forty-seven." It wasn't a planned question; it was just something that came into my head simply because of the context of what had been going on.' In 1996, Subash Shah would discover that his friend Freddie Bulsara had, indeed, died aged just forty-five. 'It was my fiftieth birthday and my father had found a newspaper cutting about Freddie Mercury, who had died five years before,' he says. 'I listened to jazz. I knew nothing about Queen. My father read the article and realised that this singer was the same Farrokh Bulsara that we had known as a child.'

In June, Shah and his family moved to Ohio, where Subash had been offered a scholarship at Kent State University. Shah recalls the Bulsaras leaving earlier, in March. As Bomi had a British passport, it's believed that the family fled, taking as many possessions as they could fit into two suitcases, before flying to England. The family settled in Feltham, Hounslow, an anonymous suburban town a little over three miles from the airport at which they'd arrived. Fellow resident Brian May's blunt description of Feltham was 'a place where nothing ever happened'. After first staying with relatives, the Bulsaras bought a Victorian terrace at 22, Gladstone Avenue. Bomi found work as an accountant for a local catering company, and Jer took a job as a shop assistant.

It would prove to be a difficult time for the family: living in modest circumstances in a cold, unfamiliar country where they were now immigrants. According to his family, Freddie was delighted to be in England. During those difficult early months, it was he that stayed upbeat, encouraging his parents and convincing them that they had made the right move. Like India, Zanzibar was now a memory. Freddie would never go back. Later, when friends wheedled information out of him, Mercury recalled his birthplace without affection. 'I'd ask him, "What was it like in Zanzibar? It must have been so exciting,"' said one old confidante, 'and he'd say, "Dirty place! Filthy place, dear."'

Freddie now had to decide what he was going to do with his life. 'He knew we wanted him to be a lawyer or an accountant, because most of his cousins were,' said Jer Bulsara. 'But he'd say, "I'm not that clever, Mum. I'm not that clever."' Subash Shah insists that Freddie never completed his education in Zanzibar because of the revolution. In England, Bulsara was desperate to attend art school;

partly, it seemed, because many English pop stars had done so. However, his lack of qualifications was an issue. In September 1964, the eighteen-year-old Freddie began an arts foundation course at Isleworth Polytechnic. If successful, it would give him the A-level he needed to be accepted at Ealing Technical College and School of Art, alma mater of The Who guitarist Pete Townshend.

According to one of Mercury's friends, 'Freddie wished his life had begun aged twenty-one in Feltham.' This is supported by the fact that he never referred to his time at Isleworth Polytechnic in any interview. Yet his stint at the college formed a crucial two years in his adult life. A 35-minute bus ride from his family home, the Polytechnic finally brought him into contact with the music, films, drama and fashions he had only read about from thousands of miles away. There were eight other students on Freddie's arts foundation course, including Adrian Morrish, Brian Fanning and Patrick Connolly. 'We all met at induction and were put into a class together,' recalls Adrian Morrish now. 'Freddie, Brian Fanning and I all became close friends. My first impression of Fred was that he was charmingly shy, but also very engaging.'

Initially, Freddie stood out from his fellow students on account of his clothes and hair. 'He dressed weirdly in drainpipe trousers that weren't quite long enough and middle-aged jackets that were slightly too small,' remembers Adrian. 'I suppose he'd brought those clothes with him from Zanzibar or India. He seemed very gauche, but he desperately wanted to fit in.'

'He struck me as quite lonely at first,' offers Patrick Connolly. 'But I liked him because he was sensitive and caring and not quite so jack-the-lad as some of the others. You could tell he'd come from a cultured background, and was just seeking a way for himself to develop.' What soon became apparent to his college mates was their new friend's musical ability. 'During break-time we would drift into the assembly hall,' recalls another ex-Isleworth student Geoff Latter. 'Fred was always playing this upright piano. He'd never sit at it. He would always stand. He could play our favourite pop songs by ear. I was into surf music, especially The Beach Boys. So he'd do "I Get Around" for me. He could just play it, off pat.'

'He'd hear a pop song on the radio in the morning before college, then come in and play it on the piano,' adds Patrick Connolly. 'Then he'd go, "But we can do this or we can do that?" and start improvising, to try and make it sound better.'

Intriguingly, the issue of the name change comes up again. Brian Fanning insists that the name Fred (rather than Freddie) was given to him at Isleworth: 'His name was Farrokh, but he felt that an Anglofied name would help his integration. I recall it seemed to be an important issue for him. So he was christened collectively by us as "Fred".'

Lectures at the Polytechnic were broken up by trips to the local cafe and pub ('Fred and I would run a critique on the latest jukebox offerings,' remembers Fanning, 'things like Otis Redding's "My Girl"'). Though in Adrian Morrish's case, lectures were sometime skipped altogether. 'There was one occasion when I was so engrossed in a young lady's charms that I decided to miss Liberal Studies. Freddie burst into the student common room, mob-handed, and he and a couple of others physically lifted me up and carried me into the lecture room. Freddie was always telling me off. His favourite phrase was always this rather effeminate, exasperated "Oh, *Adrian!*"'

By Christmas 1964 Freddie had joined the Polytechnic's youth choir (Brian Fanning had a tape of the choir's performance, sadly lost) and appeared in the role of Dimitri in *The Kitchen*. 'He was rather nervous and unsure, but, at the same time, you could tell he loved doing it,' says Morrish. 'He liked the attention and he liked being onstage because he was also quite full of himself. That was the first indication we had that he could also be an exhibitionist.'

Alan Hill appeared alongside Freddie in *The Kitchen* and again in a later college production *Spectrum*, 'a theatrical review,' as Hill remembers: 'It was made up of all different pieces. In one, we were supposed to be punting along a river in a boat. In another, we were doing a mime of undying love for this woman '

Morrish and Connolly both spent time at the Bulsaras' house in Gladstone Avenue. 'We'd sit in his room and play records and talk about the things teenagers talk about,' says Morrish. 'I recall him showing me his father's stamp collection, which had these stamps with printing errors that made them very valuable. Later on, I think they were auctioned as Freddie's collection, but I always remember them being his father's.'

Fred also opened up to Patrick Connolly about his background: 'He told me what luxuries his family had in Zanzibar, how he'd lived in a house with an ivory-white piano. I think there were times when he missed the life they'd had.' There was also a darker side to the memories. 'After the revolution, Fred said his father was under threat and was told that if he didn't leave, the rebels would cut his father's head off.'

Undeterred, Freddie was eager to socialise outside of the college ('Dances, clubs, parties, as many as possible,' recalls Alan Hill), although this sometimes meant falling foul of his parents. His sister Kashmira Cooke later remembered her brother and mother 'arguing about it constantly, but he was determined to do what he wanted. There was quite a lot of door slamming.'

'A friend of mine remembers us picking Freddie up from his house in my friend's car to go to a gig,' says Morrish. 'His parents took a very dim view of the idea, and he stormed out of the house.'

To fund his social life, Freddie found part-time work through Alan Hill. 'I used to design the artwork for the National Boys' Club magazine,' he says. 'Fred wanted to earn a bit of money, so because I had the contacts I got him some work, doing layouts.' However, Patrick Connolly is less sure about how suited he was to the job: 'To be honest, Fred was no great artist. He didn't have a clue. The thing about Isleworth Polytechnic was that you didn't have to be very good, you just had to show an interest in the subject. Art was never his thing. Fred's thing was always music and singing and being onstage.'

The Crown folk club in Twickenham staged performances from the likes of Bert Jansch, John Renbourn and Duster Bennett and became popular with some of the Isleworth students, while the Eel Pie Island Hotel, once known for its jazz and big-band acts, now played host to the fledgling Rolling Stones and Yardbirds, The Tridents (featuring the young guitarist Jeff Beck), Howlin' Wolf and the Butterfield Blues Band. Once an ornate building, now crumbling into disrepair (George Melly once likened it to 'something from a Tennessee Williams novel'), it was situated on an isle on a stretch of the River Thames in Twickenham, accessible only by a footbridge. The hotel was a short trip from Isleworth, and became an occasional haunt for Freddie's crowd on Sunday evenings.

'Fred joined us at Eel Pie a couple of times,' says Brian Fanning. 'We went to see Rod Stewart, Long John Baldry and tap-dancing one-man band Jesse Fuller. But even then Fred left early and sober . . . or comparatively sober.' Also at Eel Pie that night was a friend from outside the college, Ray Pearl. 'Fred left Eel Pie early as he wanted to practise his piano,' recalls Pearl now. 'In my memory, he was quiet and retiring and culturally very different from his college mates.' Ray Pearl's diary from 1965 offers a tiny glimpse into Freddie Bulsara's social life that year: 'It's all stuff like: "Went with Bri, Ade and Fred etc to the National Gallery and saw a great exhibition" and "Saw *The Knack* [film] in Hounslow with Ade, Shelagh [another Isleworth student] and Fred. Had a laff!"'

Although he was still compliant enough to appease his mother and go home early for music practice, by drinking in pubs, watching groups and frequenting college parties, Freddie was being, as Brian Fanning puts it, 'a curious sponge soaking up all the influences'. 'Fred was never at the centre of things in terms of drawing attention to himself,' elaborates Fanning. 'But he was trying to pick up as much as he could on the new culture that he was so desperate to become a part of.' Freddie was similarly eager to see something of England beyond his tiny corner of suburban West London. On the Easter weekend of 1965, Fanning, Morrish and Pearl planned to take him on a hitchhiking trip to John O'Groats. Whether it was parental intervention or a genuine illness that intervened, Freddie told his friends he had flu and never made the trip.

Two months later, Brian Fanning bought an 8mm cine camera to college. Over two days he shot around three minutes of silent footage of Freddie, Adrian and others fooling around in the grounds of the Polytechnic. As film was so expensive, Brian saved money by shooting only single-frame sequences at a time. Freddie features in three or four clips, still wearing the 'middle-aged jacket' that Adrian Morrish remembers, but with the quiff grown out and teased into a Beatle fringe. In one scene he slips his top lip over his teeth to conceal them; in another he flaps his arms in an almost identical gesture to one used onstage with Queen. What Fred doesn't look like is a pop star. As Ray Pearl puts it: 'Where *did* that extrovert butterfly come from?'

Neither Adrian Morrish nor Brian Fanning recall Freddie ever having girlfriends of his own while at the Polytechnic. 'But neither do I recall him giving any impression of being gay,' insists Brian. 'But then there was less acceptance in those days.' However, Alan Hill's memories differ: 'Fred was very interested in the opposite sex,' he says. 'When I went out with a girl, he used to go out with her afterwards.'

By 1966, the end of his time at the Polytechnic, Freddie had swapped the outmoded clothes for more fashionable threads. He'd also lost some of the gaucheness he'd had when he'd first enrolled. 'He'd changed his look by the end of Isleworth,' remembers Hill. 'It was all Levi jackets by then. That was the look. I had a white Levi jacket and he was forever borrowing it. I think he wore it more than I did. Before we went out together, he was always preening himself and plumping up his hair in the mirror. We were always saying, "Come on, you look good, Fred, you look good. Now let's go!"'

Fred was also showing an interest in making music again. He and another student, would-be sculptor Paul Martin, remembered by Patrick Connolly as a 'keen guitarist', had begun meeting at Gladstone Avenue and, as Connolly recalls, trying to write songs together.

'The three of us would sit around his piano and sing,' says Patrick. 'A favourite, believe it or not, was "Puff The Magic Dragon" [a 1963 hit for the folk trio Peter, Paul and Mary]. Paul could play, I couldn't sing, but Fred's enthusiasm brought us together. He'd actually encourage me: "Look, Patrick, you're singing, you can do it."' Years later, Jer Bulsara recounted finding ideas for songs written on scraps of paper, which Fred would put under his pillow before heading off to college in the morning. ('He'd say, "Don't throw it away, Mum, it's very important."')

Also by 1966, the student union was booking bands for dances at the Polytechnic. That year saw the Mike Cotton Sound and the Graham Bond Organisation playing the college hall. With Patrick

Connolly and Paul Martin's help, Freddie decided to audition musicians for a group of his own. 'I designed a poster and we sent it to all the colleges and schools in the area, anywhere we could think of,' reveals Connolly. 'I was interested in marketing rather than the music, but we had quite a response. Thinking back, that was quite something in the days before mobile phones and the internet.' Patrick can recall as many as forty would-be musicians turning up to be quizzed by Freddie in a room at the Polytechnic. 'There was this one amazing guitarist that I remember Fred really liked. Yes, of course, years later, I always wondered if it was Brian May . . .' Regrettably, any further information on the Isleworth auditions has faded from the memories of those involved. 'Keen guitarist' Paul Martin never re-surfaced in the lives of any of Freddie's classmates, and Patrick Connolly can never recall any group coming together from the auditions.

Freddie graduated from Isleworth Polytechnic with the precious A-level he needed for art school. But it was not easily acquired. His coursework painting of a crucifixion scene had been finished with a little help from his friend. 'I ended up doing some of the figures for him,' admits Patrick Connolly. 'Perhaps I shouldn't have told you that.'

By Easter of 1966 Dusty Springfield's 'You Don't Have to Say You Love Me' was blasting out of the pub jukebox where 'Fred, Ade and Bri' had once held their lunchtime music critique sessions. Three months later, British blues singer John Mayall would release his *Bluesbreakers* album, showcasing the prodigious talents of guitarist Eric Clapton. On 10 December 1966, Freddie and friends attended Isleworth Polytechnic's Christmas College Dance. The group booked to play were Clapton's new outfit Cream. They were paid £600 and had to be dragged out of the nearby pub during the interval to complete the second half of their set.

Before they both left to take up their places at art school, Freddie and Alan Hill accompanied two female friends to a college party. Once there, fuelled by loud music and booze, Freddie's attention was increasingly drawn to another female guest. His date for the night was not best pleased. Freddie's ardour, not to mention his carefully teased hair-do, was dampened when she emptied a pint of beer over his head. 'The extrovert butterfly' was starting to emerge from his cocoon.

On 16 December another influence crashed into Freddie Bulsara's life in the form of black American guitarist Jimi Hendrix, who made his UK TV debut on the pop show *Ready Steady Go*. It offered suburban England its first sighting of a musical force of nature. Just three days after arriving in the capital, Hendrix, then a complete unknown, had jammed with the house band at the Speakeasy club. Here, he'd torn into a version of The Troggs' pop hit 'Wild Thing' and a cover of the folk-rock standard 'Hey Joe', splattering both songs with wild solos and howling feedback.

Within weeks, word of Hendrix's revelatory appearance had spread among the capital's musicians. In London, Hendrix recruited an English drummer and bassist to form the The Jimi Hendrix Experience. Jeff Beck, Jimmy Page, and Paul McCartney and John Lennon were among the musicians crowding London night spots such as Blaises and the Bag o' Nails that summer watching Hendrix make, to quote one eyewitness, 'everyone's fillings fall out'. In October, Hendrix joined Cream onstage at London's Regent Street Polytechnic. Earlier in the year, the words 'Clapton is God' had been spray-painted on a wall near a North London train station. That night, though, in Clapton's words, 'Hendrix beat me, hands down!'

Freddie's attraction to Jimi Hendrix was instant: his playing, his clothes, his hair, his colour, his music ... everything about Jimi was fascinating. 'He really had everything any rock 'n' roll star should have – style, presence . . .' said Mercury later. 'He'd just make an entrance and the whole place would be on fire. He was living out everything I wanted to be.'

■ ■ ■

Brian May's house isn't the most ostentatious in the country lane. That accolade goes to his next-door neighbour, an Arab sheik, whose property is flanked by forbidding gates and a state-of-the-art security camera. May's own nineteenth-century country retreat, in the same Surrey village of Windlesham that Sarah Ferguson,

Duchess of York calls home, is less imposing. But then as the guitarist often says, 'I'm not very good at being a rock star.'

It is June 1998, May has a solo album to promote, but will patiently submit to the usual round of questions about Queen and, especially, their late singer Freddie Mercury. Today, he will admit that, yes, he does still have dreams about Freddie, and will pinpoint the exact seat on the number 9 London bus that the singer occupied during his regular journeys twenty-five years earlier.

Inside the house, the first thing you notice are the guitars and amps propped up around the living area, and the absence of what interior designers might condescendingly describe as 'a woman's touch'. May reveals that his partner, the actress Anita Dobson, is away 'doing a play' and that she rarely visits this house. In an adjacent workshop, his homemade guitar, the cherished 'Red Special', is being taken apart and reassembled; a process that, you suspect, leaves the guitarist feeling a little vulnerable. May still sports the snug jeans, the garish shirts and, of course, the hair that have become his recognisable uniform. Other things remain unchanged also. When he first lopes into the room, Brian's opening gambit is to complain of a cold ('I feel a bit fluey'). It's an excuse he's used more than once before in interviews.

But he is a paragon of politeness and good manners, and displays none of the airs and graces you suspect Freddie Mercury might have been prone to in a similar situation. But May is one of life's worriers. Being the lead guitarist in one of the most successful rock bands of all time may have bought him recognition, money, the adoration of fans and the respect of fellow musicians, but you sense that at no time has he ever sat back and just relished it all. At this stage in his career, the notion of Queen going back on the road with another singer seems incomprehensible. But without Queen, Brian May sometimes seems a little lost. 'I'd like to be viewed as something alive and relevant,' he says, with a rather harried look. 'Not some fossil.'

In December 1966, while Freddie Bulsara was still some way off from living out any musical dream, May, then a nineteen-year-old physics student and part-time guitarist, was a little closer. But although they lived just a few minutes away from each other in

Feltham, the two had never knowingly met. Later, Freddie would talk of 'scouring the country' to see Hendrix play, which suggests that he and Queen's future guitarist may have even been in the same audience when Hendrix played London's Saville Theatre on 29 January 1967.

For May, seeing Hendrix was a pivotal moment. 'I was already playing, I was in groups. Then this guy came along who was so far in advance of everyone else it was frightening,' he recalled in 1991. 'He was on the same road but almost out of sight, ahead of us all. I thought I was pretty good before I saw Hendrix.' By the end of 1967, his bandmates at the time had nicknamed him 'Brimi', such was his devotion to the guitarist.

May and Bulsara's mutual love of Hendrix was the first step towards their paths crossing. But May's upbringing in the same enclave of West London couldn't have been more different from the singer's.

Nearly a year younger than his future sparring partner, Brian Harold May was born on 19 July 1947 at Gloucester House Nursing Home in Sevenoaks, Kent. He was an only child to parents Harold and Ruth. His father was an electronics engineer and senior draughtsman at the Ministry of Aviation, working on the creation of blind-landing equipment for Concorde. Previously, Harold had served as a radio operator during the Second World War.

The May family home, in a small cul-de-sac at 6 Walsham Road, was barely a few hundred yards from the Bulsaras' house in Gladstone Avenue. At the age of five Brian began attending Hanworth Road primary school; a year later he took his first steps towards learning music when his father, a fan of wartime entertainer George Formby, began teaching him a few chords on Formby's trademark instrument, the ukelele. Piano lessons, which May always claimed to tolerate rather than enjoy, soon followed.

On his seventh birthday, Brian awoke to find 'a Spanish guitar hanging off the end of my bed'. His hands were still too small to play it properly, so Harold set about carving down the bridge. May Senior was known for his resourcefulness and ingenuity. As money was tight, explained Brian, 'my dad made everything. He was a technical civil servant. So he'd fix everybody's equipment.

Everything we had in our house was pretty much made by him; the radio, the TV, the record player . . .'

One evening, Harold came home with a Lonnie Donegan record. Donegan's 1955 hit 'Rock Island Line' bump-started the skiffle boom of the mid-fifties, with homegrown musicians playing an amalgam of American folk, blues and pop, often on homemade instruments. Thousands of miles away in India, it was skiffle that prompted Freddie Bulsara's school bandmate to make his own tea-chest bass.

Brian was hooked. 'It was something about the sound of the guitar and the voice and that sort of blues feeling,' he explained. 'I used to lay under the bed covers with my little crystal set listening to Radio Luxembourg and all this stuff that seemed very exciting and dangerous and forbidden. First time I heard Buddy Holly, there was just chills up my spine.' From here on, it was a short leap to The Everly Brothers, Brenda Lee, Little Richard and, his first crush, Connie Francis.

As an only child, Brian had the time and space to indulge his interests. He filed his records alphabetically and kept them in perfect condition. An ardent collector, he hoarded cheese labels, matchboxes, Dan Dare toys and Eagle comics (years later, a manager at EMI Records recalls May collecting hotel matchbooks while touring with Queen). The discovery of a book about astronomy by the scientist and TV presenter Patrick Moore found May, 'hooked for ever'. Combining two pastimes, Brian wrote a spoken-word monologue about the movement of the stars, which he would perform to his family to the musical accompaniment of 'Saturn – The Bringer of Old Age' from Gustav Holst's *The Planets Suite*. Before long, he would add a camera and a telescope (homemade, of course) to his collection.

Music, however, was still a hobby, and never to get in the way of schoolwork. At Hanworth Road, Brian applied himself tirelessly to his studies. 'I was a swot,' he admitted. 'I had a lot of application and I liked achieving.'

In 1958, his diligence paid off when he passed his eleven-plus exam and took up a scholarship place at Hampton Grammar. The school celebrated its 450th anniversary in 2006, and currently lists

Brian May among its former alumni; a list that includes QCs, judges, Olympic sportsmen and, bizarrely, William Page, the eighteenth-century highwayman.

During his first year at Hampton Grammar, another pupil, Dave Dilloway, heard Brian playing his Spanish guitar. 'I remember walking around one of the corridors in the upstairs wing and hearing this guy playing an acoustic guitar and singing that Tommy Steele thing, "Singing the Blues" [a hit for Steele in 1957 and Guy Mitchell in 1956]. He sounded good but I thought no more of it.'

A year later, Dilloway and May ended up in the same class together, the elite 2LA. 'Two Latin A,' explains Dave. 'It was the fast stream, which meant you could take your A-levels a year early, so you could go to university interviews with your A-level results in your pocket.'

At the time, Dilloway was learning to play his grandfather's guitar, May was still playing the Spanish guitar. 'So we found this mutual interest,' says Dilloway, 'and we got talking. He lived in Feltham and I lived in Whitton, and we'd go over to each other's houses on Saturday afternoons and learn a tune.'

As it was still the pre-Beatles era, the songs they learned were by The Shadows, The Ventures, and Les Paul. 'Mainly instrumental stuff,' recalls Dave. 'Crazy as it may now seem, I used to play the tune and Brian used to play the rhythm, as, for a beginner like myself, the chords were harder.'

A desire to mimic the electric sounds of The Shadows' guitarist Hank Marvin led to Brian and his father installing homemade pick-ups on the Spanish guitar. 'We used magnets and wire,' May recalls, 'and plugged it into my dad's radio and it sounded brilliant.'

At school, the pair talked music incessantly. 'Brian used to teach me chords in the back of the German lesson,' says Dave. 'I used to slide my shirt cuff up my arm, which is where I'd had a guitar fretboard drawn on, and I'd learn the chords that way: "Which one is this, Brian?" and he'd show me the position of the fingers on the board. The joke is that I failed German O-Level and he passed because he was such a clever sod.'

Away from lessons and playing guitar, over the next couple of years, Brian would tackle his natural shyness to become secretary

of the school debating society, and act in several school productions, 'dragging up' as a woman (twenty years before he did so in
Queen's fabled video for 'I Want to Break Free') to appear in school
productions of *The Admirable Crichton* and *The Rivals*. Years later,
when interviewed, May would often admit to feelings of insecurity
as a teenager: 'I used to think, "My God, I don't know what to do, I
don't know what to wear, I don't know who I am."'

Playing music seemed to offer a respite. With the onset of the
beat group boom, May and Dilloway weren't the only aspiring
musicians at Hampton Grammar. 'There was a scene,' explains
Dave, 'with a growing group of guitarists who would drag small
amps into school and play at lunchtimes.' Other older pupils were
already playing in bands: John Garnham, nicknamed 'Jag', owned
a handsome Hofner Colorama; Pete 'Wooly' Hammerton had a
Telecaster and, later, an SG of which Brian was especially envious.
Playing this and other friends' guitars, May began noting what he
liked and didn't like. Unable to afford his own guitar, he and his
father had already decided to make their own.

In the summer of 1963, the pair began the painstaking process of
designing and building an electric guitar from scratch. It took them
eighteen months to complete, but gave May an instrument that
became his signature for the next forty-five years. The guitar's body
was moulded from oak and blockboard; the neck was made from
an eighteenth-century mahogany fireplace salvaged from a friend's
house (two woodworm holes were plugged with matchsticks); the
fret markers on the neck were fashioned from mother-of-pearl
buttons scavenged from Ruth May's sewing box and sanded down
by hand, while the tremelo arm was made from a piece of steel
originally used to hold up the saddle of a bike and, recalled Brian,
'capped by my mum's knitting needle'. Two valve springs from a
1928 Panther motorcycle were then used to balance the strings'
tension.

The only parts of the guitar not made from scratch were the
pick-ups and the fretwire used for the strings. As Brian and
Harold's homemade pick-ups didn't give them the sound they
wanted, Brian relented and installed Burns pick-ups (as favoured
by The Shadows). 'Then I bought the fretwire from a shop called

Clifford Essex in [London's] Cambridge Circus,' he recalled. 'But everything else was junk.'

With its twenty-four frets and the customised positioning of the pick-ups, the DIY instrument had a unique sound and tonality. Once completed, and varnished a deep mahogany hue, the homemade guitar came to be known as the 'Red Special'. Showing his customary eye for detail, May photographed the construction of the instrument at every stage. In 1998, when the Special was finally taken apart to be rebuilt, Brian's guitar tech was presented with Harold May's original tool kit containing the same screwdrivers, fret saws and even the original tins of wood-stain used in its creation some thirty-five years earlier.

Showing a similar ingenuity, by early 1964, Brian and Dave had begun using two reel-to-reel tape recorders to experiment with multi-track recording; taping the guitars on one machine, then playing the tape back in the room and playing along. Dilloway now had a homemade bass to add to the mix. 'Brian or I would usually play the bass, then I'd hit anything I could find – hat boxes, strips of Meccano – to make a drum sound,' remembers Dave. 'Not sophisticated.' Between them, the duo cut rough-and-ready versions of Bo Diddley's self-titled hit, The Shadows' 'Apache' and FBI and Chet Atkins' 'Windy and Warm', among others.

Before long, the pair were scouring the school lunchtime music sessions (May: 'We used to play in the cycle sheds as we weren't allowed to play in the school') looking for like-minded players. An ad hoc group soon formed around Brian on guitar, Dave on bass guitar, classmate John Sanger on piano and an older Hampton pupil, Bill Richards, on vocals and guitar.

Their repertoire included Manfred Mann, The Beatles and The Moody Blues. Richards' tenure in the group was short-lived, after May politely told him that his guitar wasn't up to scratch and that he would have to buy a new one or leave. 'To be honest, I think Brian was being even more tactful by underplaying the problem with my vocals, which weren't right at the time,' said Richards. His replacement, Malcolm Childs, proved unreliable and lasted a few days. Before long, John 'Jag' Garnham – and his Hofner Coloroma – had arrived.

'We got talking to "Jag", who was already in a band and who was a year older than us,' recalls Dave Dilloway. 'But he also had transport, and microphones and cabinets, which was very important.'

'I'd been playing in a group with Pete Hammerton, whose nickname was Wooly — I have no idea why — but Wooly could be a bit awkward,' remembers John Garnham. 'He went off, so I started playing with Dave and Brian May. I was a year above Brian at school but with him being such a smart-arse, he jumped a year.'

While Garnham could sing, and both May and Dilloway had recorded their vocals during the bedroom taping sessions, the group needed a dedicated lead singer. A Saturday night trip to a local dance would prove fruitful. 'We turned up to watch this band playing at Murray Park Hall in Whitton,' says Dave. 'They were called Chris and The Whirlwinds. We were impressed because the lead guitarist had this very nice-looking guitar. But while we were watching we saw this chap that we recognised from school, watching in the audience. He was sitting down, minding his own business, but every so often he would start playing along to the band on a harmonica. The group couldn't hear him, but we could, and he was good. We had no idea whether he could sing but we invited him along to rehearsals to see what he could do.'

Their latest recruit was Tim Staffell from Teddington, another Hampton pupil, and, at sixteen, a few months younger than Dave and Brian. Like John Garnham, though, Tim already had experience of playing, and had been singing in a local group called The Railroaders. Unlike his more studious bandmates, Tim struggled to stay focused on school. Three years earlier, a serious road accident had kept him away from lessons and he had 'lost a lot of ground'. Tim was a keen artist, though, and already had his sights on a place at art school (a decision that would have lasting consequences on Brian May's career). He quit The Railroaders and threw his lot in with Brian and friends.

However, the group were still missing one vital ingredient: a drummer. 'So we put up a postcard saying that we were looking for one in the window of Albert's Music Shop in Twickenham,' says Garnham. They had one applicant, Richard Thompson, a pupil at Isleworth's Spring Grove Grammar School, who was already playing local youth club gigs in a group called The Fifth Column.

'Richard Thompson turned up on my parents' doorstep in his motorcycle gear,' recalls Dilloway. 'He had a mate with him who had transport, so he brought his drum kit. He seemed amenable, so he was in.'

The band began regular rehearsals at Chase Bridge primary school in Twickenham, next door to the rugby stadium, reaping the benefits of a Richmond council scheme that allowed groups to use local schools and youth clubs for a small annual fee. 'They formed this organisation called The Whitton Beat Club,' recalls Dave Dilloway. 'So we used to practise at the primary school. The hardcore of the band was now myself, Brian, Tim, Richard and John Garnham on rhythm guitar, but John Sanger was still on the periphery, playing the piano.' Their set was made up of covers of pop songs of the day, including, as Brian May recalled, 'a mixture of adapted soul stuff like Sam and Dave, and Otis Redding.'

The group had also decided on a name, 1984, taken from the title of George Orwell's post-war novel. Brian and Tim were both ardent science fiction fans, and the name stuck.

By now, after months of his schoolfriends seeing Brian polishing the guitar's neck in between lessons, the Red Special was complete. 'I first saw it when it was still a drawing on a piece of paper and a mantelpiece,' laughs Dave Dilloway. 'There's no bullshit. All those stories about his mum's sewing box and the motorcycle springs are all true. They didn't even have a lathe; they turned the motor-bridge pieces with a drill. That's Brian, though – ever the perfectionist.'

Before long, The Whitton Beat Club network had delivered a booking. 'We were asked to play a youth-club gig,' explains Dave Dilloway. 'There was a friend of someone we knew, and he and his girlfriend or wife booked us this gig at St Mary's Hall in Twickenham.' On 28 October 1964, while Farrokh Bulsara was still settling into Isleworth Polytechnic, 1984's debut concert took place, in a venue just opposite Eel Pie Island.

John Sanger tagged along to play keyboards. 'This was in the days before electronic keyboards,' continues Dave. 'At some gigs John would play the school hall's upright piano, if they had one, with a microphone stuck in the back. But at that first gig, they didn't have a piano so we borrowed a reed organ. The trouble was, it was like a glorified mouth organ with keys stuck on, and it sounded like a Hoover motor starting when you switched it on. Once you miked it up, all you could hear was this noise like a wind tunnel.'

Later, Brian would state that the 'guitar gave me a shield to hide behind' and that playing onstage as a teenager was infinitely preferable to being on the floor 'wondering whether I should ask someone to dance'. 'Brian never seemed as au fait with the world as, say, Tim and I were,' offers Richard Thompson. Yet Brian now had a girfriend, Pat, a pupil at the neighbouring Richmond Girls' School. Their relationship would survive until Brian's first year at college. It was Pat and her friend, Tim Staffell's girlfriend, that secured 1984's next booking, on 4 November in the girls' school hall.

'Tim and Brian both had girlfriends at the school, and, yes, that's how we got the gig,' recalls Dave. 'But we struggled with the repertoire. We had two hours' worth, but we had to play for three hours, so there were probably a few repeats.'

As John Garnham explains: 'We did a mix of songs in 1984, but there was no real direction. Brian and Dave liked The Beatles, and I was more into Chuck Berry and rhythm and blues, and I also took note of the soul stuff. I was always saying, "We must do stuff that people can dance to", because I liked dancing and I liked girls, and the girls liked dancing.'

While playing in the group brought them attention, John insists, 'None of us were that girl-minded. Out of all of 1984, Brian certainly never appeared to be. He did eventually have Pat, but I don't remember her being brought along to gigs, done up in a short skirt, like my girlfriend or Richard's.' (Dave Dilloway: 'John had some real crackers.')

The group's girl-friendly setlists that year veer from The Beatles' 'Help' and 'I Feel Fine' to Little Richard's 'Lucille' and Lonnie Donegan's 'Jack o' Diamonds' to Rufus Thomas's 'Walkin' the Dog', with an encore of blueser Sonny Boy Williamson's 'Bye Bye Bird'. But as Tim Staffell put it: 'The songs were dredged from all sorts of areas. Because of the nature of the material we approached, we were almost schoolboy cabaret.'

The Chase Bridge rehearsals and occasional gigs continued, but minus John Sanger, who'd taken up a place at Manchester University. 'I had no grand plans to be a musician,' he said (though he re-joined 1984 years later). The group continued as a five-piece, with Tim and Brian having weekly rehearsal competitions to see who could hit the highest note. 'Their ambition was to see who could sing higher than John Lennon,' recalls Garnham.

Brian was chaperoned to school halls and youth clubs in his dad's Javelin, while the older 'Jag' transported as much of the group's equipment as he could cram into his Isetta bubble car. 'My dad used to take my drums in the car,' remembers Richard Thompson. But on one occasion, the band came close to losing a vital piece of equipment. 'Before one gig we arranged to meet Brian on Putney Bridge,' says Thompson. 'We picked him up, drove to the venu and when we got there Brian realised he'd left his guitar, the actual Red Special, on the bridge. We got back there an hour later and, incredibly, there it was, propped up against the bridge where he'd left it. Brian could be a little scatterbrained.' For a few gigs, Garnham and Dilloway even swapped instruments, with 'Jag' playing Dave's homemade bass. 'But it was a bit of a plank,' says Garnham, 'not of the quality of Brian's Red Special.'

The 'schoolboy cabaret' also faced stiff local competition. 'There was another popular band in the area called Fire,' remembers John Garnham (Fire's guitarist Dave Lambert would later join The Strawbs). 'We all kept up with what these groups were doing, especially a group called The Others.' In October 1964 – just as 1984 made their live debut – The Others, a band comprised of five Hampton Grammar pupils, three from the same year as May and Dilloway, released a single, 'Oh Yeah!', a song recorded by Bo Diddley. 'That made them mini-heroes at school,' recalls Dave, and Garnham adds that 'they used to do early Stones stuff, things like "Route 66" . . . they had a bit of attitude.'

'The Others were big at the time,' remembered Brian May. 'They were rebels who weren't interested in the academic side. And they were very influential to me. I felt very jealous of all those people that were doing it at school, being in semi-professional groups, because all the pressure on me was to keep on with the studies. My parents thought you should stay at home and do your homework . . . and then go out when you were about twenty years old. I was a bit sheltered really.'

The Others gave the impression of being anything but sheltered. A surviving promotional photograph shows five youths with Brian Jones-style fringes and skinny ties, displaying the same surly demeanour visible on the cover of the first Rolling Stones LP. 'Oh Yeah!' was cocky English pop; a schoolboy Yardbirds, with lots of wailing harmonica and faux menace. While The Others would never crack the charts (re-emerging briefly as The Sands three years later), their tougher sound was the antithesis of 1984.

While The Others seemed to have cornered some of the 'raw sex and anger' that May so admired in The Yardbirds, Brian himself was still the shrinking violet. 'He was never an extrovert onstage,' says Garnham. 'Brian was a super-brain, a goody two-shoes at school. But he was still a quiet person when he was in the early groups. It always struck me as peculiar that once Queen got going, he was rushing to the front of the stage doing the Pete Townshend windmilling arm and being The Great Rock Guitarist. I used to think, "This is not the same person." I think Brian's outward character changed when he was in Queen, but his inward character stayed the same.'

'Brian was always serious-minded,' agrees Dave Dilloway. 'He was never the life and soul. In 1984, Tim and Richard were the loosest characters and the biggest personalities. John was just in it for fun, and I was the bass player . . .' He laughs. 'And we don't have personalities.'

As Hampton's other musos passed their exams and headed off to universities, others stepped in to take their place. 'People started slotting into other groups just to keep things going,' explains Garnham, whose pre-1984 sparring partner Pete 'Wooly' Hammerton would later find himself in The Others. In the meantime, Hammerton and Brian May circled each other on the local youth-cub scene; two hotshot guitarists eager to outplay each other. 'I wouldn't like to say who was better but both were well above average skills and speed,' says Dave Dilloway.

'There was a competition to see who could play new stuff

quickest,' said Brian. 'So when the new records came out we would all feverishly study them at home.' A Swedish instrumental group The Spotnicks offered the ultimate challenge with their 1963 cover of the bluegrass standard 'Orange Blossom Special' and another, later, single, 'Happy Hendrick's Polka'. 'We really killed ourselves, trying to play it. We'd make our fingers bleed.' Only later did they discover that The Spotnicks sped up their tapes in the studio.

This revolving-door policy would find Brian occasionally guesting with The Others, and brought May and Hammerton together for a one-off gig at Shepperton Rowing Club in 1965. 'Wooly' handled lead vocals and guitar, with Brian switching to bass and Richard Thompson playing drums. Among The Beatles and Martha and The Vandellas covers and The Others' 'I'm Taking Her Home', the trio tried their hand at a game version of The Who's 'My Generation'; a song that, among others by The Yardbirds, would signal a shift in direction for 1984 over the next twelve months.

But in autumn 1965, it was time for 1984, and its star pupil, to move on. Brian May left Hampton Grammar with ten O-levels and four A-levels, in Physics, Applied Mathematics, Pure Mathematics and Additional Mathematics. As being a full-time guitarist was not yet an option, May set his sights set on astrophysics, and was accepted for a three-year degree course in Physics and Infra-Red Astronomy at London's Imperial College of Science and Technology. Richard had already been working for some time, but John took a job at the BBC, Dave headed off to study electronics at Southampton University, and Tim enrolled on a graphics course at Ealing Technical College and School of Art.

Before Imperial College, though, Brian paid for a new amp by taking a summer-holiday job at the Guided Weapons Research Centre in Feltham. It was a position more suited to his scientific bent than his previous holiday jobs: making windscreen wipers and doling out the wages at a fire extinguisher factory.

For 1984, there began a period of, in Dave Dilloway's words, 'rehearsing by letter'. Still, they managed to play most other weekends around the West London suburbs, plugging in at Putney's Thames Rowing Club, Twickenham's All Saints Church

Hall, Feltham R&B Club . . . A gig at Southall's White Hart tavern gave them their first taste of boozy violence, when a fracas broke out in the audience and the police were called; another found them playing behind a barely-clothed female dancer with a snake. Later, they'd break up their three-hour sets by cracking jokes and fooling around onstage with plastic bricks and shaving foam; anything to stand out from the other teenage bands playing the same songs on the same circuit.

The Yardbirds' 'Heart Full of Soul' and 'I Wish You Would' had now crept into the set, while Brian's lightning-fingered rendition of 'Happy Hendrick's Polka' gave the audience something to gawp at when they weren't dancing. 'Thousands of people must have seen Brian May playing these small clubs,' reflects Dave Dilloway, 'and not had the slightest idea that he was later in Queen.'

Throughout the year, though, it was still a juggling act to rehearse, play live and find time to study. Dave, John and Brian's parents accepted their sons' musical hobby, but Tim's were less impressed by what they called 'that band nonsense'. At the end of 1965, after a year, Dave Dilloway quit Southampton University and opted for an HND electronics course at Twickenham College of Technology. Being back in West London sped up the process of getting to and from gigs.

May's college connections also brought 1984 bookings at Imperial, including one at a fancy dress party in the spring of 1966. The following year found them playing marathon sets in an upstairs room at Imperial, keeping the students dancing, while, as Dave Dilloway explains, 'the main band played the main hall downstairs'. Dashing between the two rooms during the interval, they found a way to sneak into the main hall without paying, to catch snippets of their rivals' sets.

During their final years at school, the band members had been regulars at Eel Pic and Richmond's Station Hotel, watching The Rolling Stones, Fleetwood Mac, The Tridents and The Yardbirds. 'I saw The Yardbirds at the Marquee, soon after Jeff Beck joined,' recalled May. 'Eric Clapton came on and jammed at the end. I'll never forget it.' Clapton's next band, Cream, would make an even greater impression. The trio made their live debut in the summer of

1966, unveiling their first album, *Fresh Cream*, in December. Like The Jimi Hendrix Experience, with whom they seemed locked in a dead-heat musical race, Cream's freewheeling sound and virtuosity spun the blues off into myriad directions. Between them, Clapton and Hendrix opened up May's eyes to a world of musical possibilities.

Not long after Brian saw Hendrix blow The Who offstage at the Saville Theatre, Dave Dilloway witnessed Jimi up close on 1984's home turf: Hounslow's Ricky Tick Club. 'A club smaller than the local village hall,' says Dave. 'The PA was a pair of four-by-twelves and a Marshall stack. Incredible.' Before long, Clapton and Hendrix's influence would be felt in 1984, with the latter's 'Stone Free' stripped into the set. 'Brian's influences changed dramatically from The Beatles to Hendrix and Cream,' remembers John Garnham. 'But I still had this thing in 1984 that we should do songs that people could dance to, which wasn't true of, say [Cream's] "Sunshine of Your Love". I played that crash-bang-wallop Chuck Berry style. I couldn't play the fancy Eric Clapton stuff, but Brian could.' As we had a guitarist who could play Clapton and Hendrix, that's what we did,' adds Dave Dilloway. 'We muddled along, gradually moving with the music of the time.'

A February 1967 article in the local newspaper, the *Middlesex Chronicle*, found Tim Staffell in an effusive mood, proclaiming that 'psychedelic music is here to stay'. In keeping with the psychedelic era, electronics whizz Dilloway was now experimenting with a primitive light show, inspired by the up-and-coming Pink Floyd. But 1984's student grants would hardly run to the oil slides and projectors Floyd were using. 'Our lighting rig was very basic. We had the ideas and the technological know-how, but we didn't have the money,' laughs Dave. 'We couldn't afford bigger bulbs! We used to get paid peanuts but everything we earned we ploughed back into the band. All the time Brian was with us, we didn't even have a PA: just two AC30 amps.'

If, as they freely admitted, 1984 was 'always small-time', during Brian May's final months in the band, they were lurching closer still to their musical idols. Dave Dilloway's course at Twickenham had introduced him to trainee technicians at Thames Television's studios in Teddington. The studio had invested in new equipment and needed a group to test it. Dilloway offered 1984. On 31 March, the group spent a day playing musical guinea pigs (minus the MU rates the studio would have had to pay a professional band) and recording a handful of songs, including Cream's 'NSU', Sam and Dave's 'Hold On I'm Coming', Hendrix's 'Purple Haze', and Eddie Floyd's 'Knock On Wood'. Heard now, it's May's guitar playing and Staffell's voice, loose and soulful like a wannabe Steve Winwood, that most impress. Tellingly, Staffell sounds more at ease on the soul numbers than he does on 'Purple Haze', which, naturally, gives May the chance to cut loose.

The differing tastes of 1984's singer and its lead guitarist would become a sticking point later on, but in 1967, Tim and Brian were sufficiently in tune to start writing songs. Also recorded that day were two versions of a May/Staffell composition titled 'Step On Me'. 'I didn't know then that Brian wanted to explore songwriting or that he even had ideas,' admits Dave Dilloway. 'I don't think the rest of us had those aspirations. "Step On Me" was our one original number in all the time 1984 played live.' With its dainty melody and subdued guitar solo, its overriding feature is the exquisite harmonies; like an early test drive for the sound May would explore fully with Queen.

Just weeks later, Brian was back in the studio, helping out his old Hampton Grammar schoolmate Bill Richards. Two years earlier Richards had put together a band called The Left-Handed Marriage and in January 1967 issued a privately pressed album. Two months later, Richards signed to EMI's music publishing wing, Ardmore and Beechwood, as a songwriter. Richards wanted May to help beef up the group's sound. May joined the group at a recording studio in Twickenham, playing on four songs for a planned EP. The EP was never released, but Ardmore and Beechwood stumped up for another more prestigious recording session two months later. This time, Dave Dilloway joined May, deputising for The Left-Handed Marriage's absent bass player. 'We got taken down to Abbey Road to do it,' says Dave. 'This was at the height of The Beatles' era, so it was tremendously exciting.'

Bill later recalled that an A&R man present at the session was unimpressed by Brian's playing. But, undeterred, a third session with May took place at London's Regent Sound, in July. With singer Henry Hill's enunciated vocals, The Left-Handed Marriage merged elements of The Kinks, while his co-singer Jenny Hill brought a folkier slant to the music. In the end, Bill's career as a songwriter never took off. But in 1993, the final Regent Sound sessions were included on a Left-Handed Marriage album called *Crazy Chain*, giving Queen fans the chance to hear their guitar hero in his youth; the Red Special splashing colour on a set of whimsical mid-sixties pop songs, miles away from the pomp of Queen.

In between the recording sessions, May also came within touching distance of his idol. On 13 May, 1984 were booked on the same bill at Imperial College as The Jimi Hendrix Experience, the day after the band released its debut album, *Are You Experienced?* 'Brimi' was in his element. But there would be no communication between the two; only Jimi's question to Tim Staffell as he loped down the corridor from the dressing room: 'Which way's the stage, man?' Also in Hendrix's entourage that night was Brian Jones, soon to be expelled from The Rolling Stones for too much drinking and drugging. Dave Dilloway glimpsed the ghost-like Jones tagging along behind Hendrix on the walk to the stage looking sicker than anyone he had ever seen before. Jones would be dead in less than two months.

A September 1967 booking for 1984 at the London School of Medicine would be the catalyst for another date with Jimi, after talent spotters took a shine to the band. 'To this day I have no idea who they were,' laughs Dilloway, 'but there were these three guys who fancied breaking into the music business and were looking for a band to manage. We were doubled up on the bill with another group at the London School of Medicine. I think they came to see this band, and decided to go with us instead.'

John Garnham and Richard Thompson are similarly baffled as to the identities of these 'couple of characters'. Nevertheless, their new patrons watched the band rehearse and told them they needed to sharpen up their image. Early photos of 1984 found most of the group sporting the skinny-trousered, Chelsea-booted mod look of the day, with Tim Staffell and John Garnham taking turns to wear a pork-pie hat. Curiously, it's Brian May that looks the most ill at ease; very much the suburban schoolboy, clutching his guitar like a comfort blanket and wearing a cardigan. As Tim ruefully explained, 'I never perceived Brian as having the dangerous image which was necessary at the time.'

But the band was tentatively embracing fashion. Staffell would later claim to hate the flowery-shirted 'Summer of Love' look, but he, like the others, moved with the times. On 9 September, after a boutique shopping trip, the group showed up for a battle-of-the-bands competition at Croydon's Top Rank Club looking very much the pop stars in waiting, even Brian.

The contest had been sponsored by Scotch tape, and the proviso for entering was that groups had to submit songs recorded on a reel of Scotch. 1984 submitted two tracks: The Everly Brothers' 'Crying in the Rain' and Marvin Gaye's 'Ain't That Peculiar?' On the night, they played two sets (the first as backing group to an unknown singer named Lisa Perez) and won the contest hands down. 'It was a joke, though,' laughs Dave. 'Nothing ever came of it.'

Instead the winners were gifted with a reel of Scotch tape and an LP for each band member, deteriorating in quality from Simon and Garfunkel's *The Sound of Silence* (blagged by Tim Staffell) to an album by Irish bandleader Tommy Makem, for which Dave Dilloway drew the shortest straw. 'That's all we got,' says John Garnham. 'These crappy LPs.'

Still, the winning band were photographed that night, preserving an image of 1984 that year. Twenty-year-old Brian May had a regulation Beatle hairdo and Hendrix-style military jacket. Much to his chagrin now, Tim Staffell was wearing a shirt with pink polkadots.

A similar so-called competition found the band piling into the back of Richard Thompson's works van and trekking over to East London's Forest Gate to play to one of their biggest audiences yet at the Upper Cut Club. 'It was a club run by Billy Walker the boxer,' remembers Thompson. 'The Who had opened the club, and I don't know if there even was a competition. I think it was just an excuse to get people over there. We played to a couple of thousand people that night.'

The aspiring managers disappeared as quickly as they arrived.

Still, their hustling skills were enough to secure the group a slot at the 'Christmas on Earth Continued' extravaganza. Held on 22 December at the chasm-like Kensington Olympia, 'Christmas on Earth Continued' was an all-night musical love-in starring fifteen acts, which included Pink Floyd, The Who (who never showed), The Move, Soft Machine and headliner Jimi Hendrix.

Before the gig, the band's benefactors sent them out to buy some new outfits. 'My memory is that Tim and Richard went to Carnaby Street and bought us stuff to wear,' recalls John Garnham. 'I was presented with this black shirt with a silver front.' Though Tim Staffell recalled: 'Our manager bought us velvet guardsman jackets and put us in make-up. We looked terrible.' Newly groomed, the band drove to the Olympia, parked their cars in a side street and started unloading their gear.

Inside the arena, they were told that they would be going on 'very late'. The band set up camp in the artists-only gallery overlooking the stages. The hours dragged by as they watched interminable soundchecks and, later, sets by The Move and Pink Floyd. For a change of scene, they de-camped to Olympia canteen, where they again spotted Jimi Hendrix. 'I remember thinking, "Oh, we are going up in the world,"' says John Garnham, continuing, 'At 1 a.m., we were about to go on, when this guy rushed over and said, "No, no, no . . . So it was back to waiting for another few hours.' In the end, depending which of the band members is telling the story, 1984 went onstage sometime between 4.30 and 6 a.m. on 23 December. 'Everyone was drunk or stoned and lying around, and we bounced on,' said Tim Staffell. 'I think they'd had enough by then,' adds John. 'We just plugged in and hoped for the best, and, thankfully, didn't get booed off.' 'Because we were an unsigned band and it wouldn't cost them anything, I think a snippet of our set was shown on TV,' recalls Dave Dilloway. 'Looking back, it was mediocre but very loud.'

There was worse to come. When the band returned to the dressing room, they discovered their money had been stolen. Then, when they left the Olympia, re-emerging into a frozen December morning after some fifteen hours inside, they found their cars had been towed away. According to Dave Dilloway, the band members were still in their garish stage clothes 'all tarted up in make-up', making the four-mile hike to the police compound in Hammersmith even more uncomfortable. Having paid to retrieve their vehicles, the exhausted band members spent the rest of the day in a haze, trying to buy last-minute Christmas presents. While the Olympia show had been their most prestigious gig yet, it was, in its own way, the beginning of the end.

Just a few months into the New Year, Brian May quit 1984. In the final year of his course, he felt compelled to knuckle down to his studies. It was an amicable decision. 'We weren't out to change the world,' shrugs Dave Dilloway, 'and I didn't know that Brian May wanted to set the world on fire.' The band pressed on with Tim stepping up as lead guitarist and vocalist, but before long, he would be enticed back into playing music with Brian.

Away from the stage and the recording studios, another even more important connection had been made. One of Staffell's new chums from Ealing art college had become a regular at 1984 gigs. 'He was Tim's mate and he was mad about Hendrix. He just loved the scene,' explains Dave Dilloway. 'He used to get into the gigs for free by being our roadie. He never asked to sing or play so I had no idea he was even musical.' Their roadie's name was Freddie Bulsara.

■ ■ ■

Former Guns N' Roses drummer Matt Sorum likes to tell a story about Queen's Roger Taylor. In the late 1970s, the fifteen-year-old Sorum and his friends would while away their evenings on Los Angeles' Sunset Strip. One night, the gang saw a Rolls-Royce pull up outside a Hollywood nightclub. The car door opened and Roger Taylor emerged. The drummer was wearing black sunglasses, a snow-white suit and was managing to hold a glass of bubbly in one hand while a beautiful girl hung off the other. From that moment on, said Sorum, 'I wanted to be Roger Taylor.'

Fast forward to 2005 and Taylor is sitting in the deserted upstairs bar of the Dominion Theatre, where the Queen musical *We Will Rock You* is halfway through its third year in London's West End. He strokes his white goatee and offers a rather bashful smile. 'I always felt it was my job to have a good time,' he nods, then laughs. 'Oh, God, am I a cliché?' Queen, the band, are about to go on tour again for the first time in nineteen years. Except Queen is now just Taylor and Brian May, with Freddie Mercury's place taken by Paul Rodgers, once the lead singer of sturdy blues-rockers Bad Company and, before them, Free. Rodgers is telling critics that, unlike his predecessor, he will 'not be wearing tights'. It is fair to say that Queen fans and critics are eyeing the planned union with varying degrees of concern. Taylor is, just as he was at the beginning of Queen's career, utterly gung-ho about the tour and eager to shout down any naysayers. 'To be the darling of the critics is the kiss of death,' he offers. 'Which is probably why we are still alive.'

In early 1967, while Jimi Hendrix was wowing Freddie Bulsara and Brian May in London, eighteen-year-old Roger Meddows Taylor was planning a sighting of his own. Living in Truro, Cornwall, Taylor drove 160 miles to Bristol, the nearest stop on Jimi's UK jaunt. Taylor became an instant convert, going on to see Hendrix play live a total of three times. Back in Truro, his own group The Reaction would begin radicalising their sound, stripping out the Motown and pop covers, and striving to ape the thrilling new music that was prompting Brian May to do the same with 1984. But in the summer of 1967, Taylor left Truro to begin a dentistry course at the London School of Medicine. The Reaction would continue, but Roger's move to the capital would ultimately mark the beginning of the end for a band once billed as 'The Champion Group of Cornwall'.

Roger Taylor ('Meddows' was a family name) was born on 26 July 1949 in West Norfolk and King's Lynn Hospital to parents Michael and Winifred. Michael was a civil servant at the Ministry of Food (working as an inspector for the potato marketing board), while Winifred may have had the musical gene, playing the accordion as a child. Following the birth of a daughter, Clare, in 1953, the family moved from King's Lynn to Truro, a beautiful market town and the self-appointed 'capital' of Cornwall.

Roger began attending Bosvigo School, where, at the age of eight, he began playing the ukelele. Just months later, he formed a skiffle group, The Bubblingover Boys, playing the ukelele alongside a couple of wannabe guitarists and another pupil on the inevitable tea-chest bass. They played a school dance but were, in Taylor's words, 'terrible, really terrible'. In May 1960, aged eleven, he landed a choral scholarship to Truro Cathedral School; a proviso of which was singing at all functions and in the school choir several times on a Sunday. But just four months later, he moved on after being awarded a place at the prestigious Truro School. Meanwhile, an older cousin with a Dansette record player introduced Roger to Elvis Presley and Jerry Lee Lewis. Before long, a cheap acoustic guitar had replaced the ukelele in his affections. Roger learned the rudiments of playing the guitar, but was soon drawn to another, noisier instrument.

'I remember banging on my mother's saucepans with her knitting needles,' said Roger. 'Then my father found this ancient snare drum in the storage bin where he worked. I started with that.' For Christmas 1961, Michael Taylor bought a new snare drum and a cymbal for his son. Before long, he had acquired a set of old Ajax drums: 'It consisted of one tom-tom, one bass drum, one snare and one minute cymbal.' It was enough to get him started.

In 1964, after his parents separated, Roger, his sister Clare and their mother left the family home in Falmouth Road to a new house in Hurland Road, where at least one neighbour still recalls the 'bloody noisy kid who always played drums with the garage doors open'. The thirteen-year-old Roger's curiosity was piqued again by the 1963 hit 'Diamonds' by former Shadows, Jet Harris and Tony Meehan, a wildly rhythmic instrumental that struck a chord with the young drummer. Before the year he was out, he was playing drums in a trio with two fellow Truro schoolboys, bassist David Dowding and guitarist Mike Dudley. Calling themselves, variously, The Cousin Jacks, Beat Unlimited and, possibly, The Falcons, the trio rehearsed in a barn on Dowding's parents' farm in neighbouring New Mills; working out passable covers of The Shadows hits 'FBI' and 'Apache' (just as Brian May and Dave Dilloway were doing at the same time) and Taylor's *pièce de résistance*, a snare-drum heavy cover of Surfaris' 'Wipe Out'.

At some point, the trio were joined by a singer and began playing school functions, private parties and a fundraising gig for the Truro

Young Liberals, organised by Roger's schoolfriend, the late Liberal MP David Penhaligon. 'I was involved with that gig, and we lost money on it, which might be more of a reflection on the Young Liberals,' recalled Penhaligon. Others from Taylor's school days recall a boy that was simply 'mad about drums' with, as Penhaligon said, 'a fetish for wanting to be a pop star'. 'I always wanted to be in rock 'n' roll, but not necessarily a rock star,' claimed Taylor in 1999. 'But I used to listen to the music and watch the singers and think, "I want a bit of that."'

Come 1965 and both Taylor and Mike Dudley had outgrown Beat Unlimited. Through Truro's musical grapevine, running from the town's nightspots to Ford's Music Shop via the coffee bar on Old Bridge Street, a connection was made. Roger and Mike were approached by local musician John Grose, aka Johnny Quale, and asked to join his backing band. Described by Mike Dudley as 'an Elvis-cum-Billy-Fury clone', Quale had the Presley quiff and tried to sing like his hero.

Billed as Johnny Quale and The Reactions, Taylor and Dudley (now playing keyboards) joined bass guitarist Jim Craven, guitarist Graham Hankins and saxophonist John Snell, nick-named 'Acker' on account of his love of Acker Bilk, trad-jazz's 'Grand Master of the Clarinet'. In March, after a few weeks' rehearsal, they made their debut gig at the annual Rock and Rhythm Championship at Truro City Hall, serving up a mix of Beatles, Roy Orbison and Elvis tunes, and coming fourth (out of fifteen) in the contest.

Fellow Truro School pupil, Geoff 'Ben' Daniel, was playing guitar in another local band at the time. 'There was the West Cornwall bands and the East Cornwall bands, so there were these two cliques,' he explains. 'It was highly competitive. I think Roger was pissed off that they didn't win the championship that day. His favourite saying was "I'm gonna be a pop star". He said it all the time and it used to drive everyone mad.' Taylor was already thinking ahead and displaying an ambitious streak. 'He came to see the group I was in play a gig in Camborne,' recalls Daniel, 'and he came up to me at school the next day and said, "If you ever get fed up of being in that band . . ."'

Daniel would follow up Taylor's offer, but not until the following year. In the meantime, Johnny Quale and The Reactions saw out the summer with regular gigs around Truro, Penzance and Falmouth. Listening at home, Taylor was inspired by The Yardbirds and The Who, coming to The Beatles only after 1966's *Revolver*. Onstage, his confident drumming style was an attempt to ape his hero Keith Moon of The Who. 'Moon had a totally unique style,' said Taylor. 'He didn't owe anyone anything. The Who were outrageous: real energy, real art.' When his heroes played Camborne Skating Rink that autumn, Taylor took his girlfriend to see them, trying in vain to catch Moon's drumsticks when he threw them into the audience. Later, Taylor would begin a relationship with a Truro Grammar School girl named Jill Johnson. Jill was part of a female folk-rock trio sometimes known as The Three Jays that also included Mike Dudley's girlfriend. Somewhere in Truro exists a reel-to-reel tape of Roger backing the three girls on drums and enjoying a rare excursion into folk music. On or offstage, with or without a regular girlfriend, Taylor's blonde hair and delicate features brought him female attention. Mike Dudley later recalled that, after losing the Rock and Rhythm Championship, Roger seduced the attractive go-go dancer that had accompanied the winning band.

In September, Johnny Quale flounced out of the band after a petty dispute. Quale's passion for Elvis was such that he insisted the band keep a particular Saturday night free for him to see a Presley film that was being screened at the Truro Plaza. Instead, the band took a booking which Johnny, ever the professional, felt compelled to complete. Furious, he quit straight after. Undeterred, the band found a replacement in part-time village-dance promoter/singer and full-time butcher's assistant, Roger 'Sandy' Brokenshire. 'Sandy' was an old-school showman, with a mop of wild hair and flamboyant stage clothes, who'd been performing since childhood. In truth, the 24-year-old was cut from the same cloth as his predecessor, but his sturdy voice was fine for belting out James Brown's 'I Go Crazy' and Ray Charles' 'What'd I Say'. 'Roger Taylor wasn't the best drummer I ever played with,' recalled Brokenshire, years later. 'But he was good-looking and really knew music. He used to wait for me outside the butcher's shop where I worked and we'd go off to do the gig.'

With Brokenshire often, as one band member recalled, 'still greasy from making sausages', The Reactions divided their set between high-energy soul (the 1984-approved 'My Girl' and 'Knock On Wood') and voguish rock numbers including The Rolling Stones' 'Satisfaction', on which Taylor would sing lead vocals while drumming. In March 1966, the new-look The Reaction (another name change) re-entered the Rock and Rhythm Championship at Truro City Hall. By now, guitarist Geoff 'Ben' Daniel was in. 'Everyone at school started calling me Ben after Ben-haddad, the middle-eastern king,' he says. 'I was reading his name out loud in religious studies class and I got an attack of the giggles. It stuck after that. I think there was a fall-out between Graham Hankins and the rest of The Reaction, and I slid in at the beginning of sixty-six.'

At City Hall, the group rocked up in black turtle-neck sweaters, Taylor's bass drum skin painted with a very modish target, and charged into Wilson Pickett's 'In the Midnight Hour' and The Shirelles' 'Will You Still Love Me Tomorrow?'. Even Roger Brokenshire's multicoloured trousers and pink and blue sheepskin jacket couldn't blight their performance. The Reaction saw off the competition, outshining rival Truro act The Strangers, Newquay's The Other Five and Falmouth's Kontiki Klan. They won the competition and were, according to the *West Briton and Royal Cornwall Gazette*, 'mobbed by young girls'.

As contest winners, The Reaction's bookings increased. With it came the new billing: 'The Champion Group of Cornwall'. They opened for The Kinks at Torquay Town Hall and Gerry and The Pacemakers at Redruth's Flamingo Ballroom, alongside their own gigs in Truro. Local entrepreneur Rik Evans had first encountered The Reaction playing a wedding reception. The 21-year-old Evans had just bought a marquee company and had hired out a marquee at the same event. He and Taylor became friends. 'I used to book The Reaction for any wedding events,' says Rik. 'They were a great band. You didn't see many singing drummers apart from in The Dave Clark Five, but Roger had the voice even then.'

When Reaction bassist Jim Craven was unavailable for a weekend slot supporting The Nashville Teens in Torquay, Rick Penrose stepped in. Penrose had first encountered Roger at Truro Cathedral School. As bassist with the Truro band The Strangers, he'd reconnected with Taylor on the gig circuit. At Torquay, Rick witnessed The Reaction drummer's winning way with the opposite sex. 'Roger took some girls home in our van after the gig. He went off and he never came back. So we had to unpack his drum kit and then we got thrown out on the street, with all the gear. God knows how long he left us there waiting.' Rick was similarly amused by Roger's gung-ho approach to securing his drum kit. 'We played the technical college in Plymouth, which had this beautiful polished wooden stage. Because Roger's bass drum work was so strong, the drum kept moving. So before the show, he would nail the spikes on the drum stand to the stage floor with these six-inch nails.' 'People used to go ape-shit,' recalled Mike Dudley.

Undeterred, Penrose joined The Reaction permanently and, in October, accompanied the band and their ex-singer Johnny Quale to a recording session at a studio in Wadebridge. Quale had made contact with EMI producer Norrie Paramour and wanted to send him a demo tape. 'A friend of Norrie's was running the studio,' explains Geoff Daniel. 'Johnny wanted to do an EP of his sort of music, which meant Elvis. We agreed to be his backing band but, to be honest, he'd had his day.' After accompanying Quale on four tracks, the studio engineer made an offer. 'We slipped him a few quid,' continues Daniel, 'and he let us record a couple of songs.' The Reaction played spur-of-the-moment versions of 'I Feel Good (I Got You)' and 'In the Midnight Hour', with Roger taking the lead vocal, making it the first professional recording of the future Queen drummer.

Listening back to the Johnny Quale EP highlighted some of the group's shortcomings. 'We booted John Snell out because he could never get the bloody sax in tune,' said Mike Dudley, and Roger Brokenshire soon followed. 'Sandy was an amazing frontperson because he was so full of energy. He absolutely sold the thing,' laughs Rick Penrose now. 'I don't want to stab him in the back, but he did scream and shout a lot, and run around wearing this sheepskin furry jacket thing, trying to look like Sonny Bono . . .' In the era of Dylan's *Highway 61 Revisited*, three songs from which were now in The Reaction's setlist, Brokenshire's cabaret style was seen as incongruous. 'There was a falling-out between him and Roger and Mike,' recalls Geoff Daniel, 'but I stayed well out of it.' However, others remember Brokenshire's exit differently: supposedly the rest of the band simply stopped picking him up from the butcher's shop until he got the message. Unfazed, Brokenshire changed his stage name to Rockin' Roger Dee and spent the next three decades playing the Cornish club circuit.

Like Brian May and his school group, The Reaction changed during 1967. 'We all got into Cream and Hendrix,' says Geoff Daniel, who left the band to attend university that summer. With his kit moved further to the front of centre-stage, singing drummer Taylor (now bestowed a band nickname of 'Splodge') was The Reaction's leader, with the others happy to defer to him. In addition to Keith Moon, Taylor had found another drumming hero, The Jimi Hendrix Experience's Mitch Mitchell. 'Roger was always very forward-looking,' explains Rick Penrose. 'With any band you have a few people that are just there for the fun of it, but Roger had real ambition.'

Since taking over, Taylor had worked hard at securing The Reaction the best gigs possible, signing up with a local booking agency. Realising they could save money by booking shows themselves, he ditched the agency and set about doing just that. Onstage, his desire to make an impact led to him dousing the edge of his cymbals in petrol and torching them during the show's finale. Meanwhile, the Taylors' family piano was torn out of its wooden casing, splattered with paint and transported to gigs where, during a frantic reading of Wilson Pickett's 'Land of 1000 Dances', Roger would attack it with a hammer. Taylor's tireless mantra, 'I'm gonna be a pop star', seemed more believable now.

But The Reaction's soul revue-style show would not last much longer. Rick Penrose was a year older than Taylor and Dudley and already holding down a full-time job as well as playing in the band. Rick faced further challenge when the band stripped back to become a three-piece. Inspired by Cream and The Jimi Hendrix

Experience, this new version of The Reaction came about when Mike Dudley sold the organ and purchased a white Jimi-style Stratocaster. Roger and Mike's listening habits had changed to include *The Who Sell Out*, Hendrix's *Are You Experienced?* and Cream's *Disraeli Gears*, and the setlist changed, too. 'I found it difficult,' admits Penrose. 'When there were five or six of us in the band, it was reassuring. With just three of us we had to work harder. I came to enjoy it, but by then I was under pressure from outside the group to leave.'

Rick was finding it hard to commit to the band and manage a full-time job. In February 1967 his mind was made up for him after an accident on the way to a gig. Roger was driving the group's Thames Trader van. In the back were Rick, Mike Dudley, and four other friends, including fellow Truro School pupils-cum-roadies Neil Battersby and Peter Gill-Carey. As the seventeen-year-old Taylor had just passed his driving test, Battersby, the usual driver, handed him the keys.

Driving through heavy rain and fog near the Cornish village of Indian Queens, Taylor failed to spot an unattended fish lorry parked half on the road with its lights turned off. The lorry and the band's van were turned upside down by the impact, with Roger himself thrown through the windscreen. Incredibly, he escaped largely unhurt. Meanwhile, Rick Penrose was showered with glass and sustained numerous cuts, and Mike Dudley was left with a broken nose and hand. However, Peter Gill-Carey was more seriously injured, suffering a punctured lung. Although he eventually made a recovery, he spent several months in hospital recuperating. The subsequent insurance claim took several years to settle, with the fish lorry owner refusing to take responsibility for the collision. The incident cast a long shadow over all involved. 'That dreadful accident made a big difference,' says Rick Penrose. 'People wanted me to leave the band and then that happened as well. It all became incorporated.'

For Roger and the others, there was also the issue of further education. Taylor later claimed that he was 'a lazy scholar', but in the summer of 1967 he still managed to leave Truro School with seven O-levels and three A-levels in Physics, Chemistry and

Biology, though his A-level grades were, by some accounts, not as high as expected. His old schoolfriend David Penhaligon later joked, 'It was always alleged that he [Roger] ruined four or five academic careers because he involved others in the group.' Weakening that claim is Mike Dudley, who took up a place at Oxford University. But as Rick Penrose remembers it, Taylor was now under heavy parental pressure: 'Roger was all set to go to college and his mum said to him, "You are not to go up there and start playing in a group, Roger."'

Leaving his drum kit behind, Taylor began the first year of his dentistry degree at the London School of Medicine in Whitechapel. He found a ground floor flat at 19 Sinclair Gardens, Shepherd's Bush, sharing with four others, including another Truro lad Les Brown. Fortuitously, Brown was studying at Imperial College. Taylor began his degree course, just as Brian knuckled down to his second year at Imperial and Freddie Bulsara began his second year at Ealing art college. Taylor respected his mother's wishes in London throughout the following year. Without a drum kit, he satisfied himself with trips to the Marquee, while the Sinclair Gardens flat soon echoed to the heavy 'progressive' sounds of Free's debut album *Tons of Sobs* and, later, Family's *Music in a Dolls House*.

A trip back to Truro for the summer holidays in 1968 found him reviving The Reaction, with whichever local musicians were available. Inspired by the musical 'happenings' taking place in London, Taylor struck a deal with his friend and marquee-hire company owner Rik Evans to stage a few of their own.

Billing these events as the Summer Coast Sound Experience, The Reaction would provide the music, Rik would hire a doorman, and the proceeds ('five shillings on the door per person') would be split. 'We'd take our marquee to different locations around Cornwall,' says Evans. 'The best one we did was on Perranporth Beach. The local life-savers club had a barbecue and The Reaction provided the music. Unfortunately, the council didn't want us on there, so we never came back. There were times when we'd just set up in these little coves, not even knowing who owned the land, and they'd just plug in and play, and we'd make a few bob. It was all very seat of the pants.' One such event in a secluded cove at Trevellas Port near St Agnes coincided with a massive thunderstorm, and only a handful of paying punters turned up. 'I think I saw five teddy boys dancing in a puddle,' laughs Rik Evans.

With the holidays over, The Reaction drifted apart for good: wives, families, proper jobs and universities all playing a part in its demise. Mike Dudley returned to Oxford, continued to play music but went into a career in insurance; Rick Penrose played in a cabaret band before becoming a photographer; Geoff 'Ben' Daniel worked as an engineering consultant and, later, moved to Hong Kong. Rik Evans still runs the marquee hire company in Truro. When asked about his days in The Reaction, Taylor has always seemed coy. 'My friends and I started a band at school. It built up from school until, finally, the bad bands became good bands,' he said once. 'I was always the leader. I must have been the pushy one.'

Back at the London School of Medicine in the autumn of 1968, Taylor's pushiness would come to the fore. Playing again in Truro had given him a taste of what he'd been missing. On top of this, he was fast losing interest in the dentistry course. 'I only went out of middle-class conditioning,' he claimed. 'You had to get a proper job and make a good career . . . And it was a good way to stay in London without having to work.' Eager to put together a new band, he even contacted Rick Penrose and invited him up to London: 'But I said no,' explains Rick. 'I have no regrets about that. I sometimes think your life is mapped out for you.'

Taylor wouldn't have to wait long to find new players. In autumn, his flatmate Les Brown spotted a postcard pinned to a noticeboard at Imperial College. The request was simple: 'Ginger Baker / Mitch Mitchell-style drummer wanted'. It would mark the beginning of a new life for the nineteen-year-old drummer. 'Playing in a group was always a dream for me,' insisted Taylor years later. 'I always wanted to do it, and eventually it got the better of everything else. I broke out, and that was it.'

CHAPTER THREE

A Happy Accident

> 'In the beginning I was quite prepared to starve. You have to believe in yourself no matter how long it takes.'
>
> **Freddie Mercury**

> 'I just want to go home and be a milkman.'
>
> **Mick 'Miffer' Smith, drummer in Mercury's first band, Ibex**

It was while studying at Ealing Technical College and School of Art that The Who's Pete Townshend first felt compelled to destroy an electric guitar. Pete, a student for two years until 1964, enjoyed his Eureka moment while listening to lecturer Gustav Metzger expound his theory of auto-destructive art. Metzger was one of a handful of Ealing lecturers gifted with what Townshend admiringly called 'wild thinking'. Among his similarly-minded Ealing colleagues was Roy Ascott, who once shut a group of students in the lecture theatre, bombarded them with continuous flashing lights, before leading them to the college's entrance hall, the floor of which was covered with hundreds of marbles. Ascott's aim was to challenge and disorientate. To Pete Townshend, Ascott was 'a fucking genius'.

When Freddie Bulsara rolled up at Ealing in the summer of 1966, the 'genius' at Ealing was more likely to have been Pete Townshend. By 1966, the rollcall of art-students-turned-rock stars was growing: Townshend, Ron Wood, Charlie Watts, Keith Richards, Jimmy Page, Eric Clapton . . .

A grey-brick affair on St Mary's Road, close to Ealing Green in the depths of suburban West London, Ealing didn't have quite the same reputation as its rivals. 'Camberwell and Chelsea were well known for painters,' explains ex-Ealing graphics student Renos Lavithis. 'St Martin's and Holborn were good for painting and fashion. Ealing's fashion course and industrial design course were good; its art department was not so good.'

Mark Malden met Freddie Bulsara when the two enrolled as the only male pupils among thirty women on the fashion design course. 'Fred told us that his family was of Persian origin, but he let us assume they'd lived in England for generations,' says Malden now. 'When he spoke, his accent and pronunciation was like that of someone who had attended a good private school in England.' From the start, Freddie told Mark that he'd wanted to study graphic design, but had decided to try fashion first. However, the course made little use of his Art A-level and focused instead on textile technology, fabric printing and pattern design. The pair made themselves fashionable batik T-shirts, and, later Freddie would model one of Malden's own creations, a chevroned leather and fur jacket, at the end-of-year fashion show.

On the fashion course, Freddie and Mark fell in with three other fashion students: Gillian Green, Celia Dawson and Glynnis Davies, aka 'Glyn the Pin'. The five would frequent the nearby Castle Inn pub, and gigs in the college theatre and its annexe building in Drayton Green. Freddie and Mark would travel further afield to Richmond's Crawdaddy club, where they saw a then unknown Elton John, and to a school hall in Hayes to watch their old Ealing alumnus Pete Townshend destroying a guitar onstage with The Who. At weekends, Bulsara would sometimes tag along with Gillian and Celia to the Green Man pub in Putney Heath.

Though still living at home, Fred was expected to earn some money of his own, and took a weekend job as a baggage handler at Heathrow Airport (Malden: 'I know it's hard to imagine Freddie Mercury doing manual labour'). But before long, he had discovered a more lucrative source of income, as a life model for the college's evening art class. Fred introduced Mark Malden to the job, and before long both were earning £5 for a couple of hours' work, posing naked for what Malden remembers as 'a lot of old women and a few old men'.

The year after Fred Bulsara arrived at Ealing, two budding artists from Yorkshire, Chris Smith and Paul Humberstone, showed up for their first term. Both had enrolled on the advertising and graphic design course. Smith was also a keyboard player and was studying privately for a music degree. 'I could have gone to music college,' he says, 'but I went to an art school simply because that's what Keith Richards had done.' While exploring the college on their first day, the pair stumbled across the fashion department. 'Not wishing to sound too macho, but our first thought was, "Fashion? Great. There's bound to be lots of nice women in there,"' says Paul Humberstone. 'So we stuck our heads round the door and the first thing we saw was this bloke with lots of black hair: Freddie Bulsara.'

At some point between 1967 and 1968, Fred crossed over from fashion to graphic design, joining Alan Hill, his old compadre from Isleworth. 'I still don't quite know how he managed it,' says Alan now. 'But after thinking he wanted to do fashion, Fred decided, no, he wanted to do graphics. The truth is he thought we were having more fun and going to more parties.' Mark Malden knows otherwise: 'Fred was kicked out of fashion design by the principal James Drew,' he reveals. 'But he talked his way into letting him switch to the graphics course instead. I sometimes wonder if he did it on purpose as a way of prolonging his time at the college, and deciding what he was going to do with his life.'

The course was loosely split between graphics, commercial art and illustration. Fred joined a clique of musically-minded students that included Chris Smith, Nigel Foster and 1984's lead vocalist Tim Staffell. The four of them would, as Smith recalls, 'sit in the corner and talk about music all day long. Everything from Jimi Hendrix to Igor Stravinsky.' Lunchtimes were spent flitting between the student common room, the refectory (Alan Hill: 'Freddie and I both had a thing for the same girl and used to sit there at lunch-times and wait for her to turn up'), the Castle Inn and the guitar shops on Ealing Broadway.

Tim Staffell soon introduced his new friends to 1984. After seeing the band play the college's Christmas ball at Ealing Town Hall, Chris Smith ventured his opinion: 'I said to Tim Staffell straight away, "You and the guitarist are miles ahead of the others,"' he laughs. Fred was similarly impressed by his classmate's group, and extended his friendship from Staffell to include Richard Thompson. 'I lived in Hounslow so I was near to where Fred lived,' says Thompson. 'We used to hang out together. He'd travel to 1984 gigs in the van with me, and I used to go over to his house. His dad had one of those old stereograms, so we'd sit round there listening to Fred's Beatles records.'

Subash Shah, his old schoolfriend from India and Zanzibar, had been writing intermittently to Bulsara since his family's move to Ohio. 'I never received a reply,' says Shah. 'So I made a pact with myself that if he didn't respond to me by 1968, I would stop writing. That year I wrote and told him my thoughts about the Vietnam War and everything else that was going on in the world, but he never wrote back. I realised then that he had crossed over to the other culture, and that he didn't really wish to be reminded of India and Zanzibar.'

Freddie was clearly too distracted by everything else that was going on around him. Smith, Humberstone and Mark Malden echo his Isleworth classmate Brian Fanning's description of Freddie Bulsara as 'a curious sponge, soaking up all the influences', in particular Cream and his beloved Jimi Hendrix, but it was still difficult for some to tell just how serious he was. Alan Hill became a regular with Fred at London's Marquee club: 'We went to see Cream together, and Fred always wanted to get near to the front, right by the speakers, and he'd start playing imaginary guitar. If they'd had an air guitar championship back then, he'd have won it hands down.'

'At college he'd get the ruler out and start doing his Hendrix impression,' adds Humberstone. The eighteen-inch yardstick, sometimes replaced by a T-square, was his favourite prop during those impersonations. 'The thing is, you could be talking to Freddie about something serious and then, suddenly, bang! Out came the ruler,' adds Chris Smith. 'And he even played it left-handed so he could be just like Jimi Hendrix. At times, it could get on your nerves, but it was just Fred being Fred.'

According to Roger Taylor, 'Freddie saw Hendrix fourteen nights in a row in different pubs.' While the guitarist never played fourteen pub shows in a row, no one could dispute Freddie's devotion. 'Hendrix was the reason James Drew kicked Fred off the fashion course,' says Mark Malden. 'He was taking too much time off from college to go and see him.' Malden had accompanied Freddie to his debut Hendrix gig. 'It was some obscure club in Soho in late 1966 or early 1967,' says Malden now (the likeliest venue being the Bag o' Nails in Kingly Street). 'I remember it because Fred bought an ex-RAF greatcoat to wear to the gig as it was so cold. I found Hendrix interesting, but not to the extent that Fred did. He idolised the man.'

Richard Thompson also recalls joining Freddie for a Hendrix gig at the Marquee. Chris Smith missed out on the gig after blowing a term's grant on a new amplifier ('I starved after that') but remembers seeing Fred the day after and being told about the performance in forensic detail. Alan Hill's last meeting with Freddie Bulsara was at his wedding in 1970. The two hadn't seen each other in over a year, but Freddie came bearing a wedding gift: a Jimi Hendrix LP.

Smith's observation that Tim Staffell and the guitarist were the best players in 1984 proved correct. By early 1968, Brian May had quit and Tim would soon follow. They planned to start a new group: Smith playing the organ, May on guitar and Tim Staffell handling lead vocals and bass. 'We had a meeting in the Duke of Wellington pub in Wardour Street,' remembers Smith. 'We decided to work together but we needed a drummer, which is how we came up with the idea of putting an advert on the notice board at Imperial College.'

The 'Ginger Baker / Mitch Mitchell-style drummer' they found was Roger Taylor. May met Taylor in the bar at Imperial College, later writing the drummer a letter outlining his musical ideas; a move that demonstrated the guitarist's painstaking attention to detail and love of good planning. When Staffell, Smith and May arrived at Taylor and Les Brown's flat in Kensington, they found that Roger's drum kit was still at his mother's house in Cornwall. Making do with the popular hippy accoutrement, a pair of bongos, he still managed to impress them. 'We spent an hour just talking to

Roger that night,' says Smith, 'and he also sang, and that impressed us. I remember Tim saying to me afterwards, "Oh, he's got a better voice than me . . . And he's better-looking than me . . ."'

What Taylor shared with Brian May was ambition, but, like Tim Staffell, he had a looser, more easy-going personality. 'Roger's playing was punchy and flamboyant,' explained Staffell. 'But also his personality was always "up".' For Taylor, too, making an immediate connection was a relief. 'I had gone for a few auditions but they were always very depressing affairs: eighteen drum kits in a line and so on.'

Though still commuting to Ealing from the family house in Feltham, Fred would also find a second home at Chris and Paul Humberstone's flat ('Fred lived like a gypsy,' recalled Brian May). After first moving to London, Smith and Humberstone had lived in Elsham Road, directly opposite the Kensington Tavern. Later, the pair found lodgings nearby at 42b Addison Gardens. The musos' social network soon centred around the Kensington, Addison Gardens and Roger Taylor's flat in Sinclair Gardens.

With Taylor's drums now in London, they began rehearsing in any available space at Imperial College, including, says Chris Smith, 'the broom cupboard'. 'Brian had never met anyone before who could actually tune drums,' recalled Taylor in 2002. 'He wasn't even aware that you could tune drums. Typical guitarist! But he and I clicked straight away. His playing was beautiful.'

The band adopted the name Smile, a Tim Staffell creation, which he immortalised with a self-designed logo of luscious lips and pearly white teeth. Imperial College's place on the university circuit made Smile an ideally placed support band. But their guitarist's academic career was still an issue. Tim and Chris had another year to complete at Ealing. Roger would drop out of his dentistry course, receiving the first half of his degree and appeasing his mother with a vague plan to take just a year off to concentrate on music. (He would resume his studies later, switching to biology at North London Polytechnic.) Brian, though, had now finished the final year of his degree, and wanted to remain at Imperial as a post-graduate to work on a PhD thesis on the movement of inter-planetary dust. May's future as an astronomer seemed assured: he had already spent time in Switzerland studying zodiacal light at an observatory hut, and, after graduating, had been invited to carry out astronomical research at Jodrell Bank Observatory at the request of the eminent astronomer Sir Bernard Lovell. As one of May's professors explained: 'Brian was first and foremost a bright physicist . . . There was no question of him becoming a rock star.'

His academic future may have been mapped out for him, but May was now a fixture in the audience at the Marquee, watching bands, especially their guitarists, and mentally taking notes. At least one prominent guitar player still recalls the lanky, busby-haired youth as a permanent presence at his gigs, approaching him after the show to ask technical questions about the equipment he was using. The conflicting influences in May's life appeared almost side by side on 24 and 26 October 1968. On 24 October, Brian, watched by his parents, was awarded his Bachelor of Science by the Queen Mother at the Royal Albert Hall. Two days later, Smile played a gig at Imperial, opening for Pink Floyd.

Tim Staffell has always maintained that the Floyd show was Smile's debut performance. However, Chris Smith, while agreeing that the group's debut was at Imperial, believes it was supporting The Troggs. 'We turned up and they were soundchecking,' he explains. 'If you've ever heard *The Troggs Tapes* [a bootleg recording of the band arguing in a studio], then that's exactly what they were like. Also their drummer hardly seemed to play with both hands at the same time. I remember looking at the other guys, open-mouthed. These were pop stars. They'd done "Wild Thing". We couldn't believe it. Why are we supporting them? We could blow them off!'

The group also encountered another problem: Brian's stage clothes. 'Brian had the afro-type hair by then but he still looked very much the student,' says Smith carefully. 'He turned up for the gig wearing a bri-nylon shirt and one of those knitted string ties you'd have worn in 1964. Extremely square. So Roger took him back to his flat to change. But with Roger being much smaller than Brian, there wasn't much in his wardrobe that fitted, except for this purple waistcoat . . . which he put over the bri-nylon shirt.'

As Chris recalls, Smile opened their show with a segment from Bach's *Toccata and Fugue in D Minor* played on his Selmer Capri organ.

'Then Brian hit this huge guitar chord, Roger went into a drum roll, and we did this big vamp and straight into "Can't Be So Bad" by Moby Grape.' But it was their four-part harmonies 'with Roger's lovely tenor on top' that shocked him. 'I was surprised how good it sounded. Thinking back, you had it all there: Brian's guitar sound and Roger's drums. All you really needed was a smart guy to come along with some good ideas . . . Someone like Freddie.'

'I guess Smile wanted to be heavy rock,' said Tim Staffell. 'But there was also a pressure to try and make it appear virtuoso.' Staffell's mention of this pressure summed up a potential problem with Smile's music, for both him and their keyboard player. Chris Smith and his Selmer Capri would only appear with Smile on a few more occasions.

'I loved the creativity of it, but musically it wasn't for me,' Smith offers. 'Roger was a rocker, and I liked that, but he wasn't into the blues. We'd be round his flat listening to the first Led Zeppelin album or Yes and I'd be thinking, "What happened to Muddy Waters and Otis Redding and Howlin' Wolf?" In my mind, I had this idea of playing in a little Rolling Stones. I wanted songs about the blues and love and death. I liked the seriousness of that, and it was obvious Smile weren't going to go that way.'

Tim Staffell remembered Smith being asked to leave Smile in February 1969, shortly before their gig at the Royal Albert Hall: 'We said, "Chris, we'd rather do tomorrow night as a trio," ' he told *Record Collector* magazine. Smith disputes this: 'I saw Brian on Elsham Road and said, "I'm not coming back to the band." I dare say the writing was already on the wall, but I don't remember being sacked.'

On 27 February, Brian returned to the Albert Hall, minus the Queen Mother, but with a Smithless Smile. The concert was a fundraiser for the National Council for the Unmarried Mother and Her Child, compèred by DJ John Peel. As the show had been organised by Imperial College, Smile blagged their way second from the bottom of a bill, below Spooky Tooth, Joe Cocker and headliners Bonzo Dog Band, fresh from their recent hit, 'I'm the Urban Spaceman'. Going on before Smile was Free, a new blues-rock group featuring lead singer (and future Queen collaborator) Paul Rodgers.

Smile got off to a shaky start when Tim Staffell dashed to the front of the expansive stage only to discover his bass guitar lead was too short. Having accidentally unplugged himself, it was left to Brian to play the opening chord. The trio muddled on, though, playing their own heavier, vamped-up versions of folk singer Tim Hardin's 'If I Were a Carpenter', Sonny Terry's 'See What a Fool I've Been' and Tommy James and The Shondelles' 'Mony Mony'.

In the meantime, Peter Abbey, a friend of Taylor's from his dentistry course, had been appointed as the band's manager. Abbey passed a tape on to John Anthony, then working as an A&R man at Mercury Records. Anthony had previously been the in-house DJ at the Speakeasy, a rock stars' watering hole on London's Margaret Street, immortalised on The Who's *Sell Out* album with the lyric 'Speakeasy, drink easy, pull easy . . .' He had also compèred one of Led Zeppelin's first tours.

'My boss at Mercury was Lou Reizner, who was this big Chicago records mogul,' says Anthony. 'At the time Lou had David Bowie, Eyes of Blue, which became Man, Peter Hammill and Terry Reid. When I started working for Lou, the first person through the office door was Roger's friend from his dental course, with a tape of Smile.'

Through March and April that year, Smile played three gigs at PJ's in Truro, a club owned by Roger's friend Peter Bawden. The Taylor connections had been enough to secure weekend gigs at the club and elsewhere in Cornwall; shows that were sometimes billed as 'featuring the Legendary Drummer of Cornwall, Roger Taylor'. As Chris Smith remembers it, 'When Smile did those gigs as a three-piece in Cornwall, I think they got used to the idea of being Cream.'

John Anthony accompanied the band to one of the gigs in Truro. 'Unfortunately, it ended with me getting into a fight with the locals,' he admits. 'I was the music business guy down from London with long hair and the alien clothes, and these guys started hassling me, standing on my feet . . .' A fight broke out on the dancefloor, with Anthony leaping into the back of the band's van to escape and fending off his attackers with a mic stand. 'After it was all over, we drove back to London. I said I'd get them some studio time.'

In April, Lou Reizner saw Smile in concert in London and offered them an on-the-spot one-single deal for the US only. 'It was a toe-in-the water contract,' recalled Tim Staffell. 'Just Mercury putting out a small amount of dough to see what happened.' Two months later, Smile were summoned to London's Trident Studios to record the single, with John Anthony producing. 'What I saw in Smile was a sort of "Led Yes",' he offers, 'because they had Yes's harmonies and Zeppelin's big riffs. I was sure they would do something but not in that incarnation. To be honest, I wasn't sure about Tim Staffell.'

Brian's decision to quit 1984 had been partly driven by a desire to write his own material. Tim Staffell shared this ambition with him and had been making a concerted effort to write since the previous summer. Smile's set now included 1984's one original 'Step On Me', and two new compositions 'Earth' and 'Doing Alright' (which would end up on the first Queen album). With lyrics influenced by his passion for science fiction, Staffell would later be dismissive of his early work, describing it as 'pretentious guff . . . cobblers'.

' "Earth" was a good song,' insists Chris Smith. 'It was the era of the moon landings, so that was very much in the ether. I remember Tim telling me that he'd written the song about being given the choice to go to space in a rocket ship, but the catch was you could never come back to earth. I remember he said, "If I had the choice to go and not come back I'd take it." I said, "No thanks, Tim, I'll stay here." '

At Trident, Smile cut the single, 'Earth', with a B-side of 'Step On Me' (also squeezing in a recording of 'Doing Alright'). It was set for an August release. In the meantime, though, it was back to Cornwall for another run of Smile shows. Smile's entourage for the summer trip had expanded to include Peter Abbey, van driver Richard Thompson, roadie Pete Edmunds, and, for less obvious reasons, Freddie Bulsara.

On 21 July, astronaut Neil Armstrong became the first man to walk on the moon. 'We all crowded round the TV at Roger's mum's to watch it,' recalls Richard Thompson. Winifred Taylor had agreed to accommodate the touring party for some nights, and found Roger's dandyish friend Freddie a source of endless fascination. Despite being bussed around the country in the back of a van, Fred managed to maintain impeccable sartorial standards. Said Roger Taylor: 'My mother could never work out how Freddie's trousers had such a perfect crease in them.'

Back in London, Smile signed to the Rondo Talent Agency on Kensington Church Street. While overshadowed by other Rondo clients such as Nick Drake and the fledgling Genesis, the connection at least meant more bookings. Through the remainder of the summer, the trio would gain valuable experience opening for The Climax Chicago Blues Band, Family and others, and 1984's rhythm guitarist John Garnham caught them in concert. 'They were supporting a group called Timebox who had a song called "Bake Jam Roll in Your Eye", absolute crap title and song,' he laughs. 'Smile came on and did this wonderful slow, heavy version of "If I Were a Carpenter."' As a roadie for Smile at a gig at Watford College in October, Garnham was even more taken: 'They were better than Taste [the headliners]. That was the time I thought, "Yes, they're on to something here."'

Garnham wasn't alone. From their first gig, Smile had acquired an ardent if not uncritical fan in Fred Bulsara. 'I think Freddie was there in the wings when we first played,' says Chris Smith. 'After the gigs, he'd be like, "You know that bit where the drums come in? Well, why don't you do this instead?" He was full of suggestions, full of ideas. I said to Brian, "Fred is desperate to be in this band, you know", but Brian was like, "No, no, no, Tim is the lead singer. He'd never wear it."'

Brian May has no recollection of Fred's stints as a 1984 roadie. Instead, he remembers first meeting his future singer at a Smile show. 'I don't know if it's accurate or not but in my mind's eye I remember him very much dressed like a rock star,' he said in 2005. 'But the kind of rock star you hadn't seen before − really flamboyant and androgynous. He was flicking a pompom around and being very flippant, saying, "Yes, it's wonderful, it's wonderful, but . . . why don't you present the show better, why don't you dress like this?" He was full-on from the very beginning.'

'He came over with Tim one day,' recalled Roger Taylor. 'And he just became one of the circle. He was full of enthusiasm − long, black, flowing hair and this great dandy image.'

Photographs from Ealing in 1968 support Paul Humberstone's memory of Freddie as 'not being particularly flamboyant'. Mark Malden also insists that during his time on the fashion course, Freddie was shy and never once mentioned wanting to become a musician. But Freddie's defection to the graphics course marked a change in his behaviour and ambition. In his final year at Ealing, Fred's crisp shirts and neat Levis were swapped for knotted silk scarves, satin and, as one contemporary remembers it, 'velvet, lots of velvet'. That year, another graphics student, Tony Catignani, had acquired a bespoke black satin coat. 'One of the girls on the fashion course made it for me,' says Catignani now. 'It looked like a long undertaker's jacket. Fred had his eye on it, and I swapped it with him for an LP.'

After a shopping trip to Carnaby Street, Chris Smith sauntered into college wearing a pair of newly acquired bright red trousers. 'And there was Freddie, feet up on the desk, wearing snakeskin boots and these crushed velvet trousers, just like Hendrix, reading *Melody Maker*. He saw me, glanced down and didn't say a word. I'd been aced again.'

In contrast, Smile still dressed down in split-knee jeans and scoop-neck T-shirts. Onstage, they adopted the standard pose of staring at the floor and concentrating on the music. Said Brian May: 'The fashion then was that you had to wear jeans, and you had to have your back to the audience. Freddie had the idea that rock should be a show, which was a pretty unusual idea in those times.'

Despite Freddie's grand designs for Smile, he was still without a band of his own, and his frustration was growing. Mark Malden's brother, Aubrey, was on the graphics course at Ealing and was also social secretary of the Student Union. 'Fred hung around any band that we booked for the college,' says Aubrey now. 'He was always around the guys in 1984, but we booked Free to play the rag ball at Ealing Town Hall, and I saw Fred deep in conversation with their guitarist Paul Kossoff. It was around this time that he started telling us that he was going to become a pop star. Of course, we all laughed.'

Chris Smith had seen Fred playing the college piano many times.

'He had this staccato style. It was like Mozart gone mad.' He also discovered how quickly his friend could memorise a piece of music and play it. Though Fred was still cautious about his abilities. 'When there were other musicians about, he could be quite humble,' says Chris. 'It was often, "Oh, you play, you're better than me."' Tony Catignani adds, 'I remember he was often missing from lectures. The tutors were like, "Where *is* Freddie?" And you'd always find him in the common room playing the piano.'

Before long, he struck up the courage to start singing. Fred sat opposite Tim Staffell in class, and the pair, sometimes joined by Chris and Nigel Foster, would practise harmony vocals, often to the amusement of their classmates. 'We enjoyed it, we encouraged them,' claims Renos Lavithis. 'They'd sometimes get guitars out and play. We used to tease Freddie, "Look, you'll be famous one day." You could tell he was stuck between wanting to become an illustrator and wanting to be a musician.' Tim maintains that it took time for Fred to find his singing voice; Chris Smith insists that he was 'nailed to the wall' the first time he heard Fred sing. Paul Humberstone vividly recalls a 'falsetto voice that really did sound like Mika, that guy who's on the radio now'.

According to Smith, though, while Fred could play piano and had started singing, it was still a source of annoyance to him that he couldn't write a song: 'Brian May and Tim Staffell had written a proper song, "Step On Me". It sounded like a song The Beatles would do. Freddie and I didn't know anyone that had written a song. That was something the gods did, not mere mortals. That was when Freddie said, "Maybe we could do that." He couldn't approach Tim because Tim was in Smile, and he didn't know Roger and Brian well enough yet, so he came to me.'

Back then, Chris was 'vaguely interested' in songwriting, but remembers Fred being passionate about it. 'I had the keys to the music department, so we'd meet there sometimes. Freddie would turn up with these scraps of songs that he'd put together.' Away from the college Tony Catignani was invited to Gladstone Avenue and recalls Freddie 'tinkering around on the piano, always humming a tune and trying to write songs. It was in his blood.' It was around this time that Catignani caught a glimpse of Freddie's passport. 'He'd listed his profession as "musician",' laughs Tony. 'I said, "Why have you got that in there?" He said, "Because I am going to get into music and become a musician." Looking back, Fred had this incredible energy. Sometimes it was as if sparks were coming off him – "Let's do this! Let's do that!" '

Sparks flew again when Freddie started writing songs. In June 1967 The Beatles had released *Sgt Peppers Lonely Hearts Club Band*. With tracks such as 'A Day in the Life' and 'Within You, Without You', they had expanded the horizons of what constituted pop music. 'So Freddie started linking these different scraps of music together,' says Chris Smith. 'We used the link in "A Day in the Life" – "Woke up, fell out of bed" – as we found you could link any two piece of music with that.' But it was still an arduous process and Freddie would sometimes lose patience. 'Fred would get annoyed with himself. Some days he'd have his heads in his hands, despairing, "Why can Tim and Brian do this and we can't? . . . Why am I so crap?" '

On other occasions, though, his enthusiasm would prove infectious. If there wasn't a guitar to hand, Freddie would drag Chris to a music shop on nearby Ealing Broadway: 'We'd go there at lunchtime, and Fred would just take a guitar off the wall and start playing it, showing me what he'd just written. They got fed up with us because we were in that shop every week, playing their guitars. Then we'd buy one plectrum and leave.'

The Bulsara/Smith songwriting team came close to finishing just one composition. Intriguingly, Chris remembers it as a piece called 'The Cowboy Song'. The opening line was: 'Mama just killed a man . . .' Seven years later, those words would form the opening line of Queen's 'Bohemian Rhapsody'. Smith: 'When I first heard "Bohemian Rhapsody", I actually thought, "Oh, Freddie's finished the song." '

In Harrogate, a local R&B covers band had hired Smith after they'd heard him practising the organ in a church near to their rehearsal space. In London, Chris was still studying church organ as part of his music degree. Three or four evenings a week he would practise at a church in Acton. 'Sometimes Fred would ask to go with me,' says Smith. 'He'd offer to turn the pages of the sheet music while I was playing. Or that was the idea. Once we got there and I'd been playing quietly for a while, he'd start . . . "Go on, Chris. Do 'Gimme Some Loving' . . . Do 'Gimme Some Loving'."' Eventually Smith would relent and start pounding out the Spencer Davis Group hit while 'Freddie started jumping around the empty church, going mad and doing his poses'.

Freddie's desperation had become almost tangible by this stage. One morning, Smith encountered him sitting at his desk, his eyes glazed. 'So I put my hand in front and said, "Come on Fred, you're miles away." He just looked up and said, "I am going to be mega! You have no idea how *mega* I am going to be!" I said, "Oh yeah, as mega as Hendrix?" "Oh, yes." I was like, "Well, good luck with that one."'

Every Tuesday, the college would host lunchtime concerts, where bands with at least one foot on the ladder would perform to a student audience. These gigs were a godsend for the would-be 'megastar'. 'Tim, Freddie and I would go down to the entrance to meet the groups,' remembers Smith. 'We'd tell them we were from the Student Union, a complete fabrication. We'd just help carry in their gear and hang out, see what they'd tell us, see what we could learn. It was bands like Tyrannosaurus Rex, Savoy Brown, Chicken Shack . . .'

Earlier that year, on 29 April 1969, as Smile were signing to Mercury Records, Fred and Chris had encountered David Bowie at one of the lunchtime sessions. 'This little Renault pulled up and out he came,' says Smith. 'Bowie had this little WEM PA column, an acoustic guitar, a tape recorder and a mic stand.' Once inside the college's amphitheatre, Bowie was far from happy. 'He was like, "There's no stage!"' Chris Smith, David Bowie, just two months shy of having his breakthrough hit 'Space Oddity', and the future Freddie Mercury set about pushing tables together to build a stage.

Meanwhile, the objects of Freddie's jealousy were still waiting for their big break. Smile's single, 'Earth/Step On Me', snuck out in the US in August but disappeared. Despite failing to promote the single, Mercury were still making vague noises about an album or, possibly, an EP. In September, Smile went into Kingsway's De Lane Lea studios, with a producer, the late Fritz Freyer, to cut two original songs and one cover. 'Blag' was a blood-and-thunder rocker, instrumentally in the spirit of Cream's 'N.S.U.' or Deep Purple's 'Wring That Neck'; 'Polar Bear' was a bluesy soft-rock shuffle, while the dainty ballad 'April Lady' (written by one Stanley Lucas) had been suggested by the record company. Whatever their short-comings, though, the distinct harmonies and May's snazzy guitar lines flit in and out of the songs like snapshots of the future. Staffell's keening voice is also only a few steps removed from Freddie Mercury's on Queen's earliest recordings. In the end, Smile's EP never appeared, and Mercury shelved the recordings for nearly fifteen years, only cashing in when Queen were in their pomp.

Yet Smile would have another recording session that month, which, unbeknown to them, would have lasting consequences. Terry Yeadon had been a club DJ in his native Blackburn before moving to London and a job as a maintenance engineer at Pye Studios. One night he ran into a student who remembered him from his club days and told him about a band called Smile. 'She said she was going out with the guitarist,' says Yeadon now. 'She said the band were good and persuaded me to go and see them. For once, I thought, "OK, why not?" '

Terry is uncertain, but there is some suggestion that was Christine Mullen, Brian's girlfriend and future first wife, who'd buttonholed him that night. Christine had family in the north of England, but was now in London studying at Kensington's Maria Assumpta teacher training college where she became friends with Roger Taylor's girlfriend. Christine and Brian had initially met at a Smile show.

Keen to 'have a go in the studio myself', Terry Yeadon arranged a session for Smile late one night in Pye's Studio 2. Terry and Pye's disc-cutting engineer Geoff Calvar oversaw the 'illicit session', producing half a dozen acetates of 'Step On Me' and 'Polar Bear', finishing just before the morning shift began. 'I remember Geoff and I were taken with the fact that they were writing their own stuff, which was still unusual for bands back then,' says Yeadon. 'Smile were still rough around the edges, especially Roger, but Brian was exceptionally good, even then. After we were done, they were like, "What do you think? Can you do anything for us?" But we didn't have any experience of placing bands. I was hoping I could have a career in producing, which is why I offered them the session. It was a selfish thing. I wanted some practice.' Thinking no more of it, Terry gave Smile their acetates. The band now had a top-quality audition tape with which to approach record companies. Yeadon would come back into Brian's and Roger's lives two years later, but for now, he says, 'I thought that was the end of it. I didn't expect to see them again.'

■ ■ ■

The Kensington can still be found on the corner of Elsham Road and Russell Gardens; a short stagger from Kensington Olympia, a longer trawl from Shepherd's Bush and Holland Park. It's now a gentrified bar and grill with branded canopy, lunchtime menus and 'free wireless internet access' for all. In 1969, the Kensington Tavern was just another London pub, a boxy, smoke-filled watering hole with an upstairs function room for jazz groups, and a clientele of local workers and students spilling in from rented digs, nearby colleges and the fashion hubs of the Portobello and Kensington markets.

By 1969, Smile and their extended entourage had been frequenting the Kensington for more than a year. That summer Freddie Bulsara left Ealing art college without taking his final exams. Instead, he had his sights on a very different career. In the Kensington one night, Fred saw Chris Smith walking in, and put his head in his hands, feigning despair. When asked what was troubling him, Fred replied, 'I'm never gonna be a pop star.' Chris's response was straight out of a Tony Hancock comedy routine: 'You've got to be a pop star, Freddie, you've told everyone now.' To which Fred stood up, very slowly, before raising his hands above his head in an exultant gesture. 'I am not going to be a pop star,' he announced. 'I am going to be . . . a . . . legend!' Finally, after two long years, a chance meeting in the Kensington would bring him a tiny step closer to fulfilling that dream.

Ibex were a trio from St Helens in the northwest of England, made up of guitarist Mike Bersin, drummer Mick 'Miffer' Smith and bass guitarist John 'Tupp' Taylor. Just like 1984 and The Reaction, the band had met at school, in this case Wade Deacon Grammar School in Widnes. Taylor and Bersin had started out playing soul covers in a five-piece called Colour. By 1966, and under the overpowering influence of Clapton and Hendrix, the pair had separated from their bandmates. 'They were older guys very set in their ways,' explains 'Tupp' Taylor, 'and Mike and I were into blues and progressive rock.' They found a sympathetic drummer in 'Miffer' who suggested a name change to Ibex. ('What is an ibex?' ponders Taylor. 'I think it's an African antelope. But that name only came about because "Miffer" once said, "I'm so hungry I could eat an ibex." And we were like, "Right, that's the name of the band." ')

In May, Ibex sent their demo tape to BBC Radio 1 DJ Stuart Henry and The Beatles' newly launched Apple Records label. The Beatles connection was enough to gain them a splash of publicity in the *Widnes Evening News* ('Ibex's philosophy – blues is not music, it's a way of life'), but Apple never made an offer. After a couple of local gigs and with a few months to spare before college and work commitments kicked in, Ibex, joined by their seventeen-year-old schoolfriend Ken Testi, decided to try their luck in London.

'We thought we'd go there and get famous,' remebers Ken Testi. 'Give it a few months and see what happened.' Testi already had a driving licence and previous experience of promoting school dances in and around Widnes. He was naturally gifted as an organiser, and had fallen easily into the role of unofficial Ibex manager-roadie-chauffeur. 'Ken was always very resourceful,' says Taylor. 'He sent the tape to Apple and Stuart Henry. We got some recognition in the Liverpool area, but then, nothing, so it was time for London.'

Crucially, Testi's girlfriend, Helen McConnell, was in the capital, sharing a flat with her older sister, Pat, who was at the Maria Assumpta college. 'Very sportingly Pat agreed to let half of us stay at her flat in Sinclair Road, just behind the Olympia,' explains Testi, 'while the other half were farmed out to another friend of hers, Ann McCormick, who was renting a place in Batoum Gardens off the Shepherds Bush Road.'

The day after they arrived, and keen to get hustling, Testi parked

Ibex's Commer van by a public telephone box, took out his list of numbers and started cold-calling record companies. 'I rung up Chrysalis Records and asked to speak to Chris Ellis. The woman on the end of the line was like, "Yes, this *is* Chrysalis." We didn't have a clue.' In hindsight, Ibex's timing could have been better. Many students had gone home for the summer and the lucrative London college gig circuit was lying fallow.

Through knowing Brian May's and Roger Taylor's girlfriends at Maria Assumpta, Pat McConnell had seen Smile play at Imperial College. A couple of days before her twenty-first birthday, she chose to celebrate by paying a visit to Smile's local, the Kensington Tavern. (Ken Testi: 'The reason being she's seen Smile and thinks they're quite cute and would like to meet them . . . especially Roger.') The Ibex/Smile rendezvous took place that night. Flitting around on the fringes that night was Freddie Bulsara, looking sharp in a tiny fur jacket. Like Roger Taylor in his Granny Takes a Trip threads, Fred already resembled a rock star. 'We felt like Northern hicks next to them,' laughs Testi. Smile seemed to have achieved so much already: a recording session, support slots to Yes and Family . . . 'Then they told us about this deal with Mercury Records, so we were even more impressed.'

'Brian was very, very polite,' remembers Mike Bersin, 'and Roger was a poser, in the nicest possible way.' At closing time the party continued at Pat's Sinclair Road flat. Unable to stop himself, Brian picked up Mike Bersin's unplugged guitar and started to play. 'Brian was sat there cross-legged on the floor,' continues Testi. 'I thought I had a handle on guitarists. I'd seen all the black blues guys who toured in the sixties, I'd seen everyone that had been through John Mayall's band . . . but when Brian started playing I thought I'd just missed a chapter. It was that special.'

Before long, May, Taylor and Staffell began demonstrating a couple of Smile songs, with a little help from their friend. 'They had a chum with them,' says Testi. 'And that was Freddie. He knew all the words to the Smile songs and even started singing the harmonies. From that moment, it was obvious to us he wanted to be in that band. But Smile didn't need a frontman. Ibex did.'

Like Smile, Ibex were solely about the music. Their idols were Cream, Fleetwood Mac, Ten Years After, and, like those idols, they were predisposed towards, as 'Tupp' Taylor, admits, 'soloing endlessly until everybody fucked off to the bar'. On at least one occasion, 'Miffer' Smith's drum solo was lengthy enough for the spikes on his floor tom to get wedged into the gaps between the stage boards, causing the drum to disappear lower and lower into the stage with each paradiddle.

Image-wise, Ibex had the requisite long hair, with Mike Bersin sporting a capacious afro, but beyond that, it was all flared jeans and trench coats. While 'Tupp' Taylor was confident enough to sing some lead vocals and handle the between-song announcements, neither him nor Bersin were comfortable frontmen. It didn't take long for Freddie to make his move. Taylor thinks they asked him to join in a meeting at the Kensington; Mike Bersin remembers an audition in somebody's basement flat, while 'Miffer' recalled an audition at Imperial College. 'One thing we learned later was that Freddie was very good at getting his own way,' says Bersin. 'He was very sure of himself, and he wanted to sing with us.' The deal was done.

The Smile/Ibex contingent spent July and August drifting between the flats surrounding the Kensington Tavern. David Bowie's 'Space Oddity', timed perfectly to coincide with Neil Armstrong's historic walk, gave the struggling songwriter a hit single. Back on earth, The Rolling Stones played a free concert in Hyde Park as a memorial to ex-guitarist Brian Jones, who'd been found dead in his swimming pool. At Sinclair Road, the soundtrack included the inevitable Jimi Hendrix LPs, The Who's 'Tommy' ('Tupp' Taylor: 'We wore that one out') and the Island Records sampler 'All Join Hands' with its heavy roll call of honour: Free, Spooky Tooth, Jethro Tull . . .

Before long, the presence of mysterious hairy males at the McConnell sisters' flat came to the attention of the landlords. 'So we all shipped over to Batoum Gardens,' explains Ken Testi. Here, three beds were shoved together to accommodate more bodies. 'There was nothing else going on,' laughs Testi. 'They were good Catholic girls, all totally respectable. But it was only one stop short of a squat . . . I think "Miffer" had to sleep in the bath.'

After leaving Ealing, Chris Smith had spent a couple of months in the United States. He returned to the flat he shared at Addison Gardens and was shocked by what he found. 'There were loads of people I didn't know having a party,' he laughs. 'Someone came up to me and said, "Who are you?" I said, "I live here."' Among the revellers was 'Miffer'. The Ibex drummer with the Dickensian chin-length sideburns had a couple of years on his teenage bandmates and didn't share their naivety. He'd been coaxed into giving up his job as a milkman in Widnes to try and make it as a rock star in London. As 'Tupp' Taylor puts it, '"Miffer" always seemed more worldly than the rest of us.' Having spent weeks surrounded by Smile's posse of art students, would-be physicists and part-qualified dentists, 'Miffer' sidled up to Chris and asked wearily, 'So . . . how many GCEs have you got, then?'

The relationship between 'Miffer' and Freddie encapsulated the differences between Ibex and their new lead singer. 'We were all a bit rough and ready,' admits Ken Testi. '"Miffer" especially.' Fred, in contrast, was like an immaculately groomed dandy alien. The banter was soon flying between this curious creature and the Scouse milkman-turned-drummer. 'They took the piss out of each other all the time,' explains Testi. Later, Fred presented 'Miffer' with a sketch he'd drawn of the drummer, signed 'Ponce'.

Fred's punctiliousness was another talking point among the Liverpudlians. 'Freddie had no money, just like the rest of us,' recalls Bersin. 'So he had one outfit: he always wore this T-shirt with a wide belt and trousers, and before crashing out for the night he would take them off and fold them ever so neatly so they'd be perfect for the morning. At the time, we thought it was a southern thing, an evidence of the cultural divide: OK, men in the north don't do that but men in the south do. In a way, Freddie was a star before he was a star.'

Ibex would soon discover just how much of a star Freddie thought he was. Although Ken Testi had struggled to secure any gigs in the capital, Ibex already had two prior bookings at Bolton's Octagon Theatre on 23 August and an open-air festival in the town's Queen's Park the day after. To make the trip, Ken Testi acquired a Luton transit van from Fred's friend, 1984's ex-drummer Richard Thompson. 'Richard was working for a company at Heathrow airport and it was the works van,' admits Testi.

'It was a yellow van for the company I worked for, Arbuckle Smith & Co,' remembers Thompson. 'I used to love watching bands, so we'd pile twenty people into the back and drive everywhere – gigs, parties. You could get away with doing that sort of thing in the sixties and seventies.' The van was soon filled with Ibex, their equipment and an assortment of mates, girlfriends and casual roadies, including Paul Humberstone. On a whim, Paul brought a camera, preserving the touring party for prosperity. In one of his photos the ramshackle group are lined up alongside the Arbuckle Smith & Co van. By then, Richard Thompson had made the transition from 1984's modish drummer to a fully-fledged hippy, with shoulder-length hair, Jesus beard and sandals. Backing up Mike Bersin's recollection, Freddie looks immaculate, his three-button, long-sleeved T-shirt as spotlessly white as his shoes.

The trip began after midnight, when Ken collected 'Tupp' Taylor after his shift at a record shop in Piccadilly. But the trek up north took far less time than anticipated. 'I was a little over-cautious,' says Testi. 'We arrived at about 6 a.m., and we couldn't get into the theatre until ten. I still have this one particular memory. I pulled up outside the Octagon on the cobbles, and I'm just sat there looking in the van mirror. I hear the roller shutter go up at the back and I can see various occupants climbing out . . .'

Among the first on the cobbles was Fred. Testi watched as the new singer fussed over his appearance: 'He checked his hair, fluffed the fur on the collar of his jacket, and then began checking the creases on his trousers.' Before long, though, Ken became aware of a noise in the background. 'There was this clattering sound that just kept building, getting louder and louder . . .' All of a sudden, the source of the noise became apparent: 'The night shift had just ended.' The sound was the clatter of workers' clogs on the cobbles as they made their way home. 'The context was immaculate,' laughs Testi. 'All these guys covered in dirt walking past as Freddie Mercury stands there in his fur-collared jacket fixing his hair.'

The Octagon Theatre gig was a Saturday lunchtime affair and

part of the venue's regular 'Bluesology sessions'. At lunchtime, Ibex played their debut gig with the future Freddie Mercury. 'Tupp' Taylor thinks they opened their set with, at Freddie's suggestion, a cover of 'Jailhouse Rock'. If so, then it came with a difference. 'Pat McConnell reminded me recently that Freddie had his back to the audience for half of the first number,' recalls Ken Testi. 'It was only thinking back that we realised this was his first time onstage with a band. He'd done bits at school, but nothing since.' Fred's opening gambit to Ibex had been: 'I'm a singer but I haven't got a band.' 'Looking back, it was a brilliant strategy,' Testi says. 'It was a great stroke. By the end of the first number, the shyness had gone and he was performing well.'

Brian May had been unable to make the Friday night trip to Bolton, but wanted to catch the Sunday show. The band and entourage were planning to spend Saturday night twenty-five miles away in Ibex's native Liverpool. Ken Testi had arranged to collect May from Lime Street station, and decided to park the van on a ramp leading up to the station platform. 'I figured we'd be good for ten minutes or so, but then this very senior policeman hoved into view and walked up to the driver's window. It was then I realised we were in what you might call a borrowed van and that I could be hung, drawn and quartered for having a load of people in the back.'

Having seen the agents' address on the side of the vehicle, the officer presumed that Testi was on company business, and asked if he was waiting for the train from London. 'I said we were, so this policeman said, "Righto, well, you shouldn't really park here. I'll open the gates for you so you can back it up on to the platform."' Without further ado, a group of station porters arrived and opened the gates, while Ken reversed the van onto the platform. 'When Brian got off the train he could not believe his eyes. To his credit, he realised what was going on straight away.' With the guitarist safely stashed, Testi made a swift getaway.

The evening ended with most of the group billeted at the McConnell sisters' family home in St Helens. It was at the McConnells that Brian dozed off in an armchair close to a gas fire. 'Despite his height, Brian was wearing platforms,' smiles Ken Testi. At some point in the evening, the family could smell burning rubber. 'Poor Brian was unaware of the heat until one of his soles dropped off. He was limping around with half a shoe for the rest of the weekend.'

Fred's second gig with Ibex was due to take place the following afternoon at Queen's Park. The 'Bluesology Pop-In' was an open-air event. That day, the bill also showcased such forgotten local acts as Gum Boot Smith and acid-folk band Spyrogyra. The stage was set up on the bandstand in the middle of the park, and was three times as big as the stage at the Octagon. 'When Fred stepped on that stage, he was all action,' confirms 'Tupp' Taylor. 'I thought, "Fuck, yes! This is what we want."' Mike Bersin adds, 'I was used to playing guitar solos with my eyes shut, and now there's a guy on his knees in front holding the mic up to me. Many of the moves Fred later did in Queen, he first did with us.'

While Freddie's Bolton debut was considered a resounding success, Ibex's days in London were numbered. 'Just a few weeks later, all the promise of the summer started to fall apart,' says Ken Testi. The first to go was Mike Bersin, who enrolled at art college in Liverpool ('I'd promised my parents I'd do this after the summer'). While 'Tupp' Taylor elected to remain in London, 'Miffer' Smith seemed poised to do what he'd been threatening all summer. As Chris Smith says, 'Whenever things were going badly, "Miffer" always used to say, in this real Ringo voice, "I just want to go home and be a milkman."'

Testi was also considering a place at college in St Helens. On 8 September, he hitchhiked back to Liverpool. No sooner had he arrived then he took a phone call from Mike Bersin. 'Ibex had been offered a gig, Mike had called the others and they'd arranged to borrow a van, and could I go back to London and pick them up and all the gear?' says Testi.

Undaunted, he scrounged a lift back to the M6 where he stuck out his thumb, finally making it back to London at 11 p.m. The following morning, Smile's roadie Pete Edmunds dropped off the Transit, which Ken loaded up with Ibex's gear, most of which was stashed at Imperial College in a room at the top of a spiral staircase. As Ken manhandled the amps down the narrow stairwell, 'Freddie managed a pair of maracas and a tambourine'. With the van loaded,

Testi climbed behind the wheel to make the 176-mile drive back to Liverpool. Squeezed in the seats, between Fred, 'Tupp' Taylor, 'Miffer' Smith, Pat McConnell, guitar cases, amps and a drum kit were Brian May and Roger Taylor.

Ibex's gig that night was at the Sink on Hardman Street, a dank basement club in which The Rolling Stones were said to have played their debut Liverpool gig. As Ken recalls, 'Roger, Brian and Fred were wearing what passed for fashionable in Kensington – lots of velvet and fur. That was something unknown in Liverpool. Outside the club Roger informed us that he'd been accosted by some local youths who rather took exception to the way he was dressed.' Taylor later claimed that he flashed his student library card, pretending it was a membership card to a martial arts club. 'He said, "Look! I have to show you this before I kill you . . . I'm a black belt third dan . . . in . . . *origami*," ' chuckles Ken. 'Supposedly the youths backed off.'

Testi's schoolfriend and Ibex roadie Geoff Higgins had often taped the band's gigs and rehearsals. His one surviving tape, recorded on a Grundig TK14 reel-to-reel, is Ibex's performance at the Sink. Standing stage right, Geoff draped the Grundig's crystal microphone over a rusty nail and hoped for the best. The recording has Ibex clattering through Cream's 'We're Going Wrong', The Beatles' 'Rain', Elvis's 'Jailhouse Rock' and Led Zeppelin's 'Communication Breakdown'; making up in raw enthusiasm what they lack in expertise. According to Higgins, the Sink stage was so small that Fred had to stand in front of it, not that this inhibited his moves. Listening now, Mike Bersin's crowning moment is the Hendrix/Jeff Beck blues staple 'Rock Me Baby'; 'Miffer' Smith shines at holding the beat while others are losing their way, while Fred's Robert Plant-like squeal on 'Communication Breakdown' is testament to hours spent practising and terrorising the neighbours, at home. 'Freddie had a real thing about Robert Plant and that first Zeppelin album,' says Bersin. 'He was forever wandering around the flat singing snatches of it, especially the "never never never never gonna leave you babe" bit from "Babe I'm Gonna Leave You".'

'Tupp' Taylor is less impressed: 'When I listen to that bootleg, I think, "God, we were awful." We couldn't hear ourselves properly.

Freddie was no Winwood, Marriott or Cocker, he didn't have that kind of soul, and at the beginning, his pitching was awful, but what he was fantastic at from the start was the show.' Sadly, what the Sink recording doesn't include is the encore. Geoff Higgins claimed the tape ran out just before Roger Taylor and Brian May joined Ibex for renditions of what Geoff recalls as a couple of Smile songs. 'So we had three-quarters of Queen in the place,' reflects Testi, 'although none of us knew that at the time.'

Brian May's memory of the pre-Queen Fred as 'very shy but cloaking himself in this persona' is borne out on the Sink club tape. Fred's between-song announcements are muted, hushed and achingly polite. Offstage, as well, for all his acid wit and lively banter, he could just as easily slip back into shyness, especially in the company of strangers. However, just weeks into his stint with Ibex, Fred was already plotting. The first casualty of his coup would be the band's name. Fred wanted to re-title the group Wreckage, but had met with some initial resistance. 'Then Freddie phoned me at home in Liverpool,' says Mike Bersin, 'and said he'd called everyone else in the band and they were happy to change the name to Wreckage. I said that if everyone else was OK, then so was I. I later found out that he'd called each of us and said exactly the same thing.'

His band members' approval was just as well: before making the calls, Freddie had, apparently, already stencilled the new name onto Ibex's gear. 'Good marketing, very cute,' says Ken Testi. 'That was a guy with an agenda.' On 12 October Freddie and Richard Thompson had gone to see Led Zeppelin at the Lyceum. 'I think I'd read something with Jeff Beck where he said that a heavy band needed a heavy name. Like Led Zeppelin,' says 'Tupp' Taylor. "Someone, it may even have been Beck, suggested the name Concrete Wellington as a joke. But that was the thinking behind Wreckage, it just sounded heavier.'

Going hand in hand with the change of moniker was some new material. 'Vagabond Outcast', a rather torpid heavy blues, was still in the set, but as Ken recalls, 'Freddie and Mike had started writing songs. Fred realised Mike was someone he could work with.' Existing Wreckage setlists confirm the original titles 'Green', 'Cancer On My Mind', 'Without You, Lover' (an early prototype of the Queen song 'Liar'), 'Universal Theme', 'FEWA' (which some believe stood for Feelings Ended Worn Away), 'One More Train' and 'Blag-a-Blues'; most of which went unrecorded. Mike Bersin's memory of specific songs is sketchy, but as he explains, 'We came down from the North playing twelve-bar stuff, no key changes, and Freddie said, "No, no, no, you've got to use the black notes, and what we need now is a key change because it makes it more interesting." We knew where music was, but Fred knew where it was going.'

Though Freddie had persuaded his bandmates to change their name, the geographical distance between the singer and the guitarist presented another hurdle. Previous accounts of Fred's tenure in Ibex/Wreckage claim that at some point around October 1969, Freddie moved to Liverpool for a few weeks, staying at roadie Geoff Higgins' family pub in Penny Lane. Ken Testi tactfully disputes this: 'Freddie made brief visits to Liverpool, but somehow a stopover turned into summer in Liverpool. It didn't happen.'

What is known for certain is that by the last week in October, Wreckage had lost drummer Mick 'Miffer' Smith and were limbering up for their debut gig at Ealing art college. The information was contained in a letter that Fred wrote to a friend, Celine Daley, one of the Maria Assumpta students. In it, Fred lambasts the drummer ('Miffer's not with us anymore 'cos the bastard just upped and left one morning saying he was going to be a milkman in Widnes'); reveals that he and 'Miffer' were about to start part-time jobs in Harrods; says that he paid Mike Bersin's rail fare from Liverpool for rehearsals; that Smith's replacement is ex-1984 drummer Richard Thompson ('the practice was really great. Richard collapsed halfway through . . .') and that 'the Zeppelin II LP is a knockout'. As written, Mick 'Miffer' Smith did return to his old trade, after a stint as a construction worker on the M56 motorway. Richard Thompson was an obvious choice, because, as he points out now, 'I already knew all the songs.'

Wreckage's debut in what was known as the 'Noisy Common Room' at Ealing was not particularly auspicious. Mark Malden had now left the college, but his brother Aubrey was still running the student union and had booked Wreckage as a favour to Freddie. 'They were crap,' he says now. 'I remember Freddie had bought a white suit especially for the gig, but the only good bit was when he lay on his back on the stage, took the microphone off the stand and dangled it down his throat while wailing. This was all going on in the common room, and while some people were watching, others were sitting around chatting, reading newspapers, playing table football . . . I thought they were a bit of a joke.'

Wreckage would only play some ten gigs, at other venues including St Martin's art school and Imperial College. Chris Smith saw them and was bemused: 'Tim Staffell and I saw Wreckage in a pub, I think. Freddie was doing all the posing and the strutting, which I had never seen him do before. It was a shock, though, as it just didn't work in a pub. But ten out of ten for bravery.' Interviewed in 2004, Brian May tactfully recalled a similar sighting: 'We went to see Fred sing with his own group. You could hardly keep up with him. He was being very ebullient and making a big noise, and we didn't quite know what to make of it.'

In November, 'Tupp' Taylor's sister arranged for Wreckage to play her school dance in Widnes. According to Queen mythology, it was the night Fred discovered his trademark. 'Apparently that was the gig where the bottom of his mic stand fell off. A happy accident,' says Ken Testi. Richard Thompson maintains that the base fell off and Fred simply continued without it. 'Later, Queen came up to play St Helens Technical College, where I was social secretary,' adds Testi. 'I spotted the mic stand at soundcheck. I said, "Fred, this mic stand thing? Are you sure?" He said, "It's my gimmick, dear. You must have a gimmick." I said, "Fred, you're sounding a bit like Jimmy Savile". But he was like, "No, no, no".'

For Wreckage, though, it was all over by Christmas. Two days after the girls' school show, the group are believed to have played their final gig at Richmond Rugby Club. 'The overwhelming reality is that the band wouldn't have made it,' explains Mike Bersin. 'Freddie tried to keep it together, but I wasn't that focused. However, that determination to succeed was an irresistible force in Freddie right from the start.' Fred retreated to plan his next move while Bersin dropped out of music and continued with his pre-diploma course at art college in Liverpool. By now, the old network of Kensington flats and rented digs had found a new centre of operations: 40 Ferry Road, Barnes.

'Pat McConnell and another girl called Denise [Craddock] were the original ones in there,' claims 'Tupp' Taylor. 'Then I moved in, then there was Fred, Roger Taylor and another bloke who I think was studying to be a dentist. We had the whole bottom floor of the house.'

While Fred had made the move out of the parental home in Feltham, his new lodgings were a far cry from the Bulsaras' suburban comfort zone (Freddie: 'My parents were outraged when I told them what I was up to'). The house hadn't been decorated in an age and still bore some of the gaudy stylistic traits of its previous occupants. Mike Bersin crashed there during the dying days of Wreckage, and recalls it now as 'ghastly'. Richard Thompson maintains that 'Ferry Road was a dump, but they all were. Typical student place.' The communal living room is remembered for a red vinyl sofa, the seams on which had split leaving tufts of horsehair stuffing spilling out onto the cushions. The kitchen was largely a no-go zone, whose food contents rarely extended beyond tea and milk.

Any number of waifs or strays might emerge from the bedrooms on any given morning, but, adds Mike Bersin, 'I still have no recall of where the bathroom was.' 'The old lady who owned the property lived upstairs,' remembers Taylor, 'and Sylvia Sims, the actress, lived next door. This old lady didn't like Sylvia Sims. She'd always be talking about her as "that awful woman! Thespians . . . you know, not reliable people". Meanwhile we were in this flat, playing music and making this terrible noise.'

In October 1969, before Wreckage's Ealing college debut, Richard Thompson taped the group rehearsing late one night at Ferry Road: Bersin playing an unplugged electric guitar, Taylor on amplified bass, and Thompson pattering around on what he remembers as a 'guitar case'. One of the songs played was the Bulsara/Bersin composition 'Green'; the only surviving recording of Wreckage. 'There is another song on the end of the tape,' says Thompson. 'And on the tape you can you hear their flatmate come in and complain about the noise as it's one o'clock in the morning.' What you can also hear on the Wreckage tape is Fred's cultured tones, directing his bandmates ('Listen . . . don't forget . . . after those two verses').

While dope-smoking was widespread at Ferry Road, Fred was unusually abstemious. Instead, as was his wont, he'd be up bright and early, tiptoeing over his stoned flatmates, singing quietly to himself and strumming the chords to The Who's 'Pinball Wizard' on his new guitar. 'He was like a wandering minstrel,' says Mike Bersin, 'making a nuisance of himself.'

On one occasion, when two policemen called at the house after complaints about the noise, 'Tupp' Taylor, 'playing the friendly Northerner', sweet-talked them with a cup of tea and a piece of hash cake. 'I used to buy dope on Carnaby Street,' says Taylor. "I once showed Freddie an ounce of dope and he was astounded by the size of it. But if you asked him, he used to say, "Oh, I've been through *that*. I've done all that." '

Ferry Road's dope was sometimes purchased concealed in jasmine tea. It would then fall to one of the flat's occupants to separate the leaves. On one occasion, the stash was dumped, unsorted, into the tea caddy and Fred made himself a cup, unaware of its exact contents. According to one eyewitness, Fred was found later, 'freaking out' to Frank Zappa's *We're Only in it for the Money* album, a parody of *Sgt Pepper's Lonely Hearts Club Band* with a trick segment featuring the sound of a stylus scraping across a run-out groove. This had sent Fred into a panic, as he believed he had scratched his new favourite record. 'Freddie didn't like dope,' confirms Chris Smith. 'Later on, though, he offered me speed. Freddie was like, "Have some of this Chris" . . . I'd tried it once, as it was good for playing a gig, but the comedown was terrible.'

The speed in question had been acquired in Kensington Market, the hippy emporium at which Freddie and Roger Taylor now had a stall of their own. As the year wore on, Freddie supplemented his meagre earnings with a stint at Harrods (as mentioned in his letter to Celine Daley) and occasional drawing jobs. 'I came downstairs once and saw him drawing women's underwear,' says Mike Bersin. 'He had taken a job designing fashion ads for newspapers.' Later, Fred signed up as an illustrator with the Austin Knights design agency, and was commissioned to work on a children's book that was never published.

The chic, three-storey indoor market on Kensington High Street was a hive of musicians, actors and artists, giving Fred and Roger a direct conduit to London's 'beautiful people'. Initially, the pair paid £10 a week (from Taylor's grant money) for a stall, selling artwork from Fred's college friends. 'Then we sold Fred's thesis, which was based on Hendrix,' revealed Taylor. No trace has ever been found of the artwork but, according to Roger, 'there were some beautiful things – he'd written the lyrics of "Third Stone from the Sun". . . things like that are probably worth a lot of money now.'

For a couple of months Tim Staffell also took a stall on the market, selling artwork. But he loathed what he described as its 'air of narcissistic coquettishness'. Realising that art didn't pay, Freddie and Roger tried a different strategy. 'We got into old Edwardian clothes,' explained Taylor. 'We'd get bags of silk scarves from dodgy dealers. We'd take them, iron them and flog them.'

'It was bits of tat really,' says Ken Testi. 'Victoriana, fur jackets, the odd cricket blazer, some old lady's coat sawn off and masquerading as a cape.'

Undeterred by the small scale of their operation, Fred told everyone that they were 'gentlemen's outfitters' and seemed to approach the job with the same enthusiastic zeal as he did his music. 'Fred would bring home these great bags of stuff,' recalled Brian May. 'Pull out some horrible strip of cloth and say, "Look at this beautiful garment! This is going to fetch a fortune!" And I'd say, "Fred, that is a piece of rag."'

It was at the market that Adrian Morrish ran into his old friend from Isleworth Polytechnic. 'I was on a shopping trip and suddenly heard that voice: "Adrian! Adrian!" He introduced me to Roger and I went to a party at his flat, got drunk, and that was the last time I saw Freddie. He said, "You must come and see my band", and, of course, I didn't. I was so convinced that he wasn't going to make it any more than anyone else.' It was also at Kensington Market that the possibly apocryphal story arose of Freddie, reluctant to use public transport, selling Roger's own jacket on the stall to pay for a taxi. Asked about this by an *NME* journalist in 1977, Fred refused to confirm or deny it.

In his letter to Celine Daley, Fred wrote that 'Roger and I go poncing and ultra-blagging just about everywhere', confirming how comfortable he was with the 'narcissistic coquettishness' that Tim Staffell found such a turn-off. Ex-Ealing student Tony Catignani vividly recalls he and Freddie being wolf-whistled at while promenading along Kensington High Street. Yet, in the same letter to Celine, Fred had also complained that 'Miffer the sod has told everyone down here that I have turned into a fully-fledged queer!' Mike Bersin suggests that while Fred 'may not have been out of the closet he was certainly looking through the keyhole'. Yet, according to Bersin, during the singer's time in Ibex and Wreckage, 'he still gave every appearance of being heterosexual'.

'Tupp' Taylor maintains that 'Fred had all these great girls who were his mates . . . and that was extremely handy for us . . . there was an art student called Caroline . . . two girls called Mary . . . and there was Josephine [Ranken, née Marston] from the art college, who was very over the top and looked like an artist even then.' Josephine, remembered by another of their contemporaries 'as a girl with an extraordinary bohemian sense of style', was a platonic friend of Fred's and later introduced him to a gay friend of hers. She recalled Fred being 'obviously terribly interested in homosexuality; he was also afraid of it as well.'

Yet both Paul Humberstone and Chris Smith remember the female student with whom Fred would go on to have a relationship. 'She was this red-headed bombshell called Rosemary,' laughs Humberstone. Interviewed in 1995, Josephine Ranken revealed that Fred and Rosemary's relationship became physical, but 'I heard they slept together just once, as his performance in bed was imperfect, shall we say.' Nine years later, *The Times* newspaper ran an interview with Fred's ex-amour, Rosemary Pearson, who had previously remained silent about the relationship.

Rosemary revealed that the two had met in 1967 on the same course at Ealing and struck up a friendship. 'He'd sit next to me in the canteen and be terribly attentive and brotherly,' she explained. The couple spent their time together 'rushing off to exhibitions', and going to gigs and parties. Two years later, they became lovers, back at Ferry Road. Rosemary's connection with the art world had led her into a dinner-party clique based around a London doctor named Patrick Woodcock, whose patients, friends and confidants included the likes of David Hockney, Christopher Isherwood, Derek Jarman and John Gielgud. Fred had already begun wondering, she said, 'what it would be like to sleep with a man', and was keen to be introduced to Rosemary's gay friends: 'Freddie thought that if he didn't meet them, he would never know whether he was gay.' Ultimately, Rosemary ended the relationship at some point in 1970, claiming she knew, deep down, that Freddie was homosexual: 'I think Freddie did love me, but for me it was too ambiguous, too androgynous. He liked to think of himself as two genders.'

Fred never made his dilemma public knowledge to anyone at Ferry Road. Or if he did, they're not telling. Despite the jokes and ruthless teasing that went on, as one regular explains, 'In hippy circles you didn't question anyone's sexual orientation. It was not done.'

Chris Chesney was a seventeen-year-old guitarist who became part of Fred's circle in early 1970. When Wreckage disbanded, Fred had begun scouring the music press for a replacement band, and answered a 'Vocalist Wanted' ad in the back of *Melody Maker* placed by a band called Sour Milk Sea (named after a George Harrison song from The Beatles' *White Album* sessions). The group, originally called Tomato City, had formed at St Edward's public school in Oxford by Chesney (then known as Chris Dummett) and rhythm guitarist Jeremy 'Rubber' Gallop, whose businessman father bankrolled the venture. With drummer Boris Williams and bassist Paul Milne, the group had played a handful of shows at various arts labs and 'happenings'; the sort of places where, explains Chesney, 'people would take their clothes off and scream poetry'.

Williams left the band for India and the hippy trail in 1968 (though, many years later, he would reappear in The Cure), and his replacement was Rob Tyrell, an ex-Charterhouse public schoolboy who had previously backed future members of Genesis in a group called The Anon. By the summer of 1969, Sour Milk Sea had turned professional and opened for Deep Purple and Taste. Just like Ibex, they lacked a frontman. 'We called ourselves a progressive blues band,' says Chesney now. 'At public school you listened to John Mayall's Bluesbreakers, Peter Green's Fleetwood

Mac, and Cream. Hendrix was beyond our capabilities. We wrote our own songs and I sang lead vocals, but I really wanted to concentrate on playing guitar.'

Their 'Vocalist Wanted' ad yielded results. Auditions took place at a youth club in a church in Dorking, and Chesney recalls that as well as the usual no-hopers, a couple of promising vocalists turned up, including folk singer Bridget St John. Still, there could be only one man for the job. Fred arrived in grand style, having cajoled Smile roadie John Harris into driving him to the audition. (As Ken Testi explains, 'I once asked Freddie why he never learned to drive. He said, "My dear, I don't need to drive, I'll always be driven."') Once he'd disembarked from the van, Fred strode purposefully into the youth club, Harris a few steps behind, carrying his master's microphone in a wooden box.

'When he fired up with us, it was so obvious that he was fantastic,' laughs Chesney. 'He had the long dark hair and was dripping in velvet and he was very bold.' Immediately, Fred reprised the moves he'd first used with Ibex. 'He came up to me straight away and there was this physical interaction, jabbing the mic stand at me while I played a solo. He didn't quite have the voice then, as I don't think he'd done that many gigs, but he sang falsetto, which was unusual, and I liked that.'

Chris is unsure of the precise dates but, with Freddie in tow, Sour Milk Sea played The Temple in London's Lower Wardour Street. 'I also think we opened for Black Sabbath and played the Red Lion on the Fulham Road,' he adds. A planned gig on Smile's home turf, PJ's in Truro on 18 April, was cancelled, with Smile taking Sour Milk Sea's place. Remarkably, the band's debut gig with Freddie, at Highfield Parish Hall in Headington, Oxford, in March 1970, was accompanied by an interview in the *Oxford Mail*. The gig was on behalf of the homeless charity Shelter, and as the son of All Souls philosophy don Michael Dummett, Sour Milk Sea's teenage guitarist had a certain pedigree. Remarkably, the *Mail* reporter allowed the band 'their say' at the end of the article. 'Their say' was to print the lyrics verbatim to one of Fred's songs, 'Lover', opening with the wonderfully nonsensical line, 'You never had it so good / the yoghurt pushers are here . . .' The accompanying photographs showed Chris Chesney as a baby in his pram and, posing with Sour Milk Sea, 'new vocalist Freddie Bulsara' gazing confidently into the camera lens.

'We never knew his name until later,' reveals Chesney. 'When our manager took the call for the audition, he asked him his name and he said, "Fred Bull." He stopped himself from saying Bulsara. It was not an issue for us, but he was always watching himself. Freddie never talked about his childhood and we didn't even know he came from Zanzibar.'

Six years older than Chris Chesney, Freddie soon began introducing his ideas to the guitarist. 'We were doing our own songs, which appealed to him, but straight away he was like, "I'm tossing out your lyrics and writing my own." I didn't care. I was seventeen and I welcomed the education.' Under Freddie's aegis, Sour Milk Sea changed. Paul Milne's then-girlfriend, the future novelist Judy Astley was struck by the transformation: 'I saw a rehearsal in the wilds of Surrey, and one of the gigs, and it was immediately clear that Chris and Freddie were a terrific stage act. Freddie seemed to free up Chris to be more flamboyant than before.'

Judy found Fred to be 'polite, sweet, charming and funny, but reluctant to give a lot away about himself'. In contrast, Paul Milne was Sour Milk Sea's 'pouty bassist'. 'Paul was a terrifically cool dresser,' elaborates Judy, 'buying lots of velvet from Granny Takes a Trip and shirts from Deborah and Clare. He was very fond of Chris and, I think, miffed that Chris and Fred got on so well.'

Freddie hustled the group to play songs from his Wreckage days, and rock 'n' roll covers such as 'Lucille' and 'Jailhouse Rock'. As Chris explains: 'He had this showbiz angle which was rare at the time.' With Chesney, he began writing songs with wild chord changes ('his chords broke all the rules'). Onstage, though, for all the phallic mic-stand twirling and camp horseplay, Fred's humour was much in evidence: 'He loved to wind up the audience. So he'd do this thing at the end of a song where he'd go, "Wank you . . . wank you very much", and you could see people in the audience going, "Did he say thank you or wank you?"'

Offstage, though, Fred's shameless vanity went down less well with some. Interviewed in 1996, Jeremy 'Rubber' Gallop recounted an incident where Freddie studied himself in a mirror for some time before announcing, 'I look good today, don't you think, Rubber?' 'I was only eighteen at the time and didn't think it was very funny,' he said. 'So I thought, "Fuck off!"'

In a matter of weeks, though, minor grievances turned into a major rift, with Fred and Chris on one side; 'Rubber' and Paul Milne on the other. To compound the tension, Chesney had accepted Fred's offer to move into 40 Ferry Road. 'I was from a very conventional middle-class background in Oxford, and all these guys from West London were more glamorous and interesting,' recalls Chris. 'So the others, still stuck in Leatherhead, thought that me and Fred were cooking up something in Barnes. There was an awful lot of jealousy.'

At Ferry Road, Chris and Fred 'bonded quickly'. Musically, the guitarist was intrigued by his singer's catholic tastes. At Ferry Road, the record player spun Hendrix's *Electric Ladyland* ('that was at the heart of everything'), The Beatles' *White Album*, The Move's *Cherry Blossom Clinic*, Zappa, The Who, Rod Stewart . . . 'Fred was hugely into Led Zeppelin, but he was very quick to spot pop music,' says Chesney. 'The Jackson 5 single "Want You Back" had come out, and Fred was very into that. I also remember him telling me that David Bowie was the perfect pop star, and at the time he'd only had a hit with "Space Oddity". He was very prescient.'

The pair's relationship was never sexual ('I wouldn't be embarrassed if it was, but it wasn't'), but as Fred's protégé, Chesney was happy to experience all that was on offer. At Ferry Road, he dropped LSD, marvelled at the Smile groupies drifting through the place, took care not to risk his health by venturing too far into the kitchen ('you might make a cup of coffee, no more'), and practised his guitar in jamming sessions with Brian May ('we'd lock ourselves in a room with a couple of AC30s').

It seems probable, too, that Chesney saw Fred with Rosemary Pearson: 'He had a girlfriend, not Mary Austin [Fred's soon-to-become serious partner]. They used to disappear into his room together. No one ever suggested to me he was gay.' Fred's regular announcements that he was 'off to see my bender friends' always drew some hearty ribbing from Smile's drummer, however: 'Roger loved to take the piss, but Brian was far too polite for that.' Meanwhile, according to Chesney, neither May nor Taylor were considering Fred as a possible lead singer in Smile: 'I had the impression they thought he was a bit of a joke. That he was trying too hard.'

Among the rest of Sour Milk Sea, the tension continued to grow. Fred's song 'Lover' was a particular bone of contention, as Gallop and Milne considered it too twee and commercial. Fred's musical influence was regarded as pernicious, teasing the group away from an authentic, underground sound. Paul Milne was a massive fan of Free, and, as Gallop explained: 'We were supposed to be a heavy duty blues band but Freddie was coming up with these huge harmonies.'

'Paul definitely thought Freddie was an influence in the wrong direction,' confirms Judy Astley. 'He thought he was a hired vocalist and shouldn't be influential in decision-making.' Having ploughed hundreds of pounds of his father's money into the group, 'Rubber' had further reason to feel resentful. Interviewed in 1995, Gallop (who died in 2006) was painfully candid: 'I liked Freddie a great deal. The thing was, I'd put my life into the group . . . I was in tears over it . . . Chris was an amazing lead guitarist, and I thought my chances of making it were a lot slimmer without having him around.'

Tempers frayed, punches were thrown, and though Fred tried to play the diplomat, by the spring of 1970, Sour Milk Sea was over. 'Rubber took all the equipment back,' admits Chesney. 'I had a beautiful SG Standard and a nice Marshall. All gone. Later, one day I went down to Leatherhead, shinned up a drainpipe, through the bathroom window and nicked the guitar. How I thought I could get away with it! Sure enough, before long there was a knock on the door in Barnes, and two heavies were outside.'

Fred's erstwhile band members began to go their separate ways. Gallop and Rob Tyrell went off to form another group; Paul Milne took up a place at East Anglia University, and Chris Chesney scavenged as many shifts as he could at Huntley & Palmers biscuit factory in Reading to help him buy a new instrument. Chris, Freddie and John 'Tupp' Taylor considered forming a group of their own, but without money or, in Chesney's case, a guitar, it seemed pointless. Instead Taylor found a job as road manager for the band Patto, going on to form his own management company, looking after the likes of the late Jim Capaldi, Dennis Locorriere and Joe Brown. 'After those days, I never saw Freddie again,' he says. 'And he still had a suitcase of my clothes . . . which my sister always reminds me of, as she owned the suitcase.'

Freddie was, once again, 'a singer without a band', yet the group he'd always wanted to join were now falling apart. In the two years since Smile opened for Yes and Pink Floyd, their progress had been achingly slow. Smile remained a perennial support band; a name in small print in *Melody Maker* listings, but rarely the main event. Two weeks before Christmas 1969, they opened at London's Marquee for Kippington Lodge, a band featuring Nick Lowe, a songwriter who at the time had been trailing around the same circuit with similarly diminishing returns. Despite promises from Mercury Records that the gig would boost Smile's profile, it led to nothing.

Brian May was again juggling science and music. In February 1970, as Fred was prancing his way into Sour Milk Sea, May was studying in Tenerife. As part of his ongoing thesis, Brian had joined Imperial College's Professors Jim Ring, Ken Reay and others at their observatory close to Mount Teide, the island's dormant volcano. In Santa Cruz, Brian bought a tiny Spanish guitar. 'I used to play it up the mountain where we were observing. I think Ken thought it was quite funny. He had a sly little smile on his face that said, "Obviously you'll never get anywhere . . ."'

Returning to Britain with an enviable suntan, Brian found Tim Staffell waiting to tell him the bad news: he was quitting Smile. 'The longer it went on, the more success eluded us and the more insecure I felt,' Staffell admitted. Yet Smile's lack of progress was only part of the problem. Just as it had been for Chris Smith, the music was also an issue. Staffell had been introduced to US soul and R&B and was now far less inspired by Smile's terribly English hard rock. 'We used to do a version of "If I Were a Carpenter", a bit like Vanilla Fudge, and it didn't swing,' Staffell protested. Equally, with the pompom-wielding Freddie Bulsara hovering in the wings, Tim could see the future: 'Smile wanted to go this theatrical way, and I could see I was not going into that. My idea of a musician is heads down, long hair, staring at the floor.' While the two would remain on good terms, Brian May said Smile's bass player 'had a strange driving force which was always driving him away from us.'

Surprisingly, Tim Staffell's next musical venture would be light years away from soul or R&B, fronting ex-Bee Gees drummer Colin Peterson's new group Humpty Bong. They enjoyed a minor hit single, 'Don't You Be Too Long', in August 1970, and even an appearance on *Top of the Pops*, but split without playing a single gig. A year later, after spending a few months playing in the US, Staffell returned to England, and a new gig as lead singer in the cosmically inclined progressive rock band Morgan, featuring ex-Love Affair keyboard-player Morgan Fisher. Morgan recorded the old Smile song, 'Earth', for their 1972 debut album, *Nova Solis*.

When Morgan stalled, Staffell flirted with the idea of a solo career, even going so far as to play a solo gig at the Marquee. By the late-seventies, Tim ducked out of music to pursue model-making as a career. As well as crafting numerous pieces for films and television commercials, Staffell's most enduring creations are the models he made for the children's TV show *Thomas the Tank Engine*. In 1992, he was back onstage with Roger Taylor and Brian May for a two-song Smile reunion at the Marquee; in 2003, he cut an independent solo album, *Amigos*, and is presently writing a science fiction novel.

For years Tim Staffell has graciously picked over his time in Smile for inquisitive journalists and TV documentary-makers, always insisting that he had not missed an opportunity by leaving the band. 'I did not have it in me to do what Freddie did,' he said. 'I was never the showman or the writer that Freddie was. I have regretted not being a musician but not leaving Smile.'

At Tim Staffell's house one evening in 1972, Morgan Fisher was introduced to one of his new lead singer's friends. 'Tim said, "Oh Morgan, this is the bloke who took over from me in Smile." And this extraordinary, exotic Persian guy got up from the sofa, wearing clothes that looked as if they'd all been made out of a velvet cushion cover. He smiled very shyly, barely said a word and gave me this incredibly limp handshake.' It was Freddie Bulsara.

CHAPTER FOUR

A Strange Vibrato

'When I joined Queen I had sod all to do.'

**Mike Grose, Queen bass guitarist
for three months**

'I thought they were going nowhere.'

**Barry Mitchell, Queen bass guitarist
for six months**

'Can't complain, nice house, great family and a fancy car
. . . but it would have been nice.'

**Doug Bogie, Queen bass guitarist
for two gigs**

'When I first joined Queen, the other three argued like
mad and I just kept out of it.'

**John Deacon, Queen bass guitarist
since February 1971**

In 1970, *Woodstock* the movie opened in cinemas but not every
budding rock musician was a fan. 'When I saw that film it was a
shock to realise how little I related to it,' admitted Brian May.
'Queen weren't the sort of band that would get stoned, go on and
shuffle around. In a way, we were a reaction against it,' To some in
their social circle, Bulsara, Brian May and Roger Taylor had always
been an obvious combination of musicians. 'I can remember
walking down Ealing Broadway in 1968 with those three and
thinking, 'That's it, that's the band,'' says Chris Smith.

Initially, though, Smile's drummer and guitarist were wary of
their new recruit. 'I remember thinking, "Good on showmanship,

but not sure about the singing,"' admitted May. 'Fred had a strange vibrato,' chuckled Roger Taylor, 'which some people found rather distressing.' Just as it had been with Ibex and Wreckage, it was Fred's persistence that ultimately won the day: 'Freddie was there, saying, "I'll sing and I'd do that,"' said Brian, 'and we gradually went . . . "OK."'

Tim Staffell's exit had also left Smile without a bass player. They recruited Roger Taylor's friend Mike Grose, who had been the co-owner of PJ's, the Truro music venue where Smile had been regulars. PJ's was facing closure, but Grose was a bass guitarist with the added bonus of owning a Volkswagen van and a Marshall amp. Better still, Grose had played briefly as a guitarist in The Reaction and previously understudied for Tim Staffell at a Smile gig at PJ's, after a row between the bassist and Roger Taylor.

Grose moved up to London and into a billet at Ferry Road. May hustled his Imperial College professors into signing the forms needed to let the band rehearse in one of the lecture theatres. Taylor had promised his mother that Smile would play a Red Cross fundraiser at Truro City Hall on 27 June. Neglecting to tell anyone that this was a very different 'Smile', May, Taylor, Bulsara and Grose managed to muddled their way through an uneven set in front of around 200 people in the 800-capacity hall, for which they were paid £50.

The origins of the Queen name, are, much like Freddie's sawn-off mic stand, steeped in all kinds of myth and hearsay. 'The name was mine,' maintains John 'Tupp' Taylor. 'I used to call Fred "the old queen" and I used to say to him that if he was ever in another band after Wreckage he should call it Queen, and he used to say, "Oh, do you think so?"' However, Mike Grose remembers sitting in the garden at Ferry Road when Freddie first pitched the name. Ken Testi remembers being told of the new band's name in a telephone call from Kensington Market. 'It made perfect sense to hear that he was with Brian and Roger. It should have been that way all along. I told him it was great news, and then he told me the name: Queen. I said, "You'll never get away with that, Fred." But he was like, "No, it's wonderful, dear, people will love it."'

Other contenders for the group's name included Build Your Own Boat, The Rich Kids and The Grand Dance (the last of these taken from C.S. Lewis's science-fiction trilogy *Out of the Silent Planet*). But they were no competition. 'The concept of Queen is to be regal and majestic,' Freddie later told *Melody Maker*. 'We want to be dandy. We want to shock and be outrageous.'

'The name was Freddie's idea,' said Roger Taylor in 1974. 'It was just a reflection of the social world we were in at the time, when he and I were working together on Kensington Market. In those days there was a pretty eccentric crowd there, and a lot of them were gay and a lot of them pretended to be, and it just seemed to fit in. I didn't like the name originally and neither did Brian, but we got used to it. We thought that once we'd got established the music would then become the identity more than the name . . .'

Queen wouldn't be the only name-change that spring. 'Freddie had written this song called "My Fairy King",' said Brian May. 'And there's a line in it that says, "Oh Mother Mercury what have you done to me?" And it was after that that he said, "I am going to become Mercury as the mother in this song is my mother." We were like, "Are you mad?"'

Though no official documentation has ever surfaced at the Deed Poll Office, from now on Fred Bulsara's passport would read Frederick Mercury. The transformation from gauche immigrant schoolboy to extrovert butterfly was complete. 'Changing his name was part of him assuming this different skin,' said May. 'The young Bulsara was still there but for the public he was going to be this god.'

Before long, though, Mike Grose had grown weary of the struggle. May, Taylor and Mercury had been students since the mid-sixties, and were used to living in diminished circumstances. The 22-year-old Grose liked earning a living and found what he called 'the empty days' at Ferry Road depressing: Freddie was an art student used to doing nothing; Brian and Roger still had months left to go on their courses. But Grose was used to working a day job and playing gigs in the evening. That summer, in the garden at Barnes, he had watched as his three bandmates teased out ideas for songs that would eventually find their way on to the first Queen album. Queen had written the whole of what would become their debut, and the song 'Father To Son' (from what became *Queen II*). Grose thought the band had potential but wasn't prepared to wait. He quit after a few months, returned to Cornwall, played briefly in a group called No Joke with, bizarrely, Tim Staffell, before forming his own haulage company and dropping out of the music scene.

Mike Grose's replacement would be found after a chance meeting in Cornwall. Barry Mitchell had grown up in Harrow, West London. By 1965, he was bass guitar in a soul covers band called Conviction, also featuring a young Alan Parsons on guitar. Parsons would go on to engineer Pink Floyd's *The Dark Side of the Moon* and front his own ensemble, The Alan Parsons Project. Conviction changed their name to Earth in 1967, made one unreleased album and secured a residency at the Coffin Club on London's Gerard Street.

By August 1970, Mitchell was considering giving up music altogether. His most recent group, Black (featuring a black South African Hendrix lookalike) had stalled, and he was working a day job in Soper's department store in Harrow. 'I had a good friend called Roger Crossley who worked there with me,' says Mitchell now. 'The two of us used to hang out at the art college looking for pretty girls. Roger Crossley went to Cornwall in the summer and he met Roger Taylor. They got talking and Roger Taylor said he was looking for a bass player . . . So my mate gave me his phone number.'

Mitchell made the call, caught the tube to Kensington and auditioned for Queen at Imperial College. His first thought was how blessed the group were to have access to free rehearsal space and storage; the twin holy grails for any struggling band. 'We had a couple of plays,' remembers Barry. 'We ran through some Hendrix and [Willie Dixon's] "Do Me Right", and that was it, I was in.'

Queen had a gig booked at Imperial in three weeks' time, for an audience of invited friends. A few hours before showtime, the group convened in Brian's bedsit. Here, Barry discovered that they were cooking homemade popcorn on the flat's single gas ring, which they intended to serve with fruit juice as refreshments for their guests. 'It was all quite sweet and innocent,' he grins. 'But, yes, you could say they weren't rock 'n' rollers.'

Queen's set now included a smattering of old rock 'n' roll tunes, Smile's 'Doing Alright' and 'Stone Cold Crazy', a song Freddie had worked up in Wreckage and which Queen would make their own. Their wild cards were covers of Shirley Bassey's 'Big Spender' and Cliff Richard and The Shadows' 'Please Don't Tease' (Mitchell: 'I remember thinking, "*What?*" '). John Garnham, 1984's ex-guitarist, saw the Imperial College show, and was struck by the originality of doing 'this completely straight version of a Cliff Richard song right in the middle of the set'. Garnham was also struck by Freddie's individual performance: 'His voice wasn't that dissimilar to Tim Staffell. But Tim was not a good frontman. He was always quite introverted and saying, "Oh, I didn't do that. Shall I do this or shall I do that?" But Fred just took the bull by horns.' That evening, John also remembers Queen road-testing a new song 'Son and Daughter'. His verdict matched those of many who saw Queen at the time: 'It was *very* Led Zeppelin.'

Also in the audience was John Anthony, now working as an A&R rep and in-house producer for Charisma Records. 'Roger and I had kept in touch,' he explains. 'It was always Roger that used to call me.' He knew lots of women: 'One of them gave me crabs . . . even had them in my eyebrows. But Roger would always let me know what he was doing with Smile, and then one day I got the call saying they had found a new singer and was I interested.'

Anthony vaguely recalls having seen Freddie at Kensington Market before Queen. 'He was very gushing and camp, but I didn't think anything of it. Onstage, though, he filled the whole room. It was such a difference from Smile. They more or less had their sound together, but they had a dodgy bass player. He looked like he'd be better in a heavy metal band. I said to Roger afterwards, "Look, it's not working visually, but you're three-quarters of the way there." '

In the meantime, Queen's 'heavy metal bass player' was getting to know his new bandmates. 'Brian was this fantastically nice guy and a unique guitar player,' says Barry Mitchell. 'Roger was a bit of a lad, and while his drumming was OK I thought it was a bit wishy-washy. Freddie was very sweet, but hard to get to know and incredibly self-conscious about his teeth.' Mercury had played the

Imperial College gig in a black, figure-hugging, one-piece outfit (designed by ex-roadie Pete Edmunds's wife, Wendy). He called it his 'Mercury suit', as the ankles and wrists sported little wings. 'I remember first seeing it and thinking, "Oh, you brave, brave boy,"' recalled Roger Taylor.

Prior to the show Barry had also been taken aback to find the singer teasing his hair into place with heated tongs and sporting black vanish on the fingernails of one hand. 'There was a difference right there,' he admits. Mitchell's look, such as it was, comprised jeans, T-shirts and a mop of long blonde hair. 'There's Freddie with his tongs and there's me thinking, "Here's my hair, right let's go."'

In rehearsals, too, Mitchell witnessed the band's painstaking attention to detail and willingness to bicker over those details: 'There were lots of disagreements. You could lose half an hour with them just arguing over four bars of music.' A great leveller in such situations was John Harris. Harris had been introduced to May and Taylor by Pat McConnell the previous summer. Smile's former driver/roadie Pete Edmunds was no longer with them, and Harris had stepped up as road manager, electronics wizard, sound engineer and 'fifth member'. 'He was a lovely guy who drove this long-wheeled transit van and really looked after us,' says Mitchell. 'He was always there in rehearsals and he was great at stepping in and saying, "Oh, for fuck's sake! All this over four bars. Get it together!"'

If Mitchell had any misgivings, at least Queen were working. The Imperial College gig was followed by a show at an American private school in London's Swiss Cottage, where Roger regaled Barry with stories of his romantic derring-do: 'Roger was having a thing with a young lady living in student accommodation in Kensington, and apparently he'd scaled two or three balconies to get to her room.'

On 18 September 1970, Jimi Hendrix was found dead at his girlfriend's room at the Samarkand Hotel in Notting Hill. Rehearsing at Imperial, barely a stone's throw from the scene of his demise, Queen abandoned their own set and began jamming Hendrix's 'Foxy Lady', 'Voodoo Chile', 'Purple Haze' and others. Chris Smith had seen a newspaper headline announcing Jimi's demise while travelling on the tube to Imperial: 'I was shell-shocked,' he remembers. 'And as

I walked down the corridor to the lecture theatre, I could hear them playing "Stone Free".'

Mercury and Taylor closed their market stall for a day in honour of Hendrix. Despite the noble gesture, they could hardly afford to lose the money. Fred's illustrative work was strictly piecemeal. 'He got an offer to illustrate a book about Second World War aircraft,' remembers Richard Thompson. 'So I lent him my collection of *Air Pictorial* magazines. I remember him doing some drawings, but I think he gave up on it, as it was too much like hard work.' Furthermore, any cash Queen made barely covered their overheads. They needed proper day jobs.

Alan Mair was the proprietor of the clothes stall opposite Freddie and Roger's at Kensington Market. 'They were both lovely, but that stall of theirs never cut the mustard,' he says now. 'There was more and more competition on that aisle. You had the first denim jackets with white fur collars coming in, and people were making jackets out of chamois leather, but those two were just selling a few loonpants, nothing unusual.'

While Mercury and Taylor's profits dwindled, Mair's grew. He had begun making his own leather boots in a workshop and selling them at the market. Before long, he'd enlisted Freddie to help keep an eye on his stall. Lunchtime trips to the Greyhound pub on Kensington Square found the three striking up a rapport. While Mair knew that Freddie and Roger played in a band, they didn't know that Mair had played bass guitar in a sixties Glaswegian combo called the Beatstalkers. 'One night, at my flat, the Beatstalkers memorabilia came out, and I started getting invited to all the Queen gigs.'

The Beatstalkers had been managed by David Bowie's mentor Ken Pitt, and covered a few early Bowie songs. When Bowie himself breezed into the market one day, he made straight for Alan's stall. Mair offered Bowie a pair of boots on the house ('"Space Oddity" had been a hit, but he said he had no money. Typical music biz! I said, "Look, have them for free"'). Freddie fitted Bowie for a pair of boots. It was probably the first time the two had met since Mercury helped build Bowie's stage at the Ealing college gig: 'So there was Freddie Mercury, a shop assistant, giving pop star

David Bowie a pair of boots he couldn't afford to buy.'

In October, Mair and 'everyone else in the market' descended on Kensington's College of Estate Management for Queen's weekend gig. 'And it wasn't very good,' says Alan. 'Freddie had this nervous energy that would make him push his voice, and he sang sharp the whole set. He looked awkward onstage and wasn't very rhythmic. It was the first time they had enthusiastically invited everyone down from the market, and on the Monday we were all saying, "Oh, it was OK." And Freddie and Roger were like, "Is that *all*?"' Mitchell, too, concedes that during his time in Queen, Mercury's voice left something to be desired: 'There wasn't a lot of depth there.'

Gig bookings stopped when Brian, still studying for that PhD, took another trip to the observatory in Tenerife. On his return, Queen's Liverpool connection picked up the slack. Ken Testi was still social secretary of his college in St Helens, and booking bands through his friend and fledgling promoter Paul Conroy (who would go on to become managing director of Virgin Records). Testi offered Queen two shows: a support slot at St Helens on 30 October and The Cavern the day after.

With a few hours to kill before The Cavern show, Queen trooped into a local cinema to watch a low-budget soft porn film. According to Barry Mitchell, the action and dialogue was so desperate, the group began laughing uncontrollably, 'so they threw us out'. As The Beatles' spiritual home, The Cavern still had a romantic cachet. 'It was this basement with a low ceiling and sweat everywhere,' says Mitchell, 'but it was still an iconic place.' Ken Testi thought differently: 'The Cavern DJ Billy Butler wasn't very welcoming to Queen. Having a band in seemed to be an interference to him playing his records. I hated The Cavern and still do.'

Between gigs, Queen stayed at the Testi family's pub, the Market Hotel, in St Helens. 'It is worth mentioning,' says Ken, 'that for a Northern lad to be able to introduce such idiosyncratically dressed friends from London to his mum and for them to be so well-mannered was fantastic.' Ken's sister, then aged four or five, still remembers sitting on Freddie Mercury's lap and being taught to play noughts and crosses. At Queen's next booking a fortnight later, at a teacher training college in Hertford, the group chanced their luck by requesting a bigger fee. The reason? They'd played The Cavern and were now more famous having been on the same stage as The Beatles. They were refused.

Christmas 1970 came and went. In January 1971, Queen supported art-rockers Audience at the Marquee, and Barry Mitchell found enough space on the graffiti-daubed dressing room wall to write his name. It was a watershed moment of sorts. He'd made up his mind to leave. May, Taylor and Mercury had a shared history and social circle. Mitchell was living in Kingsbury, North London, miles away from Kensington. The morning after most gigs he'd have to drag himself out of bed to start his day job as a park keeper. There was another issue. 'Their music wasn't what I wanted to do,' he says. 'I wanted something more bluesy and soulful, something with a brass section.' By now, too, Queen were playing songs that would end up on their debut album, including 'Keep Yourself Alive', 'Liar' and 'Great King Rat'. 'But it was all a bit airy-fairy,' confesses Barry. 'I didn't like that stuff. They were still like Led Zeppelin meets Yes. I didn't think they'd found their mojo yet.' It was a strange reprise of Tim Staffell's earlier misgivings about Smile.

Mitchell played his last Queen gig opening for Kevin Ayers and Genesis at Ewell Technical College on 9 January. As with Mike Grose, his bandmates didn't want him to go. In the dressing room after the show, Genesis' lead singer Peter Gabriel sidled up to Roger Taylor with a proposal of his own. Genesis were on the verge of firing their drummer, had yet to discover Phil Collins and needed a replacement. Was he interested? 'I told Roger he should take them up on it,' laughs Barry. 'But he was having none of it. He was totally committed to Queen.' At the time, John Anthony had just produced Genesis' second album, *Trespass*, but Anthony now emphatically denies ever trying to lure Taylor away from Queen.

In spring 1971, Barry Mitchell re-surfaced in a trio called Crushed Butler, soon renamed Tiger, whose street image and untutored hard rock was about four years too early for punk. Later, he turned down a job with what became The Glitter Band. Barry saw Queen opening for Mott The Hoople a year after he left, and watched without rancour or regret. When 'Bohemian Rhapsody' became a hit, he was managing an electrical store. As the song blared out, he told his incredulous staff that he 'used to be in that band'. On the journey to Liverpool to play The Cavern, Mitchell remembers Brian May fooling around with a new camera and training the lens on his bandmates as they huddled in the back of the transit. 'But there are no pictures of me onstage,' he shrugs. The lack of photographic evidence, some memento from those times, still frustrates him.

When Mitchell left Queen, it was Freddie's girlfriend that tried to persuade him to change his mind. Mary Austin had become a familiar presence, and would go on to become the most significant relationship of the Queen singer's life. According to Freddie, the pair met in 1970, when the nineteen-year-old Mary was working as receptionist for the fashion boutique Biba, then located on Kensington High Street. Biba was the brainchild of clothes designer Barbara Hulanicki, and had been at the hub of London's fashion scene since the mid-sixties. 'Part of the attraction of Biba was that the girls were so beautiful,' admitted Brian May. 'So we went in there to enjoy the scenery.'

Before Biba, Mary had worked as a trainee secretary, and had grown up with two deaf and dumb parents, learning sign language from a young age. It was Brian May that first asked her out after meeting her at a concert at Imperial. They went out on a few dates, but the relationship never went any further. Before long, Freddie begun asking Brian about her. 'He would come in to Biba, usually with Roger, and he would smile and say hello in passing,' remembered Mary. 'This went on for five or six months and finally he asked me out on a date. Five months later we were living together.'

Initially, Mary believed, wrongly, that the 'wild-looking' singer was more interested in her friend. Freddie took her to see Mott The Hoople at the Marquee that summer, and the relationship slowly grew. 'Freddie was very confident and I had never been confident,' she explained in an interview in 2000. Like Rosemary Pearson before her, Mary talked of finding safety and security with Freddie: 'We knew we could trust each other and we knew that we would never hurt each other on purpose.'

'Freddie'd had relationships with other girls,' explained May. 'But, looking back, his heart wasn't in it. It worked with Mary because they were both shy.'

Freddie moved out of the Fulham flat he'd been sharing with Roger (Taylor: 'We used to wait for a weekly hamper from his mother') and into a tiny second-floor flat at 2 Victoria Road, Kensington, with Mary and their cats, Thomas and Jerry. Freddie's small record collection included The Who's *Tommy*, *Led Zeppelin I*, The Beatles' *White Album* and The Pretty Things' *S.F. Sorrow* (Mary was a friend of Pretty Things guitarist Dick Taylor's then wife Melissa), plus the soundtrack to Liza Minnelli's *Cabaret*. Says John Anthony: '*Cabaret* was Freddie's favourite film. He used to see it repeatedly. I always thought he took the idea of painting his fingernails from Liza Minnelli.' The flat was a short walk from the market, the rent was £10 a week, and they shared the bathroom and kitchen with another couple.

Ken Testi, now back in London, helped the couple move in. 'I was driving a Mini at the time,' recalls Testi. 'So I helped taxi all their stuff to the flat in several trips. A few days later we were invited round for dinner. Mary and Freddie didn't have two ha'pennies to rub together, but what money they had they'd spent on these really nice plates! As there was no kitchen, they just served salad.' It was a momentous occasion: 'As a Northern lad, I'd not had much salad.'

For Ken and others, Mary's presence in Freddie's life scotched any doubt about the singer's sexuality: 'They were 100 per cent a couple back then.' Barry Mitchell, too, had always regarded Freddie's camp behaviour and effeminacy as a guise, 'an act, like calling the band Queen'. There could, however, be no disregarding Freddie's regal tendencies and his ability to create a scene, however reduced his circumstances. Visiting the couple's bijou flat one morning, Mike Bersin found Freddie holding court from his and Mary's bed: 'My impression of the bed is that it was a) vast and b) festooned in blowsy swags. It almost certainly wasn't but that's the effect Freddie had.'

With Barry Mitchell gone, Queen found themselves seeking their third bassist in less than twelve months. That third bassist would become the tiniest of footnotes in the group's history. Until now. In *Queen: As It Began*, the band's semi-official biography, Barry Mitchell's replacement was referred to only as 'Doug'. He lasted just two gigs before being fired for his behaviour onstage. 'He jumped up and down in a manner most incongruous,' protested Brian May.

Referred to since as 'Doug X' or, erroneously, 'Doug Ewood', Queen's mystery bass guitarist was actually an eighteen-year-old trainee telephone technician named Douglas Bogie. 'I was a serial auditionist,' says Douglas now. 'I saw an advert in *Melody Maker*, made the call, popped my Telecaster bass in a rucksack and got on the 716 Greenline bus from Weybridge to the Albert Memorial.'

The audition, inevitably, took place at Imperial, where, remembers Bogie, 'Freddie wandered in, accompanied by a really nice girl, presumably Mary, and wearing his signature grey rabbit-skin jacket.' With John Harris smoothing the way, Doug spent the next few days learning most of the songs on Queen's would-be debut album. 'I came away amazed at the strength and vitality of Roger's voice,' he recalls now. 'He was just fantastic. Speaking as a Jeff Beck fan, he would have blown Rod Stewart off the stage.' After hours, Douglas hung out with Freddie at Alan Mair's boot stall. 'This went on for a few weeks, and I thought it was all going well.' Sadly not.

On 19 February, Queen played beneath The Pretty Things at London's Hornsey Town Hall. The day after, Queen opened for Yes at Kingston Polytechnic. 'Mine and everyone's first gig with a W-Bin PA, which Queen told me they'd bought from Iron Butterfly,' remembers Douglas. 'I thought I'd done really well. These guys were older but I had energy and I was leaping about . . . Unfortunately, no one told me that what Freddie wanted was a quiet thumper at the back.'

To spare Bogie's embarrassment, Freddie instigated what Douglas now describes as the 'I don't want to do this anymore – we're breaking up discussion' in the back of the van after the gig: 'Freddie was having a conversation along the lines of "That was a terrible gig, the world is against me and I've had enough . . . I don't want to do this anymore . . ." I guess he was being nice to me being the youngster and the new boy while letting the others know that he was the leading light and needed to be consoled and massaged.' With sleight of hand and a lack of direct confrontation, Douglas Bogie was, indeed, let go after just two gigs.

In 1973, Douglas Bogie began working as a sound engineer. Two years later he signed a one-off deal with Ringo Starr's Ring'o Records and cut a novelty single as Colonel Doug Bogie ('Harry Nilsson took a liking to it'). Later, while working as an engineer in Edinburgh he secured a deal with A&M for his new band RAF ('It stood for Rich And Famous,' he laughs, 'and we had a very produced Queen/Foreigner sound'). RAF made two albums 'so hugely successful that we were never asked to do a third'. Tracking the debut RAF album at London's Air Studios in 1980, Bogie bumped into Brian May.

'I never went on about the Queen thing,' Douglas explains now. 'I was embarrassed at being dumped and felt a bit sorry for myself, and I sometimes thought that the few who knew about it might think it was a bullshit fairy story.' It wasn't. A successful career in video production and 'a nice collection of guitars' has sustained 'Doug X' ever since.

■ ■ ■

The slogan 'Behind every great man there is a great woman' seems curiously appropriate in the story of Queen. Without the machinations of the band's female friends at the Maria Assumpta, Queen's history might have taken a very different turn. In 1969, Brian May's student girlfriend had sweet-talked engineer Terry Yeadon into investigating Smile and helping them record a free demo; in the same year the McConnell sisters had brokered an introduction between Smile and Ibex, and given Fred Bulsara his first singing job. It would be five months before Queen performed live with Douglas Bogie's replacement, but, again, it was the 'good Catholic girls' at Maria Assumpta that helped the band find their man.

In late February 1971, Brian May, Roger Taylor and John Harris attended a disco at the college. Through a mutual friend, they were introduced to John Deacon, a nineteen-year-old student in electronics at London University's Chelsea College. Deacon had previously played bass guitar in a schoolboy group in his home-town of Oadby, Leicestershire, but had given up playing when he moved to London. Caught by the musical bug again, he began going for auditions but without success. In October, he had been among the small crowd at Queen's College of Estate Management gigs, where Alan Mair had winced at Freddie's singing. (Deacon said later: 'They didn't make an impression on me.')

In November 1970 he and his flatmate, a budding guitarist named Peter Stoddart, and a couple of like-minded students, had formed a band to play covers at a Chelsea College gig. Needing a name for the promotional flyers, they called themselves Deacon. It would be the last time the self-effacing bass player ever put himself at the centre of anything. Deacon would never play another gig. Queen had found their missing link.

John Richard Deacon's story began on 19 August 1951 in St Francis' Private Hospital in Leicester, where he was born to parents Lilian and Arthur. His father worked at the Norwich Union Building Society and died when John was just ten years old. Deacon spent his first nine years living in Evington before moving with his parents and younger sister Julie to nearby Oadby, a suburban town that had been slowly growing since the end of the Second World War. The family settled in a detached house at 54 Hidcote Road, and John began attending the local Langmore Junior School and, later, Gartree High School.

Fascinated by electronics, Deacon spent his time tinkering with a homemade radio receiver and a reel-to-reel tape recorder on which he would tape songs from the radio. Nigel Bullen had met John at Langmore Junior. At the age of thirteen, the two began playing music. After hearing The Beatles' 'Please Please Me', John saved up enough cash from a paper round to buy a cheap acoustic guitar. With Nigel playing drums, the two began making a noise together.

The catalyst for their first band would be Richard Young, who encountered Deacon and Nigel Bullen in the local Uplands Park in the summer of 1965. Young was older, had attended Woodbank private school and Scarborough College and, at the age of sixteen, had just started working in his father's electrical wholesaling business. Interviewed in 1996, Bullen described Richard as 'the kid with the expensive bike'.

'I'd already formed a group at Scarborough,' says Young now. 'I was working in my dad's business and that provided me with the money to finance the group. The rest of the guys were still at school.' Young put together the band: himself as lead singer and guitarist, Bullen playing drums, Deacon on rhythm guitar, and another local lad, a snappy mod dresser named Clive Castledine, playing bass.

After rehearsing in Bullen's garage, the new group made their debut at a party in Castledine's parents' house in September. Young: 'I don't remember much about Clive's party but it did dawn on me that the weakest link was, sadly, Clive.' Calling themselves The Opposition, the band went public in October with a gig at Gartree High School, followed by a bigger show in December at Enderby Co-operative Hall. By now, Richard Young had decided to switch to playing keyboards. 'My voice was capable but I began to realise the importance of a frontman,' he explains. 'Also I was playing guitar, but I felt that I was not good at it.' Young was now having piano lessons and it was a natural move to the side of the stage.

Plying their services in the *Oadby & Wigston Advertiser*, The Opposition began picking up £2–£4-a-night bookings in neighbouring church halls and youth clubs. But there was a problem: Clive Castledine's bass playing still hadn't improved. 'He found difficulty in keeping time and I think the idea of being in a group appealed to him more than mastering the bass guitar.' ('I was getting distracted by girls and bikes,' admitted Castledine, years later.)

Despite the fact that it was Clive who'd introduced Richard to his girlfriend Patricia ('Clive and his girlfriend and me and Pat all went to see *Help!* at the Odeon in Leicester'), the bass player was out. Deacon switched from rhythm to bass, and was taken to Cox's music shop on Leicester's King Street and bought a £60 EKO bass, paid for by Richard Young: 'There was a lot of groups starting up around Leicester. The only way to stay ahead of the rest was to make good music, which meant you had to have good equipment.'

The line-up shifted again with the arrival of guitarist Dave Williams in July 1966. Williams had been at Gartree High with Deacon, and Bullen had played in a band called The Outer Limits. They were older boys, and dressed like mods. Much like Brian May's 1984 and their mini-heroes The Others, The Outer Limits were something to aspire to.

That summer Deacon and Bullen moved up to Beauchamp Grammar School, but continued to play with the group, despite John's mother insisting that he did not play pubs. Richard Young's diary records an entry for September 1966, when 'Deaks wasn't allowed to do it, so Brian from The Glen [local band The Glen Sounds] stood in.' Stoic, shy, and rarely flustered, 'Easy Deacon' as he was nicknamed, was already displaying the traits for which he'd become known in Queen.

Now calling themselves The New Opposition, and fronted by singer Pete 'Pedro' Bartholomew, they could be found regularly chugging through Tamla Motown covers at the Leicester Casino. By the end of the year, they'd lost 'Pedro' and acquired a new guitarist Ron Chester, noted for a Sherlock Holmes-style deer-stalker hat from which he was rarely parted. With Chester in the band, The Opposition (the 'New' had been dispensed with) were photographed by the *Leicester Mercury*. 'We were finalists in the Midlands Beat Championships,' remembers Richard Young. The final was meant to take place at Leicester's De Montford Hall, but the promoter did a runner with the money, and it never happened: Our first experience of the shitty side of the music business.' The *Leicester Mercury* photo captures a band stuck between the sixties beat-group boom and the encroaching psychedelic era. Williams's jumbo-collared silk shirt points one way; his tweed jacket another.

With the extrovert Williams now fronting the band, The Opposition briefly acquired a couple of schoolgirl go-go dancers named Charmaine and Jenny (Young: 'the dancing girls were to create interest . . . anything to stop the music becoming stale'). Their setlist became heavier, and the band began dabbling in flower-power fashions. By March 1968, The Opposition had changed their name to Art. At the Beauchamp Grammar School midsummer ball, Dave Williams created havoc by exploding a homemade smoke bomb during a version of The Crazy World of Arthur Brown's hit single 'Fire'. By the end of the year, Richard Young was 'getting into Argent, Deep Purple, Chopin and Bach'.

The following year, Art cut a self-financed single at a studio in Wellingborough. Alongside a couple of soul covers, they knocked up an instrumental of their own, 'Transit 3'. Like the rest of the band, it was John Deacon's first time in a studio. Only two copies of the disc are known to have survived, and Richard Young's isn't one of them ('I do not have any copies of the Art single'). One rumour has it that the others used Richard's copy as an ashtray at rehearsals.

Deacon played his final gig with Art in August 1969. A month later he moved to London and into a rented flat in Queensgate. He left his bass guitar behind in Oadby. Art split, but Bullen, Williams and Young would all continue working in original groups or covers bands. The Opposition's founder member/financier now runs a piano shop in Oadby, just 300 yards from the old Deacon family home in Hidcote Road. 'It's still strange to think that one of the members of my first group made it,' he admits.

Bullen would occasionally visit Deacon in London, but was astonished when John told him he wanted to join another group, presuming that he'd given it up to concentrate on his college course. None of his former band members had considered Deacon ambitious enough to want to make a career in music. Interviewed in 1996, Bullen recalled Deacon telling him that he'd begun answering ads in *Melody Maker* but 'bottled out when he discovered they were for a name act'. As Richard Young admits, 'Little did we know when practising in a cold, draughty garage that the shy, unassuming kid, probably still paying me some of his pocket money on an instalment on his bass guitar, would become the famous one.'

Just a couple of days after their meeting at the Maria Assumpta college, Deacon showed up at the Imperial lecture theatre with his bass guitar and a tiny practice amp. His audition comprised of a lengthy blues jam and a run-through of three Queen songs, including 'Son and Daughter'. Recalled Brian May: 'Having been through a lot of hugely thunderous bass players, this quite shy guy turns up, and as soon as he started putting basslines to what we were doing, we realised it was right.'

Also present at the session was ex-Sour Milk Sea guitarist Chris Chesney. At the time, Freddie had hatched a plan to expand Queen by adding a second guitarist. 'I'd seen them play at Imperial with the blonde guy [Barry Mitchell],' recounts Chesney. 'Freddie had come up to afterwards and said, "I'd like you to join the band."' Previously Queen had supported Wishbone Ash, the denizens of progressive blues-rock, notable for having two lead guitarists. Maybe the inspiration was there, or, more likely, the rather static Brian was less of a visual foil for Freddie than Chris had been. When it came to their individual playing, 'Brian was ahead of me technically,' offers Chesney. 'But I thought I nudged him on feel.' In the absence of a guitar of his own, Chris had to borrow the Red Special. 'It was a nightmare,' he admits. Unused to the homemade guitar's unusually large neck and idiosyncratic fretboard, Chesney struggled to play properly. 'It was nice of Freddie to consider me,' he laughs.

Before long, Chesney had quit London and enrolled at university. After a spell in the US, he returned to the UK and skirted the fringes of the punk scene. A career making video and TV commercials ensued, while covers bands, session gigs and stints as a backing musician to the likes of Percy Sledge and Ben E. King kept him involved in music. After his fumbled audition with Queen, Chris would not cross paths with Freddie Mercury again until 1987.

'Easy Deacon' made his Queen debut on 2 July 1971 at a college gig in Surrey. He did not embarrass the band with any 'incongruous behaviour', and as a student himself, wasn't shackled to a day job. His bass playing was excellent (Chris Chesney recalled that at his audition Deacon didn't drop a single beat) and his electronics expertise was considered a bonus. But there was much more to it than that. As Roger Taylor observed, 'We were all so used to each other and so over the top, we thought that because he was so quiet he would fit in with us without too much upheaval.' As Deacon told an interviewer later, 'When we argue, I yell much less than the others.'

John Anthony was invited to check out the new-look Queen. 'I saw them rehearse with John. To be honest I thought he was neither fish nor fowl,' he says. 'He always reminded me of a character in the seventies TV comedy *Please Sir!* There was a school bully who wanted to beat everyone up, and he had a sidekick who was always egging him on – "Yeah! Yeah!" That was John Deacon.' At the time, Anthony was about to set up his own production company, Neptune Productions, with Trident Studio's engineers Robin Geoffrey Cable and Roy Thomas Baker: 'I told Queen I was booked up for nine months producing other bands, but that I really wanted to do something with them.'

In the meantime, John Deacon's apprenticeship would continue with a trip to Cornwall. The band rented a cottage in Devoran and played eleven dates around the county. Sometimes billed as 'The Legendary Drummer of Cornwall Roger Taylor . . . and Queen', their garish stage clothes and Freddie's mannered posturing was paraded before the personnel gathered in the NCO's mess hall at RNAS Culdrose. One pub gig was marred by a row over the volume of their PA, and the band were, literally, chased out of town by angry locals. It was all grist to the mill. Roger's old pal Rik Evans promoted an outdoor gig at Tregye Country Club near Truro, with Queen warming up the crowd for Hawkwind and Arthur Brown.

Back in London, 'Cornwall's legendary drummer' bit the bullet and went back to being a student. Taylor's year off was over, and he signed up to study biology at North London Polytechnic. Adamant that the course would not stand in the way of Queen, Roger had to give up the market stall. In Taylor's absence, Freddie closed the stall and carried on working for Alan Mair. The close proximity between the two stalls also allowed the singer to continue using the market's public telephone box as his personal office. 'You could always call Freddie on that phone and he'd answer,' says Ken Testi.

Whatever progress Queen were making as a live act, they were still even further away from a record deal than Smile had been. Two years earlier, Pye Studios maintenance engineer Terry Yeadon had recorded a demo for Smile in a late-night session. That autumn, Yeadon took a phone call from Brian May. It was the first time they had spoken since Smile, and the call was a sign of May's desperation to get something, anything, happening for Queen. 'Brian told me that he had a new band, that Tim had gone but that they had a great new singer, and could I do anything?' says Yeadon. 'His timing could not have been better.'

De Lane Lea's Kingsway Studios had closed and the studio team, which now included Yeadon, had moved to a newly built facility in Wembley, North London. But there were problems. As Louis Austin, the studio engineer, bluntly explains: 'De Lane Lea was a piece of tut, a rubbish studio, appalling. When a band played in Studio One, you could hear them in Studios Two and Three, and vice versa.'

In an attempt to fully soundproof the facility, a false wall was installed in the corridor and filled with formaldehyde chips (Yeadon: 'That stuff you embalm dead bodies with'). What the team now needed was a live rock band to test the rooms, and identify any further problems. 'I remember thinking, "Who can we get?"' says Terry Yeadon. 'At Pye Studios, I'd worked with everyone from The Kinks to Sammy Davis Jnr. I thought, "I can't get any of them." Brian phoned at the right time. I was like, "Step this way."' Queen arrived with, as Louis Austin recalls, 'a complete setlist and all the songs mapped out for a first album. We were impressed.' The deal entailed the band acting as guinea pigs, with a professional studio demo as payment. 'They said if we came along and made a noise, they could do their acoustic tests and they'd make some demos for us,' recalled Brian May.

'Thinking back, we really pissed them around,' says Yeadon. 'We had them dragging their gear from one studio to the next for about a week. Then, when we were recording, we discovered there was a problem with the new tape machines, so every two minutes we were asking them to stop and start again.'

Queen rehearsed their live show in Studio Two's mini-amphitheatre, blasting through the 100-watt Marshall PA stack the engineers had hired for them, with Freddie brazenly throwing shapes. 'Fred couldn't sing and not perform,' says Yeadon. 'Even when we were recording them I think Louis had a problem with him going off mic.' Louis Austin was used to working with hungry young bands, and had just engineered Thin Lizzy's debut. 'But

Queen were unusually confident and committed. I did think they'd get somewhere, but not with me and certainly not at De Lane Lea.'

Queen came away from the studio with sixteen-track, two-inch masters of five original songs: 'Keep Yourself Alive', 'Liar', 'Jesus', 'Great King Rat' and 'The Night Comes Down'. The demos offer a time capsule of Queen in late 1971. Most of the elements of what would become their signature sound are already present: be it the grand bombast of 'Liar', the galloping heavy metal of 'Keep Yourself Alive' or the fervent 'Jesus', an early example of Mercury's lyrical ambition; like a Cecil B. de Mille biblical epic condensed into three and half strange minutes, or Freddie's art A-Level crucifixion painting set to music.

At the end of the session, Terry Yeadon experienced a déjà-vu moment. 'Once again, they were like, "Can you do anything for us?" and we all said, "Sorry, chaps, we've got a studio to build here." But while most new bands have a crappy little demo made on a Grundig, they were walking away with these professional masters.'

'We figured that at some point an opportunity would come along,' said Brian May. 'You have to get your break, and what distinguishes the men from the boys is that some people are ready for it and some aren't. So we said, "When it comes along, everything is going to be rehearsed, we're going to know what the stage act is going to be like, the whole thing is going to be professional."'

One glimmer of hope came via John Anthony. On his recommendation, his Neptune Productions partners Roy Thomas Baker and Robin Geoffrey Cable had dropped by De Lane Lea to watch Queen in action. 'I heard "Keep Yourself Alive",' recalled Baker, 'and I immediately thought it was a hit.' Baker walked away with a tape of the demo.

In the meantime, though, the band still had to earn money from somewhere. Mercury was still reliant on Mary Austin's earnings and any pennies scraped on the market stall; Taylor and Deacon were living off their student grants, while Brian May's thesis was still not complete and his grant had run out. Before long, the guitarist had taken the radical step of getting a proper job, teaching mathematics and science at Stockwell Manor, a South London secondary school. 'It was very challenging,' he recalled. 'You couldn't get the children to attend unless they were incredibly interested in what you were saying. I had an advantage because I was young and could speak to them in their own language.' However one of May's lessons went disastrously wrong, when he allowed his pupils to use scissors to cut out shapes. 'Half an hour later they were attacking each other – blood and paper everywhere.'

Nevertheless, now that Queen had a professional demo to shop to record companies, the entrepreneurial Ken Testi came back into the picture. Testi was looking for his own way in to the music business and was now in London, sharing a flat with promoters Paul Conroy and Lindsay Brown while working part-time at a market research company. While Queen were thrilled with the demo there was one hurdle: none of them owned a tape machine on which to play it. 'Cassettes hadn't been invented,' says Testi. 'So any time they wanted to listen to it, they had to find someone with a machine. Dear Mary Austin had a friend out in North London with a reel-to-reel. Then we heard of someone looking after a flat off the Kings Road, who I think may have been the keyboard player in Genesis [Tony Banks], and he had a reel-to-reel so they let us in there. But I started to get marginally pissed off because all the guys would do was listen to these tapes. They were not making any attempt to contact record companies.'

Ken's first port of call was his flatmates, Conroy and Brown: 'They used to share a room and despite this being a stoners' flat, they were very professional and went into their room to discuss it. Then they came out and said, "Right, we don't think there's room for another Led Zeppelin." That was a knee to the groin for me.'

In Truro, Roger Taylor would receive a similar knockback. 'I had a reel-to-reel in the flat where I was living with my wife,' remembers Rik Evans. 'Roger played us Queen's demo, and I was like, "Great band, Roger, but I'm not too sure about the singer."' A bit like saying no to The Beatles.'

Frustrated, Ken began cold-calling record companies: Polydor, Island, MCA, CBS, A&M . . . 'Amazingly, I managed to make appointments at EMI and Decca. Freddie and Brian came with me. Their A&R guys listened, but didn't get it, which was amusing in the case of EMI, who ended up paying bundles for Queen in the end.'

The only company to bite was B&C, an offshoot of Charisma Records, the two-year-old label that had signed the cream of the progressive rock set, including Van Der Graaf Generator, The Nice and Genesis. Charisma's founder Tony Stratton-Smith, known to most as 'Strat', was a larger-than-life bon vivant, passionate about music, horses and alcohol. Charisma had signed The Bonzo Dog Doo Dah Band and would soon do the same for *Monty Python and The Holy Grail*. The 1971-era Queen, with their wild quirks and ferocious imagination, would have been a comfortable fit.

As Ken Testi remembers it, 'Charisma made Queen an offer of, I think, £25,000. The band went and slept on it and then came came back with a decision . . . they turned it down.' Paul Conroy, who'd helped secure the meeting with Stratton-Smith, was shocked. 'Paul thought they'd looked a gift horse in the mouth,' continues Ken. 'But Queen's view was that if they signed with Charisma they would always play second fiddle to Genesis and those other bands, which was very forward-thinking of them. I was easy with the notion that if it wasn't right for them, they shouldn't do it, and I thought that if we had one medium-to-large fish on the hook we could get another.'

'Arrogance is a very good thing to have when you're starting,' offered Mercury, years later. 'And that means saying to yourself you're going to be the number one group, not the number two.'

In the meantime, Roger Taylor had telephoned John Anthony and told him about the Charisma deal. 'I wasn't surprised that Charisma had made an offer,' he recalls. 'But when we met up, the band told me that Charisma had offered them a tour of Belgium and a new van! I told them we could do better than that. I went straight to Norman Sheffield at Trident and told them they had to sign this band or I would take them elsewhere.'

Trident Studios was in St Anne's Court, a blink-and-you'll-miss it alleyway off Wardour Street. It was right at the heart of the Soho music scene, an easy stagger to the Marquee, the Ship pub and La Chasse drinking club. Brothers Norman and Barry Sheffield had built the studio in 1967. Trident's forte was its state-of-the-art 'A'

Range consoles and Bechstein concert piano, famously used by The Beatles to record 'Hey Jude' (Ken Testi: 'Harry Nilsson would fly to England just because he wanted to use that piano'). Trident's client list included Elton John, George Harrison, The Rolling Stones and Free. In 1970 David Bowie cut his *Hunky Dory* album at Trident, and by mid-1972 was there putting the finishing touches to *Ziggy Stardust and the Spiders from Mars*. 'Trident was the best studio in the world,' insists John Anthony, 'which was why it was booked twenty-four hours a day.'

The Sheffield brothers had also established Trident Audio Productions, with a view to signing bands, giving them access to a superior studio and then arranging a distribution deal for their music with a major record label. Neptune Productions would act as the go-between for Queen and Trident Audio Productions. 'I'd seen what Chris Wright and Terry Ellis had done at Chrysalis,' explains Anthony. 'I wanted the same deal they'd had: act as a production company and when your artist sold a certain number of records the company would become a label. That's what I wanted for Neptune or Trident. I didn't care which. They key thing was the quality of the work. Roy Baker and Robin Cable had been to De Lane Lea to see Queen and they were as convinced as I was.'

If Queen hoped 1972 would be better than 1971, one of their first gigs that year left them wondering. In January, they played Bedford College, a gig booked on John Deacon's recommendation, only to perform to six paying punters. Paul Conroy threw them a lifeline with a support slot at King's College Medical School on 10 March. Two weeks later, Queen played a hospital dance in Forest Hill, South London.

'I'm sure it was a nurse's college,' says Anthony. According to John, that was the night Tony Stratton-Smith was given his marching orders. 'Norman Sheffield had heard the Queen tape and he told his brother Barry to go and see them. I said to Barry, "Bring the big car, and we'll all dress in black and put the Brylcreem on." We were all big guys, all over six feet tall, and we even had a security guy with us. So we turned up, looking like we were parodying the Kray twins, and there was Queen stood at the bar with the guys from Charisma. Queen fell over laughing when they saw us.'

Onstage, the band performed the likes of 'Son and Daughter', 'The Night Comes Down', 'Keep Yourself Alive', 'See What a Fool I've Been' (a song that had started life with Smile but would become a Queen B-side) and 'Hangman', the heavy blues track that would never find its way onto a Queen album (Taylor: 'It was very much based on Free'). The Trident entourage were impressed. 'We watched the gig, and Barry couldn't believe it when they did Shirley Bassey's "Big Spender",' says Anthony. 'Straight away, he was like, "Right, we have to sign them!"'

The studio was the bait in the deal Trident Audio Productions offered Queen. They would have use of the best recording facility in the country and Trident would supply them with a new PA and instruments. However, the deal they offered meant that Trident would also be responsible for their recording, producing, management and song publishing. While Queen insisted on the Sheffields producing separate sub-contracts for each part of the deal it still placed them in a situation where Trident controlled everything; a potentially dangerous situation for any band to be in.

The Forest Hill gig would be Queen's last for eight months. They had yet to sign with the Sheffields, but initially spent the time poring over the contracts, biding their time and possibly waiting for other offers. 'I told them to lie low,' says John Anthony. 'I wanted them to concentrate on getting their sound together, and then they could come back and play bigger gigs. Why bother with tiny clubs?'

For Ken Testi, the arrival of Trident marked the beginning of the end of his relationship with Queen. He'd had to move out of his flat in Raynes Park and was staying at Roger Taylor's place. Now, his parents were divorcing and he was needed at home. 'So I went back to St Helens, had a friend who was earning tons of money selling fitted carpets . . . Then I get the call. Queen want me to become their personal manager. I'm thinking, "This is what my life has been leading up to." But I had to say no. I had commitments to my family. I had to do what I had to do, but it is a source of regret.' Testi's entrepreneurial skills would bring him back into the music business later in the decade, when he began managing the band Deaf School and become one of the co-owners of Eric's, the Liverpudlian club that became a springboard for the likes of Echo and The Bunnymen and Frankie Goes To Hollywood.

Without another deal forthcoming, the Sheffields offered Queen the use of Trident Studios to make an album which could then be shopped to record companies. But there was a catch: Queen could only record when other artists weren't working in the studio. Following the universal instruction of tour managers everywhere – 'hurry up and wait' – Queen whiled away their days and nights, lingering over a drink in the Ship or a cup of tea in the Star Café on nearby Great Chapel Street.

'They were given what was called "Dark Time",' explains John Anthony. 'That's when an engineer can produce his favourite band or a teaboy can be used as a tape op. The trouble was, Trident was booked all the time. So Queen had these slots, starting at 11 p.m. or 2 a.m.'

It was agreed that Anthony would co-produce the album with Queen and Roy Thomas Baker. Queen told Anthony that they'd been impressed by his work on Van Der Graaf Generator's *Pawn Hearts* album. 'Next, Freddie showed me copies of *Queen* magazine [which had just become the fashion bible *Harpers & Queen*]. He said, "This is what we are about . . . But it's not just the name, it's the pictures, the articles, the whole thing . . . This is how we want our record to sound – like different topics and different photos." He had the whole thing mapped out in his head.'

Lou Reed was in Trident recording his *Transformer* album that summer with David Bowie in the producer's chair. 'We'd get a call confirming that Bowie or someone had finished early, so we'd get the 3 a.m. to 7 a.m. spot, when the cleaners came in,' grumbled Brian May. 'Literally, they'd be coming up the stairs and we'd be coming down the stairs,' remembered Roger Taylor. In a waggish moment, Bowie later told one interviewer that Mercury had asked him to produce Queen's first album; a rumour since denied by the band.

Bowie's presence at Trident was a particular thorn in their sides. Queen may have been huge Bowie fans, but were already fretting about their lack of a record deal and wider recognition, and that others, Bowie included, might gazump them. In July, Mercury and Taylor drove to Aylesbury in Roger's Mini to watch Bowie debuting his Ziggy Stardust alter-ego onstage at the Friars club. 'The first time I'd seen him was at Friars during the *Hunky Dory* era,' said Taylor. 'And he'd been dressed as a woman! Then we went to see him again and, at first, all we could see were silhouettes of the band onstage, with these alien haircuts.' A month later, a gloomy May watched Bowie at the Rainbow Theatre: 'I thought, "He's done it, he's made his mark and we're still struggling to get a record out."'

Queen recorded their first album in fits and starts that summer. But before long John Anthony was out of the picture. 'I was already recording Home and Al Stewart, and would arrive at Trident at two or three in the morning . . . I was doing all this in the middle of the Queen stuff.' One night, Anthony collapsed in the studio. He was diagnosed with mononucleosis, a strand of the Epstein-Barr virus, and ordered to rest. 'I went to Greece to eat good food, and not drink alcohol, and recuperate. So Roy took over.'

Roy Thomas Baker had started out as an apprentice engineer at Decca, before joining Trident as a staffer in 1969. He'd helped engineer hits such as T-Rex's 'Get It On (Bang A Gong)' and Free's 'Alright Now'. Fellow engineers at Trident included his Neptune Productions partner Robin Geoffrey Cable and Bowie's regular collaborator Ken Scott; all three would have a hand in Queen's debut. But they weren't alone. 'Everybody who was hanging around, including myself, was roped in to tape-operating,' says Glen Phimister, then Trident's apprentice tape op and teaboy. As a sign of Trident's belief in the band, Phimister recalls one story doing the rounds, that 'Trident had turned down a Diana Ross recording session . . . so Queen could do more demos.'

Despite their lowly position, Queen made their feelings known and squabbled with their paymasters over the miking of the guitar amps and drums. 'We wanted everything to sound like it was in the room, in your face,' Brian May told *Mojo* magazine. 'We had this incredible fight to get the drums out of the drum booth and into the middle of the studio, and to put the mics all around the room.' Trident had a trademark sound, and as May explained, 'That was the exact opposite of what we wanted to be.'

Baker's expertise of recording classical music at Decca helped create the sound May wanted for his guitar. 'We never thought of

Brian's guitar as a raunchy instrument, like most guitarists do,' the producer explained. 'It was an orchestral instrument.' The end result was a mellifluous, layered sound every bit as regal as the band's name. But the producer wasn't above, as Brian May describes it, 'blinding us with science'. When the band claimed the drum sound was too dry, Baker reassured them that it would be taken care of in the final mix: 'And we had this feeling that it wouldn't be. I wouldn't knock Roy. He did some great stuff, but we fought big battles with him.'

Ken Scott fondly remembers Queen as 'sharp, bright and on the money', and Freddie as 'outrageous, even then'. Mercury's art school pal Chris Smith attended a couple of sessions, soaking up the atmosphere and the droll humour. 'After they did one take, Freddie turned to Roy Thomas Baker and said, "What did you think?" And he replied, "Well, I think you're gonna be so famous soon you're not gonna want to talk to me."' At Trident, Mercury's camp affectations became infectious. Before long, Baker was following Fred's lead, and, as one Trident staffer recalled, 'suddenly everyone was mincing around, calling each other "dearie".' Later, one of the rejected titles for Queen's debut album would be *Dearie Me*, an homage to Baker's favourite catchphrase of the time.

Evidence of the tug-of-war between Queen and Trident can be heard on the finished album. Dissatisfied with a new take of 'The Night Comes Down', Queen insisted on sticking with the version they'd cut at De Lane Lea. Another song, 'Mad the Swine', was excised from the album completely after Baker and the band failed to agree on the final mix. Even after the album was completed, Baker and May would insist on another mixing session to iron out what they both felt were further imperfections. Said May: 'Between Roy and I, we were fighting the whole time to find a place where we had the perfection but also the reality of performance and sound.'

However, John Anthony recalls the final mix differently: 'When I returned from Greece everyone was bummed. The first thing that struck me was that the mix of the album was very schizophrenic, and the sequencing was all wrong,' he says. 'Roy had gone away, so Freddie, Brian and I came in and we remixed most of it.'

Also present was Mike Stone, recently promoted from Trident runner/tea-boy. Stone had been on the verge of getting fired, according to John Anthony', until the producer intervened: 'I said to Mike, "We have to make this sound like a live record." So I put all the faders to zero and mixed the album like a live gig. I wanted it to show the balls and the energy of Queen's live show.'

For Anthony, one of the biggest problems was the version of 'Keep Yourself Alive'. 'They'd overdubbed on the wrong backing track. It sounded like it had been done at four in the morning, especially Roger's drumming. So we re-recorded all the backing tracks and re-sequenced it.' Mike Stone was present, and, according to Brian May, his mix of 'Keep Yourself Alive' was chosen for the final album. 'We got on brilliantly with Mike and soon realised that he had the best ears in the building,' claimed May. It was the beginning of a working relationship that would endure for the next six years and a further five Queen albums.

Queen may now complain about some aspects of their debut album (Taylor, inevitably: 'I don't like the drum sound'), but it retains a boyish energy, a naivety even, which they would never quite have again. With their orchestral guitars, paint-peeling harmonies and vocal gymnastics, 'Great King Rat', 'Liar' and 'Son and Daughter' blueprinted the Queen sound. Glen Phimister recalls: 'I had just heard this huge production with sounds going backwards and forwards and huge vocal harmonies . . . and, amazingly, after the first track ended, Norman [Shaffield] says, "No, I don't think it's overproduced at all".'

Among the album's oddities were 'Jesus', re-recorded from the De Lane Lea sessions but still as baffling, a version of Smile's 'Doing Alright', which would give Tim Staffell a regular royalty cheque for life and a 1.10-minute segment of 'Seven Seas of Rhye', that would appear in full on the next album. May and Mercury were especially prolific that summer and had written several new songs which they were itching to record. No sooner was the first album finished then it was, in Queen's mind, out of date. The liner notes on the album's back cover would say as much: 'Representing at least something of what Queen's music has been over the last three years.'

During the first album sessions, Freddie Mercury had also been asked to record something on his own. Robin Geoffrey Cable had been fooling around in one of the Trident studios trying to cut his own version of The Beach Boys' hit 'I Can Hear Music'. Cable had heard Mercury in full flight with Queen and thought he'd be ideal. Straight away, Fred began making suggestions: Why not do this? Why not do that? Before long, Taylor and May were also playing on the track. The fruits of their labours, plus a second song – 'Goin' Back' featuring just Freddie – would be released a year later as an EMI single, under the name Larry Lurex (a spoof on the then popular glam-rocker Gary Glitter). The single bombed, but pre-empted Queen's debut single by a fortnight.

While the Sheffields were swift to spot musical potential, they were cut from a very different cloth to their artists. John Anthony and Barry Sheffield's ruse to dress like a couple of heavies at Queen's showcase gig tapped into the glaring difference between the Sheffields and their bands. David Bowie's producer Tony Visconti, remembering the brothers in 2010, described them 'as being like something out of the Wild West'. As songwriter and Queen's Trident contemporary Mark Ashton explains now, 'Barry and Norman were tough guys, very old school.' In a prescient move, the Sheffields had also set up a film and video company Trident Video Productions. 'I did a video with Norman and I always remember him shouting from the wings, "For fuck's sake, how much is this costing us?"' laughs Ashton. 'They were very professional people but you did not mess around with them.'

In September, Trident offered Queen a weekly wage of £20 each. 'That was the first bone of contention,' remembers John Anthony, 'because they wanted their sound engineer [John Harris] on a wage as well. I said, "No way. If you want him, you pay him."' Queen hadn't played a gig in months, and were still managing themselves. The 18 September 1972 issue of the underground magazine *International Times* carried a classified ad that month which read: 'The Queen! Wants gigs! Rock! Phone Roger 428 5617 after 7 p.m.' In the meantime, Taylor graduated with his degree in biology, and Deacon did the same in electronics (though he would remain at college to study for an MSc). May, meanwhile, was still caught between finishing his thesis, full-time teaching and playing in the band. To the shock of his colleagues, he handed in his notice at Stockwell Manor. Similar disappointment would follow at Imperial College. May's PhD thesis was, in the words of his professor, 'one last push' away from completion. 'I had it typed up and waiting to be bound,' recalled Brian. 'I showed it to my supervisor, who said I should spend another couple of months on it. Which I did. Then I took it back and he started going on again. And I thought, "This is as far as it goes." The band was happening, and I remember thinking, "If I don't quit this and give the group a chance, I'll end up regretting it."'

'I think Brian fretted a lot about giving up his job and his studies,' offers John Anthony. 'I remember sitting in The Ship with him and Roger, and he'd been offered the chance to go somewhere and study the stars, and I came out with something ridiculous like, "Look, Brian, you can study the stars or you can be one!" Roger fell about laughing.'

With their album recorded, Trident's plan was to shop Queen to potential record companies as part of a package deal with two of their other artists, Irish singer-songwriter Eugene Wallace, who was being touted as the next Joe Cocker, and Headstone, a group formed by Mark Ashton, until recently the drummer with Rare Bird, who'd had a hit in 1969 with 'Sympathy'. Both Headstone and Wallace had recorded their respective debuts, *Bad Habits* and *Dangerous*, at Trident. 'It really wasn't that unusual to offer bands to a label as part of a package,' insists John Anthony.

However, Anthony encountered the same frustration as Ken Testi, when trying to shop Queen to the major labels. 'Roy and I took them to Island, who didn't want to know. CBS's guy understood the vibe but said no when I said we needed £30,000 for lights and costumes. Someone else asked me, "Is this guy a homo?" when I told them the band was called Queen . . .'

In the meantime, Queen's publishing had been taken up by B. Feldman & Co., with Neptune Productions taking a cut. 'Feldman's had Deep Purple's publishing,' says Anthony, 'so I knew they could promote a hard rock band.' In Feldman's managing director Ronnie Beck, Queen found a staunch ally. In the meantime, the Sheffields had bought in an American, Jack Nelson, to help secure

Queen a record deal and a business manager. Before long, though, Nelson would take on the manager's job himself. In November, Queen officially signed with Trident, who arranged a showcase for them at the Pheasantry, a fashionable pub on the Kings Road, which had once housed the Russian Dance Academy. Despite the louche surroundings and the best efforts of Trident and Feldman's, not one A&R man turned up. Despite this, there were still some interested parties. But Jack Nelson had succeeded in keeping EMI's head of A&R Joop Visser interested.

When Feldman's were later taken over by EMI Music Publishing, Queen inched even closer to the record company. Nelson was also on the cusp of securing a deal for the band in North America. Three drafts of a contract for Queen had been drawn up with CBS. Then the managing director of Elektra Records, Jac Holzman, (past success stories: Love and The Doors) heard Queen's tape and was stunned. 'Everything was there, like a perfectly cut diamond landing on your desk,' he said.

John Anthony had previously worked with Jac Holzman with the band Lindisfarne: 'Jac had said if I ever had a band, I should call him.' Anthony says that he was instrumental in bringing Queen to Holzman's attention. However, interviewed now, Jack Nelson recalls that 'on my way to Carmel, California, from London, I stopped in New York and gave Jac Holzman a copy and told him that I was already in negotiations with CBS.' Interviewed in 1998 for Holzman's book, *Follow the Music*, Nelson recalled that the CBS deal stalled over a technicality, giving Holzman the chance to start hustling. 'Jac called me from Los Angeles ... Japan ... Australia and said, "I've got to have them."' In the meantime, Nelson began to doubt just how closely CBS's A&R team had listened to his act: 'One of their guys called Queen 'one of the best country bands' he'd listened to in a long time. That made me extremely nervous.'

Trident arranged another showcase gig, on 20 December at the Marquee, opening for exiled American art-rockers Sparks. Jac Holzman flew in from the US but was, he later wrote, 'dreadfully disappointed. I saw nothing onstage to match the power on the tape. But the music was still there.' Joop Visser was similarly unimpressed, but tentatively agreed to a production deal with

Queen, via Ronnie Beck, though Visser baulked at the 'five-figure' advance requested. Sparks, meanwhile, made a note of Queen's hotshot guitarist and would offer him a job later.

The stars finally aligned in Queen's favour in the New Year. In February, Feldman's radio plugger Phil Reed persuaded the BBC to record a session with Queen for DJ John Peel's *Sounds of the Seventies* show. Mercury re-recorded his vocals on four existing tracks from Trident at the BBC's Langham 1 Studio in London's West End. The songs, 'Doing Alright', 'My Fairy King', 'Liar' and 'Keep Yourself Alive' were broadcast the following week. The airplay and publicity was a boon.

In the meantime, Ronnie Beck had been granted an audience with EMI A&R executive Roy Featherstone at the annual MIDEM music business conference in the South of France. Featherstone was launching a new label, EMI Records, and later claimed that he'd been overwhelmed by the hundreds of tapes foisted on him at the conference 'from people's mothers to their howling dogs . . . nothing grabbed me'. Desperate for something, anything different, Beck forced him to listen to Queen. He was hooked. Being economical with the truth, Beck told Featherstone that other companies were already circling. Recalled Brian May: 'So we got this message from Roy Featherstone, the head honcho at EMI. He'd heard the demos and he sent a telegram saying, "Do not do anything until you've talked to me. I want this band on my record label." '

Trident, however, continue to play hardball, turning down EMI's initial offer as too low. Negotiations continued and, in the end, EMI rolled over. They took Eugene Wallace and Headstone as part of the deal (neither was a hit), and in March 1973 Queen signed to EMI, for 'a still unspecified sum'.

Future EMI managing director Bob Mercer was the company's director of A&R at the time. He could see the potential in Queen but also the pitfalls of their deal. 'What was unusual at the time was that there wasn't a weak link in the band,' says Mercer. 'Usually, the bass player is off or the drummer's a wanker. Not Queen. And then there was that startling voice which pinned you to the wall. But Queen was not a conventional A&R deal. It wasn't as if one of our guys was out there getting shit-faced in a club with them at twelve o'clock at night. The deal came straight from the Sheffields. It was an opportunistic deal for the Sheffields, and Queen had a difficult, even impossible relationship with them by the time we signed the band.'

In April, a month after they cut their deal with EMI, Jac Holzman saw Queen again at the Marquee and made a formal offer from Elektra Records. John Anthony encountered him on the way out of the gig where Holzman had some advice to be passed on to Brian May: 'Jac said, "We'll do the deal . . . but tell the guitarist to make it look harder. Kids like to think it's Beethoven."'

Though technically beaten to the punch by the Larry Lurex single, Queen made their EMI debut with the single 'Keep Yourself Alive' on 6 July. The lyrics had a simple message: don't let the bastards grind you down (appropriate in the light of Queen's struggle and Mercury's ongoing reinvention); the heavily phased guitar riff was pure Led Zeppelin, the chorus was pure pop, while Taylor returned to his schoolboy inspiration, Surfaris' 'Wipe Out', for the tribal drum fill in the middle. 'If Queen look half as good as they sound, they could be huge,' raved *New Musical Express*. Except no one was listening. The single failed to chart, and years later, May still fretted over the final mix: 'It never had the magic it should have had.'

Queen's debut album, called simply *Queen*, finally saw the light of day on 13 July. The front cover spoke volumes. It was a picture of Mercury pulling an heroic pose onstage, shot by Roger Taylor's friend from Cornwall, BBC cameraman Douglas Puddifoot. Freddie was meant to resemble 'a figurehead on the prow of those old sailing ships,' according to Brian May. Decorated with the Mercury-designed Queen crest logo, the back cover contained a montage of snapshots, including one of Mercury and Mary Austin's flat decorated with fancy Biba artifacts. Apparently, EMI's creative services manager pronounced the homemade cover 'crap'. But the design was forced through. It was an early indicator of Queen's unwillingness to compromise.

The liner notes renamed John Deacon as Deacon John and gave Taylor his full family name of Roger Meddows-Taylor; giving the band an even more regal air. It also included what would become Queen's mission statement for most of the decade: '. . . and nobody played synthesiser'. As Roy Thomas Baker explained, 'We would spend four days multi-layering a guitar solo and then some imbecile from the record company would come in and say, "I like that synth."'

Like the single, the album sold slowly and made it to number 32 in the UK (though it would chart higher following Queen's breakthrough two years later). In the press, some reviews were positive. 'A thrusting, dynamic debut,' claimed underground magazine *Time Out*. Others were less so. 'A bucket of stale urine,' said *New Musical Express*, sparking a resentment of the music press that would endure throughout Queen's career.

Relieved that they finally had a record out, Queen now wrestled with the fear that it might be already out of date. 'We were into glam-rock before The Sweet and Bowie,' Brian May told *Melody Maker*. 'We're worried now because we might have come too late.' The competition was fierce. Androgynous-looking boys in exotic clothing had become de rigueur in rock and pop. That spring, Bowie released *Aladdin Sane*, and Roxy Music put out their second album *For Your Pleasure*. Roxy, with their feather boas and art-school pedigree, had made their live debut a year earlier at the Hand and Flowers pub, a stone's throw from the Kensington Tavern. Roxy had already enjoyed one hit single and album. 'We don't want people to think we're jumping on their bandwagon,' insisted May.

That summer, London's number 9 bus became the scene for many an earnest discussion about Queen's prospects. Carrying May, Mercury and various friends, the double-decker would inch its way through the traffic on Kensington High Street, past the Royal Albert Hall and the market, and into the West End. Chris Smith recalls catching the number 9 with Mercury just after the first Queen album came out. 'Fred was getting a bit desperate: "God! I hope this band takes off. I don't know what I'm going to do if it doesn't." And he looked up at me and said, "I don't want to end up working in an art studio." We both cracked up . . . I, of course, was the one that did end up working in an art studio.'

'If you ever get on a number 9 bus and go upstairs to the front left, that's where Freddie and I used to sit,' explained Brian May.

'We used to get the bus and go up to Trident to beat them on the heads, and to ask them why they weren't doing anything about our record.'

There was some good news that summer. Mike Appleton, producer of the BBC TV music programme *The Old Grey Whistle Test*, had received an unmarked promo pressing of the Queen album. The disc had been sent without Queen's detailed press biography and photographs. Appleton liked what he heard, particularly 'Keep Yourself Alive'. With no idea of who Queen were or how to contact the band, he produced an animated sequence for the song, lifted from a cartoon which had been used to promote US president F.D. Roosevelt's election campaign. The film was broadcast on *The Old Grey Whistle Test*. An initially irate EMI and Trident both contacted the BBC, but the band were buoyed by the unexpected publicity.

In August, Mercury shaved his chest before filming a promo video for 'Keep Yourself Alive' and 'Liar'. But the grooming proved pointless. The band rejected the video, unhappy with the lighting, among other things, and reconvened in a studio in St John's Wood two months later. The final film shows Queen, daubed in eyeliner, bedecked in black satin, with May sporting the sort of opulent necklace usually found buried with an Egyptian pharaoh, and even 'Easy Deacon' in knee-length platform boots. Mercury preens, shimmies and, at one point, tosses a tambourine into the wings. It's a fabulously assured performance.

In an attempt to drum up some support for their charges, Trident hired a publicist. Tony Brainsby was a bespectacled, stick-thin 28-year-old. Rarely seen without a drink or a cigarette in his hand, he had been a teenage pal of The Rolling Stones and had a client list that included Paul McCartney, Mott The Hoople and Cat Stevens. His Edith Grove townhouse doubled as his office and was a Mecca for pop stars, writers, actors, models and liggers.

Brainsby had seen Queen live and been impressed by their conviction in front of a disinterested college crowd. He was immediately intrigued by Freddie Mercury's mannerisms ('He'd say "darling" or "my dear" practically every sentence') but also recalled the secrecy surrounding the singer's past life ('For years I believed his proper surname to be Bulsova'). Mercury was, said Brainsby, 'better at being seen, heard but not known.'

But when Brainsby took Queen on as clients, he met with hostility in the music press. 'They were called posing ponces,' he recalled in 1997 (Brainsby died in 2000). 'They were accused of getting session musicians in to cover for them because people found it so hard to believe they could look like that and be talented.' While many of their contemporaries presented an air of stoned insouciance, Queen made no attempt to conceal their intelligence, middle-class backgrounds or clarity of thought. May and Taylor would earnestly outline their game-plan, with the drummer particularly prone to outbursts: 'We are a bloody good band!'

Steven Rosen, who would go on to write for *Rolling Stone*, was spending the summer of 1973 in London trying to break into music journalism. He'd been given Tony Brainsby's name. The PR took pity on Rosen, who'd been sleeping in Hyde Park, and let him crash at Edith Grove. To help out the aspiring writer, Tony made a suggestion. 'He asked me if I wanted to interview Queen,' recalls Rosen now. 'And right away I thought the name was a bit too glam. Tony had a white test pressing of the first album and in my infinite stupidity I passed. He was like, "I could have all four guys here in the office and you'd have one of the first interviews with them." And I said, "Thanks, but no thanks." I still think about that moment.'

While critics, even the destitute ones, were broadly suspicious, Brainsby noticed that the band had a dedicated following that over the next two years would expand to include an age group much older than was associated with the traditional rock fan ('housewives, middle-aged women – I had one old woman that used to ring me up'). Queen would soon appoint Taylor's Truro friends Pat and Sue Johnstone to run their fast-growing fan club, when the deluge of mail they received via EMI became too much for the company to deal with.

In the meantime, Brainsby also wasted no time placing Queen in the teen mags. His pitch was simple: they were well-educated, fancy dressers and their guitarist had made his instrument out of a hundred-year-old fireplace. Queen may have been fuming over accusations that they weren't a serious group (Roxy Music drummer Paul Thompson had denounced them as 'too contrived'), but in October, they showed up in *Mirabelle* magazine, discussing their academic achievements, likes and dislikes. Mercury's ambition was to 'appear on *The Liza Minnelli Show*' and Taylor's was 'to go super-nova!'. 'Tall, dark, handsome' Brian May's likes are given as 'cats, Hermann Hesse and prawn cocktails . . .'

In August, desperate to start recording again, Queen had gone back to Trident to begin work on a second album. This time they insisted on and were granted proper studio time during daylight hours. Roy Thomas Baker, Robin Geoffrey Cable and Mike Stone were retained. "Jack Nelson very nicely said that we had to go and see the boys as they didn't want me to do the second album,' explains John Anthony. 'So I went to Haverstock Hill where they were rehearsing and said, 'I wish you well.' There was no hard feeling. I was working flat out anyway. But I used to still go and watch them rehearse, and advise them on the live show.'

Taylor informed *Record Mirror* that the next Queen album 'would be alright as long as our egos don't get out of control.' It would prove a prophetic statement. Not for nothing would Queen's second album have a working title of *Over the Top*. Mercury quickly gave his bandmates and Baker a glimpse of what he had in mind, escorting them to the Tate Gallery to show them *The Fairy Feller's Master-Stroke* by the Victorian artist Richard Dadd. 'It's one of the most complex paintings I've ever seen,' said Taylor. 'It had about fifty different scenarios all done by a man who was, quite literally, going bonkers.' Dadd, who believed he was acting on an instruction from the Egyptian god Osiris, had murdered his father, and spent nine years working on the painting while an inmate at the Bethlem Royal Hospital. It showed an intricate woodland scene with fairy-tale creatures lurking, sometimes almost unseen, behind the undergrowth. Mercury's song of the name would be peopled with just such creatures.

Richard Thompson had always declined Freddie's invitation to accompany him on his weekend gallery visits. But the former Wreckage drummer was still aware of Mercury's fascination with one particular artwork. 'I was at the flat with Mary Austin once, and Fred came back from the Tate with a picture postcard of *The Fairy Feller's Master-stroke*,' says Thompson. 'Freddie was most annoyed as the picture on the postcard had been printed the wrong way round!' Roy Thomas Baker was also marched to the Tate to gaze upon the Dadd masterpiece, and Mercury's instruction to the producer was simple: 'Anything you want to try, throw it in.'

The band and Baker made full use of Trident's sixteen-track facility, attempting, said Taylor, 'to break the boundaries of what people thought you could do in a recording studio'. Six-part harmonies became the order of the day, and though they stuck to the 'no synths' rule, piano, Hammond organ, castanets and tubular bells found their way into the mix (Baker: 'It was the kitchen-sink album'). May and his co-producer also took the first album's idea of an orchestral guitar a stage further on the tracks 'Procession' and 'Father to Son', creating a sumptuous din that sounded like the London Symphony Orchestra jamming with Jimi Hendrix. 'Queen were relentless,' said Baker. 'They were coming up with millions of ideas.' In the end, the title, *Queen II*, was the only simple thing about the album.

Aside from a couple of dates in July and a show supporting Vinegar Joe at Newcastle's Mayfair in August, Queen had hardly played live since March. 'We'd already driven ourselves mad playing pubs and little clubs up and down the country in Smile,' griped May. 'And we didn't want to go through that again because we thought it would get too depressing.' But it wasn't over yet. On 13 September they played London's Golders Green Hippodrome for a BBC In Concert show, road-testing most of *Queen II* on the night. A month later, they made their European debut as part of a promo trip, playing in Bonn and at Le Blow Up club in Luxembourg City.

On 4 September, Queen's debut was released in the US. Jac Holzman's enthusiasm was certainly mirrored in *Rolling Stone*'s gushing review, which frothed over Mercury's 'cocky, regal arrogance' and likened 'Deacon John' to 'a colossal sonic volcano whose eruption maketh the earth tremble', finally concluding 'Queen is a monster'. It would be a year before Queen played in the US, but it was a positive start.

As a warm-up to their forthcoming tour supporting Mott The Hoople, Queen booked two dates at Imperial College and invited photographer Mick Rock to shoot the show on 2 November. Rock, introduced to Queen at Trident on Ken Scott's suggestion, was a Cambridge University graduate who had been close friends with Pink Floyd's lost-boy singer Syd Barrett. He had gone on to photograph David Bowie and Lou Reed and had shot the covers for Reed's *Transformer* and, most recently, Bowie's *Pin-Ups* album. 'Ken Scott said, "Queen love your work, especially the things you've done with David and Lou,"' recalled Rock. 'They really want you to shoot them.'

At their first meeting, Rock was quickly swayed by Mercury and Taylor's charm offensive, but also by the band's absolute self-confidence. He noted, not for the last time, that they wanted answers for everything, and that Jack Nelson was invariably the one being questioned: 'They wanted the world and they wanted it no later than teatime on Friday.' Rock listened to an acetate of *Queen II* and agreed to shoot the album cover later. But first, at Trident's bequest, he shot some promotional photos for the forthcoming tour. Rock's first shoot had Queen huddled around Mercury, who was clutching a giant sceptre. But the royal look was too obvious for some ('Brian didn't like them and they didn't get published at the time'). Rock's next proposal was to get the band to strip to the waist. The topless look was shamelessly kitsch, but Mercury adored it. 'They wanted something sensational, an image that people would talk about,' said Rock. The naked Queen pictures would quickly find their way into *Mirabelle* and *NME*, fuelling more antagonism from the paper. But the plan worked. As Rock recalled, 'They got themselves some ink'. Better still, their sold-out show at Imperial garnered one of the best reviews of their career from *Disc*'s Rosemary Horide: 'They were forced onstage for three encores until they finally had to stop – from sheer exhaustion.'

In the meantime, EMI had broken with tradition and paid for Queen to be the support act on Mott The Hoople's upcoming UK tour. Jack Nelson was friends with Mott's manager, a fellow American Bob Hirschmann, and recalled the company stumping up £3,000. EMI's Bob Mercer claims it was between £9,000 and

£10,000: 'Queen was the first time EMI had paid for a support tour, although it became common practice after that. Mott The Hoople were as hot as bear shit, and that was the audience we wanted to expose Queen to.'

In preparation for the tour, Queen booked rehearsal time at Fulham's Manticore Studios, a converted cinema that had just been bought by super-group trio Emerson, Lake & Palmer. It was November and a jet heater had been switched on inside the studio, with parachute silks hung over the stall seats to keep the warmth in. Peter 'Ratty' Hince, who would become head of Queen's road crew, was working as roadie for Mott The Hoople at the time. Hince and his employers were already at Manticore when Queen arrived.

'It was freezing, so Mott were in there in jeans, scarves and fur coats,' recalls Hince. 'Then Queen showed up, all in their dresses, just to rehearse. We were like, "Who is this bloke called Fred prancing around with one glove and a sawn-off mic stand. Fred's no name for a pop star."' Hince was similarly intrigued by Brian May and his choice of plectrum, a sixpence coin, which May preferred to a conventional pick, possibly because of its serrated edges. 'He had a homemade guitar and an AC30 on a chair and he played with a sixpence . . . I thought, "Well, he's probably got no money . . ."' Bob Mercer tried to gatecrash the rehearsals but was refused entry. 'I didn't want to interfere or tell them what songs they should play, I was genuinely curious. But I was forbidden.' Instead Mercer would have to wait until the opening night of the tour at Leeds Town Hall.

Mott The Hoople had been together since 1969 and had been on the verge of splitting before being persuaded not to by superfan David Bowie. His song 'All the Young Dudes' gave Mott a surprise hit in 1972. A year later, with new guitarist Ariel Bender and his dyed silver hair, Mott chimed with the current craze for glam-rock. More than that, they nurtured a connection with their audience and presented themselves as regular human beings not unapproachable superstars. As Brian May put it, 'Mott were something to learn from,' and their 1973 hit 'All the Way from Memphis' included a line that could have been written for Freddie Mercury: 'You look like a star, but you're still on the dole.'

Queen's set included most of the yet-to-be released *Queen II*, 'Keep

Yourself Alive', 'Hangman' and a medley of rock 'n' roll numbers, including their uber-camp version of 'Big Spender'. The audience's response to Queen on the tour is the subject of wildly varying opinion. Joop Visser remembered that by the end of the tour Queen were stealing the show from Mott The Hoople. Bob Mercer recalls seeing one gig where 'Freddie came on and did "Big Spender" and the audience went nuts.' Backstage afterwards, Mercer remembers a spat with someone close to Mott The Hoople over how well Queen had gone down. 'He put me up against a wall and said, "They are off the tour. My band will never survive this." And I said, "Sorry, sunshine, that's your problem. I paid for them to be here." '

However, Mott The Hoople's pianist Morgan Fisher thinks differently: 'The audience's response to Queen changed from night to night. It was fifty per cent good and fifty per cent apathy.' Fisher watched Queen from the wings. He had no doubt they would go on to make it, but he nonetheless had his reservations: 'Queen were different from other groups. Thinking about it, the way they looked was very Biba. But they also wanted to work the crowd and that was their priority above everything else. The whole band were a lot more frantic back then. It was their franticness that put me off. Mott were already successful so we didn't have to try and impress all the time. But Queen were desperate to make it, and I sometimes felt that they were trying too hard.'

The two bands travelled on a coach together, where Fisher, who relished all the perks of being in a band ('I drank a lot in those days'), entertained his captive audience. 'I'd bought a copy of *The Goon Show* scripts, and I enjoyed them so much I decided I couldn't keep it to myself. So I'd stand at the front of the coach and read out a whole episode.' His soliloquies had a specific purpose: 'Queen were obsessed with their work and needed bringing out of themselves.' Eight years later, Fisher would join Queen as a touring keyboard player. 'I think my behaviour on the coach was a large factor in getting that job. Later, Freddie let himself be humorous, which was a wonderful thing to see.'

Before the gig at Liverpool Stadium, Mike Bersin visited Mercury backstage and found the singer fretting over what to say to the audience. Liverpool would become a Queen stronghold, but this was a Mott audience and one naturally suspicious of a band from London dolled up in black-and-white satin outfits. Freddie grabbed a copy of the *Liverpool Echo*, which recorded a Liverpool FC victory and a winning goal from Kevin Keegan. Flouncing out onstage minutes later, Mercury greeted the crowd with 'Nice one, Kevin.' 'The place erupted,' says Bersin.

Not every night went so well. A week later at Birmingham Town Hall, Mercury made his grand entrance, only to be greeted by a loud heckle: 'Fucking get off, ya cunt!' Birmingham was a notoriously tough crowd. Weeks before, the audience at the same venue had savaged Roxy Music's support act, budding singer-songwriter Leo Sayer, when he showed up onstage dressed as Pierrot the Clown. One eyewitness recalled seeing a male fan urinating over the balcony in Sayer's direction. Slowly, Queen managed to win over the mob, including some of the Mott diehards huddled in front of the stage. Then a misjudged high kick led to Freddie falling flat on his arse. Visibly winded, the singer pretended it was part of the act and carried on singing while lying on his back. As one eyewitness recalls, 'From that moment on Freddie was a marked man for the haters in the audience.' The final insult was a hot dog hurled from the crowd which caught the singer full in the face, splattering him with sausage and ketchup.

It was some consolation then that Queen and Mott got on well. Despite his initial reservations, Peter Hince was impressed: 'Queen really had a lot of self-belief and confidence, and, for an opening act, really pushed to get what they wanted. They were flash and posey and we certainly wouldn't call them a rock 'n' roll band, but what they were doing was interesting.' Returning to the car park after one night's gig, the band noticed a message scrawled by a fan in the dirt on the side of the coach: 'Mott is dead, long live Queen.'

On 14 December, the tour rolled into London with two shows at the Hammersmith Odeon. A second late-evening performance had been added due to public demand. At midnight, in a desperate attempt to halt the party, the Odeon's management lowered the safety curtain on to the stage while Mott were still thrashing away. Queen's performance that night is remembered as one of their best on the tour. They played to their biggest audience yet of some 7,000 people across the two performances, including May's parents, Ruth and Harold, who bemusedly signed autographs for fans.

'The opportunity of playing with Mott was great,' said Mercury. 'But I knew the moment we finished that tour [that], as far as Britain was concerned, we'd be headlining.' However, as Brian May explained, 'We went around the country getting some great reactions and thinking, "Yeah, we're finally getting somewhere," and all the while watching the single and album appear nowhere in the charts.' The band fumed, while their PR wrung his hands. As one of Tony Brainsby's associates explained, 'Queen may have been a support group but they already had the mentality of stars.'

The band saw out the year with another BBC Radio session for John Peel's *Sounds of the Seventies*. Alongside songs from the first album they threw in 'Ogre Battle', a whirling-dervish heavy metal track from the forthcoming *Queen II*. But the album's release was still three long months away. Four days before New Year's Eve, Queen sought solace with old friends and familiar faces at Liverpool's Top Rank club. They played alongside 10cc and support band Great Day, a new group featuring Mike Bersin and Ken Testi.

If Queen were already stars in their own heads, then it was appropriate that someone outside the group should acknowledge the fact. Mick Rock had been pondering ideas for the cover of *Queen II* and had acquired a set of photographs that included a shot of the actress Marlene Dietrich taken on the set of her 1932 film *Shanghai Express*. In it, Dietrich had her eyes cast upwards, her face set in a regal expression, with the spidery fingers of each hand clasping her shoulders. If Queen had not yet become bona fide stars, then replicating this picture would suggest otherwise. Mick cornered the band backstage on the Mott The Hoople tour, brandishing the photograph: 'Look at this! I know this has got to be it.' While the rest of Queen looked on aghast, Mercury was delighted. His instruction was simple: 'I shall be Marlene.'

CHAPTER FIVE
These Silly Bastards

What is your dream?

John Deacon:	'Wet.'
Brian May:	'Total understanding between people.'
Roger Taylor:	'To be rich, famous, happy and popular.'
Freddie Mercury:	'To remain the divine, lush creature that I am.'

Queen's answers to a
Japanese music magazine question, 1975

'**G**o back to Pommyland, ya poofters!' As crowd reactions go, this one could have been better. Queen had faced brutal audiences before, but not 30,000 miles from home. On 28 January 1974 the band had flown to Australia to make their debut at the Sunbury Rock Festival, a three-day musical fiesta held on a 630-acre farm in Melbourne. Somehow, Queen had been booked to play an early-Saturday evening slot to an audience who had not the slightest clue who they were. 'It was all just a series of misunderstandings,' understated Brian May, years later.

Sunbury had launched a year before and been compèred by comedian Paul Hogan, later to find fame as the comedy-movie action man Crocodile Dundee. In 1974, the bill was full of local heroes such as Buster Brown, Daddy Cool and Madder Lake; groups unknown outside their native Australia but each with a formidable reputation and staunch following. Showing their usual attention to detail, Queen had brought their own lighting rig and insisted that their own people operate it, immediately ruffling the feathers of the local crew. To get the best out of the rig, the band pushed to go on later when there'd be less daylight, disgruntling other bands on the bill.

In the end it was competition for the coveted sunset spot between Queen and Aussie pub-rockers Madder Lake that led to a fracas. Both bands' crews started trying to set up their gear at the same time. 'The Australian stage crew didn't like this and started fighting with our stage crew,' said May. Before long the festival MC had weighed into the argument: 'D'ya want these pommie bastards or do you want an Aussie rock band? . . . We've got a load of limey bastards here and they're probably going to be useless.' While Queen were met with hostility, at least one eyewitness disputes the story that they were booed offstage and claims they even managed to play an encore. Before leaving the stage, Mercury grandly announced, 'When Queen come back to Australia we will be the biggest band in the world.'

Back in England, they could console themselves with some good news in the music press. For all the critical disdain, Queen were nominated second Most Promising New Act by readers of *New Musical Express* (behind the Dutch rock band Golden Earring, who'd scored a big hit the year before with 'Radar Love') and third Best New Band in *Sounds*, losing out to weighty Scots rockers Nazareth and Blue, a Scottish pop group signed to Elton John's Rocket Records imprint.

On 19 February, David Bowie's loss was Queen's gain. When the promo for Bowie's new single 'Rebel Rebel' wasn't ready for *Top of the Pops*, the show's producer called Ronnie Fowler. Fowler's dogged promotion of Queen had continued unabated. According to Queen legend, he notched up expenses to the tune of £20,000; wining, dining and generally schmoozing various music biz players in the name of the band. Fowler pitched Queen for the vacant slot, even though their next single, 'Seven Seas of Rhye', had yet to be pressed.

In the lyrics of 'Seven Seas of Rhye', Mercury cast himself as some kind of naked avenging deity against a squall of guitar and piano. Unexpectedly, the song's finale was a chorus of the 1907 music-hall standard, 'I Do Like to be Beside the Seaside', featuring a boozy, ad hoc choir that included Ken Testi. It was the first sign of what would become a familiar theme on Queen albums. 'Growing up, Freddie and I listened to the radio,' May later told *Mojo* magazine. 'One thing that both Freddie and I listened to was *Uncle Mac's Children's Favourites* on Saturday morning. This show would have 'Nellie the Elephant', 'The Laughing Policeman' and Mantovani. It was this strange mix of novelty songs and dramatic, adult music that would appeal to kids. So we had all this stuff churning around in our brains.'

According to Eric Hall, the future football agent, then a radio plugger for EMI, 'Freddie said, "I'm not doing *Top of the Pops*. It's rubbish." ' But the rest of the band convinced him otherwise. As dictated by the Musicians' Union, *Top of the Pops* rules meant that all bands had to re-record the track they would then mime to. Queen cut a version of 'Seven Seas of Rhye' at The Who's Rampart Studios in Battersea. Knowing the group's meticulousness and how much they were already fretting, Hall claimed he slipped the original version of the song to the MU rep for broadcast: 'And he didn't have a clue.'

Wreckage's former drummer Richard Thompson was with Queen in the studio and witnessed the sleight of hand: 'Freddie was just fiddling and fiddling, waiting for this bloke to go. He said to me, "We're not really going to record. But we'll put so much effort in, he'll think we've spent hours on it." '

Two days later, Queen's television debut was broadcast on *Top of the Pops*. Passers-by on a Kensington street that night may have wondered why a gaggle of long-haired men were crowding around an electrical goods shop long after it had closed. It was Queen and their entourage waiting to watch themselves on one of the TV sets in the shop window. 'They'd been filmed just playing in front of a blue screen,' remembers Richard Thompson. 'But when we watched it on TV the BBC had stuck in a crowd of people dancing in front of them.'

Trident rushed out ten white-label pressings of 'Seven Seas of Rhye', which were quickly distributed to the BBC. Ronnie Fowler's expensive hustling had paid off. Yet after the first broadcast, Mercury spotted that the single had used a rejected mix. Jack Nelson was ordered to retrieve all copies from the radio stations and replace them with the correct one. As Richard Thompson puts it: "Freddie had this vision. It *had* to be right." His diligence paid off, and 'Seven Seas of Rhye' entered the chart at number 45. Ronnie Fowler's mission was complete. When he moved on to a new position at Elektra Records, his Queen expense account officially passed into company mythology, where it was described as a 'Steven Spielberg-style science-fiction epic'.

Yet Fowler wasn't the only one within the Queen organisation eager to spend EMI's money. With more shows booked, Mercury was determined to make a visual impact on his audience. EMI's A&R director Bob Mercer was used to buying his charges dinner ('They needed a good meal as they were always broke'), but he felt uneasy when Freddie called and asked to see him on his own. "It got me a bit upsy,' he admits. 'Except when he turned up, he wasn't on his own. He was with Zandra Rhodes, the frock-maker.'

Zandra Rhodes was a then 34-year-old fashion designer with a yen for adventurous textile designs. Her acclaimed Fulham Road boutique had opened in 1969, and was just a couple of miles from Kensington Market. Until now, costumier Wendy Edmunds and Freddie himself had been responsible for the group's stage clothes. After spotting some of her creations for Marc Bolan, Queen enlisted Zandra Rhodes to design costumes for their next tour.

'It was lovely to meet Zandra, but this was not a normal conversation for me,' explains Mercer. 'Eventually Freddie asked Zandra to go, so he and I could talk on our own. I was like, "Look, it cost us a few grand to get you on the Mott tour – how much is this going to cost us?" Fred said, "Five grand." I said, "Fucking hell!" But he was so persuasive. In the end, I agreed, partly just to get him out of the office, but I asked him to find some way of invoicing me so that we could call it something else rather than "New Frocks".'

Rhodes recalled Mercury and May arriving at her Paddington workshop in between rehearsals for the tour at Ealing Film Studios. Mercury was especially particular. 'It was quite wonderful after just dressing ladies to be asked to do something for men,' she said.

'Freddie would hold things in front of him, and just waft around the room. He was great fun to work with.' In the end, the pair settled on androgynous-looking tunics ('very Greek,' recalls photographer Mick Rock), with voluminous silk bat-wing sleeves. Within days of taking delivery, Mercury was modelling his in another Mick Rock photoshoot.

'Freddie had a lot to do with dressing Brian,' says Chris Smith. Arriving at Kensington Market, just before the tour began, Smith found Freddie standing behind the stall in his new stage outfit, arms outstretched in a Jesus Christ pose while a woman knelt below, fussing over the pleated wings. 'When she stood up, it turned out to be Zandra Rhodes,' he says. "At which point Freddie dramatically announced, "And Brian's got one, too."' For Chris and Tim Staffell, it was another reminder of the world they had left behind: 'I said to Tim, "Aren't you glad you don't have to dress up in all that gear?"' The new tour would also mark the end of Freddie's reign at Kensington Market. He was now simply too busy being a pop star.

Even though there was a tour booked, there was still no new album. In January, in response to industrial action by the National Union of Mineworkers, the British government had imposed a 'three-day week', limiting the use of electricity. This led to the first delay in pressing *Queen II*; the second came when the group spotted a spelling error on the finished sleeve. ('Deacon John' became, blessedly, 'John Deacon' and would remain that way for the duration of Queen's career.) The Queen bassist would also mark the release of the album and upcoming tour by abandoning his MSc course. 'There's quite a lot of work going for studio electronics engineers,' Deacon told one interviewer later that year. 'But I'm sticking with Queen for as long as we last.'

Queen II was finally released on 8 March, a week after the tour began at the Blackpool Winter Gardens. Finally, the fruits of what Roy Thomas Baker called Queen's 'relentlessness' was made public. The songs 'White Queen (As It Began)' and 'Ogre Battle' had already been performed live, but had since been reworked at Trident. A step forward from Queen's debut, there was greater cohesion this time, as ideas and aural tics from one song spilled over into the next. In a precocious move, the finished album was split into Side White and Side Black. May's wistful 'Some Day One Day' encapsulated the former; Mercury's gothic 'March of the Black Queen' its flipside. Taylor also followed his songwriting debut, 'Modern Times Rock 'n' Roll' on the first album, with 'Loser in the End' – perhaps one of the album's weaker songs – in which the seismic drumming was a homage to Led Zeppelin's John Bonham. 'When England had The Who and Zeppelin, we had the two finest rock 'n' roll bands in the world,' he proclaimed.

Queen II signed off with the full-length version of 'Seven Seas of Rhye'. But it was Mercury's mind-boggling 'The Fairy Feller's Master-stroke' that seemed to dominate Side Black; his fascination with the Richard Dadd painting of the same name finally realised as a similarly ambitious piece of music. The gatefold sleeve credited co-producer Baker for playing 'virtuoso castanets' and insisted that 'nobody played synthesiser . . . again'. Mick Rock's regal group portrait on the front couldn't have suited the music better.

Essentially, Queen's second album rang with echoes of The Who's *Tommy*, Led Zeppelin's fourth album and, further back, Hendrix, The Pretty Things, Yes, and Jethro Tull; anything and everything that had soundtracked stoned evenings at Ferry Road three years earlier. Yet it was these echoes that many critics focused on. In the US, where Queen's debut was now selling steadily, *Rolling Stone* magazine was mildly complimentary but also denounced parts of the record for having 'none of the wit and sophistication of Genesis' and for having 'appropriated the most irritating elements of Yes' style'. On home turf, *Record Mirror* described it 'as the dregs of glam-rock . . . If this is our brightest hope for the future, then we are committing rock 'n' roll suicide.' Naturally, the criticism stung. 'We took so much trouble over that album, possibly too much,' said Roger Taylor at the time. 'Immediately it got really bad reviews so I took it home to listen to again and thought, "Christ are they right?" But we'll stick by it.'

For the music press, the greatest obstacle to embracing Queen was the notion that, as *Record Mirror* claimed, the group 'have a giant-sized image with the music running a close second'. In reality, Mercury's obsessive nature had helped drive *Queen II*. 'Freddie didn't seem remotely bothered by the fact that there were only four of us to sing these parts,' said Taylor. 'We really were trying to break the boundaries of what people thought they could do in a recording studio.' But with their fancy Rhodes-designed costumes and their insistence on approving all publicity shots, Queen sometimes played straight into their critics' hands. After spying an unapproved band photo in one publication, Freddie buttonholed the writer: 'Look how fat my arms look!' he protested. 'My arms aren't like that at all!' Later, on tour, a Queen soundcheck was delayed after Mercury lost his favourite silver serpent bangle. The soundcheck only continued after the bracelet had been found.

At least on tour, the band's efforts weren't going unrewarded. Yet on the second night, at Friars in Aylesbury, there was a portent of trouble ahead. During the show, Brian May's playing became hampered by a pain in his arm. The band had been given injections before flying to Australia to play the Sunbury Rock Festival in January. May's right arm had swelled up. The needle used to inject him had not been sterile, and it was discovered that he had contracted gangrene. While it was treatable, the infection would impact on the guitarist's health as the tour progressed.

At Plymouth Guildhall on 3 March, Queen were joined by the tour's support act Nutz, a hard rock band from Liverpool, similarly predisposed towards loud riffing and with a corkscrew-haired frontman, Dave Lloyd, who was very much in the Robert Plant mould. There was already a double connection between the two groups: Nutz' just-released first album had been produced by John Anthony, and the band members were from the same Merseyside clique as Freddie's old sparring partners Ibex. According to Nutz bass guitarist Keith Mulholland, Brian May's opening gambit to the band was, 'I hear you rock.' At Plymouth, Mulholland and Nutz drummer John Mylett watched Queen from the wings. 'We were looking at Freddie, and we thought, "OK, he has something going on here,"' says Mulholland. That 'something' seemed to develop as the tour progressed. 'He just started getting more and more outrageous.'

Much like their mutual friends in Ibex, Nutz' approach to their music and their stagecraft was less rarified than Queen's. Dave Lloyd described it thus: 'Queen seemed very sensitive . . . we were four crazy Scousers.' Keith Mulholland watched Freddie dabbling away at 'White Queen (As It Began)' on the group's mini-grand piano during soundcheck. He was both impressed by the singer's musicality, and amused by his flamboyance. 'Freddie was reasonably shy,' says the bassist, 'but also very dramatic. There was always lots of "Oh yes, dear". He was definitely different.' Word of how different had already filtered down to the band via Ibex roadie Geoff Higgins. 'Geoff told us about Freddie and the crushed velvet flares,' says Mulholland. 'Any normal bod would just put on a pair of trousers and get on with it. But Geoff said Fred would stand in front of the mirror for ages, and make sure he got the seams straight.'

'Nutz came back home halfway through that tour,' recalls Ken Testi. 'That was when they started telling me how gay Freddie is, and I'm not having it. I'm saying, "You don't know Mary Austin', but Dave Lloyd was like, "Trust me on this one, Ken."' However, Keith Mulholland doesn't remember any specific incident. 'I think that women may have noticed it more than the fellas. He wasn't "out", but he might have been a bit "outish",' he laughs. 'We didn't care. We liked him.'

The tour progressed with a mixture of onstage highs and offstage lows. After a gig at Cheltenham Town Hall, Queen fired their lighting engineers. Trident arranged for Elton John's lighting ace James Dadd to take over, but the lighting rig would remain an unpredictable beast for the rest of the jaunt. After the Croydon Greyhound, Mercury was convinced he was 'breaking down, I was so fatigued'. Sheepishly, he told a writer from *New Musical Express* that he had thrown a glass at one of his entourage in a fit of pique, and that Taylor and May 'had a heavy scene' in the dressing room one night after the drummer squirted the guitarist in the face with hairspray.

However, despite being prone to what one tour insider describes as 'his dying-swan routine', the singer would often remain upbeat in the face of adversity. Arriving at Aberystwyth University, the road crew discovered that the event was a formal student ball, for which a steel band had also been booked, and that Queen weren't due on until after midnight. Dave Lloyd ran into Mercury at the hotel and began moaning about the booking: 'Freddie just said, "Oh David, you can be such a cunt. We'll do well tonight."'

With 'Seven Seas of Rhye' and *Queen II* inching up the charts, the timing of the tour couldn't have been better, even if, as Freddie recalled, 'Suddenly, everything escalated.' Tiny gigs in rural Norfolk and on Essex's Canvey Island began to feel incongruous, and at least one venue manager wondered whether the band would honour their booking now that they'd had a hit single. Stirling University embodied the scale of the change. 'It was a 500-capacity venue,' explains Keith Mulholland. ' "Seven Seas of Rhye" was in the charts, and the promoter had oversold the place. As soon as we walked onstage you could feel the heat of all these people. Then I saw all these guys coming back from the bar with seven-pint party cans. It was a bad combination.'

Mulholland could feel the stage moving with the combined force of the bodies pressed against it. Meanwhile, roadies crouched behind them, holding the amps upright. As soon as Queen appeared, a beer can whizzed towards the stage. 'Freddie used his mic stand like a bat,' says Mulholland, 'and whacked it back into the crowd.' After that, a hailstorm of cans landed on the stage. Later, the audience refused to leave the venue after the final encore. Queen barricaded themselves backstage, while the police were called, with fans and roadies injured during the ensuing fracas.

The following night's planned gig at Birmingham Barbarella's was postponed. A week later, the tour reached the Douglas Palace Lido on the Isle of Man. An aftershow party at the group's hotel led to a room getting wrecked. Over a more sedate drink, Mulholland became keenly aware of how different Queen's approach to the business was. 'We were talking to Freddie one night and he explained how they wouldn't let the record company backstage, and how they, as a group, were protective of every single member of the band,' he says. 'To be honest, we didn't know what he meant at the time, but, looking back, he was so clued up. Other bands didn't think that way.'

The four-week tour was due to end on Sunday, 31 March at London's Rainbow Theatre. The 3,500-capacity venue in Finsbury Park had been the place where Jimi Hendrix first set his guitar alight in 1967. Motown child-prodigy-turned-funk-superstar Stevie Wonder had played the theatre just weeks before Queen. While soundchecking during the afternoon, Freddie threw another tantrum. Keith Mulholland is convinced that the argument started over Taylor's choice of stage clothes: 'Roger had worn some top that Freddie wanted to wear that night. Freddie was furious, threw down his microphone and stormed off. I think he went and sat in the van. Brian turned up the volume and said over the mic, 'Freddie dear, come back, you old queen. Come back and sound-check."' In retrospect, though, the squabble over a shirt may have masked a bigger problem. For all his onstage bravado, Dave Lloyd recalled seeing Freddie being sick before the first gig in Plymouth. Keith Mulholland remembers it also: 'He did get nervous before a show, and he'd throw up. But everybody has their thing, their ritual, before a gig.'

On the night, though, Mercury hid any sign of such nerves. It was Queen's biggest headlining show yet, and the singer chose it to unveil the white winged tunic Zandra Rhodes had created for him. Through 'Great King Rat', 'Keep Yourself Alive' and 'Liar', Mercury did his customary prowling-cat routine, pacing from one side of the stage to the next, tossing his hair alongside Brian May before scuttling off to do the same next to John Deacon. During May's guitar solo, Freddie disappeared for a change of clothes, reappearing in a slashed black top (a second-choice perhaps, after Taylor had nixed his first), before ending the show tossing handfuls of flowers into the audience.

'He's a riveting performer,' wrote *Melody Maker*'s Colin Irwin. 'The stuff idols are made of.' But Irwin, like others, was turned off by the freneticism of Mercury's performance. John Anthony, watching Queen from the wings that night, saw how nervous the singer was. 'Fred was getting very flustered,' he recalls. 'He'd come over to the side of the stage and I'd be saying, "Calm down, Freddie, calm down . . ." I encouraged him. I said, "Freddie, you look like Nijinsky tonight, you're fucking majestic". He was like, "Oh thank you, Johnnypoos."' Backstage after the show, Mercury received his best compliment yet. 'Pete Townshend's younger brother Simon had been at the gig,' says Anthony. Thirteen-year-old Townshend Jnr was smitten. 'He said to Freddie, "You're much better than my brother's band." Fred was ecstatic.'

The show at Barbarella's had now been rescheduled to take place two days after the Rainbow, making it the official last night of the tour. The club on Birmingham's Cumberland Street would later become a hot-spot during punk and New Romantic eras. The Barbarella's stage had a catwalk, which Mercury made great use of that night. While the Queen singer paraded before his throng, Dave Lloyd and a couple of Queen roadies scampered onstage behind him. Roger Taylor had bet the Nutz singer and the crew a bottle of champagne that they wouldn't streak during Queen's set. 'So they walked onstage stark-bollock naked and mooned the audience,' remembers Keith Mulholland. 'Fred couldn't work out what was going on, until he turned round. He later said that he knew something was up as "for the first time, nobody in the audience was looking at me!"'

By April, 'Seven Seas of Rhye' had peaked at number 10, while *Queen II* had reached number 5, with Queen's debut also sneaking back into the Top 50. There was no time to bask in the glory, though. *Queen II* was released in the US, making it into the Top 50, as the group joined Mott The Hoople for an American tour. After headlining their own shows it was a wrench to go back to opening for another band, but the pill was sweetened by the promise of a trip to the States and a reunion with Mott.

The tour began in April at Regis College in Denver, Colorado, taking in a further five consecutive shows across the American Midwest at college venues and civic theatres. Barely a month before in the UK, Queen's partisan audiences had taken to singing the national anthem unprompted at the end of the group's set. Such a response was rather less forthcoming in Oklahoma City. Mott The Hoople's Ian Hunter could sense Mercury's impatience. 'He couldn't understand why Queen weren't huge immediately,' said Hunter. 'I remember him marching up and down, saying, "Why don't these silly bastards get it?" But America wasn't England; you had to tour there a few times.'

On 26 April, the tour reached Boston. Local musician Billy Squier would go on to become a hit solo artist and support Queen on their 1982 US jaunt. In 1974 he had just started fronting his own band, The Sidewinders. 'At the time I was going out with a very hip local disc jockey at WBCN called Maxanne Sartori,' says Squier. 'She was one of the first DJs in America to pick up on Queen's first record.' Squier's connections with Sartori led to him being invited to a record company dinner with Queen. Billy had already seen and heard the first album, marvelling at the photos of Freddie's painted fingernails. At the restaurant, he would be afforded his first glimpse of just how image-conscious Mercury was.

'I wound up sitting next to Freddie,' recalls Squier. 'He was wearing these white satin pants, very tight-fitting, along with some sort of brocade jacket. As we went to sit down, I can still picture him looking around furtively as if to make sure no one was watching, and then he quietly undid his trousers and took his seat. I realised his costume prevented him from sitting comfortably.'

Squier would go on to be managed by Bill Aucoin, whose clients already included Kiss, the face-painted comic-strip rockers, who also witnessed Queen on the Mott The Hoople tour that summer. There was a pattern developing among the audience. The name 'Queen' was enough on its own to attract attention from the more outré elements of the American music community. As Brian May recalled: 'We thought we were unusual, but a lot of the people that came were surprising, even to us – a lot of transvestite artists, New York Dolls, Andy Warhol – people that were creative in a way that appeared to trash everything that had gone before.'

For May, like countless British musicians before him, Queen's first US tour was a 'mind-blowing experience'. But while it was a manifestation of the dream he'd had since childhood, there was also an intensity to the experience that unsettled him. 'I hadn't learned the technique of touring,' he admitted. 'I think I was fighting against it rather than going along with it. We might have looked like a million dollars – or Fred did, I don't know about me – but we had nothing. Everything was on a shoestring, we were sharing rooms, and our manager would let us use the phone in his hotel room and call home as a treat.'

Eager to impress the natives, Queen and Elektra threw regular aftershow parties as the tour wound its way across the US. The morning after one soirée, Mott's keyboard player Morgan Fisher saw a staggeringly hungover Freddie Mercury pass out face first into his breakfast of fried eggs. For a gig at the Farm Arena in Harrisburg, Pennsylvania, a second support group, Aerosmith, were added to the bill. Aerosmith were a louche, glammy rock 'n' roll band whose lead singer Steven Tyler was an accomplished poser.

A row quickly broke out between the respective management of Queen and Aerosmith over who would play first. Eager to distance himself from the fracas, Brian May fell into conversation with Aerosmith's guitarist Joe Perry, who quickly cracked open a bottle of Jack Daniel's whiskey. Morgan Fisher was surprised: 'Brian always seemed like such a gentleman and I don't ever recall him drinking heavily.' Come showtime, both guitarists were blind drunk. May later claimed that he played the whole gig from memory, swearing never to drink 'more than a pint of beer' before a show again. Perversely, the rest of Queen complimented him on how much fire and energy he'd brought to his performance that night. May made another mental note: to 'always give it some action' in future.

Yet, the guitarist had other matters on his mind. An encounter in New Orleans led to a lifelong love affair with the Louisiana city and to a romantic entanglement alluded to in a song on Queen's next album. 'I fell in love in New Orleans,' admitted May in 1998. Thousands of miles from London, and from girlfriend Chrissy Mullen, the new object of Brian's affections would be known only as 'Peaches'. But she did find her way into the lyrics of 'Now I'm Here', a Queen song that captured the combined innocence and madness of their first US tour.

A six-night stand at New York's Uris Theater made Mott The Hoople the first rock band to play – and sell out – on Broadway. The shows also gave their support act the chance to prove themselves in front of America's hippest audience. John Anthony was in Canada producing a band of Hell's Angels named The North Ontario Paradise Riders ('that was an experience'), when he hustled a free trip to New York to see his former charges. By now more than a little one-upmanship was creeping into Queen's relationship with the headliners.

'Brian had the Zandra Rhodes costume on at the Uris,' remembers Anthony. 'The idea was that when he hit the big Pete Townshend windmill chord, the lighting engineer knew to put a spot on him which would catch the pleats of the tunic. It was a beautiful effect. One of Mott's crew knew this and started trashing the board, hitting all the faders to throw him off his mark.' The producer's fiery streak surfaced again. 'So I got hold of the guy, stuck this huge torch in his face and told him to leave the board alone.' Later, Mercury was delighted to read a review of one of the New York shows, in which the female critic had noted that 'she could tell what religion I was . . . and that I wasn't wearing any knickers.' 'They notice everything down to the pimple on your arse, dear,' he told writer Caroline Coon.

The bands travelled to Boston for the next night of the tour. But waking up in his hotel on the morning of the gig, May was barely able to move. After dragging himself into the bathroom, the guitarist saw his reflection in the mirror and realised why: his skin was yellow with jaundice. The infected arm, poor diet, late nights and the stress of touring had left his immune system depleted. May had contracted hepatitis. Queen flew back to England, where the guitarist was ordered to take six weeks' bed-rest. Meanwhile, the rest of the band, their crew, and everyone that had come into close contact with May was inoculated against the virus. Mercury returned to the UK with a health problem of his own: not a 'pimple on his arse' but a plague of boils.

'Seven Seas of Rhye' was released as a single in the US at the end of May, but with the band unable to promote it, failed to chart. PR Tony Brainsby issued a press release, expressing Queen's 'bitter disappointment' at the cancellation of the rest of the American tour, but that the group would be back in the studio by early July.

With May recuperating in hospital, Mercury, Deacon and Taylor began working up ideas for the next album. Having lasted three years in Queen, Deacon was finally shaking off the feeling that he was still, in his words, 'an outsider'. He would later tell interviewers that it was only now, with the recording of Queen's third album, that he felt convinced the band might have a serious future.

Work on the new album would take place between Trident, Wessex, Air and Sarm Studios in London, and Rockfield in Monmouth, with Roy Thomas Baker and Mike Stone again manning the board. Back on his feet, May joined the band at Rockfield, but kept leaving the studio to throw up. At Trident in August, he collapsed and was taken to King's College Hospital, where he was diagnosed with a duodenal ulcer, which had, it transpired, first developed in his teens. After an operation, May was ordered to remain in bed. Paranoid 'the band would replace me', he began writing songs while recuperating.

In his absence, Deacon proved himself an able rhythm guitarist, while Freddie paid frequent morale-boosting visits to Brian's hospital bed. But with their guitarist again out of commission, a planned run of the postponed US dates was cancelled. 'Brian has got to look after himself,' Mercury fussed to *NME*. 'We all want to make sure something like that never happens again.'

When May returned to the studio he was confronted with a 'mountain of playing to catch up on'. There were guitar parts, vocal harmonies, and countless overdubs. 'It was very weird,' he said. 'Because for the first time I was able to see the group from the outside, and I was very excited.' Despite their guitarist's absence and the fragmented nature of the sessions, Queen had a clear vision for their next album. '*Queen II* was very layered and had been difficult for people to understand,' said May. 'So much so, that when we were making the follow-up, we'd thought we'd better take it a bit easy and spell out what we were doing, so that it would be a bit more accessible.' Roy Thomas Baker's understanding of the project was clearer still: 'OK, let's have really big hit singles.'

On one of his first studio visits after leaving hospital, May was confronted by the 'big hit single' in question: 'Killer Queen'. The song was Mercury's baby and, with its dainty piano, mimicked the compositional traits of pre-war songwriters Noël Coward and Cole Porter. 'It's one of those bowler hat, black suspenders numbers,' claimed Mercury, suggesting the additional influence of his beloved *Cabaret*. Somehow in the midst of all this came chiming heavy metal powerchords and lyrics name-checking Moët & Chandon and Marie Antoinette.

'I wrote "Killer Queen" in one Saturday night,' explained Mercury. 'It's a song about a high-class call girl. Classy people can be whores as well.' The song may have been written quickly, but the recording took longer. On first hearing the track, May was unimpressed by what he described as the 'abrasive backing vocals'; all of which had to be redone. Taylor remembers 'take after take after take. The pitch had to be exactly right.' One night after a band dinner, Baker demanded that Mercury return to the studio to work on the song. 'But Freddie refused,' explained the producer. 'He said, "I'm not leaving this chair, dear!" So the road crew lifted him up and carried him to the piano. That's how we got "Killer Queen".'

Alongside Baker and Stone came two new recruits to the Queen studio team: Wessex Studio's tape operator Geoff Workman, a wry Liverpudlian who would go on to engineer Queen's *Jazz* album, and Sarm East Studio's young assistant engineer, Gary Langan. Brian May would only contribute four compositions to the finished album, but these included 'Brighton Rock' and 'Now I'm Here'; songs that would become high watermarks in the Queen catalogue. Both tracks were completed at Sarm, and gave Gary Langan his first taste of working with Queen. Roy Thomas Baker was now an expert at marshalling the band, as Langan witnessed first hand. 'Roy is the most extrovert person I have ever come across in my life,' he says. 'And to see him and Freddie Mercury together . . . He could also put the band down in a way that fired them up. He'd say, "Darlings, that was truly awful. How could you present such a dreadful performance?"

'It was very hard work,' he continues. 'You'd do fourteen- or fifteen-hour days. You'd start at twelve or one o'clock and go straight through until three in the morning, and it was total concentration for the whole time. They sweated blood.' Langan remembers that the call-and-response vocals on 'Now I'm Here' required five quarter-inch tape machines running at different speeds, which left the 'whole room humming'. The final mix of 'Brighton Rock' was heard by Langan, Baker, Stone, Mercury, May and Taylor crammed into the control booth and was, says the engineer, 'one of those "Ye gods!" moments.'

In September, May, still looking frail, made his first public appearance with Queen since New York. To commemorate sales of 100,000 copies for *Queen II*, the band were presented with silver discs at a function at London's Café Royal. With his usual keen eye for a photo op, Tony Brainsby booked Jeanette Charles, a Queen Elizabeth II impersonator, to present the band with their discs. A month later, 'Killer Queen' was released as a single in the UK. It was a double A-side, paired with another new song, 'Flick of the Wrist', but only one would find its way onto the radio. Later, Brian May shared his initial misgivings about 'Killer Queen' as a single, fretting that some fans would think it too lightweight. But, as he also admitted, 'It was the turning point. It was a big hit and we desperately needed it.' 'Killer Queen' reached number 2 in the charts, only held off by pop pin-up David Essex's 'I'm Gonna Make You a Star'. May's misgivings didn't last long: 'Fuck it! A hit is a hit is a hit.'

Adrian Morrish, Freddie's old friend from Isleworth Polytechnic, caught Queen performing 'Killer Queen' on *Top of the Pops* that summer. And there was Fred Bulsara in a fake fur blouson 'being' Freddie Mercury. 'It was the first time I'd ever seen the persona,' says Morrish. 'I knew he'd joined a band. The shock was that he'd become successful.' On the same night, Bruce Murray, once Freddie's bandmate in The Hectics, was working in a mini-cab office in South London, watching television while waiting for another fare. 'There was something about the singer in Queen,' he recalls. 'He had all this long hair now, but there was something about him I recognised . . . I suddenly realised, "My God, that's Fred Bulsara." I phoned Derrick Branche, and said, "Are you watching TV? Go and turn the TV on now!"'

Queen's third album, *Sheer Heart Attack*, was released on 1 November, just as the band embarked on their second UK tour of the year. Mick Rock had again taken the cover photograph, but the presentation was startlingly different from that of *Queen II*. 'We want to look like we've been marooned on a desert island,' Freddie told him. Rock obliged, by shooting the band from above while they lay in a circle, their faces and bare chests smeared with Vaseline and sprayed with water. When Roger complained about the appearance of his hair, extensions were added in the final picture. While Freddie's ubiquitous black nail varnish was still visible, the band were dressed down, and less overtly glam than before. 'We're showing people we're not merely a load of old poofs,' insisted Mercury. 'We are capable of other things.'

The music inside reflected the cover. This was Queen at their most concise yet. May's party pieces 'Brighton Rock' and 'Now I'm Here' opened and closed the first side of music and were the lengthiest songs on offer. 'Brighton Rock' had been in existence in some shape or form since *Queen II*, though the multi-tracked guitar solo idea dated back further to the Smile track 'Blag'. As a counter-point to the guitars was Mercury's startling falsetto vocal. 'Now I'm Here' was Queen's adventures in America set to music, name-checking Mott The Hoople and Brian's lost love Peaches with Freddie's exhortation 'Go, little Queenie' lifted straight from Chuck Berry. May's other two compositions 'Dear Friends' and 'She Makes Me (Stormtrooper in Stilettos)' were less compelling, but offered a glimpse into their composer's troubled frame of mind. May played piano on 'Dear Friends', while Mercury sung a slight lyric of love and redemption; Brian took his own lead vocal for 'She Makes Me', asking the world to 'cure his ills' over a rather leaden melody.

Even John Deacon had been coerced into writing. The bass player made his compositional debut with 'Misfire', a cheery soft-pop piece that scraped in at just one minute and fifty seconds. Not to be outdone, Taylor offered his best Queen song yet. 'Tenement Funster' was another in what would become the drummer's bottomless canon of songs celebrating the joy of the rock 'n' roll life: a hymn to loud music, 'good guitars' and 'the girls on my block'. But it was Mercury that distinguished himself as a writer on *Sheer Heart Attack*. 'Flick of the Wrist' was venomous hard rock that could have graced the first Queen album. The group-credited 'Stone Cold Crazy' was a feverish heavy metal number that dated back to Freddie's Wreckage days. In contrast, 'In the Lap of the Chords' was a pomp rock ballad (also reprised as the last song on the album) with a crowd-pleasing chorus that pre-empted 'We Are the Champions'. Tellingly, it would serve a similar purpose in Queen's live show until usurped by 'We Are the Champions' four years later.

Sheer Heart Attack's wild cards also came from Mercury. 'Bring Back That Leroy Brown' was a vaudeville pastiche, with May on ukelele-banjo, Deacon thumbing a double bass, and the singer drawing again on his boyhood memory of the novelty records he had heard on *Uncle Mac's Children's Favourites*. 'There was this feeling that we could try any kind of style,' said May, 'and shouldn't be embarrassed by anything at all.' 'Lily Of The Valley' was a delicate piano piece that hinted at the writer's inner turmoil. Twenty-five years later Brian May offered his own impressions on what the song was about. ' "Lily of the Valley" was utterly heartfelt,' he said. 'It's about [Freddie] looking at his girlfriend and realising that his body needed to be somewhere else.'

In late 1974, the singer was still living with Mary Austin, but stalling any questions about his private life in the press with the usual quips and glib aside ('I'm as gay as a daffodil, dear'). He claimed that he and his chauffeur were enjoying a flirtatious relationship, and that he played 'on the bisexual thing . . . because it was fun'. After Mercury's death, former EMI radio plugger Eric Hall would waggishly claim that 'Killer Queen' was inspired by Freddie's unrequited love for him: 'He said, "I wrote that song for you. I'm the queen and you're the killer because I can't have you!" ' According to Hall, this conversation took place in a Holiday Inn while Queen were due to appear on Radio Luxembourg. 'Freddie comes to my room in the middle of the night, tells me he's in love with me, and can he get into my bed with me,' said Hall. While agreeing to sit and 'hold his hand', Hall insists he rebuffed Mercury's advances and that Freddie accepted the rejection.

John Anthony had also found himself summoned to Freddie's hotel room one night during Queen's first UK tour that year. Anthony had travelled from London to Sunderland in the group's tour bus. One night after a show, Queen were joined by various female admirers back at their hotel. John went to bed, only to be telephoned by a frantic-sounding Freddie, who asked him to come to his room immediately. 'And there was Fred sat in bed in his pyjamas and night cap and these two girls standing around in his room,' says Anthony. 'Fred said, "Get rid of them Johnnypoos." So I told them that Fred had a big day ahead of him tomorrow and was very tired and they'd best go.' When they were alone again, Mercury told Anthony that he thought he was gay, and asked him if he would tell Mary Austin on his behalf. John refused.

On the third night, the tour reached the Liverpool Empire, where Queen were briefly reunited with the opening act from earlier in the year. Dave Lloyd was still waiting for the champagne he'd won in a bet with Roger Taylor, while bassist Keith Mulholland joined the Queen entourage in the hotel bar for an aftershow party.

'Freddie made a very grand entrance,' recalls Mulholland. 'He'd obviously gone back to his room, showered and done his hair. Very regal. I was sat at a table with Brian who was having a Jack Daniels, and Jack Nelson was pouring the champagne. I said something like, "This band is going to go ballistic", and Jack said, "Ballistic? We are going straight to the top."'

Capitalising on the success of 'Killer Queen', *Sheer Heart Attack* bettered even *Queen II*'s number 5 placing by reaching number 2 in the UK in its second week on sale (and only denied the top spot by Elton John's *Greatest Hits*). They even had some critics on their side. 'A feast, no duffers and four songs that will run and run,' extolled *NME*, which singled out 'Now I'm Here', 'Killer Queen', 'Flick of the Wrist' and 'In the Lap of the Gods' for special praise.

All four of those songs now featured in the band's setlist, spliced in among 'Ogre Battle', 'Liar' and the encore medley of 'Big Spender', 'Jailhouse Rock' and 'Modern Times Rock 'n' Roll'. Mercury managed to conceal any pre-gig nerves behind even greater displays of onstage bravado: 'Queen is back. What do you think about that?' he demanded in Liverpool. For some shows, Freddie's white stage outfit was accessorised by a chainmail-effect gauntlet on his left hand, suggesting a glam-rock falconer. After a change of costume, the singer would reappear, clad head to toe in black wearing a leather glove complete with talons on his left hand ('Do you like my claws?'). Offstage, of course, the intra-group bickering continued as usual ('Oh my dear, we're the bitchiest band on earth. We're at each other's throats,' Mercury told *Melody Maker*) but onstage, their focus was formidable, their ambition tangible.

The night after Liverpool, at Leeds University, Taylor's onstage monitor malfunctioned. Back in the dressing room, the drummer kicked a wall, bruising his foot so badly he was taken to hospital for an X-ray. During the show itself, Mercury had called a halt after fans were crushed in the scrum at the front of the stage. At the Glasgow Apollo a week later, the singer himself would be hauled into the crowd before being dragged back to safety by the security guards.

When tickets for the final night at the Rainbow sold out, a second show was added. Both nights were filmed, and while the planned live album was never released, an edited film of the gig was released in the cinema a year later. *Queen Live at the Rainbow* would play as support to Burt Reynolds' crime caper *Hustle*. It remains a fabulous period piece: Queen in their final days as a cult rock band, before the phenomenal success of 'Bohemian Rhapsody' changed their lives for ever.

Outside the Rainbow, after the show, Freddie Mercury's driver handed him a note that had just been passed to him. It was from Bruce Murray. 'I'd managed to get a message to Fred through the chauffeur,' Murray laughs. 'We both looked at each other through the car window and stared. Freddie said, "What the fuck are you doing here?" I laughed and said, "I'm here to see you, you prick!"' Murray followed Mercury's limousine to a club in Berkeley Square, where the two spoke for the first time since India. 'He told me he was skint,' says Murray. 'They were playing these shows, but he had no money.' Later, at his mini-cab office in Norbury, Murray would receive a phone call from the singer. 'He'd say, "I need to get to a party, but I have no money, will you take me?"' One night Murray chauffeured his friend to a party hosted by Elton John. 'Fred said, "Come in, come in . . ." But I said no, it really wasn't my scene. I didn't want to be a hanger-on.'

While Queen filled theatres and their singer preened from the pages of the music press, not everyone was aware of their success. Patrick Connolly hadn't seen his friend Fred Bulsara since leaving Isleworth Polytechnic in 1966. Connolly was walking past Claridges, the Mayfair hotel, one afternoon, when he heard a familiar voice: 'Patrick! Patrick!' It was Fred. 'He asked me to come in and have a cup of tea,' recalls Connolly. 'Queen were playing a concert in London that night. I was amazed by the change in him.' At Isleworth, Patrick had designed Freddie's audition posters and helped him pass his Art A-level, but, with no interest in pop music, he was completely unaware of his current success. 'I had to admit to him, "Fred, I had no idea." And he laughed and said, "Oh Patrick, you're the only person that doesn't know!"'

For the second time that year, though, Queen would go from playing to their own partisan audience to crowds that cared rather less. In November they began a two-and-a-half week tour of Scandinavia and Europe. When they arrived for a show in Munich, Queen found an audience filled with GIs from the nearby American airforce base. Queen were alternating as headliners with Lynyrd Skynyrd, a gritty rock 'n' roll band from America's Southern states, who'd just had a Top 5 hit with 'Sweet Home Alabama'. They were the antithesis of Queen, and the GIs loved them. 'For the first time in many months, I felt like I'd done a hard day's work when I came offstage,' grumbled Brian May. 'We were getting nothing back.'

While Queen found the audience's indifference draining, there was also a clash of cultures between the two groups. 'Skynyrd couldn't believe it when they saw us four caked in make-up and dressed like women,' recalled Roger Taylor. According to Taylor, representatives of Skynyrd's record label, MCA, were positioned in the audience during Queen's set. 'They would be holding up banners that said things like "Shit!" and "Queen Suck!"' he recalled. It's difficult not to be reminded of the scene in *This Is Spinal Tap*, where the hapless rock band encounter their former support act, Duke Fame, and recall an audience that 'were still booing him when we came onstage'. Yet Taylor's memory demonstrates just how at odds Queen were with most of their peers, and how determined the band were to prove that these 'four nancy boys could give [Skynyrd] a run for their money.'

After a third German date in Hamburg, Lynyrd Skynyrd were off the tour. Barely a week later Queen headlined the 6,000-seater Palacio de los Deportes in Barcelona. The gig had sold out in just twenty-four hours, and was their biggest yet.

Back at home, though, the band's bank accounts and living conditions suggested they were anything but pop stars. Taylor still rented a bedsit near the river in Kew Road, Richmond. Mercury and Mary Austin's rented flat had a grand address, 100 Holland Road,

Kensington W14, but little else. Neither Freddie's piano, which, bizarrely, doubled as a headboard for his and Mary's bed, nor the couple's collection of Biba knick-knacks could detract from the rising damp that had left the walls covered in fungus. Deacon was about to get married, but was still living in a bedsit in Parsons Green. Furthermore, Trident had just turned down Deacon's request for the £4,000 he needed to put down on a deposit for a house. ('Do you know how much money £4,000 was in 1974?' protests Norman Sheffield). Brian May's living conditions seemed to be the worst of all: a single room in a house in Earls Court, where his girlfriend Chrissy also lived. 'We lived mainly on cod in a bag and fish fingers,' he recalled in 2009. 'We had a single gas ring and no water supply, except the communal bathroom up the corridor.' More depressing still was the story that to access this bolthole, May had to enter through the building's basement boiler room.

By now, EMI's Bob Mercer put Queen in touch with lawyer Jim Beach of the law firm Harbottle & Lewis. Beach acquired copies of the band members' contracts with Trident and began looking for a way out. Mercer's relationship with Trident had become similarly troublesome. 'The Sheffield brothers had their relationship with Roy Featherstone, who had signed the band,' he explains. 'So it became something of a bone of contention when the band started saying to him, "We don't want you talking to the Sheffields." Roy felt that was the way he'd signed the band and, in the end, he and I had a pretty stand-up fight about it.'

While their lawyer began the slow process of extricating Queen from their contracts, EMI released 'Now I'm Here' as the band's next single in January. Now the melodramatic opening number in Queen's live set, it was too heavy for most daytime radio playlists but managed a respectable number 11. The day after its release, John Deacon married his long-time girlfriend Veronica Tetzlaff. The couple had been together for over three years after meeting at a party at the Maria Assumpta college, where Veronica had been a student. The Catholic wedding took place at the Carmelite Priory on Kensington Church Street. Veronica was two months' pregnant with their first child, Robert.

Deacon's best man was his old schoolfriend and former

Opposition drummer Nigel Bullen, who would watch in awe as Freddie Mercury made the grandest of entrances. The Queen singer had arrived in a stretch limo, was wearing a huge feather boa and had a woman on each arm. 'At first I thought it was the bride,' Bullen admitted. Deacon's Opposition bandmates had seen Queen play live, but they would now witness the after-effects of being in a band that had appeared on *Top of the Pops*. On a pre-wedding trip back to Leicestershire, Deacon had gone for a drink with The Opposition's ex-singer Dave Williams. Somebody put 'Killer Queen' on the pub jukebox, and within minutes 'Easy Deacon' was being pestered for autographs.

Around the same time, Chris Smith had run into Brian May at Kensington Market and taken him to the Greyhound. 'They'd had a hit with "Killer Queen", and he was getting well-known,' says Smith. 'The pub was packed, and as soon as I walked in, with Brian behind, the whispering started: "That's him from that band . . ." I sat him in a corner and went to get the drinks, and I remember thinking, "So this is what fame's like." When I sat down, Brian said, "No one's bought me a drink for a ages." I said, "Well, that's what you do. You buy the next one. That's how it is." I don't think he'd been treated normally for a while. I think Freddie and Roger could cope with fame – they seemed to love it. But I'm not sure Brian could.'

After his honeymoon, Deacon returned to the fray, and Queen reconvened for another go at the United States. *Sheer Heart Attack* had received an American release and would peak at number 12. There was still much lost ground to make up for after the earlier aborted US dates. 'We were confident that we would go down all right in the East and Midwest,' ventured Roger Taylor. 'But we were told not to expect too much in the South and far West.' 'With a name like Queen there were always questions from day one,' recalls Mott The Hoople's then roadie Peter Hince, 'especially in America. Waitresses in the Holiday Inns would be like, "Gee, you guys are great . . . are you all fags?"'

After a week's rehearsal in New York, road-testing their new PA and lighting rig, Queen opened in Columbus, Ohio, and ploughed straight into two or three consecutive gigs without a break, taking in Cleveland, Detroit and Boston. Three weeks later, after a show in Philadelphia, Mercury was losing his voice. A hospital doctor diagnosed possible nodules on his vocal cords. Freddie was told to rest, but played the following night's show at Washington's Kennedy Center anyway, managing, against expectations, to scale the high notes as before.

However, not everyone was as enamoured of Queen's lead singer. When the band had dropped off the Mott The Hoople US tour, their place had been taken by homegrown rock band Kansas. The same group would open several dates for Queen on the 1975 tour. The lead vocalist Steve Walsh would go on to praise the headline act with the exception of their frontman. 'Freddie Mercury was an asshole,' said Walsh. 'He was a prima donna.' It would not be the last time Mercury's attitude alienated some of the people around him.

With his voice causing problems, he became increasingly distraught. Mercury was in agony after Washington, and six dates were cancelled immediately. The suspected nodules turned out to be laryngitis and a strained throat, and he was prescribed painkillers and told to speak only when necessary. Despite the setback, when the tour picked up again in Chicago, Mercury's performance was as assured as ever. *Melody Maker*'s US stringer Al Rudis saw the show and was entranced by the singer's mic stand technique: 'He plays it like a guitar, aims it at the audience rifle fashion . . . wields it like a cane and a samurai sword, and pretends to break it across his knee like an Apache declaring war.'

On a day off before playing two nights at Los Angeles' Santa Monica Civic Auditorum, May and Taylor went to see Led Zeppelin at the nearby 18,000-seater Forum. 'We thought if we played the Rainbow in London we'd made it,' said May. 'Then we saw Zeppelin at the Forum and thought, "Jesus Christ, if we ever make this kind of thing" . . . Our manager was there and he said, "Couple of years' time, you'll be doing this."'

In 1975 Los Angeles' Sunset Strip was a ready-made playground for any visiting rock band. Like every English rock group before them, Queen made a pilgrimage to the notorious Rainbow Bar and Grill in West Hollywood. The Rainbow was a regular haunt for the likes of The Sweet, Led Zeppelin, The Who's Keith Moon and their attendant female admirers. 'I thought, "My God, what a strange island of odd humanity this is,"' said May. Taylor, however, loved it. As John Anthony insists, 'Roger always wanted to be a pop star, and wanted to enjoy everything that being a pop star entailed.'

Frustratingly, the tour limped rather than galloped towards the finishing line. Mercury's voice was still a problem and yet more dates had been cancelled. After a successful show at San Francisco's Winterland, the band flew to Canada, managing three gigs before cancelling the final date in Portland and flying home. Once again, a US tour had been scuppered by a band member's failing health.

While Jim Beach continued to wade through Queen's contracts, the band holidayed in Hawaii before flying on to Japan for a hastily arranged eight-date tour. However slow their progress may have been elsewhere, and however aggrieved they felt about their situation with Trident, Queen had become pop stars in Japan, the second largest market for pop music in the world.

On 17 April the band arrived at Haneda Airport to be greeted by, recalled Roger Taylor, 'thousands, literally thousands of fans' (Deacon: 'hundreds and hundreds') brandishing album sleeves, photographs torn from music magazines and homemade banners ('Love Queen', 'Welcome Roger Queen'). The tour was book-ended by two sold-out nights at the 14,200-capacity Nippon Budokan Hall. During the first, Mercury was forced to stop the show to prevent over-excited fans getting crushed in front of the stage. Part of the second show was recorded by a local TV station and captured May and Mercury trading moves in their now well-travelled Zandra Rhodes frocks. 'The noise was enormous,' recalled John Deacon. 'The screaming and the throwing presents onstage.' 'Something just clicked in Japan,' said May. 'Suddenly we were The Beatles.'

Offstage, they were assigned a personal bodyguard (Mercury: "Mine was called Hitami. He was very sweet and gave me a lovely Japanese lantern') and filmed for the *Star Senichya* TV show, looking politely baffled as they recited personal messages to the camera, and sat cross-legged for a traditional Japanese tea ceremony. As Brian May explained at a press conference in Tokyo: 'We are overwhelmed . . . we have never experienced anything like this in any other country.' Queen returned to England with their complimentary Japanese kimonos, and back to the harsher reality of what Brian May called 'our crummy basement flats'. 'We encountered something like Beatlemania,' Taylor told *Mojo*. 'We'd never seen anything like that, and we came back after playing the Budokan and I went back to my bedsit in Richmond. We were still on £60 a week.'

Chris Smith visited May at home straight after the Japanese tour. 'Brian was shell-shocked,' he remembers. 'He said, "I was just in The Beatles. We got this amazing reception, even at the airport. Now I've gone from that to *this*." And then he took me into the bathroom, and there was all this fungus on the walls. He said to me, "I've got no money, you know."' Walking into May's room, Smith was then confronted by dozens of toy penguins. 'Brian had done an interview in some magazine and told them he liked penguins, so fans had sent them to him. So there's fungus on the wall, the room is tiny, but it's full of penguins – small ones, big ones, six-foot ones . . . just loads of penguins.'

'That first tour of Japan was what changed it,' says Mark Ashton. 'Queen had gone down extremely well, and the office gossip was that Freddie, especially, was very angry with Jack [Nelson]. I used to hear Fred in the office and he'd be very loud and very irate about Trident's failings.' Interviewed now about his time with Trident and Queen, Jack Nelson offers a noncommittal 'the whole experience was very interesting'. Nelson would move back to the US for a job with EMI, before continuing in management for Chaka Khan and Blackstreet. 'We parted on amicable terms,' he said. 'Brian and I talk all the time.'

In May 1974, the American rock group Sparks had enjoyed a number 2 UK hit with 'This Town Ain't Big Enough For the Both of Us'. Queen and Sparks had shared a bill at the Marquee, and Sparks' quasi-operatic rock wasn't so far removed from some of Queen's work. A year later, Sparks could smell blood. 'They came round and said, "Look, it's pretty obvious Queen are washed up, we'd like to offer you a position in our band, if you want,"' recalled May. 'And I said, "Well, I don't think we're quite dead yet."'

But May was still deeply frustrated. 'After three albums people thought we were driving around in Rolls-Royces,' he later told *Q* magazine. 'That's when we started to feel resentful. There was also a huge drawback in the fact that your manager is your record company, so you don't have anyone that can represent you to the record company. So you have an impossible situation. It generated friction in every department.'

Furthermore, any money invested by Trident was recoverable before any profits could be shared out. As Norman Sheffield points out: 'Trident invested over £200,000 in Queen, probably the largest sum ever invested in an up-and-coming band.' Effectively, Queen had to pay back Trident. Having the best recording facility, the best stage show, indeed the best of everything, came at a price. *Sheer Heart Attack* had supposedly cost £30,000 to make. When Queen finally had hits, they expected to make money, only to hear that they actually owed Trident. 'We were deep in debt,' said May.

'I don't think it was the deal that was wrong, it was the interpretation of the deal,' offers producer Ken Scott. 'Trident spent a fortune on that band. But some of it was chargebacks. The artist gets charged for things that they think are in-house. The artist looks at it and goes, "We are not paying that back." It's the age-old story and it happens again and again in this industry.'

Adding salt to the wound, on 12 May, 'Killer Queen' went Top 20 in the US. A week later, Freddie Mercury was presented with an Ivor Novello award for the same song.

On tour in the US, Queen had reportedly met with the late Don Arden, manager of Black Sabbath and E.L.O., and a music business impresario whose brutal reputation has earned him the nickname of 'The Al Capone of Rock' (Arden's daughter Sharon would later manage Ozzy Osbourne and launch a worldwide TV career). In a 2002 interview, Arden claimed he went to see the Sheffields and in an hour convinced them to release Queen from their contract. Trident agreed in principle, and Queen signed a letter authorising Arden to act on their behalf. At some point, however, both parties changed their mind. John Anthony recalls 'pleading with Queen not to sign with Arden'. Whether they heeded his advice or not, any deal with Don was soon off, but, said the band, 'by mutual agreement'. Despite his reputation, there were no known reprisals from the Arden camp.

Around the same time, Queen's management wish-list included 10cc's manager Harvey Lisberg, The Who's tour manager Peter Rudge, and the late Peter Grant, Led Zeppelin manager and co-founder of Zeppelin's Swansong record label. One of the stipulations of any contract with Grant would have included Queen signing to Swansong. Queen were also conscious of their possible place in a management pecking order that also included Bad Company and Led Zeppelin.

In the end, it was John Reid who took on the role of Queen's new manager. Reid's managerial career had begun just four years earlier when he took on a young singer-songwriter christened Reg Dwight and now known as Elton John. 'We knew we were in a difficult position management-wise, but we were in a good position overall,' explained Brian May. 'So we went around and saw everybody that we could, and the only situation that was suitable for us, really, was John Reid.'

In August 1975, Queen signed an agreement with Trident that separated them from all of their deals. Queen's publishing was now in the hands of EMI Publishing (which had taken over Feldman's), while their record deals, with EMI in the UK and Elektra world-wide, were no longer processed through Trident. Inevitably, it came at a cost. Trident received a severance pay of £100,000 covered by an advance from EMI Publishing. Trident also retained the rights to 1 per cent of the royalties on Queen's next six albums.

The bitter aftermath of Queen's Trident deal still lingers. As recently, as two years ago, Ken Scott was waiting in the lounge at London's Heathrow Airport when he spotted John Deacon. 'So I went up to him and said, "Hi, John, do you remember me? I was an engineer from Trident called Ken Scott?" And John snapped back at me, "Yes, and I have nothing whatsoever to do with any of that any more!"'

CHAPTER SIX

A Vulture's Crotch

'Fantasies? Perhaps I'd like to be Rudolf Nureyev.'
Freddie Mercury

'. . . Has all the demented fury of the Balham Amateur
Operatic Society performing *The Pirates of Penzance*.'
Melody Maker **review of 'Bohemian Rhapsody', 1975**

Rockfield Studios still looks like the working farm it once was. Tucked away in the Wye Valley near Monmouth, its barns and sheds were converted into a recording facility in 1963. The farm's owners, Charles and Kingsley Ward, had a group of their own, and realised it would be cheaper to record at home than trek down to London. Once the Wards had converted further outbuildings into living quarters, Rockfield became one of the first residential studios in the world. By the mid-seventies Rockfield had chalked up its first hit single with Dave Edmunds's 'You Hear Me Knocking', and had become a Mecca for many of the flagship heavy bands of the era.

At the beginning of August 1975, just before heading to Rockfield, Queen set up base at a country house in nearby Herefordshire for three weeks of rehearsal. Queen's stay at the house would be recalled in novelist Tiffany Murray's 2010 memoir *Diamond Star Halo*. To make ends meet, Murray's mother had rented the house to rock bands during the seventies, and Freddie Mercury 'with his fleshy lips and feathered hair' was remembered as always being the first one up in the morning, and of commandeering the piano to play a new piece of music to the six-year-old Tiffany which turned out to be 'Bohemian Rhapsody'. ('Do you like it?' he asked. 'It's fantastic,' I said. 'It's a bit long,' he replied.)

If Queen would be remembered for one song alone it would be this one. 'Bohemian Rhapsody' is the third biggest-selling British single of all time, whose worldwide sales tipped over two million following Freddie Mercury's death in 1991. But the band had little idea of what lay in store when they checked into Rockfield on 24 August to begin work on their fourth album, *A Night at the Opera*. They arrived just after John Anthony's protégés Van Der Graaf Generator finished their own stint at the studio. Billeted in a row of converted barns adjacent to the studio, and with only the Old Nag's Head pub in Monmouth within stumbling distance, distractions were few and far between.

'They spent their free time playing Frisbee in the main yard outside the studio,' remembers Kingsley Ward. 'Freddie also used to play the old upright piano we kept in what was then the horse tack and feed room.' Later, Roger Taylor would set up his drums in the same room, with yards of cable fed across the yard back into the studio.

The tranquillity of the Wye Valley offered Queen some respite from the turmoil in their professional lives. With the demise of their deal with Trident and the departure of Jack Nelson, another US tour had been cancelled. 'It was an enormous blow,' admitted Roger Taylor. New manager John Reid's instruction to Queen that summer was simple: 'I'll take care of the business; you make the best record you can.'

On the day Queen were due to start work at Rockfield, Roy Thomas Baker made a phone call of his own to Trident: 'I told them I didn't want them to manage me any more . . . I think it was the only time I actually got a return call from them,' he said in 1982. Baker, too, would sign himself over to John Reid Enterprises. With one less business problem to distract him, the producer turned his attention to the job in hand.

The seeds of what became 'Bohemian Rhapsody' went back to the half-written piece of music that Freddie and Chris Smith had fooled around with at Ealing more than five years earlier; the piece Smith remembered Freddie calling 'The Cowboy Song' after its lyric 'Mama just killed a man'. Roy Thomas Baker had first heard the song early in 1975 during a visit to Freddie's flat. The pair were due to go to dinner, but Mercury insisted on playing him 'something he'd been working on. So he sat down at his piano, played the first part and said, "This is the chord sequence", followed by the interim part, and I could tell it was going to be a ballad. He played a bit further through the song and then stopped suddenly, saying, "This is where the opera section comes in." We both just burst out laughing.'

As a studio apprentice at Decca Records, Baker had helped record the D'Oyly Carte Opera Company, an ensemble known for their performances of Gilbert and Sullivan's light operas. It was an experience he wanted to draw on for the recording of 'Bohemian Rhapsody'. 'Queen came up with so many ideas,' he said, 'but my job was to organise those ideas in order to make them work.' He had also adopted another mantra: 'Ideas weren't problems. They were challenges. I'd never say, "That's not possible."'

Baker's never-say-die attitude was a godsend. By now, Queen's working practices were well established. Each band member would write alone before bringing their song ideas to the others for suggestions, improvements, rejection even. It could be, said Roger Taylor, 'a lonely process'. During the making of *A Night at the Opera*, the drawbacks of this method would become apparent. On some occasions, band members would end up working in pairs, sometimes even in different studios. 'You lose a bit of the group feeling,' May told *Melody Maker* in 1975. 'I can point to things on this album that suffered from not having us all there at one time and because there was too much responsibility on one.'

Therefore, when Mercury descended on Rockfield's Studio 1 with 'Bohemian Rhapsody', his bandmates had no idea what to expect. Freddie had written down his ideas for the song in the notebooks his father Bomi used for his accountancy work. 'It wasn't standard musical notation,' recalled Brian May. 'But As and Bs and Cs in blocks, like buses zooming all over bits of paper. He seemed to have the whole thing worked out in his head.'

The finished article would find room for a cappella vocals, tender balladry, scything heavy metal and an operatic mid-section that would take supposedly 180 overdubs. The basic backing track was recorded at Rockfield, with, as Taylor recalled, 'Freddie conducting'. The first section, after the a capella intro, was straightforward enough, comprising just piano, bass, guitars and drums. Once completed, Baker left a thirty-second strip of tape on the reel for later use on what was already being called 'the opera section', unaware of just how involved that section would become, before the group recorded the song's closing, heavy rock coda, with May playing a Mercury-written riff in E-flat; a difficult key for any guitarist. But, in keeping with Baker's mantra: it wasn't a problem, it was a challenge . . .

'We were all a bit mystified about how he was going to link these pieces,' admitted May. In 1969, Freddie had co-opted The Beatles' instrumental breakdown from 'A Day in the Life' to link his different ideas for 'The Cowboy Song'. This time, he'd written his own pseudo-operatic midsection ('mock opera' he said), with lyrics name-checking the seventeenth-century Italian comedy mainstay Scaramouche, the Spanish and Portugese folk dance the fandango, the Italian astronomer Galileo Galilei, and Rossini and Mozart's operatic character Figaro. For added multiculturalism, he threw in the Arabic noun *bismillah*, commonly used in Islamic prayer. It was the first time Mercury had explicitly referenced his ethnic background in a song for Queen. Interviewed in 1996, Queen PR Tony Brainsby claimed that 'Freddie avoided at all costs mentioning Zanzibar. He just didn't think it fitted the image.' Not that his bandmates were ever privy to what he was singing about. 'We didn't speak to each other about lyrics,' admitted May. 'We were too embarrassed to talk about the words.' To this day, no one connected with the band has ever revealed where the song's title came from.

In the pre-digital age, Queen had just twenty-four analogue tracks to work with. However, to complicate the process, they then had to record the backing vocals before the lead vocal. 'That wasn't a regular way of doing things,' admits Baker. 'But we wouldn't have had enough tracks left for the rich backing vocals if we hadn't gone down this route.' The process became even more involved when, as Roger Taylor explained, 'Freddie started adding more and more "Galileos".'

'Every time Freddie added another "Galileo" I would add another piece of tape to the reel,' said Baker. In the meantime, Baker's endless loops of tape had begun to resemble 'a zebra crossing whizzing by'. After numerous playbacks, it sounded as if the song was gradually fading away. What happened next has passed into Queen mythology, like the origins of Freddie's sawn-off mic stand.

The exacting process of recording one vocal harmony at a time had required, in the parlance of studio engineers, 'bouncing' each harmony on to another track, and so on. Brian May explains: 'The original tape had actually worn thin. People think it's this legendary story, but you could hold the tape up to the light and see through it. Every time the tape went through the heads, more of the oxide was worn off.' The tape was hurriedly transferred, but as May wistfully recalled later, 'Every time Freddie added another "Galileo" we lost something.'

Queen rolled out of Rockfield in September. The studio's traffic of loud rock bands continued, as ex-Hawkwind bassist Lemmy rolled in with his new group Motörhead. While the Queen album was far from complete, the band had found a potential name for it. According to Roy Thomas Baker, after a particularly tense day at Rockfield, the producer had persuaded the group to relax at his rented house nearby. Baker had one of the first video players, and over a few drinks, the group watched the 1935 Marx Brothers comedy movie *A Night at the Opera*. Considering the epic 'Bohemian Rhapsody', 'the title seemed terribly apt'.

Back in London, Queen began a marathon spree of overdubbing at Sarm East and Scorpio Studios. Sarm's assistant engineer Gary Langan (who, with Gary Lyons, would also help engineer part of the album) had first met Queen during *Sheer Heart Attack*. Working on *A Night at the Opera* was an even greater eye-opener. Sarm East was a tiny studio at the bottom end of Brick Lane in London's East End. Day after day, the studio would be filled with an assortment of roadies, while Mercury, Baker and Mike Stone (Langan: 'Rag, Tag and Bobtail') would take up residence at the Trident-B console (later sold at an inflated price as 'the board used to mix "Bohemian Rhapsody"').

'Freddie would only leave when Brian moved in,' says Langan

now. 'For the rest of the time, he'd be sat there, for hours on end, drumming his painted fingernails on the desk, in his black satin trousers with the top button undone.' Langan was taken aback by how Mercury dressed up even for a working session at the studio. Others also recall that Freddie's hairbrush took up its place on the mixing desk in front of him.

Gary encountered the same level of perfectionism when May arrived at Sarm. 'People talk about Michael Jackson spending two weeks on getting a drum track, but I can tell tales of Brian May spending a week on a guitar solo,' he insists. Langan was also intrigued by the band's dynamic. 'For me, any band is made up of different chemical elements. In Queen, there was Roger Taylor, who was very much this wild child, and at the other end there was Mister Methodical Brian May. 'I'd offer to make tea or coffee, and I'd go round the room taking orders from Freddie, Roger, Mike and whatever other hangers-on were there, and then I'd ask Brian what he wanted. Then there'd be this pause and then he'd ask, "How many teas are you making? How many coffees? . . . Two? . . . Three? Is it easier for you to make another coffee or another tea?" You could spend ten minutes just doing this. He was trying to make it easier for me, but in the end I'd be like, "Brian! Just tell me what you want!" '

It wasn't until every section of 'Bohemian Rhapsody' was spliced together that anyone, even Mercury, realised quite what they'd created. For Gary Langan, hearing the song in its six-minute entirety was 'a red letter day – my jaw was on my chest'. But it left others perplexed. Ian Hunter had quit Mott The Hoople, and was about to co-opt most of Queen into playing on his next solo album, when he dropped by the studio.

'They unleashed it on us in four huge speakers,' he recalls. 'I couldn't make head nor tail of all that pomp and circumstance. It was like being run over by a truck. Fred said, "What did you think?" I didn't have the faintest idea. He was like, "Did you not hear the third harmony in the second verse? There's a slight variation there." I just looked at him aghast and said, "Give me a break." He just didn't realise. He'd been in the studio three days solid.'

Unflinching, Mercury announced that 'Bohemian Rhapsody'

would be Queen's next single. He had the rest of the band's support, or nearly all of them ('There was a time when the others wanted to chop it around a bit'). Interviewed in the early 1990s, the late Peter Brown claimed that John Deacon was against releasing the song as a single without editing it down. Reportedly, when John Reid played 'Bohemian Rhapsody' to Elton John, the singer's response was: 'Are you fucking mad?'

However, for a band, whom Freddie claimed, 'argued about everything – even the air that we breathe', Queen presented a united front to EMI. Behind the bravado, they knew they were fighting for survival: they'd been bruised by the Trident deal and another US tour cancellation, and had to make an impact with their next release. 'Tell me one other group that has done an operatic single?' Mercury demanded. 'I can't think of anybody.'

Roy Thomas Baker defended the choice of 'Bohemian Rhapsody' as a single by citing Richard Harris's 'MacArthur Park', a 1968 hit that had tipped seven minutes. But his reasoning cut little ice with EMI: 'Their comment was that the BBC wouldn't play a song that long when the current formula was three and a half minutes.'

Paul Watts, general manager of EMI's international division, was among the doubters. 'I was expecting something very special,' he said. 'So when they played me "Bohemian Rhapsody", my reaction was: "What the fuck's this? Are you mad?"' Watts and Queen's staunch EMI ally Eric Hall both suggested an edit for radio. Queen flatly refused.

Eric Hall said that he smuggled a copy of the song to Kenny Everett, then a DJ on London's Capital Radio. Roy Thomas Baker also claims that he invited Everett over to Scorpio Studios on London's Euston Road to hear the song and solicit his opinion. Everett (who died in 1995) was apparently so impressed he told the band it was a guaranteed hit. He asked for a copy and the group agreed, on the half-hearted proviso that he didn't play it on his radio show. The following day, Everett played a few seconds of 'Bohemian Rhapsody' before teasingly telling his listeners that he wasn't allowed to play any more. After playing more snippets, Everett aired the whole song – all 5:55 minutes of it – a total of fourteen times over the weekend.

Ex-1984 guitarist John Garnham first heard 'Bohemian Rhapsody' on the radio. Like Ian Hunter, he wasn't sure. 'I rang up Brian and said, "What have you put out this load of rubbish for?"' he laughs. 'That showed my judgement. But then I'd always had this thing in 1984 about playing songs that people could dance to. "Bohemian Rhapsody" seemed more removed from that than even Hendrix and Cream. I just didn't get it at the time.'

Fans who went to buy the single the next morning were told that it wasn't out yet. EMI's hand had been forced. Everett had played the song repeatedly, scuppering the record company's argument that 'Bohemian Rhapsody' was too long for radio. EMI relented and on 31 October, 'Bohemian Rhapsody' was released as Queen's fifth single. It entered the chart at number 47. Ten days later, and with the single rising to number 17 and then 9, Queen realised they couldn't perform the song live, and approached director Bruce Gowers to shoot a promo that could be sent to *Top of the Pops*. Gowers had previously directed the film of Queen's Rainbow gig. In 1975 pop promo budgets normally ran to £600. According to Gowers, 'Bohemian Rhapsody' cost £3,500; excessive for the time, if piddling by today's standards.

Gowers and his crew arrived at Elstree film studios where Queen were rehearsing for their next tour. The premise of the video was simple: to shoot the band playing live on the soundstage and to bring the cover of *Queen II* to life, animating the band members' four heads and capturing Mercury in his Marlene Dietrich pose. While its multi-angle shots and trippy visual effects were pioneering for the time, the shoot took just three hours. 'We started at seven-thirty,' said Gowers. 'Worked until ten-thirty and were in the pub by quarter to eleven.'

Among all the 'Scaramouches', the 'bismillahs' and 'Galileos' one question remained unanswered: What was 'Bohemian Rhapsody' about? Evasive as ever, Mercury insisted that 'people should just listen to it, think about it and then decide what it means'. Taylor claimed, 'It's obvious what it's about.' May had his own take on the song: 'I don't think we'll ever know and if I knew I probably wouldn't want to tell you anyway. But the great thing about a great song is that you relate it to your own personal experiences in your own life. I think that Freddie was certainly battling with problems in his personal life, which he might have decided to put into the song himself. But I don't think at that point in time it was the best thing to do so he actually decided to do it later. I think it's best to leave it with a question mark in the air.' By late 1975, there were significant changes taking place in Mercury's personal life, but he had no intention of making them public.

In the meantime, EMI's head of press and promotions, Martin Nelson had been shepherding Queen to gigs and interviews since *Sheer Heart Attack*. In November, with the tour about to begin, Nelson was instructed to find a studio where Reid could meet the band and play them the final mix of *A Night at the Opera*. 'I managed to get Radio City in Liverpool,' recalls Martin. 'We were given an off-air studio, but the studio itself was still being built and no one told me that the equipment had not yet been fully wired up. We all congregated at 11 a.m. John Reid turned up in a Rolls-Royce from London. There were no seats in the studio so we all had to sit on the floor. Then the tape machine was working, but only in mono, so it was just coming out on one speaker. Not the best way to hear your new album back for the first time. John was incensed.' Nelson escaped the full extent of the manager's wrath when Reid went outside and saw his car. 'I was lucky. The studio was in Stanley Street, which could be a bit rough. Someone had stolen John's hubcaps, so he became distracted by that.'

Queen began their 24-date tour on 14 November with two nights at the Liverpool Empire. In keeping with the grandiosity of their new single, the band's stage set included more lights, more magnesium flares and more dry ice than before. Taylor's kit was accessorised by a giant gong (just like John Bonham's), while his snare drum would be filled with lager to create a fountain of liquid during his solo.

The show would begin with a taped introduction from best pal Kenny Everett ('Ladies and gentlemen . . . a night at the opera') and a recording of the operatic section of 'Bohemian Rhapsody', before the band careened onstage to finish the song, minus the final verse. 'Bohemian Rhapsody' would be reprised after a run of songs including 'Ogre Battle', 'Flick of the Wrist' and 'Killer Queen'.

Later, 'Bohemian Rhapsody' would be played in one piece, with the band leaving the stage for the taped operatic section (Brian May: 'It gave us a chance to change the frocks') and returning for the finale.

This time, Freddie's stage outfits ran the gamut from the winged Hermes suit and slashed-neck black number, to eye-wateringly tight satin shorts ('Rude? Meant to be, dear,' he told a writer from *Melody Maker*) to a £200 Japanese kimono. Three dates in, at the Coventry Theatre, the kimono's sash disappeared into the audience, and Pete Brown was dispatched to find a replacement; Mercury had to make do with a silk scarf. As Jonh (sic) Ingham wrote in *Sounds*: 'Freddie reacts to his audience like an over-emotional actress – Gloria Swanson, or perhaps Holly Woodlawn playing Bette Davis. At the climax of the second night in Bristol, he paused at the top of the drum stand, looked back over the crowd and with complete, heartfelt emotion, placed his delicate fingers to lips and blew a kiss . . .'

Queen's road crew now included Mott The Hoople's ex-roadie Peter Hince, who had been appointed to look after Mercury and Deacon. Peter soon became au fait with Freddie's perfectionism. 'If something wasn't working, then Freddie would immediately order another new one,' he recalled. 'Everything had to be the best, to do the best work.'

This attention to detail also extended to the employment of a personal masseur named Steven, a moonlighting physiotherapist who had once worked for Rudolf Nureyev. However Queen's PR Tony Brainsby was no longer required. Brainsby claimed that first hearing 'Bohemian Rhapsody' left him 'feeling like a father whose wife had just given birth'. He'd looked after the band for three years, but with a change in the management regime, Brainsby's place would be taken by a PR from John Reid Enterprises, Caroline Boucher. 'Queen were so easy and pleasant and willing and keen,' says Caroline now. 'Elton John was just getting into quite a bad drug phase, so Queen were much simpler to deal with than Elton. But Freddie could have his moments if things weren't going his way, as he was such a perfectionist.'

On 20 November, *Top of the Pops* broadcast the promo for 'Bohemian Rhapsody'. On a day off between dates in Cardiff and

Taunton, Queen and members of their support band Mr Big gathered in a hotel room to watch it on TV. It was the first time any of Queen had seen the finished promo. 'There was much hilarity,' remembered Brian May, as the group crowded around the set, watching themselves in action, their four disembodied heads 'singing' the operatic section, even the head of John Deacon, the one member of Queen who never sang in the studio, and whose microphone was always turned down onstage.

'I loved the video. I thought it was wonderful,' recalls Mr Big's lead singer Jeff Pain, who performed under the stage name Dicken. In 1977 Mr Big would have a Top 5 hit with the single 'Romeo'. In 1975, they were being managed by Mott The Hoople's handler Bob Hirschman and touting their debut album *Sweet Silence*, a much heavier record than their later hit would suggest. 'Fred told us how much he liked *Sweet Silence*, particularly a song of ours called "Zambia". They used to keep putting the album on when we were travelling in the bus together. I used to feel embarrassed: "No, no, Freddie, please play *Sheer Heart Attack* . . ."'

The two bands had met at Elstree just before the tour was due to start. 'Queen were farting about onstage, and it sounded awful,' says Dicken. 'We watched them and thought, "Oh, we're gonna blow them offstage." Then we got to Liverpool, and I stood at the side when Queen were on and just went, "Oh!"'

On 21 November, the day after 'Bohemian Rhapsody' debuted on *Top of the Pops*, EMI released *A Night at the Opera*. While overshadowed by its epic single, the rest of the album hardly trailed behind in the scope of its ambition. In later years, it would become a clichéd statement for rock groups to make, but Brian May's explanation 'we wanted *A Night at the Opera* to be our *Sgt Pepper*' was no exaggeration. The album had been created in six different studios, with, on occasion, three studios being used simultaneously. Its cost was estimated at a then unheard of £40,000, leading to a rumour that it was the most expensive album ever made (later denied by the band). Such was the band's ceaseless meddling that they'd missed their deadline of a release in time for the tour. No sooner had the band premiered *A Night at the Opera* at a press reception at London's Roundhouse Studios, than Roy Thomas

Baker whisked the tapes back into the studio to continue the process of fine-tuning. 'This album combines the outrageousness of *Queen II* and the good songs of *Sheer Heart Attack*,' Mercury told the press. 'The finest songs ever written.' As a final flourish, the album artwork featured a very regal crest, incorporating lions, fairies and a swan over the band's Q logo. 'The advertising side of me comes out in that aspect,' Mercury explained. 'We look upon it as a campaign, a project.'

The album's opening song was outrageous enough. Written by Mercury 'Death on Two Legs (Dedicated to . . .)', found the singer spitting bile about blood-sucking leeches and decaying sewer rats, and seemed to have been inspired by some perceived wrong-doers. It wasn't until the album sleeve had been manufactured and an EMI executive read the lyrics that the label had doubts (Paul Watts: 'Someone said, "Are you sure about this?"'). The song's lyrics were so vicious that Mercury recalled May 'feeling bad singing it'. But 'Death on Two Legs' was very much the singer's baby. 'In the studio, Freddie was insistent on having the headphones so loud in order to reach the high notes that his ears started bleeding,' recalls Gary Langan. (Mercury himself told a reporter that it was his throat that bled.)

The camp vaudeville of 'Lazing on a Sunday Afternoon' came as light relief, and Queen explored a similar mood with 'Seaside Rendezvous' and 'Good Company'. The rest of the album also illustrated the eclectic nature of the band's songwriting. Mercury's 'Love of my Life' was the subtlest of ballads that paid lip service to his great passion for classical music. Mercury even coerced May into playing the harp on the song; a process fraught with difficulty as the instrument kept slipping frustratingly in and out of tune.

After the inconsequential 'Misfire' on *Sheer Heart Attack*, John Deacon's 'You're My Best Friend' sounded like the work of a completely different songwriter. The antithesis of 'Bohemian Rhapsody', it was a disarmingly simple pop song, dedicated to his wife, and featuring its composer playing electric piano (Taylor: 'Freddie thought the electric piano was vastly inferior to the grand'). 'You're My Best Friend' managed to sound unlike anything Queen had done before, but still wholly convincing; a trick the band would achieve again and again in years to come.

John Anthony's belief that Roger Taylor was Queen's most obvious pop star seems confirmed by his contribution to *A Night at the Opera*. But 'I'm in Love With My Car' was actually inspired by the band's soundman John Harris – a 'boy racer to the end', said Taylor – whose pride and joy was his Triumph TR-4, although Taylor sampled the sound of his own Alfa Romeo on the song. 'I'm in Love With My Car' was eventually chosen as the B-side of 'Bohemian Rhapsody', earning the drummer considerable royalties. As Brian May explained, 'At the time, we'd always work on each other's songs, but when it came to credits, the person who came up with the original idea would go, "I wrote the fucking song, so I'm taking the writing credit." A lot of terrible injustices take place over songwriting. The major one is B-sides. "Bohemian Rhapsody" sells a million and Roger gets the same writing royalties as Freddie because he did "I'm in Love With My Car". There was contention about that for years.' Queen would finally change this rule for 1982's hit single 'Under Pressure'. 'A wise decision,' said Taylor, 'as that financial side of things can be very divisive.'

The rather one-dimensional 'Sweet Lady' aside, Brian May's writing on *A Night at the Opera* was as varied as that of his bandmates. The straight-ahead folk song '39' was sung by May with lyrics supposedly inspired by German poet and novelist Hermann Hesse. 'It's a science fiction story,' May told a BBC interviewer. 'It's about someone who goes away and leaves his family, and when he comes back, he's aged a year and they've aged a hundred years.' Not for the last time, the guitarist had written a song expressing his misgivings about being away from his home and his family.

However, May's greatest coup was 'The Prophet's Song', a number of more than eight minutes. 'It's this outrageous, mammoth track,' Mercury told Kenny Everett. May claimed the song had been inspired by a dream, and that it tapped into his fears about the human race: their lack of empathy and interaction. 'People don't make enough contact with each other,' he explained. With its Wagnerian riff, biblical feel and an a cappella vocal interlude featuring countless overdubs, it had all the ambition of 'Bohemian

Rhapsody', but not the pop hook. After 'Bohemian Rhapsody', the album closed with Queen's own short version of the national anthem. At the playback party, Mercury, typically, leapt to his feet during 'God Save the Queen' and demanded the press do the same: 'Stand up, you *cunts!*'

Onstage, the singer had become especially quick-witted. After Mercury was heckled at Manchester's Free Trade Hall ('You fucking poof!'), he ordered a spotlight to be turned on his tormentor ('Say that again, darling'). On 25 November, four days after *Top of the Pops*, the news broke that 'Bohemian Rhapsody' had reached number 1. 'We'd just played in Southampton,' remembers Dicken. 'It was a wonderful moment for them.' On a rare day off, a Queen and Mr Big entourage went to see the funk band Hot Chocolate in concert. Their hit single 'You Sexy Thing' had been scaling the charts, but had now been stopped at number 2. 'Their singer Errol Brown came up to us after the show and said to Brian, "You bastards! That was my chance of a Christmas number one."'

Back on the road, high spirits took over when one member of Mr Big acquired a carpenter's plane, and began shearing off chunks of wood in one of the hotel lifts. 'I think we were in Birmingham,' says Dicken. 'But he was seen doing it by the comedian Dickie Henderson, who was staying at the hotel. Dickie went and reported it to the management and he got us all banned. Freddie was not best pleased.' Dicken also saw how distanced Mercury could be from everyone else, when the mood took him. 'On the coach, he'd spend most of his time with his minder and Mary Austin. Me and Mr Big's drummer John Burnip would be allowed into his dressing room, but we were the only ones from the band.' Regrettably, the tour's five-night run at London's Hammersmith Odeon was marred when the Mr Big singer fell into the orchestra pit. 'I landed on a photographer,' he explains, 'and broke my guitar.'

A few days later, the tour bus was pulled over by the police between Newcastle and Dundee. One of the crew had been fired earlier, and is believed to have placed an anonymous call claiming there were drugs on the bus. Some of the crew were found with tiny amounts of amphetamines, but Queen and Mr Big had nothing, bar a bottle of Southern Comfort and a packet of aspirin. Freddie would soon discover cocaine, but, as Peter Hince recalls, 'drugs were very taboo amongst the band back then'. When asked by one of the officers whether he indulged, Freddie, dolled up as ever in fur coat and eyeliner, replied, 'Don't be so impertinent, you stupid little man!'

The tour ended with two nights at the Glasgow Apollo, but promoter Mel Bush threw in another Christmas Eve show at the Hammersmith Odeon. The concert would be broadcast live on BBC radio and also on *The Old Grey Whistle Test*.

'Bohemian Rhapsody' spent seventeen weeks in the charts, nine of them at number 1. For Bruce Gowers, the brains behind the promo video, it was a slightly hollow victory. In 1973 Gowers had directed an Emmy-winning documentary, *Aquarius: Hello Dali!* with Salvador Dali. 'But my phone never rang,' he said. Then came 'Bohemian Rhapsody'. 'I did one lousy six-minute video and the phone never stopped.' Gowers would go on to become a director on the US reality TV show *American Idol*.

For EMI's Martin Nelson, Queen's success was validation for all their efforts. 'I'd spent hours on the road with them,' he says. 'All of them crammed into my company Ford Cortina estate, where Brian had to sit in the bit behind the passenger seat as his legs were so long. But they'd done everything asked of them. Freddie may have become outrageous later, but what I'd seen was a very dedicated working vocalist. It was a work of genius to get "Bohemian Rhapsody" on Capital Radio, because after that other DJs thought it was OK to play the record, but only after Kenny Everett.' As EMI's Bob Mercer admits: 'It was all Queen's doing. The only thing EMI were smart enough to do was say, "Yes."'

Some of the press pounced on the amount of money and studio time spent on *A Night at the Opera*. 'It sounds as if the production team were having a little too much fun in the control room,' wrote *Melody Maker*. *NME*'s Tony Stewart concluded: 'If it is the most expensive album ever made, it's also arguably the best. God save me.' With the single at number 1, it took three weeks for *A Night at the Opera* to follow it to the top of the charts. Critical suspicion remained, but readers of all the music papers would nominate

Queen for the likes of Best British Single and Best Band in the months ahead.

With another US tour due to start in the New Year, *A Night at the Opera* had been released in America in December. Kris Nicholson, writing in *Rolling Stone*, praised 'Queen's willingness to experiment, even when they fail', concluding that of 'all the heavy metal groups . . . Queen is obviously the strongest contender in the field'. The album would go on to spend seven weeks in the US Top 10, peaking at number 4.

Back in England, Mercury scooped another Ivor Novello Award for 'Bohemian Rhapsody', which had just shifted over one million copies. But when he received his gold disc commemorating *A Night at the Opera*, he was suspicious. Believing the powers-that-be at EMI were too miserly to provide the real thing, Mercury was convinced the disc inside the frame was not his own album. He broke it open and put the record on a turntable, shocked to discover that it really was *A Night at the Opera*.

Such suspicion and erratic behaviour seemed to have become part of the Freddie Mercury persona. Bruised by his experience with Trident, Freddie, even more so than the rest of the group, questioned everything and everyone. Somewhere inside, behind the fur coat, the hair, the nail polish and the endless 'darlings' and 'dears', he was still Fred Bulsara. 'I seem to have created a monster,' Mercury said at the time. 'When I'm performing I'm an extrovert, yet inside I'm a completely different man.'

Despite his public relationship with Mary Austin, Mercury was now struggling with his sexuality. In the spring of 1975, the singer had met 25-year-old record executive David Minns through a mutual friend. Minns worked for Paul McCartney and had recently begun managing a singer-songwriter named Eddie Howell. One night, while drinking at a club on the Kings Road, Mercury kissed him on the cheek. Minns was openly gay, but he was surprised that a male pop singer would display such public affection for another man (although, as *EMI*'s Martin Nelson recalls, 'My wife remembers Fred kissing me on the cheek. That's just what he did').

Minns was invited to the studio to hear a playback of 'Bohemian

Rhapsody'. Before long, David and Freddie had become lovers. 'Freddie was a very sweet guy,' said Minns in a 2004 interview. 'He was highly sexed and just latched on to you.' Unfortunately, Freddie had been a little economical with the truth regarding his home life. Minns was introduced to Mary Austin, believing her relationship with Freddie to be platonic. But when the three of them went back to the Holland Road flat, David was shocked to see only one bedroom: 'There was clearly more to the relationship than he had been able to tell me.'

Interviewed in 2000, Mary recalled a shift in Mercury's behaviour towards her as early as the release of the first Queen album. 'Things were never the same after that,' she said. 'Our relationship cooled. When I came home from work, he just wouldn't be there. He would come in late. We just weren't as close as we had been.'

The even greater success of 'Bohemian Rhapsody' and *A Night at the Opera* seemed to magnify the distance between the couple. While Queen struggled in penury, Mary had been the breadwinner. Now Mercury had money, recognition and fame. When the singer joined his sister Kashmira for a day out in York, he found himself trailed by schoolchildren who recognised him. Yet he could no longer hide in private, either. At some point, Mercury confessed all to Mary. 'He said, "I think I'm bisexual,"' Austin recalled. 'I told him, "I think you're gay." And nothing else was said. We just hugged.'

Brian May's theory that 'Bohemian Rhapsody' reflected the battles Mercury was having in his personal life is supported by Peter Freestone, Mercury's personal assistant through the 1980s and 1990s. 'If you look at the way "Bohemian Rhapsody" is written, it's in three parts that describe Freddie's life,' said Freestone. 'Living with Mary, his coming to terms with his desire for men, and his actual sleeping with men.' Mick Rock, who had always presumed that his friend 'liked boys and girls', saw the song as indicative of something more: '"Bohemian Rhapsody" changed everything, That was when he threw all caution to the wind.'

Through his new boyfriend, Mercury worked outside of Queen for the first time. Minns's client Eddie Howell had recently been signed as a songwriter to Warner Brothers. Mercury was in the audience at Howell's showcase gig at Kensington's Thursday Club in the autumn of 1975, and was especially impressed by a new composition called 'The Man From Manhattan'. He asked if he could produce the song.

In the end, Mercury and Mike Stone would co-produce the track during sessions for *A Night at the Opera* at Sarm East Studios. Freddie played piano with Brian May contributing the guitar solo. Howell marvelled as Mercury worked out intricate harmonies in the same idiosyncratic notation Queen had seen him use for 'Bohemian Rhapsody'. Meanwhile, even at £60 an hour, the singer seemed unperturbed by the cost of the session. When a bell he wanted used for the final note of the song turned out to unsuitable (Howell: 'D was the correct note and there wasn't a D-pitched bell in the studio'), a studio minion was sent off to find the right one. Several hours and hundreds of pounds of extra studio time later, the song was completed.

The lyrics for 'The Man From Manhattan' had been inspired by Mario Puzo's hit novel *The Godfather*; musically it took its cue from The Kinks. However, under Mercury's direction the song veered closer towards Queen, becoming something that wouldn't sound out of place on *A Night at the Opera*. 'It was great, but I did make a conscious effort not to include John Deacon and Roger Taylor,' said Howell. 'They would have played on it, but I wanted the song to retain some of my own identity.'

Freddie's parting shot to Howell — 'You should sue Warner Brothers if this isn't a hit' — didn't help. Released in 1976, the song sank due to lack of promotion after it was discovered that the American bassist playing on the session didn't have a work permit. 'The Man From Manhattan' would find its way into Queen's soundchecks, and appear on a Queen box set in 2000. Meanwhile, following his brush with royalty, Eddie Howell would return to an under-the-radar career as a songwriter for hire.

By the time the North American leg of the *A Night at the Opera* tour began in late January 1976, 'Bohemian Rhapsody' had been in the US charts for three weeks, inching its way up to number 59. During the weekend that Kenny Everett had blanket-bombed the airwaves, Paul Drew, programme director of the RKO group of American radio stations, was in London and heard the record.

Drew acquired a tape of the song and began playing it on air in the States. Queen's label, now Elektra/Asylum, just like EMI a few months before, had been forced into releasing it as a single. 'It was the same in America,' said Mercury. 'A six-minute single? You must be joking! Oh, you just got away with it in Britain.'

The tour took in theatres in Waterbury Connecticut, Boston and Philadelphia before reaching a four-night run at New York's Beacon Theater. Here, they joined Ian Hunter and Roy Thomas Baker at Electric Ladyland Studios, where Mercury, May and Taylor performed on one song on his upcoming *All American Alien Boy* album. With Jack Nelson gone, Queen had now appointed Hendrix's former road manager Gerry Stickells as their tour manager, while Roger Taylor had acquired his own drum tech, Chris 'Crystal' Taylor. Personal assistant Pete Brown's duties now extended to removing the thorns from the roses that Freddie regularly tossed into the audience, and appearing as a Freddie look-alike onstage during 'Now I'm Here'. The vocal echo used on the song would be accompanied by Brown flashing into view on one side of the stage, before the real Mercury appeared on the opposite side. However, dressing up as Mercury and tending his flowers would be the least of Brown's problems on the tour. Coping with the singer's airs and graces presented a far greater challenge.

Queen were a far bigger act in the US now than they had been even twelve months before, but aftershow parties in their honour still required attendance from the band themselves. While the rest of Queen would show willing and press the flesh, Mercury became increasingly prone to, as David Minns recalled, 'turning on his heel and flouncing out' at the first sight of Queen's record company paymasters, assorted hacks and hangers-on. According to Minns and others within the entourage, the crux of the problem was lack of control. At his own parties, Freddie would happily play the attentive host. At parties thrown for him, he would become as shy and tongue-tied as the eighteen-year-old Farrokh Bulsara showing up for his first day at Isleworth Polytechnic. Unlike his teenage student self, Mercury could now throw a tantrum without fear of parental reprisal. He was the singer, the pop star, and he was indulged accordingly.

Interviewed in New York for American TV, though, it was Mercury that answered the questions while the rest of the band sat mute beside him. 'Is this the future? Is this where rock is going?' asked his interviewer. Fussing with his hair, the singer fired back: 'There's no message, I'm not trying to put anything across.' He grinned. 'It's just rock 'n' roll.'

Queen had acquired two Elektra/Asylum support acts for different legs of the tour. Both Southern soul duo The Cate Brothers and Detroit rockers Bob Seger and the Silver Bullet Band were quite unlike the headliners. The US press was bemused by the 'Jekyll and Hyde pairing' but the tour progressed without bloodshed or a repeat of the previous year's spat with Lynyrd Skynyrd.

Onstage, Mercury showed no reticence whatsoever. 'I'm going to sing until my throat is like a vulture's crotch,' he forewarned one reporter. Between songs, he threw thornless roses into the throng and toasted them with champagne. At one show, a female fan rushed to the front and began waving at him between songs. Eventually, Mercury sidled over and asked haughtily, 'Yes, my dear, what do you want?' When it became apparent that she just wanted to touch him, he took the teenage girl's hand daintily before whispering, 'For you, a gentle touch.'

Closing with four nights at Santa Monica Civic Auditorium and a final show at San Diego Sports Arena, the press applauded Queen's 'purist hard rock' and predicted that the band would be filling 10,000-seaters next time round. By the end of the tour, 'Bohemian Rhapsody' had made its way into the Top 20, ultimately reaching number 9. But America's love affair with the song would never equal Britain's, at least not until it was re-released following Mercury's death. *Rolling Stone*'s Steven Turner marvelled at the overdubs and lyrics that were 'simultaneously violent and mystifying', but there was still a suggestion that Queen were a European phenomenon and that Mercury's 'queenly stage demeanour' could hold them back in America.

In the UK, Queen's concert film from the Rainbow began playing in cinemas across the country, just as the band began another eight-night tour of Japan. Greeted with even greater adulation than on their first visit, the trip gave Mercury the

'We all wanted to be Elvis': Farrokh (né Fred) Bulsara (right) with fellow pupils and Hectics bandmates Victory Rana and Bruce Murray, St Peter's School, Panchgani, India, circa 1958.
Courtesy of Bruce Murray

The 'charmingly shy' Fred Bulsara (third right), with his earliest friends in England, including Patrick Connolly (fourth right), Brian Fanning (second right) and Adrian Morrish (far right), Isleworth Polytechnic, 1965.
Courtesy of Adrian Morrish

Fred Bulsara with fellow students (clockwise, from left) Tim Staffell, the late Paul Fielder and Chris Smith (back to the camera), Ealing Technical College And School Of Art, London, 1969.
Courtesy of Mark Haywood

Fred Bulsara and friends, impersonating The Shadows outside 42b Addison Gardens, Shepherds Bush (from left): Paul Humberstone, Richard Thompson, Bulsara, Tim Staffell (in Hank Marvin-style glasses) and Chris Smith, circa 1969. *Courtesy of Mark Haywood*

Fred Bulsara (far right) on the weekend of his first gig as a lead singer, with members of Ibex and their entourage, including Mick 'Miffer' Smith (far left) and Ken Testi (third left, seated), Bolton, August 1969. *Courtesy of Mark Haywood*

Four fifths of 1984 (from left): Richard Thompson, Tim Staffell, Brian May and John 'Jag' Garnham, at an airfield in Hertfordshire, 1964. *Courtesy of Richard Thompson*

Sour Milk Sea, photographed for the *Oxford Mail*, March 1970. From left: Fred Bulsara ('He told us his name was Fred Bull'), Chris Chesney (né Dummett), Jeremy 'Rubber' Gallop (seated), Paul Milne and Rob Tyrrel.

'Super-brain' Brian May (bottom, right) with 1984 bandmates (from top left) John 'Jag' Garnham and Richard Thompson and (bottom left) Dave Dilloway, circa 1968. *Courtesy of Richard Thompson*

The Reaction, winners of the Cornwall Rock and Rhythm Championship, 1966. From left: Jim Craven, Geoff 'Ben' Daniel, Roger Brokenshire, Roger Taylor, Mike Dudley and John 'Acker' Snell.
Courtesy of Geoff Daniel

The Opposition: (from left) Nigel Bullen, Richard Young, Ron Chester, Dave Williams, and a 16-year-old John Deacon, photographed for the *Leicester Mercury*, 1967.

The one that got away: bass player Tim Staffell, recording with Smile, Trident Studios, London, June 1969.
Courtesy of Mark Haywood

'I felt a bit sorry for myself': Douglas Bogie, Queen bassist, fired after just two shows in 1971. *Courtesy of Douglas Bogie*

'They wanted the world, and they wanted it no later than teatime on Friday': Queen, Imperial College, London, 2 November 1973. *Mick Rock/Retna Pictures*

QUEEN INVITE YOU TO A NIGHT AT THE OPERA

TH ODEON

Rock Opera: London's famous Hammersmith Odeon, during Queen's sold-out five-night run, November to December, 1975. *Peter Hince*

'I yell much less than the others': John Deacon, Wessex Studios, London, Autumn 1976. *Peter Hince*

Queen go gospel: recording the video for 'Somebody to Love', Wessex Studios, London, Autumn 1976. *Peter Hince*

Peter 'Ratty' Hince, future head of the Queen road crew, inspecting John Deacon's bass, 1977. *Peter Hince*

Court jester: Freddie Mercury and John Deacon, A Day at the Races tour 1977. *Rex Features*

Love of my life: Freddie Mercury with former girlfriend Mary Austin, Hotel Eden Palace au Lac, Montreux, 1978.
Peter Hince

Queen's state-of-the-art lighting rig, 'The Pizza Oven', being fired up before its first use at Dallas Convention Centre, 28 October 1978.
Peter Hince

Queen, at Mountain Studios, Montreux, recording the *Jazz* album, 1978. The band would buy the studio in 1979. *Peter Hince*

Freddie Mercury hiding behind his own image, Musicland Studios, Munich, Spring 1979. *Peter Hince*

'I wasn't quite Baryshnikov': Freddie Mercury rehearsing with the Royal Ballet Company, London, October 1979. *Rex Features*

Brian May breaks Queen's 'no synthesisers' rule, Mountain Studios, Montreux, Autumn 1981. *Peter Hince*

Freddie Mercury and producer Reinhold Mack ('His job was to make it fresh and new and exciting'), Musicland Studios, Munich, 1981. *Peter Hince*

Roger Taylor relaxing during the recording sessions for Queen's David Bowie collaboration, 'Under Pressure' ('A clash of the titans'), Mountain Studios, Montreux, 1981. *Peter Hince*

Queen celebrating the last night of the Hot Space tour at Seibu Lyons Stadium, Tokorozawa, Japan, 3 November 1982. *Peter Hince*

On the set of Radio Ga Ga, Shepperton Studios, January 1984. *Peter Hince*

Freddie Mercury lights up ('He smoked like a schoolgirl') on the set of the 'Radio Ga Ga' video shoot, Shepperton Studios, January 1984. *Peter Hince*

Huge plastic falsies: Freddie Mercury and a make-up assistant, on the set of the video for 'I Want To Break Free', Limehouse Studios, London, March 1984. *Peter Hince*

Freddie Mercury on the set of 'our worst video ever' for 'It's A Hard Life', Munich, 1984. *Mirrorpix*

'I have to win people over': Freddie Mercury grapples with the BBC cameraman, Live Aid, Wembley Stadium. *Rex Features*

Freddie Mercury and Brian May performing 'Is This The World We Created?', Live Aid, Wembley Stadium, 13 July 1985. *Getty Images*

Freddie Mercury with musical collaborator Billy Squier, Sarm East studios, London, 1986. *Peter Hince*

Queen get airborne: Freddie Mercury and inflatable friend, Knebworth Park, Stevenage, 9 August 1986. *Getty Images*

One last fling: Freddie Mercury and Brian May, Knebworth Park. *Getty Images*

By royal appointment: Freddie Mercury in crown and ermine, London, 1987. *Peter Hince*

A night at the opera: Freddie Mercury and Montserrat Caballé performing Barcelona, 1987. *Rex Features*

Freddie Mercury with Brian May and Roger Taylor, BPI Awards, February 1990. *Getty Images*

LOGAN PLACE

Fans' tributes on the door of Mercury's former property, Garden Lodge, 1 Logan Place, Kensington, London. *PA Photos*

George Michael, Lisa Stansfield and Brian May, A Concert For AIDS Awareness as a tribute to Freddie Mercury, Wembley Stadium, 20 April 1992. *Rex Features*

The show must go on: Liza Minnelli with Roger Taylor and Brian May, The Freddie Mercury Tribute: A Concert For AIDS Awareness, Wembley Stadium, 20 April 1992. *Rex Features*

Brian May performing 'God Save The Queen' on the roof of Buckingham Palace, the Queen's Jubilee Concert, 3 June 2002. *Rex Features*

Freddie Mercury's statue outside London's Dominion Theatre, home of the record-breaking *We Will Rock You* stage musical. *Rex Features*

Paul Rodgers and Brian May, the Q + PR tour, Budapest, Hungary, 23 April 2005. *Rex Features*

'Goodnight and sweet dreams':
Freddie Mercury, the Magic
tour, 1986. *Rex Features*

opportunity to indulge in some retail therapy. 'The Japanese call it "crazy shopping",' he explained. 'I walk around like the Pied Piper with hordes of people following me, shouting out, "You crazee shopping!"' Accompanied by the Japanese promoter's wife, Mercury's spending sprees would be conducted in empty department stores which had been left open for his pleasure. It would then fall to Pete Brown to freight the antique chairs, clothes, artworks and Japanese woodcuts back to England.

'Pete was a fantastic tour manager,' explains Caroline Boucher. 'But he was also massively dyslexic. How he managed with all those sheets of paper and itineraries and timings . . . especially in Japan. Apparently, he used to memorise the shapes on each of the band's hotel keys as a way of knowing whose room was whose.'

Gary Langan witnessed a similar episode of 'crazy shopping' in London. 'I think Queen had finally got their royalty cheques out of Trident,' he recalls. Mercury had raided Harrods before moving onto Christopher Wray on the Kings Road and acquiring a set of Tiffany lamps. 'When he came back he said, "Darlings, I couldn't spend another penny more!"

'Fred did enjoy his money,' agreed Roger Taylor. 'But he also exaggerated about his spending, because he knew that it would get right up people's noses. He did it on purpose.' After years of scraping by, every *objet d'art*, every Louis XIV chair purchased was a riposte to the critics, the Sheffields, the doubters at Ealing art college.

With just a week to get over the jet-lag, Queen followed Japan with a short tour of Australia in April. It would be their first visit to the country since the ill-fated Sunbury Festival two years earlier. At that gig, Mercury had told the audience that when Queen returned to their country they would be the biggest band in the world. While not quite the case, both 'Bohemian Rhapsody' and *A Night at the Opera* had sold well in Australia and New Zealand.

Queen had also sold out the majority of the shows in Perth, Adelaide, Melbourne and Brisbane. But before their first gig at the Hordern Pavilion in Sydney, Mercury threw an extraordinary tantrum. An annual fair was taking place in the grounds of the venue, making it inaccessible by car. When the band was advised to make the short trip through the fairground to the venue on foot, Mercury refused. Instead, his limousine nudged its way through hordes of people, while Freddie sat in the back seat, sipping champagne and ignoring the insults and catcalls from those outside. Inside his dressing room, the singer, in a rage, grabbed a mirror and smashed it over Pete Brown's head, supposedly showering the room with glass. Recounting the incident in 1996, Brown simply explained: 'He just had to take it out on someone, and that time it was me.' Peter Hince remembers the incident, but points out that had it been a full-size mirror, Brown would have been seriously injured: 'I do believe that Freddie made Pete sweep up the glass afterwards.'

'Pete Brown could have a pretty short fuse at times,' offers Caroline Boucher. 'But I think he was good at keeping it in check around the band. But both he and his brother Steve, who was Elton John's first producer, came from a Salvation Army background. That must have taught him an enormous amount of patience and fortitude.'

In May, during a three-month break, Brian May married girlfriend Christine Mullen at St Osmund's Roman Catholic church in Barnes. By now, he had left the dismal Earls Court bedsit and bought a modest semi-detached house for the couple in Suffolk Road, Barnes. His bandmates' living conditions had also finally improved. Deacon, his wife Veronica and son Robert had their own Victorian semi in Putney. Roger Taylor, soon to become flush from the royalties for 'Bohemian Rhapsody' and its B-side 'I'm in Love With My Car', had rather more money at his disposal, and moved into a house in upmarket Fulham, later adding a Surrey countryhouse to his property portfolio.

By the end of the year, Mercury and Mary Austin's relationship would change for ever. Freddie moved out of their shared flat and in to another at 12 Stafford Terrace, Holland Park. As a parting gift, Mercury later bought Mary a £30,000 flat nearby. But as she explained, 'I could see Freddie's own flat from my bathroom. I thought, "Oh, I'm never going to get away."' Mary would also go on to work for Mercury in his newly formed production company Goose Productions.

Mercury and Austin's relationship would outlast almost all of the singer's relationships with men. Their friendship endured, despite their change in circumstances. To the press and to the public, they were still a couple. By playing up his campness, Mercury had become even more adroit at deflecting intrusive questions about his private life and sexual orientation. In 1976, when asked whether he was straight, gay or bi-sexual, the singer replied: 'I sleep with men, women, cats, you name it . . .'

In June, EMI released the single 'You're My Best Friend'. It reached number 7 and, later, number 12 in the States. As one EMI insider explains, 'It was the anti-"Bohemian Rhapsody".' A charming love song, free of operatics and running to a manageable length, it was unlikely to scare the horses.

Queen, restless as ever, were already moving on to the next project. In July, they booked into the Manor studio, in Oxfordshire, owned by Virgin Records supremo Richard Branson, to start work on another album. Roy Thomas Baker's four-album contract with Queen had now expired. By mutual agreement, Queen would produce their fifth album themselves, with Gary Langan and Mike Stone engineering.

'Roy's ego was exploding,' laughs Langan, 'and he went off to America.' Baker had signed a deal with CBS Records, and was busily producing the likes of Ian Hunter. Over the next few months, though, he would drop in and out of Queen's lives, checking on their progress and offering advice. The relationship between the two parties seemed to be that of a parent looking on, anxiously, as their child heads off to make his own way in the world. 'Taking more responsibility has been good for us,' Mercury explained. 'Roy's been great, but we simply felt that it was now or never.'

Queen had proved themselves as a hit album and hit singles band. Yet they now faced the challenge of repeating that success, without being seen to repeat the ideas they'd used before. Roy Thomas Baker's mantra of 'no problems just challenges' seemed an appropriate mission statement for the job ahead.

'Queen took the success of *A Night at the Opera* in their stride,' says Gary Langan. 'It wasn't like dealing a team of football players, where you take a player off the street, give them a huge wage and they go off the rails. Queen were intelligent guys, and because of their aptitude they dealt with it very well.' Nevertheless, the pressure-cooker environment of making a Queen album still took its toll. 'There were huge rows some days,' explains Langan. 'Freddie could throw the biggest tantrums of all – pure rage. But it was all about the music.'

Others would see a different side to the singer that summer. One afternoon at the Manor, Mercury asked to be driven back to London to visit Mary. Without his regular car or chauffeur on hand, Peter Hince agreed to drive Freddie in a car borrowed from the studio. Approaching a roundabout in West London, the brakes failed and the car smashed into a pile of drainpipes stacked next to some roadworks. Unhurt, Freddie clambered out of the car, marched to the nearest house and asked to use the owners' tele-phone. 'I'll never forget him standing by the roadside,' says Hince. 'He hadn't shaved for two days, he was wearing white clogs, blue jeans and a Japanese kimono with "Queen" written on the back.' Astonished to find Queen's lead singer on the doorstep, the resi-dents let him use the phone and made him a cup of tea, but only after Hince had scavenged a few coins for their gas meter, which had just run out. EMI's Brian Southall later heard from someone in the Queen camp that Mercury arranged for several hundred pounds in small change to be sent to the flat, by way of a thank you.

A month into the sessions, the band realised that they were behind schedule, and that a planned summer release was impossible. With a full tour postponed, Queen agreed to play two open-air shows and two nights at a theatre. The outdoor shows would be held in September at Cardiff Castle and London's Hyde Park. The warm-up shows were at the Edinburgh Playhouse, a venue now being sponsored by John Reid, and into which he had block-booked a week of his own acts, including Elton John. Before then, though, Mercury celebrated his thirtieth birthday with a lavish party at a cabaret club on the Kings Road, treating his 150 guests to caviar, lobster and Cristal champagne, after personally handwriting every one of their invitations.

At Cardiff Castle, Queen were joined by Manfred Mann's Earth Band, Frankie Miller and Andy Fairweather-Low. Like a scene out of *This Is Spinal Tap*, ex-Deep Purple guitarist Ritchie Blackmore's new band Rainbow withdrew from the bill when refused permission for their 35-feet stage prop of a giant rainbow. Onstage, Queen premiered two new songs, fresh from the Manor sessions. 'You Take My Breath Away' was a highly dramatic showcase for Mercury's piano and voice with lyrics that are now impossible to ignore in the light of the singer's tangled love life. Brian May's 'Tie Your Mother Down' was also given its first public airing. The song's riff dated back to the summer he'd spent working at an observatory in Tenerife. 'I was on top of a mountain, playing some riffs while the sun came up, when the words to that song came into my head,' he says. 'I thought it was a crap title, but Freddie said it meant something to him, so he knows the answer, and who am I to argue?' 'Tie Your Mother Down' would become a mainstay of Queen's live set on the tours that followed.

The free Hyde Park show was held a week later, on the sixth anniversary of Jimi Hendrix's death, and had been organised by Richard Branson. Brian May had watched Pink Floyd at the inaugural free concert in the park in 1968. A year later, The Rolling Stones had played the same event. Queen agreed to an hour-long headlining slot on an eclectic bill that also included Kiki Dee, Steve Hillage and a Liverpudlian funk band called Supercharge. Their guitarist Les Karski had been at Ealing art college with Fred Bulsara, but although he met him backstage, Karski was unable to recognise Freddie Mercury such was the reinvention ('He'd changed so much since those days').

Over 150,000 people filled the park, while Capital Radio broadcasted live with Queen fan Kenny Everett among the DJs commentating. For Roger Taylor, there was an added attraction to playing Hyde Park: Richard Branson's beautiful personal assistant Dominique Beyrand, with whom he would begin a relationship.

After being smuggled into the park in the back of a laundry van, Freddie's pre-show nerves boiled over in the backstage area. Before long, he was hurling abuse at the freeloaders and demanding they go out front and watch the show. David Minns would describe such behaviour as 'Freddie pitting himself against an imaginary foe to get the adrenalin going'. Onstage, Queen found room for 'You

Take My Breath Away', but their set was cut short after they over-ran by thirty minutes and broke a police curfew. Mercury was threatened with arrest if he set foot on the stage again. Although furious at being denied his encore, as tour manager Gerry Stickells recounted, 'the thought of being in jail in tights didn't appeal to Freddie at all'.

Reviewing the Cardiff Castle show, *Record Mirror* wrote: 'Queen don't worry about competition. Queen don't worry about any-thing.' Unfazed by the size of their audience, the band positively embraced the scale of the event. They wanted more. 'We always said we wanted to be the biggest band in the world,' explained Roger Taylor. 'That was the object of the enterprise. What else are you going to say? We'd like to be the fourth biggest!'

■ ■ ■

'I thought it reeked of sequel.' Roy Thomas Baker's impression of Queen's fifth album was less than complimentary. 'It wasn't a dis-appointment,' their former producer insisted. 'Just an observation.' Then again, Queen had set themselves up for the comparison. Released in December 1976, *A Day at the Races*, like its predecessor, was named after a Marx Brothers movie and presented in a sleeve that reprised the crest logo and typography used on *A Night at the Opera*. The band would fight their corner as always, but as Brian May said later, 'I wish in some ways we'd put *A Night at the Opera* and *A Day at the Races* out at the same time. The material for both of them was written at the same time. So I regard the two albums as completely parallel.'

A Day at the Races avoided a rewrite of 'Bohemian Rhapsody' or another 'Prophet's Song'. In the main, it comprised brisk, expensive-sounding pop-rock ('It cost as much as the album before,' confided Roger Taylor), with singles that would sit comfortably on a radio playlist between Electric Light Orchestra, Rod Stewart or Wings.

'Tie Your Mother Down' was a swashbuckling opener that defined Freddie's 'no message, just rock 'n' roll' maxim, by being a modern-day rewrite of the Chuck Berry/Eddie Cochran formula: teenage rebellion, disapproving parents and a bit of sex. The rhythm section delivered a song each: Deacon's 'You and I' was pleasant enough but unlikely to supersede 'You're My Best Friend', while 'Drowse' had Taylor recalling a restless childhood, daydreaming about something, anything, happening. Now that something had happened, the drummer sounded strangely disenchanted.

Brian May's disenchantment was palpable on 'Long Away'. Once again, the guitarist sounded like Queen's liberal conscience, on a quest for greater human understanding while everyone else was popping champagne corks and shopping for Rolls-Royces. For all his good intentions, though, May's song 'White Man' was unintentionally condescending; nobody really wanted to hear Freddie Mercury pleading the plight of the Native American people. Finally, 'Teo Torriatte (Let Us Cling Together)' was a plaintive love song that even included some Japanese lyrics, a thank you to the country's fans.

It seemed as if Mercury was better at the shopping and the popping of champagne corks, but behind the frivolity there was so much more going on. 'Some of A Day at the Races is a baroque masterpiece,' May later told Mojo, before adding, 'mainly the stuff I didn't write.' May's false modesty aside, Mercury excelled himself.

'The Millionaire's Waltz' was a song inspired by John Reid, in which May spent weeks creating an orchestra of guitar sounds as per Freddie's instruction (Brian: 'It staggers me the stuff that Fred put into it. I can't even remember how I arrived at all that stuff'); on 'You Take My Breath Away' the singer turning himself into a one-man choir, while 'Good Old-Fashioned Loverboy' was a playful ragtime jazz, in which Mercury, unknown to the outside world, serenaded boyfriend David Minns.

Some of the credit for the vocals on A Day at the Races rests outside the band. 'Mike Stone was the vocal guy,' said Roger Taylor. 'Mike was a rock,' confirms Gary Langan. 'All those stacked-up vocals were his work. Roy Thomas Baker had a way of getting people to jump through hoops, but it was Mike's ability as an engineer that made those moves happen.'

Bigger and brasher than everything else on the album was 'Somebody to Love'. A rolling, piano-heavy soul tune that, incredibly, recalled Ray Charles (with May and Taylor as his Raelettes) and Freddie's personal favourite Aretha Franklin. Six years earlier, Sour Milk Sea's guitarist Chris Chesney had listened to Fred Bulsara praising the Jackson 5 in a house filled with dope-smoking Who fans. 'Somebody to Love' was a realisation of the singer's passion for soul music. On paper, the idea — Queen go gospel — sounded terrible; in the studio it worked.

'Somebody to Love' had been released as a single in November as a trailer for the album. Within three weeks it was at number 2. Kenny Everett conducted a joshing interview with Mercury on air, between playing the whole of the new album, while *A Day at the Races* was launched with a soirée of free booze and food at Kempton Park racetrack. The 86-year-old Groucho Marx sent a telegram at Pete Brown's behest congratulating the band ('I know that you are very successful recording artists. Could it, by any chance, be your sage choice of album titles?') Bruce Murray attended a playback party for *A Day at the Races*, and ran into Mary Austin. It was the first time Murray became fully aware of the significant changes in his old schoolfriend's life. 'I knew he was gay, but I also didn't know,' offers Murray. 'That was the night that Mary told me they were splitting up. She said, "I think the pretence has gone on long enough, Bruce."'

On 1 December, Queen were booked to appear on the early-evening TV show *Today With Bill Grundy*. When Mercury had to make a rare visit to the dentist (his first in fifteen years), the band pulled out, leaving EMI promoter Eric Hall with a problem. In Queen's absence, Hall offered EMI's latest signing, the punk rock group, The Sex Pistols. Plied with free booze and encouraged by Grundy, the band swore like naughty schoolboys. The fallout was extraordinary: the show attracted a record number of complaints and caused a Liverpudlian lorry driver to smash his TV set in disgust; Grundy's TV career was over, and The Sex Pistols became household names overnight.

The next day the *Daily Mirror* blazed with the headline "THE FILTH AND THE FURY" and asked 'Who are these punks?' Musically, they took their cue from The Who, The Rolling Stones and American garage-rock: short, sharp songs with a nihilistic message. It was punk's anti-fashion that caused more concern: cropped hair, ripped clothes, anarchist slogans . . . The image and the idea for The Sex Pistols had both been cooked up by their manager Malcolm McLaren and his girlfriend, the designer Vivienne Westwood, in their boutique, SEX. The shop was on the Kings Road, just a few doors down from Freddie's favourite gay haunt Country Cousin, but Pistols' singer Johnny Rotten, with his bleached hair and blank stare, was a world away from Mercury and his rarefied existence.

In the late 1960s, rock music had moved away from three-minute singles to forty-minute albums and musical experimentation. In the late 1970s the pendulum swung back again. Punk didn't require 180 vocal overdubs or a virtuoso guitarist, and claimed to hold up a mirror to real life. In 1976 Britain was in the grip of an economic crisis, with widespread unemployment and inflation at 13 per cent. In 1977 it would get even worse. Many musicians from the punk era would grow rich, famous and complacent, and inverse snobbery was rife, but a band singing a song called 'The Millionaire's Waltz' and toasting an audience with bubbly was seen by some as incongruous, and even offensive. Queen defended their music as 'escapist'; critics deemed them 'out of touch'. In November, as Queen released the single 'Somebody to Love', The Sex Pistols released 'Anarchy in the UK'.

Queen's already fractious relationship with the music press would become worse. *New Musical Express* now had a weekly readership of around 200,000, and its writers had been championing punk for some time. There was a backlash against the likes of Led Zeppelin and Pink Floyd, but it was Queen that attracted the most disdain. Nick Kent, writing for *NME*, denounced *A Day at the Races* as 'grotesquery of the first order'. But what Kent objected to most of all was the singer: 'Almost everything bearing the composing moniker of one F. Mercury seems to drip with that cutesy-pie mirror-preening essence of ultra-preciousness.'

Eight years before at Ealing art college, Fred Bulsara's fascination with harmony singing had bemused some of the blues-loving students. A year later, when he was singing in a band of his own, he'd insisted on including unfashionable Little Richard covers in their set, while Shirley Bassey's 'Big Spender' had been a mainstay of Queen's show for years. The clues were all there. Mercury loved the unexpected, and had no intention of being restricted by the rock format. Early on, he'd told one reporter, partly in jest, that Queen 'were more Liza Minnelli than Led Zeppelin'. His songwriting and performance on *A Day at the Races* suggested as much, with a side order of Chopin, Mozart, Gilbert and Sullivan, and Noël Coward. This wasn't just rock 'n' roll. On *A Day at the Races*, more than any Queen album before, you can hear why, nearly thirty years later, Mercury's music would be performed on the West End stage. But it was too much for some.

Furthermore, while *NME* dismissed Queen as 'masters of style, void of content', Mercury seemed to fuel the fire, claiming that his music was disposable and throwaway, likening it to a Bic razor, even a used tampon. 'There was more to this than meets the eye,' said Brian May. 'It's like when Fred was first asked if he was gay by a writer and he said, "I'm as gay as a daffodil, dear." It neatly sidestepped the whole question. The fact that he said his song was disposable dispelled any pretension and stopped him having to talk about it. I knew Fred pretty damn well and I know a lot of what was going on, and there's a lot of depth in his songs. That false modesty shouldn't mislead anyone. Even the light stuff and the humour had an undercurrent.'

Despite *NME* and The Sex Pistols, Queen celebrated the New Year with *A Day at the Races* at number 1 in the UK album charts. In January, Queen flew to Milwaukee for the opening night of their American tour. Their support band would be Thin Lizzy. It was an inspired pairing. Formed in Dublin by lead singer and bass guitarist Phil Lynott, Thin Lizzy played hard rock, tempered with folk, blues and Celtic ballads. Lizzy had enjoyed a Top 10 hit a year before with 'The Boys Are Back in Town', and had just released a new album *Johnny the Fox*, but their plans had hit the skids when guitarist Brian Robertson was injured during a fracas at the Speakeasy.

With Robertson temporarily out of the band, Lizzy had reinstated their old guitarist Gary Moore. Lizzy joined the tour in time for a gig at Detroit's Cobo Hall. Mercury was clearly in his element. His entourage now included a 250lb American bodyguard, his masseur, personal assistant Paul Prenter (appointed by John Reid Enterprises, who would go on to become Freddie's personal manager), and Dane Clarke, a show-dancer that Mercury had picked up and who was now on the payroll as his hairdresser.

Thin Lizzy's tour manager Chris O'Donnell was stunned by what he saw: 'He had this coterie of people around him, and it was all "Yes, Freddie", 'No, Freddie",' he says. 'Dane Clarke would prepare his clothes, take him to the car, put him onto a plane, and then into another car, and then on to the soundcheck. Most people would soundcheck at five o'clock, then have a meal from backstage catering with the road crew. But Queen would sit down after a gig and have a full meal with silver service. After a while, Brian and Roger got fed up with it and were asking to go with us to hang out at some clubs after the show. This left Freddie sat alone at this huge expensive meal, furious that his band had abandoned him. He had this concept that you always had supper after a first night . . . so he decided you should do it every night. I had never encountered anything on that level.'

On 28 January, the tour reached Chicago, encountering sub-zero temperatures, snow and ice. The band's equipment trucks had been delayed from the previous gig. But despite the cold, Mercury ignored the promoter's plea and refused to allow the audience queuing outside into the venue until Queen had completed a lengthy soundcheck. 'The others didn't do anything because Fred ran the show,' recalls O'Donnell. Later, at the gig, Queen came under attack from a dozen eggs hurled onto the stage, causing May to slip over during 'The Millionaire's Waltz', after which Mercury berated the audience ('You motherfuckers!'), putting paid to their usual second encore.

Behind the scenes, Phil Lynott was impressed by his Queen counterpart's behaviour. 'Freddie set Phil off on a very difficult trail,' says Chris O'Donnell. 'He got it into his head that if you were not difficult you wouldn't get anywhere. But being difficult and demanding isn't so easy when you're in the support band and it can't be so easily accommodated.'

Temptation on tour would also contribute to the end of Mercury's relationship with David Minns. America, more than England, allowed the singer the freedom to indulge himself. Interviewed in 2004, Minns admitted, 'Freddie was clearly having flings with other people.' During the tour, he took up with a 27-year-old chef named Joe Fanelli.

'We were on tour in the States and suddenly he's got boys following him into his hotel room instead of girls,' said Brian May. 'We're thinking, "Mmmm . . ." and that really was the extent of it. I always had plenty of gay friends, I just didn't realise that Freddie was one of them until much later.'

'The thing is, I remember Freddie before Queen,' adds O'Donnell. 'It was interesting how you can invent this androgynous personality. Boy, was he a hustler. Hanging out at Kensington Market, hanging out with Mary Austin, with whom he was in a loving relationship . . . But there was not a smidgeon of Freddie being gay. It wasn't until he signed with John Reid Enterprises and moved into that circle, with Elton, that he became more flamboyant and found more of an expression in the gay community.'

Brian Southall, EMI's head of promotion, accompanied a posse of journalists to New York for a sold-out gig at New York's Madison Square Garden before flying on to shows in Syracuse and Boston. 'I'm sure Freddie was "out" within the band,' maintains Southall. 'By 1977, there was no question of him not being gay, but it certainly wasn't an issue. But there was very much an attitude from the others of "We do what we do, and Fred does what he does".' Southall recalls that the band 'came together for the gig rather like a football team'. The rest of the time they operated individually: 'Brian was with Chrissy, and he always travelled with English tea and biscuits. He also used to collect matchbooks. There wasn't much frivolity with Brian.' As well as his matchbooks, tea and biscuits, Brian carried a large map of the United States over which he had superimposed the tour itinerary to include flight and hotel details and stopover times.

John Deacon was also travelling with his wife and son. 'I went to a Japanese restaurant with John,' remembers Southall, 'and he had some new fancy Seiko digital watch that had a calculator, so he could add up Queen's royalties in four different countries. Queen, especially John, were always interested in how the business was going. I remember thinking, "Marc Bolan was never like this . . ."'

On a night out, Southall accompanied Phil Lynott and Roger

Taylor to CBGBs, the hub of the New York punk scene. 'There was always frivolity and fun with Roger, but also questions being asked in the house. Roger was the party animal, Brian and John were not, and Freddie was his own party animal.' While the tour was relatively drug-free, Mercury was using cocaine. Fired up on the drug, it was easier for Fred Bulsara to 'be' Freddie Mercury.

Bruce Gowers flew to Miami to shoot a promo film for the next single, 'Tie Your Mother Down'. A fortnight later, Queen sold out two nights at The Forum in Los Angeles. Between the gigs they visited Groucho Marx to present him with a gold disc for sales of *A Night at the Opera* and *A Day at the Races*. It was a timely photo opportunity, with Marx dying just five months later.

After playing San Francisco, Mercury suffered a recurrence of the throat problems that had plagued Queen's last US tour ('I have to take it easy on the red wine,' he told one journalist). Some gigs were cancelled – but the tour resumed for a final run in Vancouver and Alberta. Despite a mutual respect, Queen and Thin Lizzy each gave the other a run for their money. Madison Square Garden was Queen's night; Nassau Coliseum was Lizzy's . . . But as Chris O'Donnell admits: 'However good Thin Lizzy were, once Queen came on with the full production, they wiped the floor with us most nights.' *A Day at the Races* hit number 5 in the US charts, with 'Somebody to Love' at number 13.

The tour also reunited Freddie with one of his friends from pre-Queen days. Mark Malden from Ealing art college had been living in Canada since 1969. He bought tickets for Queen's show at Montreal Forum and managed, after hours of waiting, to make contact with his old friend for the first time in eight years. Mercury was astonished to see him. 'After the show I got a phone call from Dane Clarke, saying, "We are in the lower lobby bar and Fred wants you to have a drink,"' says Malden. 'Our conversation went on for a long time, but the first thing Fred said to me was, "So, Mark, what do you want?" I said, "I don't want anything." He replied, "Everybody from the college that has come to me wants something. One of them wanted me to model their clothes . . . I had to say no and they were upset . . ." At that point, I vowed I would never take anything from him.'

Malden could see the pressure his friend was under, and just how much he was being indulged by his coterie of assistants, gofers and hangers-on: 'The trouble is everybody wanted something from Fred, and that had made him suspicious of everyone. But, to me, he wasn't Freddie Mercury. I still thought of him as Fred Bulsara.' The problem was, as Queen's success grew, fewer and fewer people knew who Fred Bulsara was.

When Queen returned to the UK, they found a country divided. It was Queen Elizabeth's silver jubilee year. To celebrate her 25-year reign, the nation's shops were filled with commemorative mugs, plates and tea towels. It seemed as if every saleable nick-nack had been embossed with the monarch's Mona Lisa smile. Plans were now underway for countrywide street parties in the summer. In the opposite corner, EMI's *enfants terribles* The Sex Pistols were gearing up for their second single release, 'God Save the Queen', a song that would reach number 2 in the charts in May and which, some suggest, was deliberately denied the top spot to save embarrassment in a year of royalist celebrations.

'Tie Your Mother Down' was released in March, but was a minor hit (barely making it into the Top 50 in the US). It was a surprise flop, losing out not to The Sex Pistols or any of the new punk upstarts but to David Bowie, Bryan Ferry and Queen's onetime support band Mr Big, whose single 'Romeo' made the Top 5 that month.

Queen went back on the road, playing eight dates across Scandinavia and Europe, quickly followed by eleven shows in the UK. Mercury, as always, was in his element. He toasted the audience with the ever-present champagne and tossed carnations into the stalls. He switched outfits from his white kung fu jumpsuit to his tiny silk shorts and matching kimono to an exact replica of a costume worn by the Russian ballet dancer Vaslav Nijinsky. Behind him, the rest of the band played up a storm. 'Death On Two Legs', 'Brighton Rock', 'Liar' and 'Keep Yourself Alive', for example, were flashy, bombastic, heavy metal tracks that sounded wonderful in big arenas.

At Earls Court, Queen debuted their most ornate stage prop yet: a specially commissioned lighting rig in the shape of a crown that would ascend at the beginning of the gig and descend at the end, amid industrial quantities of dry ice. The rig weighed two tons and cost a bank-breaking £50,000. Beyond the visual spectacle, the whole thing could also be perceived as a forthright 'fuck you' to their detractors. Behind the scenes, though, one of EMI's senior executives recalled meeting Mercury after a show at the Glasgow Apollo: 'He told me he didn't understand the whole punk thing. It wasn't music to him.' The executive suggested that punk 'would settle down to its place in the market. It's only the kids telling you what they want.' After all his onstage bravado, it seemed odd to find Freddie Mercury expressing doubts about anything.

In June, Queen released their first EP. It included 'Good Old-Fashioned Loverboy' backed by the older tracks, 'White Queen (As It Began)', 'Death on Two Legs (Dedicated to . . .)' and 'Tenement Funster'. To Queen's relief, it made number 17 in the charts. When pitted against the music press, Mercury remained comically defiant. Interviewed by *NME*'s Tony Mitchell that summer, he defended Queen's broad musical style ('I'm into this ballet thing'), his aloof attitude towards fans ('What do you expect? Somebody to go round and have tea with the front row?'), and the accusation that *A Day at the Races* was a pallid sequel to *A Night at the Opera* ('We haven't dried up!').

Writing just twelve months earlier in *NME*, Tony Mitchell had poured praise on *A Night at the Opera*. But now he felt alienated by their lead singer's attitude. 'I thought Queen were a pioneering rock band,' said Mitchell, years later. 'But Freddie Mercury treated me with utter contempt. He had lost touch with reality.'

The *NME* interview ran under the infamous headline: 'FREDDIE MERCURY: IS THIS MAN A PRAT?'

CHAPTER SEVEN

'Boom-Boom Cha!'

'I'm going backstage, maybe get a blow job . . .'
Freddie Mercury, New Orleans Civic Auditorium,
31 October 1978

'People think we take ourselves a lot more seriously
than we do.'
Roger Taylor, the morning after, 1 November 1978

Centrepoint, the 35-storey office block, has loomed over London's Charing Cross Road for more than forty-five years. Tourists and sightseers emerging, blinking, from Tottenham Court Road tube station have used it as a marking post for just as long. Opposite stands the Dominion Theatre. In the autumn of 1957, Judy Garland staged a one-month run of her live show here. In 2010, Queen's musical, *We Will Rock You*, is enjoying its eighth year.

Above the door of the theatre, dwarfing the musical's distinctive gold logo, stands a statue of Queen's late singer Freddie Mercury, duplicating an original piece by sculptor Irena Sedlecka that can be found on the shores of Lake Geneva in Switzerland. Regrettably, the face resembles a random selection of moustachioed men of the twentieth century, including Josef Stalin, Saddam Hussein and, bizarrely, actor Tom Selleck. However, Sedlecka's statue recreates the ubiquitous Freddie pose, with the right hand raised in a clenched-fist salute and the left clutching a short microphone stand. The pose is enough to achieve the necessary deception. Just don't look too hard at the face.

The notion of a statue of Freddie Mercury fighting it out with Centrepoint as a West End landmark would have seemed incomprehensible in the twentieth century. But then, stranger still, *We Will Rock You* is now the longest-running musical in the history of the Dominion Theatre. How many times, you wonder, did Ealing art student Fred Bulsara glance up at the same theatre hoarding before ducking down into Soho for a gig at the Marquee? Later, in Queen's earliest days, Mercury and Brian May would pass the Dominion, then screening *The Sting*, *The Towering Inferno* and every Hollywood blockbuster of the time, as they travelled on the number 9 bus from Kensington to Trident Studios.

'We Will Rock You', the song that gave the Queen musical its name, was recorded in the late summer of 1977. After completing the final stretch of their European tour, Roger Taylor, eager to keep working, had made demos of four tracks for a possible solo project. One of these was a cover of The Parliaments' 1967 song '(I Wanna) Testify'. Taylor's version was co-produced by Mike Stone, and slipped out as a solo single in August. It cost him £5,000, failed to chart, but was, Taylor explained, 'simply a bit of fun'. Then again, he could afford such luxuries.

Taylor was in a relationship with Dominique Beyrand, but didn't yet have the same commitments as some of his colleagues. Veronica Deacon was pregnant with her second child. By the end of the year, Brian and Chrissy May would be expecting their first child. Mercury's complex love life would find David Minns replaced by the American Joe Fanelli, who, as one of Mercury's friends later explained, 'was a sweet, naive kid, uprooted and dragged into Freddie's lifestyle'. While May, especially, fretted over going back out on tour and the pressure this placed on his relationship, Taylor and Mercury were itching to get back out again.

'We got very insular, shut off, self-protective,' the drummer admitted a year later. 'I suppose we had too much time on our hands. We were holed up in England and we're always at our most depressed when we're not working. We got a bit fed up and lacking in inspiration.'

Publicly, as ever, Queen would defend *A Day at the Races* and *A Night at the Opera*, but, in a less guarded moment, Brian May admitted 'they may have been overproduced'. The plan was to make, as the guitarist put it, 'a more spontaneous album'. Regardless of musical trends and critical disdain, Queen had gone as far down that path as they could. As Roger Taylor admitted, 'I thought *A Day at the Races* was the most brilliant thing we'd done, but it hadn't sold better than *A Night at the Opera*, and that didn't seem the way things should be going.' At least one of Taylor's home demos would point the way ahead.

Alongside '(I Wanna) Testify', Taylor had cut three originals: the single's B-side 'Turn on the TV', 'Fight From the Inside' and 'Sheer Heart Attack'. As its title suggested, the last of these had been kicking around since Queen's 1974 album of the same name. Newly completed, 'Sheer Heart Attack' was a fiery rock 'n' roll song that replicated the verve and energy of the contemporary punk scene, but predated those bands by nearly four years. While Mercury had supposedly told one EMI executive about his dislike of punk, his bandmates were slightly more accepting. The now 28-year-old Taylor's yen for songs about teenage rebellion was evident in his own work. He would tell interviewers that he liked 'The Sex Pistols and raw rock 'n' roll' but was suspicious of the hype. May, similarly, would applaud The Pistols' 'passion and energy' but was vexed by the music's self-destructive element: 'Maybe I'm a sheltered soul, but I was a bit bewildered by all this stuff around them. The whole punk ethos was a bit manufactured and I never took it seriously.'

John Deacon, as always, said nothing. However, by the following year, the bassist had adopted a drastically short haircut, which would earn him the soubriquet 'Birdman', after the shaven-headed prisoner 'the Birdman of Alcatraz', portrayed by Burt Lancaster in the film of the same name. There was a comparison to be made with Charlie Watts, The Rolling Stones' unlikeliest hippy, who'd recently dispensed with his own flowing locks for the album *Black and Blue*. Like Watts, Deacon was Queen's eternal pragmatist. He shunned publicity, seemed to abhor the frippery and pretension of the music industry, and was content simply to play music and earn enormous amounts of money. On Queen's next tour, Deacon would model a shirt and skinny tie of the kind he might once have worn with The Opposition. Bizarrely, in 1978, it made him look like a member of The Jam, one of the most critically lauded new bands from the punk scene.

With Taylor snapping at his bandmates' heels, Queen imposed a deadline of just over two months in which to make their new album. Booking a US tour for November left them no option but to complete the record. The process would begin in July and finish in September and would be split across West London's Basing Street Studios and Wessex Sound Studios, a converted Victorian church hall in North London. Working quickly would, it transpired, also allow Freddie more time for antique shopping and bidding at Sotheby's.

The new Queen album would be called *News of the World*, after Groucho Marx reportedly rejected the group's request to borrow the title *Duck Soup*. 'The story goes that Groucho cabled them,' says EMI's Bob Mercer, 'and told them he didn't want the next Queen album to be called *Duck Soup* but said, "I would like it to be named after my next movie: *The Rolling Stones' Greatest Hits*." '

By autumn that year, the UK album charts were a curious mix of diva Barbra Streisand, Swedish pop titans Abba, and the progressive rock band Yes, who inspired Queen in their early days. Only the presence of The Stranglers in the Top 10 hinted at punk's growing popularity. That would soon change. Bob Marley and The Wailers had just completed their *Exodus* album at Basing Street, while Queen's supposed nemesis The Sex Pistols were putting the final touches to their debut, *Never Mind the Bollocks (Here's The Sex Pistols)* in Studio B at Wessex Sound.

Andy Turner would go on to become programme director for London's Capital Gold radio station. In the summer of 1977, though, the eighteen-year-old had just started work as an assistant sound engineer at Wessex ('Basically, I was Queen's tea boy'). On his first day in the job, he was told he would be working with the band for the next two months. 'I was a fan,' says Turner now. 'I was in awe of Brian May after hearing "Keep Yourself Alive" on *The Old Grey Whistle Test*.' While spontaneity may have been the buzzword for the new album, in Queen's world, nothing was that spontaneous. 'On day one, a lorry arrived with Roger Taylor's drum kit. We unloaded it, set it up in Studio A, and spent the best part of the next two days getting the right drum sound. Roger sat there with his drum tech, hitting drum after drum after drum . . . That was on Monday, and the rest of the band weren't due to arrive until Wednesday. I remember thinking, "Bloody hell! You're being charged £200 an hour for this."'

As with *A Day at the Races*, Queen planned to co-produce with engineer Mike Stone. 'Wessex always used to use in-house producers, so that was unusual,' recalls Turner. 'So there was very much this thing of having the Big American Producer brought in for the project.' One of the first changes Stone made was to bring in a new set of studio speakers. 'I don't think there was anything wrong with the ones they already had. But Mike managed to blow a set. Then again, I guess Queen could afford it . . .'

Paying £200 an hour also gave Queen other privileges. 'One of my duties for Freddie was to go down to the bakery on Dalston High Street every morning before he arrived and get him some Mr Kipling almond slices to go with his tea,' explains Andy. After one late-night recording session, Mercury invited Turner and the studio's young maintenance engineer, Howard, to accompany him to a party. The pair politely refused, but Andy would still be accorded privileges of his own during the recording sessions. 'Basically, Freddie told me that no one else in the band was allowed any of his almond slices, but that I could help myself. To be honest, I thought this was just Fred being Fred . . .' Then, one afternoon, Brian May crossed the line. 'Brian took an almond slice without asking, and there was a minor row about it. Freddie made this big announcement: "No one is allowed to touch my almond slices, no one . . . except Andy!"'

Back at work, Roger Taylor's 'Sheer Heart Attack' was soon finished, with the drummer playing everything except the guitar solo. Taylor's other new track, 'Fight From the Inside' was weaker, and sounded like a swipe at fly-by-night musical trends, including, inevitably, punk. But before long, Queen would have their close encounter with rock 'n' roll's latest public enemy number one. Roadie Peter Hince remembers meeting Sex Pistol Johnny Rotten (real name: John Lydon) at Wessex in 1976 when Queen were working on *A Day at the Races* ('He seemed like a pleasant sort of

bloke. What was all the fuss about?'). Mercury's interview with
NME in June the year before ('IS THIS MAN A PRAT?') had quoted the
singer discussing his passion for ballet.

According to Hince, The Sex Pistols' bassist, born John Ritchie,
better known by his stage name Sid Vicious, had stumbled into the
control room at Wessex and drunkenly asked Mercury, 'Have you
succeeded in bringing ballet to the masses yet?' 'Fred then said,
"Aren't you Stanley Ferocious or something" and threw him
out . . .' The story varies depending on who is telling it. Others
remember Mercury replying to the question with the withering
put-down, 'Oh yes, Mr Ferocious, dear, we're doing our best.'
Another possibly apocryphal tale has Vicious and/or Rotten
crawling into the studio on their hands and knees while Mercury
was playing the piano.

'We used to bump into them in the corridors,' said Brian May. 'I
had a few conversations with John Lydon, who was always very
respectful. We talked about music. I don't remember everything
about Freddie's legendary conversation with Sid Vicious. But I
remember Sid looking like such a boy. Straight out of school.'

Roger Taylor recalls Queen and The Sex Pistols 'looking at each
other with real distrust', before finding a common ground with
Pistols' guitarist Steve Jones and drummer Paul Cook. 'They were
down-to-earth guys,' said Taylor, 'but Johnny had a big charisma
about him.' Beyond the haircuts, the clothes and the bank
balances, the two lead singers had more in common than either
would care to admit. Johnny Rotten, like Freddie Mercury, was a
self-made creation. Both Lydon and Bulsara appeared to be funda-
mentally shy boys who had acquired a larger-than-life persona to
mask all sorts of insecurities.

Queen's ex-manager Jack Nelson once said of his charges: 'When
we'd get into an airport, one would stop, one would go right, one
would go left, and one would go straight ahead.' *News of the World*
was the first Queen album to truly highlight those differences.
Queen's diversity had previously been a selling point; now it
resulted in an album that didn't always gel. Almost the equal of
Sheer Heart Attack was Brian May's 'It's Late', a strutting rocker with
a dramatic lyric about a love triangle (May: 'It's about all sorts of

experiences that I had'). It backed up the guitarist's belief that 'News of the World would help Queen get back to basics and find some vitality again', but not everything would succeed as well.

John Deacon's rather trite 'Who Needs You' (described in the music press as like something from 'a Carmen Miranda forties musical') and Mercury's 'My Melancholy Blues' were fine but undistinguished. Deacon did better with his big-hearted pop song 'Spread Your Wings'. May's 'All Dead All Dead', with its orchestral guitar fills, was better than the faux blues of 'Sleeping on the Sidewalk'. 'It was the quickest song I've ever written' said the guitarist, but it was just as quickly forgotten.

Mercury's 'Get Down, Make Love' was far better. The sparse piano fills and funk groove suggested the R&B and dance music that soundtracked New York's gay club scene. The lyrics sounded like a celebration of sexual abandonment ('New York is Sin City. I slut myself when I'm there,' Freddie said). Meanwhile, sticking to the band's 'no synthesisers' policy, Brian May helped accompany the tale of the sexual escapades with some unearthly noises coaxed out of the Red Special and an effects pedal.

In October, Queen were presented with a Britannia Award for 'Bohemian Rhapsody', which tied with Procol Harum's 'A Whiter Shade of Pale' as Best British Single of the Last Twenty-Five Years. In the same month, they released the first two songs on News of the World as the two sides of their new single: 'We Are the Champions' and 'We Will Rock You'. Rock 'n' roll bands declaring their invincibility was nothing new. But rarely had any group sounded so utterly assured of that invincibility.

' "We Are the Champions" is the most egotistical song I've ever written,' Freddie admitted. He had, he said, been inspired by the crowd singalongs at football matches, and wanted to write something for, as he called them, 'the masses' at Queen concerts. 'I suppose it could be construed as my version of [Frank Sinatra's] "My Way",' he added. 'We have made it, and it certainly wasn't easy.'

'I was quite shocked when I heard the lyrics,' Brian May told Mojo. 'I remember saying, "You can't do this, Fred. You'll get killed." Freddie said, "Yes, we can."' He was correct. Mercury's conviction drives 'We Are the Champions' from its dainty opening verse to its ridiculously overblown conclusion. Not once does he sound like a man suffering one iota of self-doubt. Queen filmed a promo for the single at the New London Theatre in front of an audience of nearly a thousand invited fans, with Freddie conducting the masses in his Nijinsky stage suit. After just one take, the crowd reacted as if they'd heard the song as many times as 'Keep Yourself Alive' or 'Seven Seas of Rhye'.

The bold declaration of 'no time for losers' seemed a defiant snub to Queen's critics ('In their moneyed superiority, they are indeed champions,' wrote *Rolling Stone*'s Bart Testa, as if throwing up his hands in surrender). Taylor and May would always insist that Mercury's tongue was in his cheek when he wrote the song, and that, as the drummer said, the 'we' was 'a collective "we". We are all champions.'

If audiences felt patronised, it didn't show. 'We Are the Champions' gave Queen a number 2 hit in the UK, a number 1 in France (for a record-breaking twelve weeks) and a number 4 in the US. A song that at first, as Brian May said, 'had us on the floor laughing' would go on to become 'an international anthem for sports, politics . . . everything.'

The single's flipside had been written by Brian May, but was every bit as self-assured. 'I woke up after a momentous gig at Stafford Bingley Hall when the audience had kept singing after we'd gone offstage,' recalled May, 'and I had the idea for "We Will Rock You" in my head. Freddie and I both thought it would be an interesting experiment to write a song with audience participation specifically in mind.' Until the arrival of the stuttering guitar solo, the track relied only on Mercury's vocal and the collective hands and feet of his bandmates and anyone else that happened to be in Wessex Studios that day. 'There are no drums on the track,' revealed May. 'It's just clapping and stamping on boards, overdubbed many times over with many primitive delay machines.'

'"We Will Rock You" truly showed the creative side of Mike Stone,' remembers Andy Turner. Over the course of some fifteen takes, Stone recorded everyone he could find at Wessex performing the two foot stomps and a handclap that comprised the song's rhythm. 'Early one evening, they came and rounded up me, Howard, and Betty the tea lady, who lived in the council house next door to the studio, and got us all up on these drum risers,' laughs Turner. 'We all stood there and did the "boom-boom cha" take after take after take.'

At EMI's autumn sales conference that year, Brian Southall made use of both songs. 'Our conference was themed around "We Are the Champions" and "We Will Rock You", so we handed out football scarves to everyone,' he explains. In keeping with the spirit of the occasion, Southall had also hired sports pundit Dickie Davies, presenter of *The Big Match*, to record links for the conference. 'Then we played both tracks. Everyone was on their feet, totally fired up.'

After spending over six months in the US singles charts, 'We Are the Champions' would be adopted by the New York Yankees baseball team as their anthem. Thousands of miles away from London in North Carolina, ex-Panchgani pupil Subash Shah would hear Queen's rallying cry of 'We Will Rock You' every time he watched his baseball team over the next few years. Shah was a jazz fan with no great interest in pop music, and, until after Mercury's death, had no idea that he was listening to his childhood friend 'Buckwee' Bulsara.

Defiant as always, Queen refused EMI's request to put a picture of the band on the sleeve of *News of the World*. Instead, they hired American artist Frank Kelly Freas to pastiche his artwork for a 1953 edition of *Astounding Science Fiction* magazine. Freas re-created his original doleful-looking robot, now attempting to cradle the members of Queen in his mechanical claw. As a gimmick, EMI created promotional robot clocks. 'They were big grandfather clocks,' says Brian Southall. 'Very expensive. But that's what we did in those days. There was no expense spared. The policy was, "How much money can we spend to make the band and us feel good?" '

By 1977, Southall and EMI's Bob Mercer had become acutely aware that Queen were an entirely different beast from the groups they'd encountered earlier in the decade. 'Queen came to marketing meetings for one thing,' laughs Mercer. 'They hunted as a pack.' For Brian Southall, a squabble over an album sleeve was merely a sign of the times. 'There was a point in the 1970s where record companies lost control of their artists. You could blame it on *Dark Side of the Moon* if you like. So it was a perfect time for Queen to take advantage of that, albeit in the nicest possible way. Like Pink Floyd, Queen delivered the album, delivered the album cover, and your job was to do the work of the worker ants and sell it. They were perfect animals for the seventies.'

One lunchtime, Southall and his marketing assistant took Mercury to lunch in a French restaurant close to EMI's offices in Manchester Square. 'It was a great restaurant, wonderful food, but I think Freddie asked for a piece of lettuce,' chuckles Southall. 'After lunch, it was a lovely day, Freddie decided that he was going to walk back to the office. It was about fifty yards around two sides of Manchester Square. But his limo had to drive, cruising at the same speed, with the door open in case Freddie got tired. He was a star, but a bigger star than anyone I ever met.'

In November, despite EMI's robot grandfather clocks and the omnipresent 'We Are the Champions', *News of the World* only reached number 4 in the UK, Queen's lowest chart placing since *Queen II*. In a comic reversal of fortunes, it was their Wessex studio mates, The Sex Pistols, who took the top spot with their debut album. By then, Queen were on tour in the United States. The blow was softened when *News of the World* gave them their first American number 1. 'Any band from that era that says they weren't competitive are liars,' said Roger Taylor. 'We were always like, "Shit, I wish we could be where Led Zeppelin are." Or we'd be looking at groups like Yes and wanting to do better.'

When Queen had sold out New York's Madison Square Garden in March, they'd set themselves a goal to better Yes's record of selling out three nights at the same venue. In December 1977, they managed two nights. 'We were always trying to take the next step,' said May. 'A million records this year, two million next year; one night at Madison Square Garden this time, two next time . . .'

For Brian, the concerts were a personal victory. May's father, Harold, had struggled with his son's choice of career, and Queen's hit singles and albums had done little to change his point of view. One of his projects at the Ministry of Aviation had been designing the blind landing equipment for Concorde. While John Reid arranged for a group of the band's friends and employees to fly to New York for the shows on Freddie Laker's Skytrain, May went one better. 'I flew my dad over on Concorde to see us play. He'd worked on Concorde for all that time but had never actually flown on it. He saw us play at Madison Square Garden, and after the show he came up to me and said, "Yes, all right. I get it now." That was a wonderful moment.'

Onstage, Queen still subscribed to their usual policy, expressed by Freddie as 'the bigger, the better – in everything'. May and Mercury opened the show alone with 'We Will Rock You'. The tribal rhythm boomed hypnotically across the vast arenas, before the rest of band weighed in for a sped-up, almost punk-rock version of the same song. By then, Queen's 60-feet 'crown' had achieved lift-off and hovered over the stage, beaming out shafts of light through a fug of dry ice. Four months later, cinema-goers would see a similar effect in Steven Spielberg's *Close Encounters of the Third Kind*.

At Madison Square Garden, Freddie Mercury paraded in a crowd-pleasing New York Yankees baseball jacket. In Portland, the audience took over the vocals on 'Love of my Life'. Before a gig in San Diego, a worse-for-wear John Deacon stuck his hand through a plate glass window, but had it patched up sufficiently to play the show. On most nights, Queen's cover of 'Jailhouse Rock' was now dedicated to Elvis Presley, who had died suddenly in August.

After watching the first night in New York, *Rolling Stone*'s Chet Flippo wrote that 'Queen songs cannot decide whether to be The Who, Led Zeppelin, The Beatles or tortured chanting Gregorians. Based on audience appeal, they get the job done. I'm just not sure what that job is.' In America, Queen were still perceived as a heavy rock band with an unusually theatrical lead singer. Some of their musical quirks, the throwbacks to *Uncle Mac's Children's Favourites* or The Temperance Seven, didn't translate as well as they did in the studio. The good folks of Norfolk, Virginia, preferred to be blasted senseless by 'We Will Rock You', 'Brighton Rock' or 'Now I'm Here'. After the opening night, Queen's newest curio 'Sleeping on the Sidewalk' was shelved for the remainder of the tour.

Offstage, ex-Hectics singer Bruce Murray caught up with Mercury at the Aladdin: 'My mother was living in Las Vegas, and I saw that Queen were playing.' Backstage, though, Murray could see that how different his old friend's life now was. 'I didn't want to become a hanger-on,' he says. 'Freddie was into the whole gay thing now, and to be honest, there was, I think, a feeling backstage of "us and them".' The two parted on good terms, but it would be the last time Murray saw or spoke to Fred Bulsara.

Onstage, Mercury sold the show as hard as always. Described in the US press as both 'obnoxious and joyously camp', the singer modelled a fashionably shorter haircut, while his new wardrobe included a leather biker's jacket. Freddie would sign off shows with 'Thank you, it's been a pleasure doing business with you', a quip that annoyed some critics who thought it too cynical. Ian Hunter caught the show at Toronto's Maple Leaf Gardens, and burst out laughing after one incident. 'Brian May's amp had exploded,' recalled Hunter. The guitarist dashed over to tell Mercury, who was at the piano, unaware that his microphone was switched on and that the audience could hear every word. As Hunter recalled, 'Fred waved Brian away, saying, "Oh, just jump around a bit and the silly bastards won't know the difference!"'

On 22 December Queen played the LA Forum. It was their final night in Los Angeles, the last of three shows that had seen them play to total of 64,000 people. The band encored with a hastily rehearsed 'White Christmas', joined onstage by their bodyguard dressed as Santa Claus, manager John Reid disguised as an elf and assorted roadies as reindeers. They flew home a day later. However much 'slutting' there was still to be done in America, Mercury had other things on his mind: 'My mother would kill me if I wasn't home for Christmas. I haven't missed one yet.'

■ ■ ■

'There's nothing wrong with going to bed with somebody of your own sex. I think everybody's bisexual to a certain degree.'

In October 1976 Elton John discussed his sexuality in a candid interview with *Rolling Stone* magazine. It was a bold move by a mainstream pop star for the time. A year later, Elton announced his decision to retire from playing live and had broken up his songwriting partnership with lyricist Bernie Taupin, dropping out of the public eye to plan his next move.

Behind the scenes and unknown to the public at the time, Elton was also dealing with the end of his tempestuous personal relationship with John Reid, also his manager. Professionally, there was also another issue to contend with. As Reid's former PR Caroline Boucher explains, 'Freddie and Elton got on very well, but you couldn't manage Freddie *and* Elton.'

'It was obviously going to end in tears,' adds Bob Mercer. 'If John Reid was in my office with Freddie, then inevitably there would be a phone call from Elton: "What's he doing with *her*?" As another insider recalls, 'If Elton had a tour, then that took priority, and with the different personalities in Queen, you can imagine how that went down.'

With lawyer Jim Beach negotiating, Queen's separation from John Reid Enterprises was underway before their second US tour in 1977. Reid would receive a substantial pay-off for the early termination of the management contract, plus 15 per cent of the royalties generated by the Queen albums already released. Queen were also still paying a percentage of royalties to Trident; an arrangement that would only expire with the release of their next album.

Queen's relationship with John Reid had been fruitful for both parties, but they were wary of signing with another manager. Reid delivered the paperwork to the back garden of Roger Taylor's country house in order to get the necessary signatures. At the time, Queen were filming a promo for 'We Will Rock You' and their next single, 'Spread Your Wings', attempting to mime in the bitter cold and under a dusting of snow, and after Freddie had consumed the best part of a bottle of brandy. The band themselves squeezed into the back of Mercury's Rolls-Royce and signed the documents.

Initially, they decided to manage themselves, with Pete Brown and Paul Prenter assisting. Before long, their circumstances would change again. Queen's lawyer Jim Beach gave up his position with Harbottle & Lewis and was soon installed as the band's business manager. 'Jim took me out to lunch and told me he was thinking of becoming Queen's business manager,' remembers Bob Mercer. 'I was very encouraging. I'd been on the suffering end of the whole Freddie Mercury-John Reid-Elton John thing, and I could please absolutely no one.' Two years later, Brian May would admit, 'I think we were in real danger of splitting up when the John Reid situation got really sticky.'

Jim Beach established three new companies: Queen Productions Ltd, Queen Music Ltd and Queen Films Ltd; the last of which was created in response to the growing trend for pop promos. Queen would now finance their own films and maintain control over licensing and video rights. Unsurprisingly, it was John Deacon that guided his bandmates through such matters. 'John keeps a very close eye on our affairs,' Mercury told *Circus* magazine. 'He knows everything that's going on and shouldn't be going on. The rest of the group won't do anything unless John says it's all right. We've all become businessmen. Even though it's against our better judgement.'

When asked whether Freddie had ever taken care of the finances when running their stall at Kensington Market, Roger Taylor once replied, 'Bloody hell, no! That would have been an absolute disaster.' In 1978 Taylor claimed that the Queen singer 'has absolutely no idea about money, the value of it or anything.' That said, one of Jim Beach's first assignments was to renegotiate the terms of Queen's deal with EMI. One company insider has described the resulting deal as 'in the millions. A vast amount for the day.'

By 1978, though, Prime Minister James Callaghan's government had imposed a top tax rate of 83 per cent on earned income and 98 per cent on unearned income in the UK. As Roger Taylor grumbled, 'We had to think about leaving the country.' Queen would follow the lead set by other musicians in recent years, including The Rolling Stones, David Bowie and Bad Company, and become tax exiles, spending less than 183 days a year in the UK, and touring and recording overseas to avoid paying tax on their earnings.

Although Freddie Mercury had applauded it 'as John Deacon's best song to date', 'Spread Your Wings' barely made it into the Top

30 in February. Deacon would have some better news that month with the birth of his second son, Michael. But come April and the start of the new tax year, Queen were in Stockholm for the first night of a three-week tour. In Rotterdam, their gargantuan lighting rig malfunctioned. 'There was the explosion and loads of smoke,' recalled Brian May, 'and one side of the crown majestically rose while the other majestically fell. I think it helped break the ice.' Three days later, matters improved when Queen played France for the first time. 'We Are the Champions' and 'We Will Rock You' had been in the charts for weeks, but the country had been resistant to the band until then. Following a triumphal performance at Pavillion De Paris, Mercury was overheard to remark, 'Well, that's Paris ticked off.'

The UK would be served by two Queen shows at Stafford Bingley Hall and three at Wembley Empire Pool in May. It was now costing around £4,000 a day to keep Queen on the road. The *Daily Mail* revealed that they were only turning a profit in the United States, where the venues could hold as many as 20,000. Mercury gave an unusually candid interview to the *Mail*'s Tim Lott. While not discussing his sexuality with the same frankness as Elton John in *Rolling Stone*, he claimed, 'My sex drive is enormous. I live life to the full', and admitted that he and Mary Austin had broken up ('After seven and a half years we have come to an understanding. Mary should have a life of her own'). Though always good for a flippant bon mot ('I enjoy being a bitch'), Mercury confessed to 'all kinds of paranoia', explaining that he couldn't bear to go anywhere on his own, and that he had to have someone with him at all times.

Freddie's circle of gay friends provided him with the constant company he needed. Some would have the singer's best interests at heart; others would abuse his trust and, in one case, ultimately betray him. Interviewed by Kenny Everett to promote *A Day at the Races*, Mercury had broadcast a coded dedication to 'Sharon, Beryl, Phyllis, Serita . . . all the lovely people.' Freddie's 'lovely people', gay and straight, had all acquired female names: 'Sharon' was Elton John, 'Beryl' was John Reid, 'Phyllis' was Rod Stewart. Mercury himself was known as 'Melina' (after the Greek actress and political activist Melina Mercouri), Roger Taylor was 'Liz' and Brian May was 'Maggie'. Intriguingly, John Deacon was never given a name, while, in a comic reversal of gender, Mary Austin was called 'Steve' after Steve Austin, the hero of *The Six Million Dollar Man* TV series. 'Oh God, Queen and the girls' names,' sighs Brian Southall. 'You'd be having this conversation and you'd have no idea who this Brenda or Beryl was or what they were talking about.'

'Serita' had been a part of Mercury's life for some time. It was the nickname given to Peter Straker, a Jamaica-born singer and actor who had appeared in the original stage production of the musical *Hair!* In 1977 Mercury formed his own production company, Goose Productions, and stuck £20,000 of his own cash into Straker's debut album, co-producing the record with Roy Thomas Baker. Peter's music had one foot in the dwindling glam-rock scene, the other in campy West End show tunes. The album, *This One's On Me*, was released in 1978, but barely sold.

For Southall, Peter Straker was another example of EMI cosseting one of their star acts. 'In those days, you did things because your artists said so,' he explains. 'EMI signed Kate Bush because Dave Gilmour said so, which was wonderful. But then Goose Productions brought us Peter Straker. God bless him, Peter had a sense of humour. I remember we sent him on a huge tour, got to Birmingham Odeon and we'd sold thirty tickets. We were like, "Come on Peter . . ." But he said, "No, no, my loves, I must go on . . ." He had the feather boa and the heels, and he used to do a version of "That Old Black Magic" with a box of Black Magic chocolates. That night he went out with a bag of Revels . . .'

Straker's musical career continued in fits and starts, but he would spend the next few years in Mercury's inner circle, alongside mainstays Joe Fanelli (aka 'Liza') and personal manager Paul Prenter ('Trixie'). Mercury was twenty-nine years old when he'd begun his relationship with David Minns. As one of his former entourage explains, he was 'very keen to make up for lost time'. Freddie may have craved companionship and romantic love, but his fame and money brought him endless attention and offers of sex.

Writing in 1992, Freddie's close friend David Evans described Mercury's time in his thirties as 'hectic, late-night and greedy'. By

1978, Freddie was in the position of having anything and everything he wanted. One night, at a friend's birthday party in a London restaurant, the singer broke off from his conversation and uttered one word, 'Ciggy'. In seconds, packets of cigarettes were thrust in his direction. Later, Mercury stopped again, and said, 'Pee-pee.' Within seconds, he was being shepherded towards the lavatory.

It was all rather different in Brian May's world. In June that year, May and his wife celebrated the birth of their first child, James. While Mercury bragged to the *Daily Mail* of spending '£100,000 over the last three years', May lived a more frugal lifestyle. 'I called round Brian's house in Barnes,' says his old bandmate John 'Jag' Garnham. 'I hadn't been there before and didn't know he was away on tour. It was just an OK, detached house, and I remember thinking, "Where is all the money?" There were no extravagant objects in the house at all. Brian's dad Harold turned up, and I said, "Are you still living in Feltham?" He said, "Oh yes, Jag, we are. We don't let Brian pay for anything, only the airfare sometimes so we can go and see him in concert." '

Inevitably, as Queen's fame escalated it became harder to maintain relationships with schoolfriends and former bandmates. As Chris Smith says, 'I never knew Freddie Mercury. My mate was Fred Bulsara.' After a show at the Liverpool Empire, Ken Testi persuaded Queen to visit his new club, Eric's. Deacon, Taylor and Mercury arrived to reminisce with the old friend that had nearly become their manager. But Testi was amused to notice that they came, and went, in three separate limousines. In July 1978, Roger Taylor celebrated his twenty-ninth birthday with a party in Montreux. High on life and anything else on offer, Freddie Mercury supposedly swung from a cut-glass chandelier, telling stunned onlookers, 'I just couldn't resist it.'

■ ■ ■

'The one about the dwarfs and the bald heads and the cocaine is not true,' insists Roger Taylor, between conspiratorial chuckles. He hesitates. 'Actually, it *could* have been true.' Taylor is being chauffeured around the Lake District. It is now summer 2008, he has been coaxed onto the campaign trail to support Queen and Paul Rodgers' album and tour. The drummer cruises through some of the most beautiful countryside in rural England, a mobile phone pressed to his ear, patiently taking a trip back thirty years to one of Queen's most debauched parties.

On Hallowe'en night, 31 October 1978, Queen celebrated the release of their seventh album, *Jazz*, in New Orleans. At midnight, a Dixieland brass band marched into the ballroom of the Fairmont Hotel, where over three hundred guests were already gorging on oysters, shrimp creole and champagne served by liveried waiters. Following the trumpet-playing retinue were the four members of Queen, fresh from their sold-out show at the Municipal Auditorium. Before the event, Queen's publicist had been ordered to trawl the bars and clubs around Bourbon Street in the city's French Quarter with an instruction to round up 'every available freak' and invite them to the party.

As Queen arrived, a flock of transvestites, fire-eaters, dancing girls, snakecharmers and strippers dressed as nuns, appeared from the wings. The Rolling Stones' disco hit 'Miss You' blared out of the speakers, as various female revellers shed their clothes on the dance-floor. In the *Sun* newspaper, a week later, Freddie Mercury, clad in braces and checked shirt (the de rigueur dress code in US gay circles) was photographed autographing a bare female behind under the headline "WAY DOWN YONDER IN NUDE ORLEANS". The festivities rolled on until daybreak, with groupies dispensing blow jobs to music biz bigwigs in a back room, and one party girl stripping off to 'smoke' a cigarette in her vagina. Or so the story goes . . .

Over the last three decades, the tale has taken on a life of its own to include all manner of bacchanalian excess: public sex, naked mud-wrestling, a nude woman served on a salver of raw meat, and, most infamous of all, dwarfs, sometimes described as 'herma-phrodite dwarfs', ferrying cocaine on trays strapped to their, possibly bald, heads . . . 'Look, if it's true I never saw it,' admits Roger Taylor, eventually. 'But I have to say that most of the stories from that night are not *that* exaggerated.'

EMI's Bob Mercer had flown to New Orleans especially for the bash. 'The party was outrageous,' he admits. 'The story about the gnomes and cocaine is apocryphal. As far as I know, I was the only one there that had any blow [cocaine], because all night I kept getting tapped on the shoulder by certain people and I kept having to go with them to my hotel room . . .'

At round 3 a.m., Mercer remembers escorting Brian May and Roger Taylor on a trip to 'some of the seedier parts of the French Quarter'. Mercury was also 'trolling in the same village', in the company of Queen's old PR Tony Brainsby and *Sounds* journalist Sylvie Simmons with whom he was competing to spot the best-looking men ('He's mine!'). May, however, remembers the night differently. Eager to get away from what one eyewitness called 'the groupies and fame-worshippers', the guitarist left the party and headed off on what turned out to be a wild goose chase.

'You know that feeling, where everything's going on, everything's wonderful, fabulous, but inside there's this big hole?' said May in 1998. 'So it was great, it was outrageous, but I remember thinking, all is not quite right.' Brian went looking for Peaches, the woman he had met in New Orleans on Queen's first US tour. 'I'd fallen in love some years before in New Orleans and I expected that I would see her, but she wasn't there. I didn't find her but she found me later on.' Recalling the party in 2008, May still sounded dreamily wistful. 'New Orleans is a party town, and I still have a huge emotional attachment to the place. I still feel a tug on the heartstrings when I go to that city.'

The arrival of a new day brought with it a $200,000 bill, and the mother of all hangovers. Hardened bon vivant Bob Mercer returned to his hotel room at 6 a.m., only to discover that he had been robbed. 'I used to carry what we called a "nancy bag",' he explains. 'Men in those days carried all their gear in these bags because our pants were too tight to put anything in the pockets. I opened mine and I had no money, no credit card, no passport . . . I was supposed to fly to New York to catch a plane to London to go with Kate Bush to Holland for some record awards. Believe it or not, I got home. How? I don't know. I was like one of those marines who's dropped in the middle of a forest at night and told to find their own way back.'

While Mercer plotted his escape from New Orleans, a bleary-eyed Queen held a press conference. 'The party was deliberately excessive,' said May later. 'Partly for our own enjoyment, partly for friends to enjoy . . . and partly for the hell of it.' But as Taylor ominously admitted, 'The trouble was, as time went on, we just got better and better at having a good time.'

Sessions for what became *Jazz* had begun four months earlier and, for tax purposes, would be split between Mountain Studios, overlooking Lake Geneva, and Superbear Studios in Nice. In Mike Stone's absence, Queen had reunited with Roy Thomas Baker. 'Mike had been like part of the band,' explained Brian May, 'but by the time we were going to start *Jazz*, Mike had fallen in love and then had a period of falling apart.' Stone's later worked with Journey and Asia, bands who made great use of the stacked vocals and harmony techniques he had first used with Queen. Sadly, Stone died in 2002 and would never get the chance to work again with Queen.

By the summer of 1978, Roy Thomas Baker was basking in the success of his latest project, The Cars' debut album. The Cars, from Boston, Massachusetts, were part of what record company marketing departments were calling 'new wave'; the radio-friendly successor to punk. It was now the era of Elvis Costello, Blondie, and The Police. 'Roy came back with a huge amount of confidence,' said May. 'He'd done The Cars' album really quickly, and was like, "Oh, I tossed that off in two weeks and it was a massive hit!"'

Queen wanted to retain the spontaneity of *News of the World*, without creating an obvious sequel. With The Cars, Baker had fused huge harmony vocals with sparse backing tracks. Queen would employ a similar technique for *Jazz*. 'It was the first time we'd done an album away from home,' said Brian May. 'The idea being that there would be no distractions, but of course there were even more distractions. Just different kinds.' According to May, one of Freddie Mercury's distractions was the Tour de France: 'Fred got quite worked up about it, though we couldn't understand why, and then he came back with this delightful creation.'

The delightful creation was 'Bicycle Race', a song with lyrics that name-checked *Jaws*, *Star Wars*, cocaine, Superman, the Vietnam War and the Watergate political scandal. If that wasn't enough, it had a schizophrenic rhythm, pure Gilbert and Sullivan vocals, and, said May, 'about a billion chords'. The song was exquisitely camp. 'I'm not saying who was sleeping with whom and when,' insisted May, but a popular rumour still persists that 'Bicycle Race' was composed after Mercury enjoyed a tryst with one of the Tour de France cyclists. 'If anything, Freddie's personal life spilled over into his work in a positive way, the part that made it theatre,' suggested Roy Thomas Baker. 'His horizons were broad, and being gay was one extra thing he could draw upon.'

Brian May delivered the perfect companion piece with 'Fat Bottomed Girls'. 'I wrote it with Fred in mind,' he said, 'as you do when you have a great singer that liked fat bottomed girls or boys.' The song swung from thigh-slapping country-rock to heavy metal, with Mercury singing about his sexual initiation at the hands of one 'Big Fat Fanny'. 'Fat Bottomed Girls' evoked a Donald McGill saucy seaside postcard and an old *Carry On* film, with a mugging Kenneth Williams about to be pounced on by Hattie Jacques' predatory Matron.

With 'Fat Bottomed Girls' and 'Bicycle Race', Queen had acquired a double A-side single that would return them to the UK Top 20. But *Jazz* divided opinion within the group. Interviewed in 1984, John Deacon described it 'as an album I dislike'. Roger Taylor was equally unimpressed. 'It's not one of my favourites,' he admitted later. '*Jazz* was an ambitious album but I never felt as if it lived up to its ambition. The double A-side single was good, but I was never happy with the sound on *Jazz*, it never thrilled me.'

Interviewed in 2005, Roy Thomas Baker insisted, 'I thought everyone had a great time. I thought their songwriting was equally as good as what they'd done before.' One of the high points of the sessions for Baker was working again with Freddie Mercury. At Mountain, the control room was on a different level to the studio, which irked the singer. 'We installed a close circuit TV,' explained Baker. 'When Fred and I had worked together before, I wouldn't sit behind the recording console but between the console and the window, so that Freddie could tell from my facial expression if I thought a particular vocal was good or not. Freddie wanted a camera on my face, so we could maintain that relationship.' Baker found that Mercury was still 'intense and strong-willed, but great to work with. He'd write everything down on bits of paper so he was always focused, and then play me little things, like a cymbal smash of some record, and say, "How do we get that sound?" '

The singer's imagination worked overtime for the opening track, 'Mustapha'. Here, Mercury offered a rare nod to his heritage, scatting away in Arabic and broken English over a frenetic backing of drums, bass, guitar and piano. It was unlike anything Queen had attempted before, and a strikingly original, if uncompromising way to begin an album. 'I thought it was fantastic,' said May simply. 'Intrinsically difficult, but fantastic.'

Elsewhere on *Jazz*, Mercury displayed the usual split personality: playing the weary romantic on the ballad 'Jealousy', while bragging about whoring himself out to an audience on the smoke-and-mirrors hard rocker 'Let Me Entertain You'. When Roger Taylor said that Queen were getting better and better at having a good time, one band member seemed better at it than most. The 'good time' being enjoyed by Mercury would be extolled in the future single 'Don't Stop Me Now'. In the twenty-first century, the song has been used to sell Cadbury's chocolate, sung on reality TV talent shows, and voted The Greatest Driving Song Ever by viewers of the BBC's petrol-head programme, *Top Gear*. Mercury describes himself as a tiger, an atom bomb, and a sex machine travelling at 100mph, suggesting that the song's two greatest inspirations were sex and drugs. Interviewed in 2010 Brian May admitted that although the song was full of optimism, 'lyrically it represented something that was happening to Freddie which we thought was threatening him.' Namely: his lifestyle.

May's contributions to *Jazz* swung from bruising heavy rock, 'Dead On Time' (which included the sound of a thunderstorm recorded over Montreux) to 'Dreamers Ball', a light, jazzy shuffle that apparently prompted a heated row in the studio between May and Taylor, who didn't like the song. 'Around the *Jazz* album we were all getting into our own things and nobody much liked what the other guys were doing,' admitted May. 'To be honest, there were times when we couldn't tolerate each other offstage.' On 'Leaving Home Ain't Easy', May played his straightest hand yet with a song seemingly inspired by the the drawbacks of being a globetrotting rock star. Elsewhere, he delivered an epic guitar solo to John Deacon's 'If You Can't Beat Them' that was arguably the best part of the song. Deacon's other composition, 'In Only Seven Days', stuck to the same pop middle ground as 'You're My Best Friend'.

Roger Taylor has always saved his strongest criticism of *Jazz* for his own tracks, 'Fun It' and 'More of That Jazz'. 'My songs are very patchy,' he said. 'Instantly forgettable.' 'Fun It' was Queen's first foray into dance music and included a syn-drum, the electronic gizmo that would briefly revolutionise the sound of so much pop music in the next decade. Taylor's second effort was the rather sullen 'More of That Jazz', which reprised snippets from the tracks that had gone before but ended the album on a very downbeat note. 'I don't think we were as much of a group at the time,' he said. 'We were all living in these different places in a different country.'

The days of Queen bussing in to London from their respective bedsits for a recording session at Trident were long gone. In July, May had been forced to leave the UK for tax reasons soon after the birth of his son. He had flown to Canada for a break, before joining the rest of the band in Montreux. Deacon now had two children and the same commitments as May. Jack Nelson's earlier description of the four band members entering an airport ('one would stop, one would go right, one would go left, and one would go straight ahead') seemed even more apt. *Jazz* had a fractured feel, as if all the pieces didn't quite fit and everyone was pulling in their own direction. Interviewed in 1982, Baker recalled the sessions less for the songs than for the local nightlife: 'Every night we'd go to this club on the corner that had the most amazing stripper, so we had to stop the session at eleven o'clock, watch the stripper, and then go back to record again.'

Baker's co-production gave *Jazz* a crisp, cold sound, not that distanced from his work with The Cars. The choruses were as big as before, but everything else felt shrunken, as if it had been condensed, especially Taylor's drums. It was a modern sound far removed from the bombast of *Queen II* or *A Night at the Opera*, which is what all parties had been striving for before. But as Roger Taylor said: 'Jazz was disappointing . . . I don't think it really worked with Roy.'

Billy Cobham and Gilbert Gil had been among the star attractions at the annual Montreux Jazz Festival that summer. Away from the studio, Queen had spent time at the festival, which was the inspiration for the album's title. The monochrome cover artwork was Roger Taylor's idea, and came from graffiti he'd spotted while crossing through Checkpoint Charlie in Berlin. Once again, though, EMI were denied a photograph of the band on the cover.

'Our biggest disappointment was the cover,' admits Brian Southall. 'This one was particularly bizarre, as was the title Jazz, which we thought might indicate some sort of mad move into jazz and confuse people.' EMI were understandably relieved when they finally heard the album, especially 'Don't Stop Me Now', but their fears were raised once again when they learned of the proposed video shoot for the 'Bicycle Race' and 'Fat Bottomed Girls' single.

On 12 September, Queen arranged for a total of sixty-five naked female models to be filmed energetically cycling around the track at Wimbledon Stadium in southwest London. Queen's nude cyclists ran the full gamut of shape, size and race. Images from the shoot would be used in the promo video, on the cover of the 'Bicycle Race' single and also in a poster to be given away free with every copy of the album. 'It was a fun idea,' says Southall. 'And a great day out with a bunch of naked ladies on bikes. There was an enormous amount of media interest, but there was a backlash.'

There was also a problem the day after when Queen's people returned the bikes to the Halford's store from where they were borrowed. Queen were informed that, for reasons of hygiene, they would have to pay to replace all sixty-five saddles. When EMI baulked at a naked female behind on the single's cover, Queen relented and arranged for a pair of black knickers to be drawn on to the offending rear. But the free poster with its gaudy array of naked breasts and buttocks prompted a furore in America, and would be withdrawn from US copies of Jazz. 'I guess some people don't like to look at nude ladies,' quipped Mercury.

'That wasn't our problem,' laughs Southall. 'That was Elektra's.

But what was a problem for EMI in the UK was getting the video on *Top of the Pops* or Saturday morning kids' TV. Queen, of course, couldn't be bothered with "little things" like that, and were never going to compromise what they wanted to do.' In the end, 'Bicycle Race' reached number 11 in the UK and number 24 in the US.

In Britain, *Jazz* was released on 10 November, coming out four days later in America, where Queen's next tour was already underway. *Jazz* drew more critical flack than even *News of the World*. Dave Marsh's savaging of the album in *Rolling Stone* took great exception to the air of elitism, concluding, 'Queen may be the first truly fascist rock band. The whole thing makes me wonder why anyone would indulge these creeps and their polluting ideas.' With Britain still in the grip of widespread unemployment, a left-leaning music press bristled at a group of tax exiles hiring women to strip off and ride bikes around for their amusement, and throwing $200,000 parties in New Orleans. Accusations of sexism were thrown around, while the music didn't fare much better. *NME* advised its readers to buy *Jazz* only if they had 'a deaf relative'. Queen's most sensitive soul Brian May would admit to being wounded by such comments ('We are quite excessive, but in a harmless way'); Roger Taylor would agree that, yes, it rankled but it didn't matter as 'people kept on buying the records'. *Jazz* made it to number 2 in the UK and number 6 in the US.

In America, Queen were now touring without an opening act and were booked into the biggest sheds to maximise ticket sales and profits. Mercury was still experiencing problems with his voice, which he blamed on the nodules that had plagued him on earlier tours, but which others said were being aggravated by his lifestyle. In 2005, a former road manager told *Uncut* magazine: 'Around 1978 and 1979, when Queen became huge, Freddie's appetites soared. He was non-stop sex and drugs. Before a show, after a show . . . Even between songs. Before an encore, he'd nip backstage, have a few lines of coke, get a quick blow job from some bloke he'd just met, then run back to the stage and finish the gig. The man had stamina.' Even allowing for exaggeration, one observer from the time described Mercury as being 'full of volcanic, pent-up energy'. 'Christ! Fred was full of something,' admitted Roger Taylor. 'Such a joy and great fun to be around.' At Madison Square Garden, the show included the arrival of nine half-naked women on bicycles for 'Fat Bottomed Girls'. As Mercury sang, the girls circled him, trilling their bicycle bells. The press griped: 'How far will Queen go to keep people from noticing that it's not only the bicycling beauties that are bare?'

On Queen's 1977 US tour, Brian May had augmented his map of the United States with what one journalist recalled as 'a sliding tour schedule, ingeniously fashioned from cardboard and staples, and containing timetables and stopover details.' In 1979, May's sliding tour schedule must have resembled one of Heath Robinson's contraptions. Queen spent most of the year on the road promoting *Jazz*. Two weeks after Christmas they began the six-week European leg in Germany, going on to play Holland, France, Switzerland, Spain and, for the first time, Yugoslavia. By the time they returned to the UK for part of the days allocated under their current tax status, Freddie's anthem to excess, 'Don't Stop Me Now', was at number 9 in the charts.

The 1979 tour saw a pronounced change in Mercury's image. Gone were the sequinned jumpsuits to be replaced by a leather biker's cap, jacket and trousers and a heavy chain necklace. It was the singer's interpretation of an ultra-masculine look (initially known as the 'Castro Clone') that had originated in San Francisco's Castro district and had become popular in America's gay communities. As Queen played Europe in January that year, the New York disco group Village People scored a huge mainstream hit with Y.M.C.A., a coded anthem to a popular gay cruising spot. The group's members included the late Glenn Hughes (aka 'The Biker') who took the clone look even further with a heavy moustache, and whom Freddie had encountered one night at a hardcore New York gay club, The Anvil.

If one moment encapsulates the vibe of Queen's 1979 tour it's the leather-clad Mercury snarling his way through a nihilistic 'Let Me Entertain You'. The rest of Queen all played good cop to Freddie's bad. May, with ringlets and white waistcoat; Taylor the eternal blond Peter Pan; and Deacon, static on the drum riser and looking, in his shirt and tie, as if he'd just come to fix the photocopier. Above them, Queen's new rig, bathed the band in red, white and green lights, and at such a ferocious temperature that the crew nicknamed it 'the pizza oven'.

The 1979 tour would be Pete Brown's last stint as Queen's tour co-ordinator. One of his tasks for the European dates had been to ensure that the four band members had accommodation of exactly the same standard. But it was an impossible task. 'It didn't matter what I did,' said Brown. 'It was never right.' Brown eventually became a comedy agent and formed the production company, Talkback. Tragically, he died after a brain haemorrhage in 1993.

In April, Queen travelled to Japan for seventeen shows, including three at Tokyo's Budokan. Japan was a safe haven after the drubbing they'd received in the UK and US press. To honour the occasion, 'Teo Torriate (Let Us Cling Together)' was introduced into the set. Queen's standing in Japan was such that other bands were able to break into the same market almost by association. The American hard rock group Cheap Trick had opened for Queen on the US *News of the World* tour. Japanese journalists who'd flown to America to cover the tour had been impressed. Six months on, Cheap Trick were selling out the Budokan.

In June, EMI released *Live Killers*, a concert album spliced together from Queen's European shows. There had been talk of a live album since the recording of the Rainbow Theatre gigs in 1974, but the fear had been that a live Queen album couldn't match the meticulous standards of their studio work. It didn't. But in the mid- to late-seventies, most of Queen's contemporaries had made hay with live recordings: Led Zeppelin's *The Song Remains the Same*, Thin Lizzy's *Live and Dangerous*, Genesis' *Seconds Out*. 'Live albums are inescapable really,' said Brian May. 'Everyone says you have to do them.' With no immediate plans to follow up *Jazz*, EMI wanted a Queen product to tide the audience over until their next studio visit.

Live Killers was an undoctored account of Queen in concert spread across four sides of vinyl. It was loud and messy. In concert, Queen would leave the stage midway through 'Bohemian Rhapsody', giving the audience lights and smoke while they played a tape of the song's operatic section over the PA. It worked live, but without the visual extravaganza, fell flat on record. Brian May insisted there were no overdubs, but what *Live Killers* missed in finesse it made up for in energy. 'I still find it extraordinary,' said Roger Taylor, 'that the four of us could make so much fucking noise.' *Live Killers* is now a time-capsule recording of Queen in the 1970s. In the next decade the band became a very different beast.

By the time Queen reconvened to headline the Saarbrucken Festival in Germany in August, the prolific John Deacon had become a father again (to daughter Laura) and Roger Taylor had been the victim of a bizarre hairdressing accident after over-bleaching his hair on the morning of the show. The decision to play a rare one-off festival date had been taken to boost Queen's profile in Germany. They headlined over Irish guitar hero Rory Gallagher (whose old band Taste had once played above Smile), Ten Years After, and The Commodores. To the delight of Freddie Mercury, Taylor played the gig with near luminous green hair.

Taylor and Mercury would see out the summer of 1979 enjoying all the perks of moneyed rock stardom. They were among the spectators watching Bjorn Borg win the men's singles final at Wimbledon. Days later, the Queen office approached the All England Lawn Tennis Club for permission to play a gig on Centre Court. They were refused. Later, Taylor and Dominique Beyrand holidayed in the South of France. On the drive down to St Tropez, the engine on Taylor's new Ferrari blew up, rendering the car a wreck (a similar fate would befall his Aston Martin). In September, Mercury celebrated his thirty-third birthday with another lavish soirée and began plotting his next career move.

Queen's lead singer was going to become a ballet dancer.

CHAPTER EIGHT
Four Cocks Fighting

'Freddie's new moustache suggests he is looking for a
spare-time job as a waiter in the Fulham Road.'

Evening News, December 1980

'Fuck the cost darlings! Let's live a little!'

Freddie Mercury

Sunday, 7 October 1979. London's Coliseum Theatre. The Royal
Ballet Company has acquired a new male dancer: Freddie
Mercury. Reportedly, his footwork is terrible, but what he lacks in
natural ability he compensates for in enthusiasm and commitment. Outside, in the music world, The Police and Blondie are
conquering the singles and album charts while Led Zeppelin have
just played what would be their final British gig for twenty-eight
years. But in the rarefied world of classical dance, Queen's lead
singer was about to make his debut with one of the world's finest
ballet companies in front of an audience of nearly two and half
thousand people.

Mercury had been recruited to perform at the gala charity event
by one of the company's principal dancers, Wayne Eagling. To
drum up publicity for the show, Eagling wanted to enlist a
performer from outside the world of dance to make a cameo
appearance. When Kate Bush turned him down, Eagling was
offered Freddie Mercury. The singer leapt at the chance, but, as he
later admitted, 'I thought they were mad!' For his first rehearsal in
a studio at Baron's Court, Mercury made the most regal of

entrances, reporting for duty already wearing ballet shoes and tights. 'Finding out what it involved really scared me,' he said. 'They had me rehearsing all kinds of dance steps. I was trying to do, in a few days, the kind of things they had spent years rehearsing, and let me tell you, it was murder. After two days, I was aching in places I didn't even know I had.'

Mercury appeared at the gala to perform 'Bohemian Rhapsody' and Queen's next single, 'Crazy Little Thing Called Love'. With his hair slicked back, and wearing a slashed V-neck one-piece, he began his routine on the shoulders of three bare-chested male dancers, singing live to an orchestral accompaniment of the song. For the song's grand denouement, Mercury reappeared, barefoot and clad in a silver catsuit, before being flipped 360 degrees by his partners to sing the song's final lyric upside down. 'I wasn't quite Baryshnikov, but wasn't bad for an ageing beginner,' he claimed. 'I'd like to see Mick Jagger or Rod Stewart trying something like that.'

Sitting in the audience was Roger Taylor. 'There was only one person in the world that could have gotten away with it,' he recalled. 'Freddie was performing in front of a very stiff Royal Ballet audience, average age ninety-four, who did not know what to make of this silver *thing* that was being tossed around onstage in front of them. I thought it was very brave and absolutely hilarious.' It wouldn't be the last time Mercury donned his ballet shoes and tights.

Earlier, that summer, Queen had spent their time between London, Geneva and Munich. The Mountain Studios complex in Switzerland had been put up for sale. Shortly before flying to Japan, Queen's accountants approached the studio's shareholders on Queen's behalf. In the light of a recent hefty tax bill, they considered it prudent for the band to own their own studio. The deal would be completed by the end of the year, with Queen also inheriting Mountain's resident engineer David Richards.

In early June, though, Queen arrived at Munich's Musicland Studios. They were still on their tax year out and had no firm plans to make another album, but a session had been booked following the Japanese dates. Musicland was an underground complex that had been established by the Italian producer Giorgio Moroder.

German producer Reinhold Mack (known to all as just 'Mack') was recording in Los Angeles with guitarist Gary Moore when he received a message about working with Queen at Musicland. When he phoned the studio to check, no one seemed to know what he was talking about. On a whim, he bought a ticket anyway and flew to Munich.

'After *Jazz*, we felt we had to get away to new territory,' said Brian May. 'We asked Musicland who they had, and they said Mack. He turned out to be a real find.' Arriving at Musicland, Mack found the studio crammed with boxes, amps and flight cases, flown in from Japan, and three-quarters of Queen: Mercury, Taylor and Deacon. 'They had no plans to make an album,' says Mack, 'but Freddie said to me, "If you're up for it, I've got an idea. But let's do it now before Brian arrives."' Mercury strummed out the opening chords to what would become 'Crazy Little Thing Called Love'.

The song had taken shape just hours before. Peter Hince had flown into Munich from London, bringing Mercury with him: 'Fred never travelled alone. There always had to be someone with him.' A strike at Heathrow Airport had delayed all flights, and Mercury was especially anxious as he'd used up his allotted days under UK tax laws. When they finally reached Munich, the pair checked into the Hilton hotel. No sooner had Mercury disappeared to take a bath before he was calling out to Hince: 'Ratty! Ratty! Get me a guitar now.' Mercury emerged from his bathroom, draped in towels, picked up his acoustic guitar, and began humming and picking out the chords. Mercury didn't want to lose the moment and they went straight to Musicland.

Mack secretly recorded Mercury's first run-through of the song. When the singer asked if he was ready to start recording, Mack offered to play him back what he'd just done. For Queen, this was a brand-new way of working. Backed by Deacon and Taylor, Mercury sang and played acoustic rhythm guitar. ' "Crazy Little Thing Called Love" took me five, ten minutes to write,' said Mercury. 'I was restricted by only knowing a few chords. It's a good discipline, as I simply had to write in a small framework.' The discipline and restricted framework gave Queen a song that was the polar opposite of 'Killer Queen', 'Bohemian Rhapsody' and 'Bicycle

Race'. 'Crazy Little Thing Called Love' was a fun rock 'n' roll pastiche, like something Fred Bulsara might have worked out on the college common room piano after hearing Elvis on the radio at Gladstone Avenue that morning.

Mercury's parting shot to Mack was: 'Brian isn't going to like it.' When May arrived at Musicland, Freddie was proved right: 'He didn't like it at all.' Unaware of the balance of power and diplomacy required around Queen, Mack asked May to ditch his hallowed Red Special and AC30 amp, and play the song's solo on a Telecaster (borrowed from Roger Taylor), which he would then put through a Mesa-Boogie amp rather than Brian's favoured AC30. The idea was to give the song a more authentic rockabilly feel. 'I wasn't happy,' admitted May. 'I kicked against it, but I saw that it was the right way to go.' In the space of just four hours, Queen recorded the song that would become their first American number 1.

Over the next month at Musicland, they worked on three more tracks, recording without a deadline, but to have material ready for when they decided to make a new album. 'It's a way of getting out of the rut of album, touring Britain, touring America . . .' explained May. One track, Roger Taylor's 'Coming Soon', began during the *Jazz* sessions. It was slick, modern power-pop, with shades of Mack's recent production clients, E.L.O. In contrast, May came up with 'Save Me' and 'Sail Away Sweet Sister', two heavy ballads that offered a nod back to the Queen of old.

'One of my fortes is I work really fast,' Mack explains, 'and Queen work very slowly. I only discovered how slow later on. My plan was to get them to change because they'd become so stuck in their ways.' Under Queen's old rules, backing tracks were recorded over and over again until they were perfect. Even the group realised that the end result could be sterile and too precise. 'I said, 'You don't have to do that,'' explains Mack. 'I can drop the whole thing in. If it breaks down after half a minute, then we can edit it in and carry on if you just play along with the tempo.''

'We thought that was a joke at the time,' admitted May. 'But doing it Mack's way we were able to get a complete backing track down in half a day.' Unhappy with many aspects of *Jazz*, Taylor had a clear idea of what was needed: 'Mack's brief was to make it fresh and easy and not to use too many microphones. We wanted him to make us sound like a band again.'

'Crazy Little Thing Called Love' impressed EMI, who hurried it out as a single in October, a fortnight after its premiere with Mercury and The Royal Ballet. Back in England, Queen filmed a promo at Trillion Studios in London's Soho. Their image was as strikingly different as the song: everyone was in black leather, everyone had gone under the barber's scissors (even Brian), while Freddie straddled a motorcycle and shimmied with a group of male and female dancers choreographed by Arlene Phillips, later to become a BBC reality TV judge, but then the boss of TV dance troupe Hot Gossip.

Mercury and the dancers promenaded along a catwalk into which holes had been cut through which clapping hands emerged (belonging to various members of Queen's entourage). To augment his campest performance yet, Mercury's T-shirt was riddled with strategically placed holes, while his PVC trousers were accessorised by skateboarders' kneepads. 'It was the era of skateboarding,' says Peter Hince. 'Fred would pick up influences from all over the place.' *Top of the Pops* viewers who'd last seen Queen in the promo for 'We Will Rock You' would bear witness to the singer's transformation from glam-rock pimpernel to Castro Clone in just two years.

'Horrified or thrilled, audiences couldn't always believe their eyes with Freddie,' said Taylor. 'But we let him get on with it. Despite the arguments, we were a very tight-knit group. Our attitude was always: if that's what he wants to do, go for it.' By the end of the month, 'Crazy Little Thing Called Love' had peaked at number 2, only denied pole position by Dr Hook's country-pop smoochie 'When You're in Love With a Beautiful Woman'. Queen's Elvis spoof broadened their audience almost overnight. 'Suddenly, we've got a lot of younger people coming to our concerts,' said Brian May.

The Queen *Crazy* tour ran for eighteen dates across the UK in November and December. Two years before, Queen's homecoming had been marked by just a handful of arena shows. This time, Gerry Stickells had been instructed to find smaller venues.

'We'd been accused of being too grand,' admitted Roger Taylor. 'So this was our way of getting closer to the audience, and to prove to critics, "Fuck you, we can go down just as well in a 1,400-seater." ' The name of the tour didn't just relate to the single, but 'to the fact that we were crazy for doing it,' he adds, 'It was *Crazy* as in we could have done a couple of nights at Wembley instead.'

The tour opened at larger venues in Dublin and Birmingham before moving on to what Brian May called 'the daft ones'. On 13 December, Queen pitched up at the Lyceum in London, only to find a problem fitting their lighting rig into the 2,000-seater theatre. 'The Lyceum roof was too small to fit all our lights,' recalled Taylor. 'So we asked the manager if it would be OK to drill two holes in it. He was fine about it, as long as we paid for the holes. Then we got a call from Paul McCartney saying that Wings were playing there next week, and they'd need a hole in the roof too, so could he pay for one of them? We became the first ever group to sell Paul McCartney a hole.'

While Queen could see the whites of their audience's eyes, there was an incongruity between the jetset rock band and the humbler surroundings of Tiffany's Ballroom in Purley, Croydon. Mercury's entourage now included former Royal Ballet wardrobe assistant Peter 'Phoebe' Freestone. Writing in *Freddie Mercury: An Intimate Memoir*, Freeman remarked: 'Tiffany's in Purley? I think the only Tiffany's that Freddie knew about was on Fifth Avenue in New York.'

Onstage at the Lyceum, though, Mercury must have been aware of how far he'd travelled. Ten year earlier, on 12 October 1969, Fred Bulsara had been to see Led Zeppelin at the same venue. Back then, he was just out of college, paying the rent with a part-time job at Harrods, and trying to become a rock star with the band Ibex. Back then, too, he had kept one aspect of his sexuality a secret. After Queen's show at the Brighton Centre, Mercury picked up a blond motorcycle courier named Tony Bastin at a gay club and took him back to his suite at the Grand Hotel. For all the one-night stands in America, Mercury's closest friends always maintained that, ultimately, he wanted a long-term relationship. Smitten by the 28-year-old, though unable to stay completely faithful, Mercury moved Bastin into Stafford Terrace, where he became a fixture for the next few months.

The *Crazy* tour wound up at London's Alexandra Palace. Yet, just four days later, on Boxing Day, Queen played the Hammersmith Odeon. The venue was hosting a series of concerts to raise funds for the people of war-torn Kampuchea (now Cambodia). Paul McCartney had helped recruit Queen to play the first night, before gigs by The Who, The Clash, The Pretenders and Elvis Costello, among others. Showing little sign of fatigue, Queen played one of their best shows of the year, with Mercury trashing the monitors during 'Sheer Heart Attack', and re-appearing for 'We Will Rock You' on the shoulders of a roadie dressed as Superman.

While the tour was deemed a success, it came at a cost. Gerry Stickells collapsed backstage at the Lyceum, suffering from exhaustion. The pressure of tending to the band's exacting needs and, at times, trying to defy the laws of physics to fit Queen's stage show into tiny provincial ballrooms proved too much. Ignoring doctors' advice, Stickells stayed to oversee the rest of the tour. 'That's what they pay me for,' he said. 'To work miracles.'

Others weren't so fortunate. Sound engineer John Harris, the inspiration for 'I'm in Love With My Car', and once described by Brian May as 'the fifth member of Queen', had been taken ill at the end of the *News of the World* tour. His replacement was the American Trip Khalaf, who would remain with the band until the end. Harris was devoted to Queen, and, unusually, had been rewarded with a financial deal that involved him receiving a percentage of the band's live shows. He returned for the *Crazy* tour but ill-health forced him to quit again at the end of the year. Harris was offered the chance to run Mountain Studios, but declined. 'John succumbed to a mysterious illness which all but immobilised him and put an end to his touring days,' said Brian May in 2009.

For Queen, inevitably, there was no time to reflect. Just like 'Bohemian Rhapsody' before, American radio DJs had begun playing 'Crazy Little Thing Called Love', even though Elektra had no plans to release it as a single. The label relented, and by Christmas 1979, it was at number 1. It was a relief, especially as 'Don't Stop Me Now' had failed even to crack the Top 50. But it was also indicative of musical changes ahead. Queen's last US Top 5 hit had been 'We Are the Champions'. Now they were back, but with a knockabout rockabilly number. 'No doubt there are those who hate the new single, but like what we've done in the past,' said a cautious May. 'But I think that tends to happen, unless you're totally predictable. You lose some, you gain some.' In January, 'Save Me', a more traditional Queen ballad, was released as a single, reaching number 11 in the UK.

The success of both singles brought with it the pressure to keep working. Queen returned to Munich in February for a four-month recording session. It was the longest amount of time they'd spent in one place working on an album (working title: *Play the Game*). 'Between 1979 and 1984, I probably spent about a year of my life in the Munich Hilton,' says Peter Hince now. 'Ratty' was there to assist John Deacon as part of what was called the Bass Department. The Gentlemen's Department comprised Mercury and various members of his entourage. The Guitar Department was May and his tech Brian 'Jobby' Zellis, while the Drum Department included Roger Taylor and his technician Chris 'Crystal' Taylor. 'There was a certain amount of rivalry, banter and competition – professionally and socially,' says Hince.

Queen were unusually prolific in Munich. Some claim as many as forty songs were submitted for what would become a ten-track album, eventually titled *The Game*. As Mack observes, 'There were two camps of songwriting: Freddie and Brian. Fred was easy. We thought along similar lines and it took him fifteen to twenty minutes to come up with something absolutely brilliant. Brian, on the other hand, would come up with a great idea and get completely lost in insignificant details. Keeping the focus was difficult at the best of times with this mixture of personalities.'

Mack's request that May use a Telecaster on 'Crazy Little Thing Called Love' wasn't the only time the two butted heads. 'There was some conflict,' conceded May. 'I had a lot of disputes with him over how we should record guitars. I just wanted to record it the way I always recorded it. I wasn't even thinking about it. But Mack said, "Look, try my way." Eventually we did compromise and get the best of both worlds.'

Discussing Queen's tax year out to record *Jazz*, Brian May recalled the band thinking that recording overseas would take away the 'distractions' of working at home. However, in Munich, there were more distractions than ever. 'When we did *The Game*, everything was fun and new and shiny,' remembered May. 'But the problems started with, "Let's have a drink after the studio", which was nice, at first . . .'

The regular routine at Musicland would begin with representatives from each of the 'departments' meeting at six o'clock, when Brian 'Jobby' Zellis would start mixing cocktails. Cocktails would be followed by dinner, more drinks and then on to a club. Mercury and other members of the Gentlemen's Department would often head for Old Mrs Henderson (known as Henderson's), a popular gay nightspot on Munich's Rumfordstrasse. The rest of Queen, 'Crystal', 'Jobby', 'Ratty' and Mack would usually make for the Sugar Shack, 'the hottest disco in the world,' as Taylor called it at the time.

'The Sugar Shack became known as "The Office",' laughs Mack. 'We'd be down there after the studio at least every other day.' On many occasions, the night would carry on after the club had closed. 'After the Sugar Shack we might head to the market that was just opening up and have a bottle of champagne,' remembers Hince. 'Then back to the Munich Hilton where we'd meet up with Freddie.' At the hotel, the fun would continue in either Taylor's suite (nicknamed HH, the Hetero Hangout) or Mercury's (PPP, the Presidential Pouff Parlour.) 'Then we'd go to bed, get up in the afternoon and have breakfast . . . and we lived like that for a year.'

One night, after the Sugar Shack, the band returned to the studio to work on a new piece of May's called 'Dragon Attack'. The lyrics to the song even mentioned 'the shack'. 'Brian was a vodka-and-tonic man,' laughs Mack. 'I don't think I ever saw him take a drug. But if Brian was loaded he could lose his thread completely.' 'Dragon Attack' was assembled out of thirty minutes of alcohol-fuelled jamming. If the band were under the influence, the song didn't suffer. It had the same limbrous groove as some of the funkier tracks on the next Rolling Stones album. May played a brawny guitar solo while Mercury dispensed a little Robert Plant-style orgasmic grunting. It was a comfort to any Queen fan turned off by the frippery of 'Crazy Little Thing Called Love'.

The Sugar Shack had other attractions beyond the obvious. 'We would take tracks down there after hours and play them over their system to see how they worked,' said May. 'Anything with a bit of groove and space sounded good.' One of the club's crowd-pleasers was 'Feel Like Makin' Love', a hit for Bad Company, the band fronted by Paul Rodgers after Free. 'Bad Company sounded brilliant in there because there was a lot of space in that song. We played some of our stuff, like "Tie Your Mother Down", and it didn't work because it was crammed with so many things that there was no space. After that we became obsessed with leaving space in our music and making songs that would sound great in the Sugar Shack.'

But it was John Deacon's latest creation that would pass the Sugar Shack test with honours. In the studio, Taylor, Mercury and May would share their ideas for songs, humming choruses or demonstrating melody lines, looking for feedback from the others. Deacon preferred to remain silent while composing, leading Mercury to nickname him 'Ostrich'. 'He was like a bird who stays quiet until it finally lays a perfect egg,' says Mack. For *The Game*, Deakey laid his best egg yet: 'Another One Bites the Dust'.

Bernard Edwards, the late guitarist of US funk band Chic, remembered Deacon dropping by New York's Power Station Studios while Chic were recording their 1979 album, *Risqué*. From those sessions, Chic landed a huge hit with 'Good Times'. Like 'Good Times', 'Another One Bites The Dust' was a sparse dance track, driven by much the same bassline. Of course, Deacon's inspiration for the song could be traced back further to his days playing Motown covers with The Opposition. 'I listened to a lot of soul music when I was at school,' he said. 'I'd wanted to do something like "Another One Bites the Dust" for a while, but all I had was the line and the bass riff.'

'I must admit,' said May, 'that the rest of us had no idea what Deakey was doing when he started this.' Nevertheless, with the rest of the group assisting, the track took shape. Typically, Brian May remembers Roger Taylor being most resistant to the song: 'I remember Roger hated it: "This isn't rock 'n' roll, what the hell are we doing?" He didn't want Queen to become funky.' Interviewed in 2008, Taylor insisted that what he was opposed to was not the song, but putting it out as a single: 'It wasn't to everyone's taste, but it was the second time we'd put our toe in dance music. I'd had a rather ineffectual pop at it with "Fun It" [on the *Jazz* album].'

Deacon and Taylor worked together on the backing track. Deacon wanted the drums to sound as dry as possible. It was the antithesis of how Queen normally recorded, but Taylor acquiesced, stuffing the drums with blankets to muffle the sound. 'Roger laid down this beautiful drum loop,' explained May. 'It was a very unusual sound for him, as he always liked big, ambient drums. I was fine about doing it, as my job was to inject these dirty little guitars around Deakey's percussive riff.'

Deacon played the rhythm guitar, leaving May to add the flourishes, while Mack worked the sound of backwards piano, cymbal crashes and handclaps into the mix. The last sprinkle of magic dust came from Freddie Mercury. 'Fred had a feel for dance music,' said May, 'and he was starting to fall in love with singing that way. He was so into what we were doing with "Another One Bites the Dust" that he sang until his throat bled.'

'Another One Bites the Dust' wasn't the only departure from the norm. After years of resistance, Queen had succumbed to the synthesiser. 'I'm afraid that was my fault,' said Taylor. 'I'd bought this Oberheim polyphonic synth. I showed it to Fred, and immediately he was like, "Oh, this is good, dear . . ."' The Oberheim OBX would be used on several tracks, including Taylor's 'Rock It (Prime Jive)'. Taylor described the song as his 'most basic ever'. Like 'Coming Soon', it was no-frills rock. But 'Rock It' would become the source of disagreement in the studio. Taylor wanted to sing the lead vocal, but Mack wanted Mercury. Two versions were recorded. After hearing both, May voted for Mercury's, but Deacon wanted Taylor's. As a compromise, on the final version, Mercury would sing the intro before Taylor took over from the first verse.

The drummer also wanted 'Coming Soon' to be released as a single and replaced on the album by another of his own tracks, 'A Human Body'. The rest of the band disagreed, and 'A Human Body' was held over for a future B-side. 'Roger was the one in search of a new sound,' says Mack. Taylor was also the one that would work most closely with Mack in finessing his compositions, with some of his rejected songs from *The Game* finding a home on his first solo album. Taylor's attitude to punk had softened since *News of the World* days. In 1980, he enthused in the music press about The Clash's latest single 'London Calling' and new bands such as The Pretenders. But, as Brian May explained, 'In Queen, in the studio, you only got 25 per cent of your own way at the best of times.'

'If there was ever a big disagreement it was generally between me and Roger,' said May. 'As the original two that put the band together, we were like brothers. And we would always find things to have these violent disagreements about. But it was almost always music. That feeling that you're not being represented, you're not being heard.'

May reportedly walked out of the band during the Munich sessions: 'I left the group a couple of times just for the day. I'm off and I'm not coming back! We've all done that. You end up quibbling over one note.'

'There were huge rows in the studio,' agreed Taylor. 'Usually over how long Brian was taking . . . or whether he was having an omelette. We all drove each other nuts.'

Mercury described the dynamic within Queen more succinctly: 'Four cocks fighting. Lovely!'

Much like the physics student he was once was, May believed that recording was an exact science. 'Brian would spend ages getting it right,' recalls Peter Hince, 'and then getting it *more* right, after that.' While others swapped Musicland for the lure of the Sugar Shack, May could sometimes be found at the studio on what he calls 'an eternal quest for perfection'. It was a lonely undertaking. 'I was always the one sat there at three o'clock in the morning trying to make something work,' he recalled. May sang lead vocals on his own 'Sail Away Sweet Sister', a rather downbeat song with a stirring chorus.

Unfortunately, at times, Freddie Mercury sounded as if he was far too distracted by the Munich nightlife. The glib rockabilly of 'Don't Try Suicide' was the weakest song on *The Game*. The album's opening track, 'Play the Game', was certainly better. A regal ballad, supposedly inspired by Mercury's romance with Tony Bastin, only the synthesiser dated it as being from 1980 rather than 1975. John Deacon couldn't hope to better 'Another One Bites the Dust', and his 'Need Your Loving Tonight' was default-setting MOR rock sandwiched between 'Another One . . .' and 'Crazy Little Thing . . .' on the album's final tracklisting.

The Game was released in June 1980. Like *Jazz* and *News of the World*, it yo-yoed between styles and sounds, as each of its four writers hustled for space. But this disjointedness was fast becoming a key ingredient of the Queen sound. *The Game* skipped through power ballads, heavy rock, disco, pop and rockabilly on its first side alone. 'For me, the band was functioning well at this point,' said Taylor. '*The Game* was much more of a piece than *Jazz*. Our songwriting was much better.'

EMI also had the album cover they'd always wanted: a black and white shot of Queen in their 'Crazy Little Thing Called Love' get-up. It was the anti-*Queen II*, selling the group hard as a relevant pop band for the 1980s. In the press, there were murmurs of discontent about *The Game* including two already available singles, but it made scant difference to sales. Within a fortnight, Queen would have a number 1 album in Britain. Ten weeks later, it achieved the same in the US, where *Rolling Stone* damned it with the faintest of praise: 'Certainly *The Game* is less obnoxious than Queen's last few outings.'

'We have great fun, laying down bets on chart positions,' Roger Taylor told *Sounds*. The ever-competitive Taylor was especially pleased to discover that *The Game* was outselling The Rolling Stones' latest, *Emotional Rescue*, which had beaten *The Game*'s release by ten days, but would only make it to number 9 in Britain. Away from Queen, Taylor had something more personal to celebrate. In May, he joined May and Deacon by becoming a father, when girlfriend Dominique gave birth to his first son, Felix Luther.

Meanwhile, Freddie Mercury showed up for a silent cameo in friend Kenny Everett's TV show, pouncing on the DJ during a comedy skit and wrestling him to the ground. It was a rare TV appearance outside of Queen. Elsewhere, he indulged himself with a little more 'crazee shopping'. During his tax year out, the singer had instructed Mary Austin to look for another property for him in Kensington. She found Garden Lodge, 1 Logan Place, an eight-bedroom Georgian mansion, complete with three-quarters of an acre of garden, hidden away from the outside world by high brick walls. Mercury was enchanted, and paid £500,000 in cash, without flinching. 'I saw it, fell in love with it, and within half an hour it was mine,' he said. 'It's full of marble floors and mahogany staircases. I call it my country house in town. I'm not into all this country air and cow dung.' Almost immediately, he hired an architect and began instigating widespread renovations and conversions to the property.

The single 'Play the Game' was less immediate and radio-friendly than 'Crazy Little Thing Called Love', but reached a respectable number 14 in the UK. Of greater interest than the song was Mercury's latest fashion statement. The singer had completed the Castro Clone look by growing a thick moustache. In protest, the band's offices were inundated with packets of razors as fans voiced their protest. 'It's funny how he got more press out of growing a moustache than he would have done from walking naked down Oxford Street,' remarked Roger Taylor.

Queen's next American tour was due to open in Vancouver at the end of June. The Who were touring the US at the same time. Their support band was The Only Ones, a group featuring bass guitarist and former Kensington Market stallholder Alan Mair. Mair's old employee Fred Bulsara was now Freddie Mercury, millionaire rock star, but Alan would catch a rare glimpse of the old Freddie during the tour.

'I'd stayed in touch with Queen for the first couple of years, but then I joined The Only Ones and I remember seeing Freddie again and he'd got a bit too into himself, under the influence of whatever he was taking,' recalls Mair. When The Who played the LA Forum, Mair spotted members of Queen arriving backstage. 'My initial instinct was to go over and say hi, but then I remembered that the last time I'd seen Fred he'd been such an arsehole, so I looked away.' Mair left the party to walk back to the band's trailer. 'Suddenly, I heard these heels clicking behind me, and it was Fred. He'd seen me turn away. He was extremely friendly, asked me why I'd walked away and said, "Was it because I was such a cunt last time I saw you?" And I said, "Yes, Freddie, it is and you were" . . . He laughed. But after that I started to see him again.'

When Queen's own tour began, Mercury's facial hair would attract yet more attention. At some gigs, fans threw disposable razors on stage. As the tour wound on, Mercury began asking audiences what they thought of the new look, twitchily grinning at the chorus of cheers, boos and cat-calls. 'D'you girls like this moustache? . . . D'you boys like this moustache? . . . A lot of people hate it. I don't give a fuck!' Meanwhile, those unsure about who was playing the drums in Queen need only look at Roger Taylor's bass drum skin, which was helpfully decorated with a picture of his face ('Just in case he ever got amnesia, he'd know who he was,' said drum tech 'Crystal').

Six songs from *The Game* had been worked sporadically into a set that now opened with 'Jailhouse Rock'. 'Another One Bites the Dust' was played, but, at first, only occasionally. It was difficult to replicate the dry studio drum sound onstage, and the song's funkier approach rankled with some of Queen's audience. 'They thought it "not very rock 'n' roll",' admitted Brian May. A year earlier, Detroit radio DJ Steve Dahl had launched the 'Disco Sucks!' campaign in protest at rock being squeezed out of radio playlists by dance music. It culminated in a ceremonial burning of Bee Gees, Chic and Village People records at a baseball stadium in Chicago. Nevertheless, it illuminated the dividing line between rock and dance traditions in America, with an uneasy sub-text of white versus black music. In a bizarre twist, New York dance station WBLS had picked up on 'Another One Bites the Dust', unaware of Queen's history, and playlisted the record. 'They thought we were a black act,' said May. The response was so favourable that other stations followed their lead. When 'Play the Game' stiffed at a bully number 42 in America, the band had nothing to lose by such increased exposure.

According to 'Crystal' Taylor, it was the band's crew that first suggested 'Another One Bites the Dust' as a single, after hearing it at Musicland: 'But the band just glared at us and told us to mix some more cocktails.' Roger Taylor remembers it differently. After one of Queen's four shows at the LA Forum in July, the band's backstage visitors included Michael Jackson. 'I remember Michael and some of his brothers in the dressing room going on and on about "Another One Bites the Dust",' Taylor insisted. 'They kept saying we must release it as a single.'

Not for the first time, the record company bowed to outside pressure. A performance video for the song was shot during the soundcheck in Dallas. A week later, the single was released in the US. Eight weeks on, Queen had their second US number 1 hit. In the UK, 'Another One Bites the Dust' made it to number 7, losing out to The Police, Madness and Elvis Presley. But it would make the top spot elsewhere in Argentina, Spain, Mexico and Canada. As Brian May admitted, 'Roger and I would probably never have gone in that musical direction had we not been coerced by John and Freddie.' 'I never thought it would be a hit,' admitted Taylor. 'How wrong was I?'

'Another One Bites the Dust' would achieve multi-platinum status, while giving Elektra its first three-million-selling single. But Chic's Bernard Edwards had mixed feelings about the song. As John Deacon freely admitted, 'Another One Bites the Dust' had borrowed its bassline from Chic's 'Good Times'. 'That's OK,' Edwards told *NME*. 'What isn't OK is that the press started saying that we had ripped *them* off. "Good Times" came out more than a year before, but it was inconceivable to these people that black musicians could possibly be innovative like that. It was just these dumb disco guys ripping off this rock 'n' roll song.'

As well as his new son, Taylor had another welcome distraction outside of the band. During a three-week break from the tour, he flew to Mountain Studios to work on a solo album, later released as *Fun in Space*. Taylor had been piecing together ideas since the first sessions for *The Game* in 1979. Throughout the rest of the year, he would return to Mountain during downtime from Queen, and would put together ten tracks on which he sang and played all the instruments, with engineer David Richards adding additional synthesiser. The instrument that Queen had avoided for so long would take centre-stage on *Fun in Space* and on Queen's next studio outing.

The US tour reconvened in Milwaukee in early September, with

Queen basking in the glory of a number 1 hit. Mercury, usually bare-chested or in a figure-hugging vest and PVC trousers, continued to goad the audience about his moustache before introducing 'Fat Bottomed Girls': 'I hate skinny chicks . . . the bigger the tits the better!'

Offstage, of course, the *Spartacus Guide*, a worldwide directory of gay-friendly bars and clubs, would dictate his nightlife in each city. During a stop-over in New York, Mercury had a fling with a male nurse named Thor Arnold. The 'good time, good time' he had sung about in 'Don't Stop Me Now' continued at a pace. 'We all knew what was going on and with whom,' chuckled Roger Taylor. 'We were all in each other's lives.' On 28 September, Taylor would realise his dream of Queen matching Yes's record at Madison Square Garden. Queen filled the Garden for three consecutive nights, with Mercury spraying the front row of the audience with champagne and cheerfully calling them all 'cunts'. The final night's aftershow party saw male guests served by topless waitresses in black stockings and high heels, while female guests were tended to by male waiters clad only in gym shorts. As one eyewitness remarked: 'Queen didn't want to be accused of sexism.'

Implausibly, after coming straight off the back of a 46-date American tour, Queen would spend most of October and November in a recording studio. The year before, film director Mike Hodges had approached the band about composing a soundtrack for his forthcoming science-fiction movie, *Flash Gordon*. The band agreed, and Hodges pitched Queen to the film's Italian producer Dino De Laurentiis. No great fan of rock music, the producer's immediate response was, 'But who are the queens?'

Flash Gordon was a comic-strip superhero created in 1934. Taylor and May were both fans of science fiction and comic books, with Taylor especially gung-ho about breaking Queen into a new medium. 'We wanted to write the first rock 'n' roll musical soundtrack,' he said. 'No one had ever used rock music in a film unless it was something like *The Girl Can't Help It*, where it was a movie about music. Nowadays it's the norm, but we thought we were breaking a bit of ground.'

Queen were shown twenty minutes worth of film footage. They

demoed some initial ideas in Munich while working on *The Game*. 'Then Dino De Laurentiis heard the demo tracks and was like, "No, this is not my film!"' recalled Brian May. 'But Mike Hodges stuck with it and convinced him it would be great.' De Laurentiis' doubts stemmed from his desire to make a heavyweight sci-fi epic and Hodges' intention to create something more kitsch. Queen's demos were tailored with Mike Hodges' vision in mind.

The soundtrack was patched together at various London studios in two months with Brian May and Mack producing. 'It was very seat-of-the-pants,' admitted May. Not least for composer Howard Blake, who was brought in to write a last-minute orchestral score, after Bowie's string arranger Paul Buckmaster quit, in the belief that it would be used alongside Queen's contributions. With the Royal Philharmonic Orchestra already booked into a studio, Blake was presented with a crippling deadline. He produced a ninety-minute score in 10 days, staying awake for the last four days straight. 'I remember Freddie Mercury singing the idea of "Ride to Arboria" in his high falsetto,' said Blake. 'And I showed him how I could expand it into the orchestral section now on the film.' After three days conducting the orchestra in the studio, Blake collapsed with chronic bronchitis brought on by exhaustion and stress.

In the end, Taylor's enthusiasm for the polyphonic synth used on *The Game* would dictate many of the sounds on the album. When Howard Blake recovered, he discovered that much of his score had been replaced by Queen's synthesised music. 'A disappointment,' he understated. But it would be May that would see the project to completion: 'Everyone else got drawn into other things, and as I also had the longest attention span it was to left to me to hold the baby.' 'It was a technical nightmare,' adds Mack. 'There was just me and Brian and so many tape recorders and tapes and cassettes with bits and pieces of dialogue . . .'

'We wanted the soundtrack album to make you feel like you'd watched the film,' said May. 'So we shipped in all the dialogue and effects and wove it into a tapestry.' In 1994, the soundtrack to Tarantino's *Pulp Fiction* would make spectacular use of the film's dialogue, but Queen's soundtrack to *Flash Gordon* premiered the same trick fifteen years earlier. When they finally synced the music with the finished rushes, De Laurentiis was convinced. Mike Hodges had succeeded in bringing the camp comic strip to life. There were over-the-top sets and dialogue; there was Shakespearean actor Brian Blessed hamming it up in gold hot pants; there was Ingmar Bergman protégé Max von Sydow playing Emperor Ming, and there was the beautiful Ornella Muti as Princess Aura getting strapped to a table and whipped. With its tongue-in-cheek humour and frisson of S&M, *Flash Gordon* was made for Queen, and vice versa.

'Flash's Theme' was a Top 10 hit in November. The chorus was nursery-rhyme simple, the prodding rhythm had just the right air of cinematic menace, putting some in mind of the approaching shark in *Jaws* five years earlier, and there was plenty of loud guitar. Meanwhile, dialogue whizzed in and out of the mix with Brian Blessed's Prince Vultan delivering the immortal line, 'Gordon's Alive!' 'It was a very camp film,' admitted Taylor. 'But I thought our music suited the film in all its camp awfulness.'

When Queen flew to Zurich to begin rehearsals for the European tour, they brought with them their new toy: a synthesiser. It would fall to Brian May to play the synth on 'The Hero', 'Flash's Theme' and 'Battle Theme', the three Flash Gordon tracks that had been worked into the setlist. Their opening act for the tour would be Straight Eight, a West London pub-rock band who'd been signed to Pete Townshend's Eel Pie Records. The label had stumped up an eye-watering £30,000 to buy Straight Eight on to the tour. Not that anyone in Queen took much notice.

'Brian was charming and friendly and offered us compliments and advice,' recalls Straight Eight guitarist Rick Cassman now. 'John Deacon was almost invisible, and I don't think Freddie said a word to me or any of the band for the entire tour. Right from day one I noticed that Freddie was rather aloof. He always arrived by separate limousine with his own group of hangers-on. But every performance he gave was faultless. Roger Taylor was a little like Freddie in that he seemed to move in his own circles and arrived at gigs with his own entourage. I detected massive egos with both him and Freddie.'

The tour included six dates in Germany, one at Berlin's Deutschlandhalle, the 9,000-seater arena built for the 1936

Olympics. 'It was where they used to hold Nazi rallies,' recalls Cassman. 'That was surreal. Ahead of me I could see nothing but darkness until the entire audience raised their lighters and became a giant illuminated mass. Wonderful!' Freddie's party-piece for the encore of 'We Will Rock You' now involved arriving onstage on the shoulders of a roadie dressed as *Star Wars* villain Darth Vader. *Star Wars* creator George Lucas caught wind of the stunt, and threatened to sue, forcing Queen to scrap the act.

In December, *The Game* tour reached England. The Birmingham NEC was a newly opened 1,300-seat venue, making Straight Eight the first band ever to play there. But the support band were always going to be overwhelmed by the headliners. 'Queen used that old trick of turning the PA volume up to double what it was when we performed,' says Cassman. 'So that immediately made them appear bigger and brasher than us. They were 100 per cent professional, and the main thing we learned from them was to use the whole stage and try to make ourselves appear bigger than we actually were.'

At Birmingham, Mercury took such brashness to new heights by re-appearing for the encore wearing the tiniest leather shorts he could fit himself into. Backstage, crew members took bets on whether or not he'd split them. 'Onstage, Freddie was 100 per cent energy and charisma,' says Cassman. But he couldn't help but notice how different he was offstage. 'He seemed distant, even to the other band members. I never remember Queen laughing or joking about during soundchecks.'

On the night of 8 December, John Lennon was shot dead outside his apartment building in New York. The day after Queen played Wembley Arena and performed a quickly rehearsed version of Lennon's 'Imagine'. Mercury fluffed the lyrics and May forgot some of the chords. Away from the braggadocio of his live performance, Mercury was still playing down the importance of his songwriting in any interview, and Lennon, more often or not, was his yardstick. 'I don't believe that I have a talent to write deep messages,' he said. 'John Lennon can do that but I can't.'

Queen's *Flash Gordon* soundtrack was released on 8 December. In the UK, it would match the single's Top 10 placing but stopped shy of the Top 20 in America. It had Queen's name on its cover, but it wasn't a Queen album in the conventional sense. Though, oddly, it attracted some of their best press yet ('Wham! Zam! Thok! An album of truly epic proportions!' raved *Record Mirror*). *Flash Gordon* only contained two full-length songs, 'Flash's Theme' and 'The Hero', with the rest given over to short, incidental pieces; ideal for the film, but unlikely to hold the attention without the visual spectacle. Also, not everyone in the band seemed to share May and Taylor's passion for Flash Gordon. When one of Queen's crew stuck the album on during a late-night drinking session, a refreshed John Deacon slurred, 'Who is this?'

Back in Germany for the tour's final dates, Straight Eight were invited to Queen's after-hours party at Berlin's Black Cat club. For a pub-rock band from Shepherd's Bush, it was something of an experience. 'It was a strip club and very hardcore,' recalls Rick Cassman. 'The atmosphere was one of high decadence, with drink and drugs flowing.' A Playboy centrefold model invited to the party proved a charming distraction. 'I couldn't resist asking her for a dance,' admits Cassman. 'Imagine the girl in the cartoon of *Roger Rabbit* dancing with a stick-thin, wasted punk rocker. After about three minutes, Roger Taylor came up and whisked her away.' Up onstage, male and female strippers had sex, while down on the dancefloor, Straight Eight's roadie ('a big lad from Birmingham') passed out after too much over-indulgence and had to be carried out of the venue.

Like jaded Roman emperors, Queen viewed it all with the dispassionate air that came from years of witnessing such excess. That night, while most of the band basked in the seedy delights of the Black Cat, Mercury was off elsewhere enjoying his own misadventures. They all had plenty to celebrate. By the end of 1980, Queen had sold in the region of 25 million singles and 45 million albums internationally. They had also been accorded an entry in *The Guinness Book of Records* as Britain's highest-paid directors of a company (reported annual salary: £700,000 each). With *The Game* now five times platinum, Queen owned the world. But as Brian May wearily admitted: 'The excess was starting to leak into the music.'

Queen's 1981 began with the Japanese premiere of *Flash Gordon* and five nights at the Budokan in Tokyo, picking up a waif-and-stray English pop star along the way. Gary Numan had scored a run of hits since 1979 with his Bowie-influenced synthesised pop. Numan had flown to Tokyo on an invite from the rock band Japan. 'I was supposed to be guesting onstage with them,' he says. 'But when I got there it was all a misunderstanding, and they didn't want me with them at all.' On a whim, Numan managed to get a ticket for Queen's first show at Budokan. 'Someone must have spotted me, because Queen's security guy came over and invited me backstage.'

Queen asked Numan to join them for dinner at one of Tokyo's swankiest restaurants. 'But I was incredibly shy and a plain eater,' he admits. Daunted by the Japanese food and having to use chopsticks instead of cutlery, he chose to go without. 'So Freddie noticed and asked what I wanted to eat. I had to tell him: McDonald's.' Mercury called over his chauffeur, checked with the restaurant manager, and fifteen minutes later Numan was tucking into a cheeseburger and French fries, while Queen savoured the sushi and Mercury entertained the whole table with racy anecdotes. After hours, Freddie gave his credit card a workout at Tokyo's prestigious Shibuya Seibu department store, which had been closed to the public to allow him to shop in peace. Before long, though, Queen would be spending an even larger amount of money to buy their way out of trouble.

■ ■ ■

In Werner Herzog's 1982 film *Fitzcarraldo*, the lead character, a rubber baron and opera fanatic, journeys into the heart of the Peruvian jungle to find a remote crop of rubber plants from which he hopes to make his fortune and build his own opera house. Having travelled as far as he can by river, Fitzcarraldo enlists the natives to help him drag his ship through the jungle and across the Peruvian mountains. It is a punishingly slow, arduous and yet strangely compelling task. In 1981, Queen's road crew would experience their own Fitzcarraldo moment, attempting to move over 100 tons of their paymasters' equipment by air, sea and road, and even through the jungles of South America. Just months later, they would go back to the continent for a second run. This time they would be lucky to get back alive.

Queen's first trip to South America in February 1981 finally came together after nine months of meticulous planning. 'South America had been mooted a few times,' recalls Peter Hince. 'But there were always offers coming into the Queen office to play unusual places; Moscow was another one. The band were always keen, but this time they were up for it because they were so buoyed by the success of *The Game*. At that point Queen really were the biggest band in the world.'

By 1981, many of the bands that had inspired Queen had either split or were in the process of falling apart. With the death of drummer John Bonham in 1980, Led Zeppelin had closed down; The Who were limping on without Keith Moon, but would only last to make one more album before throwing in the towel (albeit temporarily), while Pink Floyd's *The Wall* tour would be their last live shows for six years. The arrival of punk and new wave had led to huge critical opprobrium, but Queen had survived.

In 1980, guitarist Peter Frampton and the funk band Earth, Wind & Fire had played shows in Brazil and Argentina. However, both had performed on a small scale and at indoor venues. 'Another One Bites the Dust' had been an unexpected number 1 hit for Queen in Argentina and Guatemala, and they were now officially the biggest-selling band in South America. Queen's plan was to transport their full show and perform at the nation's outdoor sports stadiums. Road manager Gerry Stickells and Queen's business manager Jim Beach made several exploratory trips to the continent, and a temporary production office was established in Rio de Janeiro.

It was unknown territory in more ways than one. As Hince recalls, 'There were so many people involved, you didn't really know who was in charge or what was happening.' Jose Rota, based in Buenos Aries, was appointed as the tour's main promoter, and given the task of liaising between the Queen office and local promoters elsewhere on the continent; a process fraught with difficulty, when it was quickly discovered that one promoter was unable to pay the band their guaranteed fee. Dates were scheduled, re-scheduled and cancelled.

Queen's production manager, Chris Lamb, had flown ahead to Argentina, but ran into trouble at Customs. Lamb aroused suspicion by having a canister of flash powder; an essential pyrotechnic for the show. He was also carrying the crew and backstage passes, which featured a picture of two topless women and a banana. One story claims that Lamb was forced to doctor the offending passes with a marker pen before being allowed into the country. 'I think it was the usual thing,' offers Hince. 'You paid someone and they let you in. Everything was done in US dollars, and the Queen office made sure there was plenty to go around.'

After Japan, while the band members kicked back with a week's holiday, the crew began the tortuous operation of transporting 20 tons of equipment from Tokyo, and 40 tons from Miami, to Buenos Aires for the first date at Vélez Sársfield football stadium. A DC8 was chartered to make the 35-hour journey from Tokyo to Buenos Aires, with the crew flying to Argentina from Tokyo via New York. As soon as they arrived in Buenos Aries, Hince and the rest of the crew were given strict instructions: 'Basically, we were told, "Right, you are not going to Drug Heaven, the laws here are very strict, and please remember this is a Catholic country."'

As well as their gear, Queen also had to provide a hundred rolls of artificial turf to cover the precious pitches of South America's biggest football stadiums. 'That was half the problem,' said Brian May. 'Trying to get permission for the audience to actually stand on the pitch.' On the way to Vélez Sársfield, one of the equipment trucks overturned. It took forty-eight hours to locate a crane big enough to clear the load. Meanwhile, at the stadium, Queen's sixty-strong crew, aided by local workers, were tasked with constructing a stage (100 feet high, 140 feet long and 40 feet deep) from scratch in the 80-degree heat.

'I took a photo of the first piece of wood and a measuring tape on the ground of the empty stadium,' says Peter Hince. 'Even the locals that were helping us out didn't believe that the gig was actually going to happen. They were convinced the whole thing would be called off at the last minute. So all of us were feeling edgy the whole time.'

The crew's paranoia was understandable. According to Peter, Queen were also provisionally booked to play shows in Cordoba and Belo Horizonte (Hince: 'These got blown out for whatever reason') and the Maracana Stadium in Rio de Janeiro. Queen were desperate to play Maracana as it was the biggest stadium in the world, but the gig was pulled when the governor of Rio declared that the venue could only be used for events of sporting, religious or cultural significance. These included appearances from the Pope and Frank Sinatra in 1980, but not Queen in 1981. In the end, Queen would play three shows in Buenos Aires, a night each at Mar del Plata and Rosario, and two in São Paulo, Brazil.

Queen ('SUPERGROUPO NUMERO UNO!' declared the *Sun*) arrived in Buenos Aires to an extraordinary reception. After being escorted off the plane by security guards and a government official, the band were fast-tracked through Customs. 'As we walked into the airport building, we couldn't believe our ears,' said Freddie Mercury. 'They stopped all the flight announcements and were playing our music instead.' Queen were accompanied by a small group of reporters from the music and national press, including *Melody Maker*'s Ray Coleman and the *Sun*'s Nina Myskow. But, from the moment they set foot on Argentinian soil, their every move would be shadowed by local TV and radio crews.

Queen would be hustled from airport to press conference to the Sheraton Hotel to gig in armoured vehicles. 'They were these battleship-like personnel carriers, bristling with machine guns poking through holes in the metal,' wrote Nina Myskow. 'Fleets of motorcycle cops sirened their way alongside the circus.' While Queen were hungry for their own personal victory by beating their contemporaries to become the first rock band to play huge gigs in a new territory, there was vast political capital to be made out of their visit. General Roberto Viola was in the process of becoming de facto president of Argentina, and it was Viola that had arranged for Queen to be met at the airport. Queen's visit was being sold as Viola's personal PR coup. In a country under military rule and with such a volatile political climate, it was little wonder that the

Argentinian secret service were monitoring the band's visit.

Prior to the opening night at Vélez Sársfield, promoter Jose Rota was taken aside by secret servicemen and asked what he would do if a terrorist put a gun to Freddie Mercury's head during the show and ordered him to shout 'Viva Peron!' in honour of the former Argentinian leaders. 'There were worried that with such a vast audience it might become political,' quipped Mercury. 'So they pleaded with me not to sing "Don't Cry for Me Argentina".'

In the end, Queen walked onto a stage flanked by armed soldiers. However, nothing could quite prepare them for the response from the audience. Every Queen album was now in the Argentine Top 10 and every song they played was treated like an encore, with the language difference no barrier to the 54,000-strong crowd echoing every word. Despite the stifling heat, Mercury performed part of the set in his leather bike jacket, over a vest branded with the logo of the London gay club Heaven. (His companion for the South American stint was a male model who also worked as a bouncer at Heaven.) The second night's gig at Valez Sarfield would be broadcast live to a TV audience of over 30 million in Argentina and Brazil. Backstage, the band were introduced to Argentine football hero Diego Maradona, who would, five years later, handball the English football team out of a quarter-final world cup victory.

Photo opportunities with local sporting heroes were all part of the game; but so too was dinner with General Viola. Amnesty International had earlier estimated that anywhere between 10,000 and 20,000 people had been tortured or abducted at the behest of the Argentine military junta. But, in the end, all of Queen, bar Roger Taylor, dined with Viola at his home.

So successful were the shows at Vélez Sársfield that Queen would return a week later to play a third night. In the meantime, they holed up in Rio de Janeiro and waited for their next move. With gigs in Cordoba cancelled, they rolled out the artificial turf for shows at the municipal stadium in Mar del Plata and Rosario, playing to over 76,000 people. Still determined to play the 81,000-seater Maracana Stadium, negotiations only broke down when Queen's offer of a fat donation to the governor of Rio's wife's favourite charity was refused. 'That one was a case of "hurry up and wait",' recalls Hince. 'We are playing . . . we're not . . . we are . . . we're not.'

Two more shows had been confirmed at Sao Paolo's Morumbi Stadium for 20 and 21 March. The band decamped from Rio, while the crew began the Fitzcarraldo-style task of transporting over 100 tons of equipment to Brazil by road and through the jungle. At the Brazilian border, Customs officials were determined to examine every piece (a process that would have meant cancelling both shows). Somehow a deal was struck, presumably involving US dollars, and the trucks were allowed through with just thirty-six hours to go before the first night. In São Paulo, John Deacon's personal security guard introduced himself with the information that he had killed over two hundred people. Queen had been assigned bodyguards drawn from Brazil's infamous 'Death Squads'. 'They were the heavy, heavy police who actually kill people at the drop of a hat,' recalled Mercury. 'Someone took a photo of John with "Doctor Death",' says Peter Hince. 'There's Deakey and there's this guy with a gun stuffed down his trousers.'

Backstage before the first night at Morumbi, the redoubtable Gerry Stickells finally cracked. Infuriated by the lack of a working telephone, he tore one off the wall and threw it out the window. The police were called and Queen were forced to remain in their dressing room until minutes before showtime. In the end, they would perform to more than a quarter of a million people across two nights in Brazil. Alongside their own gear, Queen were loaned spotlights by the show's organisers. On closer inspection, they saw that they were stenciled with the words Earth, Wind & Fire, and had been impounded during their tour a year before.

Fearful that Queen's equipment would be confiscated, the crew took emergency measures. While the stadium staff were busy helping themselves to the band's artificial turf, the crew broke down the stage and managed to transport all the gear to the airport. 'Our freight agent in LA had chartered a jumbo jet from a company called Flying Tigers,' recalls Peter Hince. 'It had a top deck and the guts of the plane had been turned into a hold. Unfortunately, when we arrived with all the gear, we discovered that they didn't have the right pallets to fit the equipment.' Hince spent eighteen hours at the airport, guarding the precious load, before it was flown back to the US, via Puerto Rico. Despite running costs of between £20,000 and £25,000 a day, Queen grossed $3.5 million for their South American venture, and scored a major PR victory. 'SOUTH AMERICA BITES THE DUST!' proclaimed the trade magazine *Music Week*. 'Clinical and machine-like they may be,' wrote *Melody Maker*. 'But what matters more is that Queen did it.' Seven months later, they would try and do it all again, but with rather different results.

With a planned *Greatest Hits* album deferred until the end of 1981, Roger Taylor's solo debut, *Fun in Space*, surfaced in April, preceded by a single, 'Future Management'. The album sleeve showed a goggle-eyed alien. Unknown to both parties, the model had been created by Taylor's old Smile bandmate Tim Staffell. 'I didn't know what it was for, and I didn't discover until years later,' said Staffell. 'That was peculiar.'

When 'Future Management' inched into the UK Top 20, Taylor appeared on *Top of the Pops*, miming uncomfortably with an electric guitar. 'My God!' he groaned in 2008. 'I always hated *Top of the Pops*.' The song had shades of The Police's white reggae, and both the single and album demonstrated Taylor's love of the musical here and now, but neither would really trouble the charts. *Fun in Space* was the first evidence that Queen as a whole was worth more than the sum of its parts.

In May, Chrissy May gave birth to a daughter, Louisa. Just weeks later, Brian joined the rest of the band and Mack at Mountain Studios. As with the first sessions for *The Game*, there was no pressure to complete another album. Mercury was busy collaborating with John Deacon on a pure soul track titled 'Cool Cat', which was even further removed from seventies-era Queen than 'Another One Bites the Dust'. For Brian May, Queen's rock conscience, the sessions would mark the start of an especially challenging period. 'It wasn't easy,' he said. 'It wasn't easy at all.'

July brought the welcome distraction of another Montreux Jazz Festival and an encounter with David Bowie. Mountain's engineer David Richards had worked on Bowie's *Heroes* album, and Bowie had booked a session at Mountain to record the track 'Cat People

(Putting Out Fire)'. It was almost inevitable that he would drop by a Queen session. 'David came in one night and we were playing other people's songs for fun, just jamming,' recalled Roger Taylor. 'In the end, David said, "This is stupid, why don't we just write one?"' According to Freddie Mercury, talking about the Queen/Bowie collaboration 'Under Pressure' in 1985, the resulting session lasted nearly twenty-four hours, fuelled by 'a few bottles of wine and things'. Mack's memory is clearer: 'There was so much blow [cocaine].'

■ ■ ■

Interviewed in 1984, John Deacon largely credited 'Under Pressure' to Mercury and Bowie, while claiming that it was Bowie who composed the song's now much-sampled bassline (Deacon: 'It took me a certain amount of time to learn it'). Roger Taylor said that nothing was written in the studio and that the song was originally titled 'People on Streets'. Another unreleased Queen track, 'Feel Like', from the same sessions, included a piano line that would end up on 'Under Pressure'.

'We felt our way through a backing track all together as an ensemble,' recalled Brian May. 'When the backing track was done, David said, "Okay, let's each of us go in the vocal booth and sing how we think the melody should go – just off the top of our heads – and we'll compile a vocal out of that." And that's what we did.' Some of these improvisations, including Mercury's memorable introductory scatting vocal, would endure on the finished track. Bowie also insisted that he and Mercury shouldn't hear what the other had sung, swapping verses blind, which helped give the song its cut-and-paste feel.

'It was very hard,' May admitted in 2008, 'because you already had four precocious boys and David, who was precocious enough for all of us. Passions ran very high. I found it very hard because I got so little of my own way. But David had a real vision and he took over the song lyrically.'

Bowie also decided that instead of 'People on Streets' it should be called 'Under Pressure'. On hearing of the collaboration,

EMI/Elektra were delighted. Two weeks later, Bowie, Mercury and Mack were at New York's Power Station studios trying to agree on a final mix. 'Roger was also along to keep the peace,' remembered May. 'I had given up by that time.'

'I started mixing with Bowie, and there's him out *there* and me in *here*,' laughs Mack. 'It didn't go too well. We spent all day and Bowie was like, "Do this, do that." In the end, I called Freddie and said, "I need help here", so Fred came in as a mediator.'

'I wasn't involved, but the desk broke down,' revealed May. 'The song was cobbled together and it was a monitor mix that went out as a single, which was fiercely battled over by David and Freddie.' At some point, Bowie wanted to re-do the song; at another point he was reluctant for it be released as a single. In the end, 'Under Pressure' would be released October, giving Queen and Bowie a UK number 1. ' "Under Pressure" is a significant song for us,' said Brian May in 2008, 'and that is because of David and its lyrical content. I would have found that hard to admit in the old days, but I can admit it now . . . But one day, I would love to sit down quietly on my own and re-mix it.'

■ ■ ■

After the chaos that accompanied the recording of 'Under Pressure', the offer of a return trip to South America in September offered a welcome break from the sessions. Not that Mercury needed much persuasion. Prior to the trip, the singer celebrated his thirty-fifth birthday with a five-day party at New York's Berkshire Place Hotel at which £30,000 worth of champagne was consumed. Mercury was now in the process of buying an apartment in the city. With his hangover only just subsiding, he joined the others in New Orleans for rehearsals, before Queen flew to Caracas, Venezuela, where they were booked to play three nights at the indoor sporting arena, Poliedro de Caracas.

However, they arrived just as Venezuela's ex-president and national hero, Romulo Betancourt was dying in a hospital in New York. The gigs went off without a hitch, and Queen were invited to appear as non-performing guests on a live TV pop show on

28 September. Mercury categorically refused, but the others agreed. Unable to speak or fully understand Spanish, May, Taylor and Deacon looked confused as an announcer dashed onstage to declare that Betancourt was dead, and demanded a two-minute silence. With the cameras still rolling, a second announcer appeared just minutes later to declare that it was a false alarm: Betancourt was still alive. In the end, the 'Father of Venezuelan Democracy' passed away later that night, plunging the whole country into a period of national mourning. 'This meant no music for two weeks,' explains Peter Hince. Queen's remaining shows in Venezuela were immediately cancelled, leading to a fall-out over their fee with the promoter.

The next run of gigs was due to take place in Mexico nearly ten days later. The band decamped to Miami, Florida, before an eighteen-strong group of crew members made their way to Loredo, Texas. From here, they travelled to the Mexican border. 'Under normal circumstances you can visit Mexico on a US driver's licence,' says Peter Hince. 'But the crew were told that we all needed visas.' To complicate matters further, they were also informed that the authorities could only issue a total of six visas a day. 'The official line on the visas was that we were "assisting Mexican technicians". I still have the visa application and there was some unbelievable stuff on there: a mugshot, a profile picture, fingerprints, mother's maiden name, shape of eyes . . . It was just an excuse for someone to get some cash.'

After the visas, and more money, had been successfully negotiated, the crew were ferried into a no-man's land compound outside the border and ordered to wait. 'My mate and I got bored, wandered through a gate into Mexico, bought an ice cream and came back,' laughs Hince. 'Eventually, they let us through, and we drove about 60 miles before we reached another checkpoint . . . and more money had to change hands.'

Queen were booked to play the 56,000-capacity Estadio Universatario stadium in Monterrey, nicknamed 'The Volcano'. 'Tickets had only gone on sale two days before, and they were selling the tickets through supermarkets,' says Peter Hince. 'The organisation was terrible.' After the gig, a bridge outside the stadium collapsed as the crowds were leaving. There were no fatalities but some fans sustained injuries. 'So the police locked the stadium gates and wouldn't let us leave. Once again, so someone else could get some money. If it hadn't been for Gerry Stickells, we would never have got the gear out of there.'

A second gig at 'The Volcano' was cancelled. A week later, Queen arrived at Pueblo where they would play two nights at the 22,000-capacity Estadio Ignacio Zaragoza. Asked about Queen's trip to Mexico, Brian May told *Mojo* magazine in 2008 that 'a whole lot of trouble happened that I don't even want to go into.' Roger Taylor said: 'It was a miracle we made it; there were some monstrous corruption issues.' One rumour has it that the promoter was kidnapped following the gig in Monterrey. But according to *Queen: As It Began*, the 1992 book 'written in co-operation with Queen', the band's 'promoter was arrested and thrown in jail the day before the Pueblo gig. They had to pay $25,000 to get him out of bail so the tour could continue.'

There was worse to come at the gig itself. 'The stadium had been built for the Olympics and it was virtually defunct,' says Hince. 'The pitch was covered in rubbish and there were no working toilets.' To aggravate matters, the crew had been billeted in the worst hotel in town ('When you flushed the chain, the shit came back up through the shower'), leading to cases of food poisoning and dysentery. With nearly twice the capacity crowd inside the stadium, and many in the audience 'out of their heads on mescaline and tequila', the atmosphere before the show was dangerously tense. It didn't improve when Queen arrived onstage. Many in the audience had been allowed to bring in ghetto-blaster cassette recorders, with which they were recording the gig. When the batteries ran out, they began throwing them at the band. Before long, the stage was covered in batteries, rocks, dirt and even shoes. 'It's not that they didn't like the band,' ventures Hince. 'It's just that a rock gig was an excuse to go completely wild.' Queen managed to complete their set, but Mercury was incensed: '*Adios, amigos*, you motherfuckers!'

'After the show, the band went absolutely apeshit,' remembers Peter Hince. 'They said, "That's it, we are going home." Gerry calmed them down and explained the situation: "We have another show tomorrow, then a day off, and then another one after that . . . If we don't do the show tomorrow, it's going to be very hard for us to get the gear out of the country. You won't see it again. Do the show, and on the day off we will get out."'

On the second night, the police were instructed to search the crowd, and to confiscate alcohol and batteries from the ghetto-blasters before letting anyone into the stadium. Once inside the venue, the crew spotted that the police had set up stalls to sell back the confiscated batteries and bottles of tequila. Despite this, the second night's show was relatively peaceful. But due to outside issues, later blamed on 'problems with tax and currency', Queen would not be paid for the gig. With more US dollars changing hands to hasten a speedy getaway, the stage was stripped down, the trucks loaded and Queen's gear driven from Pueblo to Texas under an armed guard. The third show was forgotten, the promoter was irate, but Queen and their crew escaped in one piece.

Back in Munich, there was what Peter Hince describes as 'an inquisition'. The band had lost a significant amount of money, estimated, by some, at around a million dollars. 'In a sense,' says Hince, 'it bought them back down to earth.' As Brian May put it, 'We thought we could repeat what we'd done in South America, but we escaped by the skin of our teeth. All of us.'

■ ■ ▩

After the trauma of Mexico, the band's nerves were soothed by the success of 'Under Pressure' in October. In the meantime, EMI busied themselves for the release of *Queen's Greatest Hits* and a corresponding collection of their finest promos, *Greatest Flix*. Both would be released to mark Queen's tenth anniversary; the band discounting their first year with other bass players and marking the beginning of the band as 1971, when John Deacon had joined. In November, the band flew to Canada and played two gigs at the Montreal Forum, filmed for their first concert video release, *We Will Rock You*. By the end of the month *Greatest Hits*, packaged with a portrait of the band by Princess Margaret's ex-husband Lord Snowdon, was at number 1 in the UK.

Before Christmas, Queen were back in Munich to complete work on a new studio album. Among the new songs was Deacon and Mercury's blue-eyed soul number 'Cool Cat' and 'Back Chat', written by John Deacon and yet another excursion into funk. As with *The Game*, much of the new material was written to pass what Brian May called 'the Sugar Shack test'. This time, Mercury was pushing even harder for a change of direction. 'Fred's thing was: less is more, make it more sparse, and play less guitar,' said May. The choice of album title, *Hot Space*, would seem very appropriate.

Sessions for *Hot Space* picked up again in the New Year and continued until March 1982. But there was more to contend with than just time-honoured musical differences. 'Munich became almost another home, and a place in which we lived different lives,' said May. 'Emotionally, we all got into trouble in Munich. Every single one of us.' The band's after-hours activities had escalated to the point where it was seriously impinging on the working day. 'We'd go out after the studio and then we weren't getting back until eight in the morning,' complained May. 'So you don't get much work done the next day . . . and then it's time to go out drinking again.' Interviewed in 2008, even Roger Taylor conceded: 'We had got fairly decadent by then. We started work at all sorts of odd hours. The days drifted into the nights into this endless cycle.'

The walls of the Sugar Shack were now decorated with gold discs for *The Game*, and with its glamorous clientele of fellow rock musicians, sports stars and models, it exerted a magnetic pull on some of the band. 'The latter days in Munich were lost in a haze of vodka,' recalled May. 'There were no drugs in my case, but there were so many drugs around.' After one drunken interlude, May returned to Musicland to complete the solo on 'Put Out the Fire', one of the few rock tracks on *Hot Space* in which he sounds as if he's allowed to slip the leash.

May fought his corner again on 'Back Chat', urging John Deacon to compromise on the song's pure funk sound. ' "Back Chat" is supposed to be about people arguing and it should have some kind of guts to it. It wasn't angry enough,' said the guitarist. Ultimately, Deacon was persuaded to allow May to 'get some heaviness into it'. But the arguments wouldn't end there. 'I remember John saying I didn't play the type of guitar he wanted on his songs. We struggled bitterly with each other.'

Mercury had his own emotional distractions to contend with. These included his latest lover, a New Jerseyite named Bill Reid, whose relationship with Freddie was fiery, even in the studio. Yet Freddie could often become what May calls 'a wonderful diplomat' by stepping in to mediate. 'Fred was the only one who could come along and say, "Now dears, we can do this and we can do *this*, now just fucking do it!" And it would always work,' said Brian. 'For a person who was famous for saying, "We don't compromise, dear", he was a great mediator in the studio. He would always cut through everything with such humour: "Oh, for God's sake, what a stupid business!"' Recalling one such episode during the making of *Hot Space*, Peter Freestone remembered Mercury losing patience with May's tireless request for more volume: 'Suddenly he exclaimed, "What the fucking hell do you want? A herd of wildebeest charging from one side to the other!"'

Mack remembers 'heated discussions about everything and the whole thing was close to breaking up'. But part of the problem was that everyone was working to a different schedule. 'Making *The Game* was the last time the four of them were in the studio together. After that, it felt like it was always two of them in one studio and two of them in another. You'd come in one day and say, "Oh, where's Roger?" and someone would say, "Oh, he's gone skiing."' Mack became so frustrated over how long the album was taking that he began measuring it against his wife Ingrid's pregnancy. 'I told Queen, "It's easier to conceive and give birth than it is to get this album finished."' A week before the sessions were complete, Ingrid gave birth to their first child, John Frederick. Mack immediately asked Freddie to become the boy's godfather.

The first evidence of *Hot Space*'s brave new direction came in April with the release of a single, 'Body Language'. The song reprised the finger-clicks and handclaps of 'Crazy Little Thing Called Love', but its synthesised funk rhythm and processed drums put it even further left of field than 'Another One Bites the Dust'. Furthermore, if Brian May was playing on it, then he was virtually inaudible. The accompanying video was dominated by Mercury and a pack of shimmying dancers, while May looked as if he couldn't quite bear to make eye contact with the camera. The single's picture sleeve depicted a close-up of two naked bodies, which caused a fuss in the US, but not enough to stop the single reaching number 11. In the UK, 'Body Language' stalled outside the Top 20.

'I can remember having a go at Freddie because some of the stuff he was writing was very definitely on the gay side,' said May, when asked about 'Body Language'. 'I remember saying, "It would be nice if this stuff could be universally applicable, because we have friends out there of every persuasion." It's nice to involve people. What it's not nice to do is rope people out. And I felt kind of roped out by something that was very overtly a gay anthem. I thought it was very hard to take that in the other way.'

Just a few days before *Hot Space*'s scheduled release, Queen received an urgent message from David Bowie. As well as 'Under Pressure', Bowie had sung backing vocals on 'Cool Cat'. When Queen informed him that the song was on *Hot Space*, he insisted they take it off the record, claiming he wasn't satisfied with his performance. 'Unfortunately, he didn't tell us until about a day before the album was supposed to be released,' said May, 'I toured with Bowie after he'd recorded with Queen,' recalls Queen's then official photographer Denis O'Regan, 'and he didn't have great memories of the experience. It was too much of a clash of the titans.' A version of the song, without Bowie's vocals, was promptly substituted. But the delay meant that the album wouldn't be out in time for the first half of Queen's European tour.

The band would be joined for the tour by an old friend, ex-Mott The Hoople keyboard player Morgan Fisher. 'I was living in Belgium,' says Fisher. 'I was having nothing to do with making music but then I felt the need to get back into it and make some money.' Fisher sent letters enquiring about work to friends and contacts, including Brian May. 'Lo and behold, Brian sent me a telegram saying, "Do you want to tour with us?" I'd sent letters to a few Brians, so I was thinking, "Which Brian is that?" '

A couple of days later a box of Queen cassettes arrived and Fisher started practising. Before long, he was in Los Angeles for an audition. 'But there were only two of us: me and Roger Powell from Todd Rundgren's band, Utopia. Roger was a synthesiser wizard and way ahead of me, but he hadn't been in Mott The Hoople, and that's what got me the job.'

With *Hot Space* still to be released, Queen faced the task of playing material with which the audience was unfamiliar. The funk track, 'Staying Power', was an especially hard sell. The album version included a horn arrangement recorded in New York by Aretha Franklin's producer Arif Mardin. Onstage, May would inject more of the 'anger and violence' he believed missing from the studio version. But Queen's more conservative audiences were less impressed. When the song's announcement was greeted with jeers at Frankfurt's Westfallenhalle, Mercury rounded on the hecklers: 'If you don't want to listen to it, fucking go home!' Offstage, Freddie was living as large as ever, flying his barber, Denny Godber, from London's hip Sweeney's salon, into Wurzberg just so he could have a haircut, and inviting him to hang out with them for as long as he wanted.

Queen's support act were Malcolm McLaren's latest protégés, punk-pop band Bow Wow Wow. After hecklers threw bottles at the stage, the group took matters into their own hands and threw them back. They were swiftly replaced by a safer proposition, Christian rockers After the Fire. Brian May was appalled. 'A certain section of our audience found Bow Wow Wow very modern,' he told *Record Mirror*. Mindful of the reaction some of Queen's new material was attracting, he added, 'Our audience is perhaps a little narrow-minded in that way.'

There were problems, too, for Morgan Fisher. 'I played the music professionally,' he says, 'but something wasn't working right.' Both Queen and Fisher had expected to find each other unchanged since 1974's Mott The Hoople tour. 'The trouble was I wasn't the same Morgan Fisher they'd known back then, getting pissed and reading out Goon Show scripts. I had been out of the scene for a while, I was much quieter, I was involved in Indian spirituality and I was meditating every day. Queen weren't the same, either. Freddie was as outrageous as ever, but the others all had kids. At the hotels, there were mums and dads and babies. It had all become very cool and calculated and professional.' Nevertheless, one night, as Fisher came off stage, he glanced down and saw that the crew had chalked a large arrow pointing left next to his stool. Alongside it was the word 'EAST'.

Playing in such large venues, it would take too long to walk from the stage to the main dressing room during the taped section of 'Bohemian Rhapsody' and Brian's solo spot. Queen's crew had constructed a makeshift mini-dressing room close to the stage, nicknamed 'The Tent' or 'The Doll's House', and made out of black fabric draped over scaffolding poles. May's lengthy guitar solo was a fixture of all Queen shows. 'Brian would fight the good fight to get his solo into the set and I always think he got the sense he'd had a victory,' says Brian Southall. While May soloed, the others would congregate in their makeshift hidey-hole.

Fisher, who was now leading an abstemious lifestyle recalls. 'The trouble is Brian's solo could go on for fifteen, twenty minutes. I remember one night, Freddie was sat there and he couldn't stand it any longer. His eyes were rolling upwards, his teeth were sticking out and his hands suddenly flailed forward and he shouted, "For God's sake, let's go shopping! Get me outta here!"'

Behind the scenes, business manager Jim Beach had re-negotiated Queen's contract. The band were now signed to EMI on a new six-album deal. *Hot Space* would finally be released on 21 May, just before their UK shows. It was Queen's most experimental album yet. Deacon and Mercury's soul and funk dominated most of the first half, with May all but relegated to the sidelines. Tellingly, all four band members and Mack would be credited with playing synthesiser. Mercury had celebrated his sexual appetite in the past on songs such as 'Get Down, Make Love' and 'Don't Stop Me Now'. 'Body Language' and 'Staying Power' would do the same on *Hot Space*. 'It's all narcissism of a decidedly tongue-in-bumcheek style,' wrote Sandy Robertson of *Sounds*.

Mercury showed more restraint on 'Life Is Real (Song for Lennon)', and Taylor offered a haunting feelgood pop song, 'Calling All Girls', that wouldn't have sounded out of place on *Fun in Space*. But, for the first time, there would be no Taylor or May lead vocals. Mercury sang lead on everything. May nudged the album closer to hard rock with 'Dancer' and 'Put Out the Fire', before turning the clock back to *A Day at the Races* era with the album's most traditional-sounding track, 'Las Palabros de Amor'. With an English sub-title of 'The Words of Love', this would be Queen's next single. It was a scarf-waving anthem, but the fireside guitars and Spanish title evoked a slight air of the Costa del Sol and, oddly, Abba's hit 'Fernando'. Surprisingly, Queen performed it on *Top of the Pops*, their first real-life appearance in five years on what Roger Taylor called 'that shit programme'.

In the press, *Hot Space* would be both praised and denounced. *Rolling Stone* pointed out that 'Queen have always been ruled by sound instead of soul', while the *Washington Post* saluted the album's 'mesmerising *rechauffé* disco'. For many fans, though, the change of direction was too much. '*Hot Space* wasn't easy,' said May. 'But I'll stand by it. It got us out of a rut and into a new place.' Roger Taylor's judgement remains coloured by the album's cover as well as the music inside. Taylor and Mercury wanted *Hot Space* to mimic a design they had seen on an old Motown record sleeve, but something went awry. 'It's our worst cover by miles,' he said. 'Absolute shit.' Despite such reservations, *Hot Space* would make it to number 4 in the UK. Six months after its release, Queen fan Michael Jackson reappeared with *Thriller*, an album that, like *Hot Space*, merged funk, pop and rock. Jackson told May he loved *Hot Space*. As Mack points out, '*Hot Space* is very underrated, and about nine months ahead of its time.'

Back on home turf, the tour ran into problems when Queen were refused shows at Arsenal FC's home ground in North London and Manchester United's Old Trafford stadium. Amusingly, the reason given was that Pope John Paul II was on his own UK tour and had hired all available portable toilets. Meanwhile, a proposed show at London's Royal Albert Hall, the scene of one of Smile's earliest gigs, was knocked back when the venue's managers saw the scale of Queen's lighting rig and feared it would damage the historic building.

In the end Queen would manage just four shows, including Leeds FC's Elland Road stadium and the recently built Milton Keynes Bowl. Tyne Tees TV filmed the Milton Keynes gig, which would eventually find its way out as an official DVD. Seen now, it's a striking reminder of how contrary and unique Queen looked and sounded in

1982. At the back, Roger Taylor, with his spiky mop and red bandana, looking like one of The Police; at the front Brian May, still the seventies guitar hero, as if preserved in aspic since the days of 'Killer Queen'; John Deacon resplendent in gaudy turquoise jeans and T-shirt, like an engineer on dress-down Friday; and Freddie Mercury presiding over the show like a camp circus ringmaster. The music, too, is all over the place, pin-wheeling from pomp rock ('Save Me') to gospel ('Somebody to Love') to heavy metal ('Sheer Heart Attack') to the weird white funk of 'Under Pressure'. Odder still, it works.

The only time Mercury dropped his guard was to introduce songs from *Hot Space*: 'Most of you know we've got some new sounds out last week . . . and for what it's worth we're gonna do some songs in the black funk category, whatever you call it . . . People get so excited about these things it's only a bloody record.' Onstage, though, May gave 'Staying Power' and 'Back Chat' another lease of life. ' "Staying Power", in particular, became a fantastic live track,' he said.

At Milton Keynes, though, one of Queen's support acts would experience the disapproval of their less tolerant fans. While Joan Jett and The Blackhearts and Heart played user-friendly hard rock, the Liverpudlian psychedelic pop band Teardrop Explodes were a far more outré proposition. 'The audience were incensed that we were playing,' said vocalist Julian Cope. 'We were bottled mercilessly from beginning to end by heavy metal bum boys who shouted at me, "Fuck off, you queer!" Wow, they dig Monsieur Freddie and call me queer?'

Teardrop Explodes wouldn't be the only ones to experience violence. Mercury and boyfriend Bill Reid had a screaming row before the gig, culminating in Reid sinking his teeth into Mercury's left hand. The wound was hastily patched up for the show. The singer's tortuous relationship with Reid was a source of both concern and amusement. Morgan Fisher still recalls hearing the same argument at every post-gig dinner. 'Every night, sat in the restaurant, Fred's boyfriend would tell him, "Freddie you have got to stop smoking", and every night Fred would snap, "Oh, shut up!" and light another cigarette. And so it went on.' Bafflingly, Mercury had begun smoking in 1980. 'I don't know why he started so late in life,' says Peter Hince. 'Maybe it was a stress thing, another prop to use. But Freddie never smoked like Keith Richards, like a rock star. It was more like a schoolgirl.' Mercury himself would tell anyone that asked that he smoked to give himself 'the husky singing voice' he so admired in other singers.

Queen's US tour was due to start in July, but the Milton Keynes show would be Morgan Fisher's last with the band. Maybe it was the daily meditation sessions, maybe it was the teetotal lifestyle. 'I was all set to go to America,' he recalls. 'So I went on holiday and I was lying on a beach when a telegram arrived from the Queen office: "Terribly sorry, Morgan, but we don't need a keyboard player for the US tour." I was furious. I had all the songs we were playing live on these cassettes. So I went back, piled them on the floor and jumped up and down on them, until there was miles of tape everywhere. Then I made sure I got my money.'

In truth, Queen always had every intention of touring America with a keyboard player, and had already lined up Fisher's replacement. A Canadian session musician by the name of Fred Mandel had been hired for what was being billed as the *Rock'n'America* tour. 'Queen were too embarrassed to say, "Sorry, Morgan, something is not right, we would rather get someone else,"' laughs Fisher. 'I never asked them why: I was too bloody repressed.'

Fred Mandel had been working with Alice Cooper and had co-written their 1980 album, *Flush the Fashion*, which had been produced by Roy Thomas Baker. 'I was asked to go to this office on Sunset Boulevard to meet Gerry Stickells,' says Mandel. 'We sat down, talked for about two minutes, and then Gerry said, "Oh, you'll do." I said, "What? Don't you want to hear me to play?" He said, "No, that's OK, I just want to make sure you're OK to hang out with." I went to Montreal on the Sunday, had two days' rehearsal. On Wednesday, I met Freddie Mercury for the first time in the dressing room of the Montreal Forum and walked out to play in front of 7,000 people.

'I had a week to learn how to play a new synthesiser,' he adds. 'I was also playing bass as John was doing rhythm on a couple of tracks. Things like "Back Chat" and "Body Language" were pretty challenging. It wasn't like learning a couple of pop tunes. Nowadays I'd baulk at taking something like that on. But back then

I was ignorantly blissful.'

When Queen rolled into Boston for a gig at The Gardens, the Mayor declared it 'Queen Day' and awarded them the keys to the city. In New York for two nights at Madison Square Gardens (one less than on *The Game* tour), they agreed to a rare in-store appearance, showing up at Crazy Eddie's, an electronics store. A photograph of the band, surrounded by TV sets and banners for *Hot Space*, captured some uncomfortable body language; this was not the sort of promotion Queen were used to doing. The aftershow party at Madison Square Garden was another night of excess, and included female mud wrestlers. But all was not well. *Hot Space* wasn't selling. Too dance-oriented for US rock radio, the album wasn't getting airplay. It had peaked at number 22, and, despite the tour, was slipping down the charts.

Queen's opening act was Billy Squier, whom they'd first met at a promo dinner on the US Mott The Hoople tour. Their paths had crossed again when Mack produced Squier's *Emotions in Motion* album. Squier had a pretty-boy image and played sophisticated hard rock, which, like Queen, was big on harmonies and dynamics. To salt the wound, *Emotions in Motion* was speeding up the charts as quickly as *Hot Space* was going down. 'Whatever disappointments the members of Queen may have been feeling, they never took any of it out on me,' insists Squier now. 'In fact, I remember Roger Taylor coming up to my room after our show in Boston, to thank me for "saving our ass on this tour".' As Taylor recalled: 'I remember suddenly realising we weren't packing them in quite as much as we used to.'

Nevertheless, Squier was a rabid Queen fan and was in awe of Freddie Mercury. 'I used to stand and watch him and think, "How do you do that? Just how do you get away with it?" ' Queen's show still had 'Now I'm Here', 'Tie Your Mother Down' and 'We Will Rock You', but there was also 'Body Language', 'Staying Power' and Freddie's moustache.

'One reason Queen were able to be so adventurous over the years was because they established their rock credibility early on,' says Squier, 'and they maintained a healthy dose of it along with whatever else they were exploring musically. *Hot Space* upset this balance and left American audiences wondering what they were listening to, and Freddie's dramatic image change undoubtedly contributed to the band's woes. When *Hot Space* came out, there was a fair degree of homophobia. Queen's male audience likely felt betrayed, or duped . . . or both.'

As well as a poor-selling album, there were other issues to contend with. Inevitably, there was a growing distance between Mercury, thirty-six years old and still living the life of a man ten years younger, and his bandmates, with their wives, girlfriends and young families. *Rock 'n' America* covered thirty-three dates in three months. As Brian May put it, 'You were always trying to find a work/life balance. There was a continual life-or-death battle going on there.' May found touring an emotionally dislocating experience, and had earlier told the band that where possible he no longer wished to travel by private plane. Onstage in New Jersey, after breaking a string on the Red Special, he broke another on his replacement guitar. In a rare fit of pique May threw the instrument into the wings.

Backstage, Fred Mandel would overhear what he tactfully calls 'discussions' over how certain songs were going down. 'My little joke was to walk into the dressing room and say, "Hey! I really enjoyed playing that song tonight", and then walk out and listen to the arguments. There was still a rock 'n' roll element to Queen, but it wasn't like Guns N' Roses — always talking about downing a fifth of Jack Daniels. With Queen, you could just as easily find them arguing about the wingspan of a butterfly.'

Mercury, however, had grown weary of touring and was becoming prone to increasingly irrational outbursts. One night, fired up after another fracas with Bill Reid, Freddie rounded on Gerry Stickells and told him that the front row of the audience that evening had been too ugly. 'Apparently, he didn't want to see that at a Queen show,' recalls Peter Hince. 'He said we'd need a casting session before we let them in. And for ten minutes, he was serious.'

Ex-Ealing art college student Mark Malden visited Mercury in his dressing room after the opening night in Montreal. Malden was still living in Canada, and the two had maintained contact since meeting again in 1977. But this time it was different. 'The dressing room was very dimly lit and Freddie had changed his clothes, and all his entourage were dressed identically to him,' says Malden. 'When he spoke it became apparent that I wasn't speaking with Fred but with "Freddie Mercury". I'd never seen him like this before and I was shocked.' Matters weren't helped by the fact that Mercury sat on his hands, being spoon-fed spaghetti from a bowl by one of his aides. 'I didn't recognise this person. This was someone else.' When Mercury made a cutting remark to him, Malden walked out.

In a repeat of what Alan Mair had experienced with Mercury two years before, Malden heard footsteps in the corridor behind him. 'It was Fred. I stopped and turned. He walked up to me and said, "I'm sorry, Mark. I didn't mean it . . . When this is all over we'll see each other again." When I looked back behind him I saw Paul Prenter at the dressing-room door with a smirk on his face.' Prenter's pernicious influence on Mercury was becoming more and more apparent. 'He was extremely controlling and he led Freddie by the nose,' believes Malden. 'There were so many users and hangers-on around Fred, so many advantage-takers.'

Rock 'n' America ended with two nights at the Los Angeles Forum, playing to an audience that included Elizabeth Taylor and Michael Jackson. But despite such a glittering guest list, Queen's fortunes hadn't improved. Their last UK single 'Backchat' had stopped outside the Top 40, while their US single, 'Calling All Girls', had stalled at number 60. Though none of them knew it at the time, the LA Forum shows would be the last time Queen with Freddie Mercury ever played in the United States.

As always, Queen could console themselves with Japan, where *Hot Space* had been better received. Queen played six shows in October despite Fred Mandel being felled by such bad jetlag he telephoned his wife convinced he was sick. 'It was the first time I'd gone overseas with any band,' he laughs. 'We got into Narita Airport, the rest of them all went off to clubs, and I went to bed and woke up an hour later in a pool of sweat.' Mandel wasn't the only one feeling the pressure. Onstage in Osaka, Mercury struck up the piano intro to 'Spread Your Wings', and then stopped. He simply couldn't remember the chords. With the tour finally done, the band members returned to their separate lives. As Brian May would later admit: 'We hated each other for a while.'

CHAPTER NINE

Huge Plastic Falsies

'What am I going to do in twenty years' time? I'll be
dead, darling! Are you mad?'

Freddie Mercury, *Melody Maker*, **1984**

Back in 1966, Simon and Garfunkel's '59th Street Bridge Song
(Feelin' Groovy)' could be heard ringing out of Isleworth and
Ealing pub jukeboxes. As a student, it's unlikely that the nineteen-
year-old Fred Bulsara could ever have imagined living in an
apartment that overlooked the bridge celebrated in the song. But
in early 1983, Freddie Mercury purchased a forty-third floor apartment in the Sovereign Building at 425, East 5th Street, and from his
balcony he could see 59th Street Bridge.

New York, like Munich, was now Mercury's playground. When
in Manhattan, he would be ferried from club to bar in the company
of four male friends whom he called 'my New York daughters'.
With Bill Reid gone, Mercury would soon fall into another tempestuous relationship, this time in Munich with a restaurateur named
Winnie Kirchberger.

The beginning of 1983 found Queen basking in the luxury of
having several months in which to do nothing. But before long, all
of them, bar John Deacon, would start solo projects. In Munich,
Mercury was approached by Giorgio Moroder and asked to
contribute to the soundtrack to a proposed re-release of the 1926
science fiction movie *Metropolis* for which Moroder had acquired
the rights. Mercury agreed, and the two would compose the song
'Love Kills', on which most of Queen ended up playing. By March,

Roger Taylor would be back at Mountain Studios working on a follow-up to *Fun in Space*. A month later, Brian May checked into Los Angeles' Record Plant to work on his own album. Deacon, meanwhile, had other matters to occupy his time: his wife would soon be pregnant with their fourth child, Joshua. All would present a united front to the outside world, insisting that Queen had not split up, but that they were taking a temporary break. As Mercury quipped: 'It would be silly to start a new band at forty.'

Apart from having the freedom to make solo albums, there were other benefits to being a member of Queen. Through most of 1983, Roger Taylor would extend his unofficial role as the band's resident man-about-town. Taylor would captain a team on the UK TV show *Pop Quiz*, beating rival team captain David Gilmour. His love of speed now extended to include a new hobby: powerboat racing. But a trip to Monaco to watch the Grand Prix was less successful. Taylor, accompanied by drum tech 'Crystal' Taylor and Status Quo guitarist Rick Parfitt, accepted an all-expenses-paid trip to Monaco from a TV producer making a documentary about Formula 1 team-mates, Derek Warwick and Bruno Ciacomelli.

The producer wanted to film a couple of rock stars at the Grand Prix; in return, the stars were promised a Lear jet to Nice, with champagne and caviar, followed by a helicopter ride to Monaco. No such perks were forthcoming, and after a marathon flight from Biggin Hill Airfield and even longer car journey through France, an inebriated Taylor and Parfitt briefly ended up in jail.

Brian May's more sober pursuits included a stint working with Scottish heavy rock band Heavy Petting, briefly pitched as Polydor Records' answer to Def Leppard. May and Mack would produce the group's debut album, *Lettin' Loose*. The album didn't sell, but the band, like Def Leppard, were from a generation of younger musicians that had grown up on Queen in the 1970s. As the 1980s wore on, more and more bands would materialise, naming Queen, and May in particular, as an inspiration.

At the end of 1982, Queen's overseas deal with Elektra had begun to unravel. They refused to re-sign with the label for Australia and New Zealand, and by the spring of 1983, had done the same for

Japan. Queen signed with EMI for all three territories which just left their Elektra deal in the United States. Mercury, in particular, had been unhappy with Elektra's handling of *Hot Space* (although, within a year, Taylor was telling interviewers that '*Hot Space* was a step in the wrong direction'). Privately, the singer had informed the others that he would not make another album for Elektra. Jim Beach began negotiating Queen out of the remaining deal, while setting up a one-off solo deal for Mercury with CBS in the UK and Columbia in the US. By October, Queen would be signed to EMI affiliate Capitol in America, having paid $1 million to Elektra to be released from their existing deal.

The first Queen-related release for Capitol would be a mini-album, *Star Fleet Project*, credited to Brian May and Friends. 'This is not a Queen album. This is not a solo album. This is a record of a unique event,' read the sleevenotes. The album came out of a jam session between May, keyboard player Fred Mandel, bass guitarist Phil Chen and drummer Alan Gratzer (both moonlighting from the US rock band REO Speedwagon). May's extra-special friend was guitarist Eddie Van Halen, whose titular band had co-opted some of Queen's musical derring-do and whose lead singer, Dave Lee Roth, rivalled Freddie Mercury in the posing stakes.

Star Fleet Project had been inspired by a children's TV show popular with Brian's son, Jimmy. The album featured just three tracks: a rock version of the show's theme tune, a new piece of May's titled 'Let Me Out', and 'Blues Breaker', an epic jam credited to all of the players and inspired by John Mayall's 1966 album, *Bluesbreakers with Eric Clapton*; required listening for the teenage May at home in Feltham, and Eddie Van Halen, growing up on the other side of the world in Pasadena, California ('Two words you never heard in the studio with those guys were: "piano" and "solo",' laughs Fred Mandel). May insisted the project was not originally intended for commercial release. But with the Queen connection, it was inevitable. *Star Fleet Project* sold modestly but was a gift for guitar aficionados.

■ ■ ■

Freddie Mercury's superstar friends that year included Michael Jackson. But their brief collaboration would never be granted an official release. In the spring, Mercury would record three tracks with Jackson at the singer's home studio in Encino, California. Jackson's *Thriller* album had been released at the end of 1982. Where *Hot Space* had failed, Thriller's hybrid of funk, pop and rock had succeeded. Less than a year later, it had sold in excess of 29 million copies in America alone. According to Mercury's aide Peter Freestone, also present at the session, 'Freddie was in awe of Michael', and managed to curtail his chain smoking so as not to upset the host. The duo worked on three songs, with a plan to complete them at a later date. So what happened? 'We never seemed to be in the same country long enough to actually finish anything completely,' said Mercury vaguely. In 1987, Freddie's then ex-personal manager Paul Prenter would sell a story to the *Sun*. One of Prenter's claims was that the sessions were abandoned when Jackson caught Mercury snorting cocaine through a $100 bill in the lounge. Mercury, in turn, would say that he and Jackson grew apart after *Thriller*: 'He simply retreated into his own little world. We used to have great fun going to clubs together but now he won't come out of his fortress and it's very sad.'

'There's a bit of history there,' admitted Brian May in 2008. 'But I do know that Fred came out of it all a little upset because some of the stuff he did with Michael got taken over by the Jacksons, and he lost out.' Of the three songs, 'There Must Be More to Life Than This' would appear on Mercury's first solo album, while 'Victory' and 'State of Shock' would appear on the Jackson 5's 1984 comeback album, *Victory*. For 'State of Shock', Jackson acquired a new duet partner, Mick Jagger.

By the time of the Mercury/Jackson collaboration, Freddie was in Los Angeles preparing for another Queen album. Initially, the band had been offered a second film soundtrack: Tony Richardson's adaptation of John Irving's coming-of-age novel *The Hotel New Hampshire*. Mercury and Deacon had a first meeting with Richardson and agreed to the project. In the end, the planned film soundtrack would act as little more than a catalyst to get Queen working together again. During an eight-week stint at the Record Plant, the soundtrack idea was shelved, when Richardson revealed that the film's budget wouldn't stretch to a Queen soundtrack. 'Keep On Passing the Open Windows', a Mercury composition intended for the film, would make it onto the final cut of the next Queen album, to be titled *The Works*.

Eighteen months apart from each other had helped, but, as ever, tension still ran high. According to Brian May, it was only Queen's new Capitol US deal that had enticed Mercury back to the studio: 'Freddie was so depressed about the Elektra situation, it was doubtful if he would have agreed to make the album at all.' Once in the studio, Mercury embraced the task. 'Every album that's ever come out of Queen, we've come up with a batch of songs, and we pick the best,' he said. 'If I have five songs that are better than one of Roger's songs, I'll say, we won't have his one song. Roger wrote three or four songs, and as far as I was concerned, they weren't good enough.' Mercury instructed Taylor to come up with something better. According to Freddie, this led to him writing the album's first single, 'Radio Ga Ga'.

The song's title was a play on words. The drummer recalled that his three-year-old son Felix, whose mother Dominique was French, had uttered the words 'ca ca' (French for, as Taylor put it 'something that comes out of your bottom') after his parents had switched on the radio. The title struck a chord with Roger's misgivings about modern radio.

At first, May and Taylor co-operated on the song, before they split and May used his ideas for another track, 'Machines (or Back to Humans)'. Taylor recalled hiding away in the studio for three days with a synthesiser and a drum machine. 'I think Roger was thinking about it as just another track,' said Mercury. 'But I instantly felt there was something in there — a really good, strong, saleable commodity.' Like the young Fred Bulsara playing 'I Get Around' or 'Paperback Writer' on the college piano after one listen, Mercury's flair for a good hook kicked in. Apparently, Taylor went skiing, and told the singer: 'Do what you want.' Fearful that radio stations wouldn't play a song called 'Radio Ca Ca', Queen amended the song's title, but the nursery-rhyme lyric would remain. 'If you listen closely, that's what we're singing: "radio ca ca",' admitted Taylor.

With its Linn drums and synthesisers, *The Works* wallowed in the fashionable technology of the time. 'Machines (or Back to Humans)' tackled the theme of man-versus-technology in its lyric and its musical composition, as traditional drums and electric guitars fought it out with drum machines and Fairlight synths. 'We got too hung up on new technology,' admitted Roger Taylor. 'In the eighties, there was always a new machine, and they were all out of date and being used as coffee tables within six months.'

Nevertheless, the new album was a conscious steer away from the soul and funk of *Hot Space*. ' "Another One Bites the Dust" started us in that direction, and we went too far,' Taylor told one radio interviewer. 'Everybody in the band feels that way now.' Perhaps none more so than Brian May. The guitarist's 'Tear It Up' was as subtle as its title, and found a good home for a riff May had been throwing into the live version of 'Fat Bottomed Girls' on the last tour. 'Hammer to Fall' was exuberant heavy metal with a social conscience; the lyric exploring May's boyhood fears of nuclear destruction during the 1962 Cuban missile crisis. Unusually, the guitarist would share a rare songwriting credit with Mercury on 'Is This the World We Created?', a ballad that Freddie envisaged as a 'Love of My Life' for the new decade.

'In the studio Freddie was full of ideas and lateral thinking,' explained May. 'But he didn't have the greatest attention span. He would always peak at a certain time. If you had Fred for an hour when he was peaking, he was absolute gold dust. But then you'd hear, "Oh look, dear! I've done this. I have to go now", and you knew you'd had your slice of Freddie.'

Mercury would take a sole writing credit on three songs. 'Keep On Passing the Open Windows' had been earmarked for *The Hotel New Hampshire*. With its optimistic lyrics and driving rhythm it was the kind of self-empowerment anthem much heard in mid-eighties film soundtracks. 'Man on the Prowl' was forgettable rockabilly, saved by a glorious piano finale from Fred Mandel. For the first time, Queen had allowed another musician into the studio for a credited performance. 'Freddie and I both played on "Man on the Prowl",' says Mandel now. 'But Fred said to me, "Why don't you take over later and play that rock 'n' roll stuff. You do that better than me. Besides, they will all think it's me, darling!" I didn't care. I was being paid.'

The singer would save his best work for 'It's a Hard Life', another of those ceremonious half-ballads in the mould of 'Play the Game' or 'Killer Queen'. The song's opening line was based on a line from an aria in Ruggero Leoncavallo's opera *Pagliacci*. 'This is one of the most beautiful songs Freddie ever wrote,' said Brian May in 2003. 'It's straight from the heart.' May worked closely with Mercury, sitting with him 'for hours and hours, trying to get the most out of it.' It's not difficult to fathom the song's appeal for May. Mercury had stopped crowing about his sexual prowess ('Staying Power') and Bacchanalian lifestyle ('Don't Stop Me Now') and was singing about his desire for romantic love. Mercury would never admit as much. 'But I almost believe that every songwriter in the world has something to say when they write a song,' said May. 'All sorts of stuff creeps in there. Fred was no different.'

Fred Mandel would play on 'Radio Ga Ga' and 'Hammer to Fall', but his most enduring contribution to *The Works* would come elsewhere. John Deacon, Queen's resident 'ostrich', had laid another golden egg. 'I Want To Break Free' ('Was he trying to tell us something?' joked Taylor) was the strongest evidence yet of what Fred Mandel calls 'Queen's secret weapon, John Deacon'. Like 'Another One Bites the Dust', it was the simplest of pop songs, stripped back to its bare bones.

Unusually, Deacon asked Fred Mandel to play the song's solo on a synthesiser. 'This was controversial, as no one did solos apart from Brian,' recalls Mandel. 'But the band were out to dinner, so I did it. I didn't think anything of it, as I'd done the same on Alice Cooper records. It was no big deal, but I think people thought it was a big deal.' Deacon wanted the synth solo to stay, and there it remained. Several years later, while touring with Elton John, Mandel was browsing in a music store when he spotted a new Roland synth. 'It had a pre-set button that read "May Sound". I realised that Roland had heard the solo to "I Want to Break Free" and thought it was Brian on guitar, not realising it was actually done on one of their own products, and copied it on to their new synth.'

Intra-band relations during the making of *The Works* would be as fraught as they had been during *Hot Space*. 'But then we'd all come back to the idea that the band was greater than any of us,' explained May. 'It was more enduring than most of our marriages.' 'I Go Crazy', one of May's heavier tracks, was rejected by his bandmates. 'The other three hated it so much they were ashamed to play on it,' he admitted. The song would wind up on the B-side of 'Radio Ga Ga'. But outvoted three to one, May had no choice but to accept that it wouldn't make it on to *The Works*. 'Deep down, they were all rational guys,' adds Fred Mandel. 'I think Queen were like the Four Musketeers: whatever was good for the group . . .'

With Mack co-producing, there was always a mediator on hand. 'Mack was like Roy Thomas Baker, Part Two,' says Mandel. 'He was as important to the second half of Queen's career as Roy had been in the first half. Mack and Roy came from a world where you had to get down on the studio floor and know how to fix the wires. Not every producer came up that way. They were ideas guys as well as technicians. It was a formidable force. Mack could achieve the things Queen asked of him.'

But, at times, even Mack needed a refuge. 'There was a nudie bar over the road from the studio,' he says now. 'It became an office for me and John Deacon to go and get a little peace and quiet.' For Mercury, in particular, Los Angeles was another playground in which he could indulge his every whim. 'The gay scene in LA was incredible,' chuckles Mack. During one of his many nights out in West Hollywood's 'Boystown' district, Mercury met a biker known as 'Vince the Barman'. Vince would join Mercury at his rented mansion on Stone Canyon Road, but refused to ditch his bar job and accompany the singer on Queen's next tour. For the first time ever, Mercury had been turned down. From here on, within the singer's close circle, Vince would always be regarded as 'the one that got away'.

'The house Fred was renting was Elizabeth Taylor's old place,' remembers Mack. 'And one day, Freddie threw a table through its glass doors.' For his thirty-seventh birthday, Mercury held a party at Stone Canyon Road, covering the mansion with lilies and inviting Rod Stewart and Elton John, among others. On Mercury's past form, it was a comparatively sedate affair, but Queen's overall spending in LA was causing concern. 'The accountant said that he'd never seen people burn through so much money,' laughs Mack. 'He started asking questions like, "Why do you have nineteen rental cars when there are only eight of you?"'

In order to finish *The Works*, Queen and their entourage decamped to Munich and back to what May had called 'the emotional distractions'. 'We got to the studio one day and John had left a note on his bass,' recalled May. It simply said: 'Gone to Bali.' Weary of the grind, the bass player had fled to an Indonesian island for some respite. 'There was no note on his bass,' disputes Peter Hince. 'Yes, he did go to Bali, for personal reasons that I don't wish to go into. I put him on the plane and I got him back.' 'We were OK about it,' added May, 'as we were all going mad as well. John could be wonderfully unpredictable: very quiet and shy a lot of the time, but then suddenly he'd break out and you didn't know what he was going to do next.'

Meanwhile, Mercury's complex love life became even more complex. In January 1984, he began a relationship with the late Austrian actress and model Barbara Valentin. The blonde Valentin had been one of film director Rainer Werner Fassbinder's leading ladies. Six years Mercury's senior, Valentin had once been described as 'the German Jayne Mansfield'. The pair met on the Munich club circuit. 'Barbara and I have formed a bond that is stronger than anything I've had with a lover for the last six years,' he said in 1985. 'I can really talk to her and be myself in a way that's very rare.' The pair would later purchase an apartment together on HansSachs Strasse, in the middle of Munich's club zone. While his relationship with Valentin was sexual, Mercury was still embroiled in an on-off romance with Winnie Kirchberger. Determined not to be dominated by his millionaire rock star boyfriend, Kirchberger would often treat Mercury badly.

'Winnie was primitive, the truck-driver type that Freddie preferred,' said Valentin in 1996. 'They'd have terrible fights and both would pick up unsuitable guys to make the other one jealous.' But Valentin's relationship with Mercury could be similarly crazed. Theirs was a close and treasured friendship, but as die-hards on the Munich club scene, they would egg each other on: more booze, more drugs, more sex, with each other, with other people. On one occasion, Mercury blacked out at the apartment, supposedly after too much alcohol and cocaine. Undaunted by the episode, he carried on indulging. It would be some time before he discovered the truth about his long-term health.

On 23 January, Queen released a taster of *The Works*, the single 'Radio Ga Ga', the lyrics and sentiment prompted by Roger Taylor's frustration with the music business. 'It deals with how important radio used to be. Before television, it was the first place I heard rock 'n' roll,' he said. 'Today it seems that video, the visual side of rock 'n' roll, has become more important than the music.'

Nevertheless, Taylor's misgivings hadn't stopped Queen making a video for the single. Director David Mallet's memorable promo for 'Radio Ga Ga' spliced footage from Fritz Lang's film *Metropolis* with images of Queen gadding around in a futuristic flying car. Taylor piloted the space-age vehicle, but seemed, at times, as if he was struggling to keep a straight face. Behind him, May simply looked uncomfortable while a similarly uneasy-looking Deacon showed off the results of his newly acquired perm. Only Mercury looked at home, hamming it up like a grand dame, possibly buoyed by the vodka and tonic he'd stashed unseen inside the vehicle. The film's most striking sequence, shot at Pinewood Studios, had Queen conducting a mass rally of 500 handclapping fan-club members. As *Mojo*'s David Thomas later pointed out: 'It was eerily reminiscent of some Leni Riefenstahl film of a Nazi night-rally.''

The comic irony of a song bemoaning the importance of video over radio, while being promoted with a lavish video, would prove no deterrent to airplay or sales. *NME* were swift to condemn the video's militaristic aspect, decrying 'Radio Ga Ga' as 'arrogant nonsense'. Yet within a fortnight, the single was at number 2 in the UK. After years of watching his three bandmates write hit singles for Queen, Taylor had finally written one of his own.

The Works was released on 1 February. Mercury had indulged his obsession with old-school Hollywood by getting photographer George Hurrell to shoot the artfully airbrushed cover. Hurrell was an industry veteran who had photographed Marlene Dietrich,

Marilyn Monroe and Greta Garbo. Before long, *The Works* had followed the lead set by 'Radio Ga Ga' and also reached number 2. A month later Queen made their first 'live' appearance since 1982, sharing a bill with Culture Club at Italy's televised San Remo Festival, and miming animatedly to 'Radio Ga Ga'. Backstage, tension simmered over into what Peter Hince describes as a 'minor disagreement' between May and Taylor. 'Brian and Roger would row quite often,' he says. 'But it never got physical, unlike some bands. I can't remember what the row in San Remo was about — probably who had the biggest hotel suite.'

'Radio Ga Ga' would give Queen a number 1 hit in Italy, Belgium, Germany, Ireland and Sweden. In America, where Queen's fortunes had taken such a blow with *Hot Space*, there were also signs of recovery. *Rolling Stone* magazine declared *The Works* 'a royal feast of hard rock without that metallic aftertaste', but sales were slow with the album eventually peaking at number 23. 'Radio Ga Ga' had fared better, inching up to number 16 in the US. But the bubble would soon burst.

'We had spent a million dollars getting out of our deal with Warner-Elektra to get into Capitol in the US,' explained Brian May. 'Then Capitol got themselves into trouble with a dispute in the early eighties over the alleged corruption of independent record promoters in the US. Capitol got rid of all its connections to the independent radio promoters. The reprisals from the whole network were aimed directly at all the artists who had records out at that time. They got very upset and dropped "Radio Ga Ga". That week it dropped like a stone.' Five weeks after reaching number 16, the single was barely in the US Top 100.

There were other contributing problems inside the Queen camp. 'The guy that looked after Fred was very good at looking after Fred's interests but trampled all over everyone else,' said May in 2008. 'So any press people and promoters in the US were treated with disdain. They thought Fred was doing it. So Fred lost a lot of friends while we were touring, and we didn't even realise it was happening. Meanwhile, the radio people were also being told, "Fred doesn't want to talk to you." ' While May would never name the guilty party in interviews, it was Mercury's personal manager

Paul Prenter. The outcome of Prenter's attitude was an added blow to Queen's relationship with the US radio networks. 'Prenter could be very effective and he did get some good scoops for the band,' says Peter Hince. 'But he could also be difficult and he was very fickle, and he had these delusions of grandeur.'

Yet there would be worse damage to come. In April, Queen released *The Works*' second single, 'I Want to Break Free'. With director David Mallet, Queen created a video so memorable it would even rival the promo for 'Bohemian Rhapsody'. 'Most videos we regarded as a complete chore,' said Roger Taylor. 'The only one we enjoyed and didn't stop laughing at was "I Want to Break Free".' It was Roger's then-partner Dominique who had mooted the idea of Queen 'dragging up' as women in a pastiche of the TV soap opera *Coronation Street*.

Queen's dysfunctional female family unit would cast John Deacon as a matriarchal grandmother; Brian May in hair-rollers, dressing gown and fluffy slippers; Roger Taylor as a troublingly easy-on-the-eye blonde schoolgirl (Taylor: 'I was quite shocked myself when I first saw it'), and Freddie Mercury as a frustrated housewife or a spoof of *Coronation Street*'s brassy barmaid Bet Lynch, in leather mini-skirt, figure-hugging pink top and false breasts. As an added prop, Freddie shunted a vacuum cleaner around a house while the others looked on. The punchline was that Mercury kept his trademark moustache for the drag act, but shaved it for a later sequence where he romped with members of the Royal Ballet in a routine that borrowed from *The Rite of Spring*.

'I Want to Break Free' went straight to number 3 in the UK, where audiences had been weaned on Carry On films and TV sitcoms in which English gents routinely dressed as women. 'We wanted people to know that we didn't take ourselves too seriously,' explained Taylor. It was a U-turn after years of Queen presenting themselves as a band who took themselves very seriously, but it encapsulated the same contrariness and contradiction that also made the group tick. As one insider explained: 'Queen would criticise themselves and each other all the time, but woe betide if anyone from outside did it.'

In the US, it was a very different story. 'They hated the video,'

May told *Mojo*'s Mick Wall. 'It was received with horror in most of America. They just didn't get it. To them it was boys dressing up as girls and that was unthinkable, especially for a rock band. I was in some of those US TV stations when they got the video, and a lot of them refused to play it. They were visibly embarrassed.'

'I'm Canadian, so I understood,' laughs Fred Mandel. 'To me it was just Benny Hill, typical British humour. I liked seeing Roger as a schoolgirl and I especially liked seeing Freddie doing housework.' Nevertheless, the all-powerful music channel MTV chose not to screen the video, and 'I Want to Break Free' limped to just number 45 in the US. 'Middle America felt that Freddie might be gay, and Middle America was very important,' says EMI's Brian Southall. 'That was the trouble: you could be terribly arty in New York or Los Angeles, but don't try it in Kansas.'

'For the first time in our lives we were taking the mickey out of ourselves,' protested Mercury. 'But in America they said, "What are our idols doing dressing up in frocks?"' 'Queen were asked to do another promo for "I Want to Break Free",' says Peter Hince. 'They were told, "This one isn't right for America, will you do a performance video?" And they said, "No." They should have done it, because it killed them in the US.'

Hince accompanied John Deacon and Roger Taylor on a world promo trip for *The Works*. 'We did Japan, Hong Kong, Australia, TV and radio. I think they flew to New York for a week and did a press day somewhere else, but it was as though they didn't want to do press in the US. Of course, everyone wanted to interview Freddie and Freddie wasn't doing any interviews. Prenter was going around, saying, "I made 'Radio Ga Ga' and 'I Want to Break Free' into hits." Their attitude to America was like, Oh fuck 'em, we don't need 'em. It was so strange, as they had just signed to EMI in the US. Maybe they thought EMI would be like a magic wand.'

'Freddie didn't want to go back to America and play smaller venues than we'd been before,' admitted May in 2005. 'He was like, "Let's just wait and we'll go out and do stadiums in America as well." But it was one of those things that wasn't to be.'

■ ■ ■

By the spring of 1984, Freddie Mercury had returned to Munich with Mack to complete work on what would become his first solo release, 'Mr Bad Guy'. A month later, Taylor put out his second solo album, *Strange Frontier*. The drummer had apparently rejected some of his own original songs for the project, and had co-written others with his new production partner, Mountain's resident engineer David Richards.

For a rock star whose reputation suggested one of carefree abandon, Taylor sounded remarkably dour. Wringing his hands over man's inhumanity to man and the threat of nuclear Armageddon, one song, 'Killing Time', even suggested a bored, dissolute rock star in paradise watching his life pass by. There were covers of Dylan's 'Masters of War' and Springsteen's 'Racing in the Street' to sweeten the pill, but *Strange Frontier* was terribly worthy and not much fun. The album would only just make it into the UK Top 30. In the music press, *Sounds* offered a rather blunt if ultimately fair assessment: 'He can write the songs, but he can't sing them like Freddie does.'

Taylor had even less to smile about when Queen reassembled to make a promo video for their next single 'It's a Hard Life'. Filmed in Munich, Mercury enlisted many of his friends and fellow clubbers, including Barbara Valentin, as extras in a lavish set that seemed a cross between an Elizabethan wedding banquet and the Sex Maniacs' Ball. 'I didn't like it,' said the plain-speaking John Deacon, but the bassist got away reasonably lightly. In one scene, Taylor, trussed up in tights and a regency ruff, looks mortally embarrassed ('I tried to get my scenes cut out,' he later admitted), while in another, poor Brian May poses with a skeleton-style guitar.

Meanwhile, Mercury's costume, a dramatic slashed scarlet tunic decorated with feathers and twenty-six eyes, was modelled on an outfit once worn by the French torch singer Mistinguett. Unfortunately, it made the Queen singer resemble what May later described as 'a giant amorous prawn'. 'It was one of my favourite songs of Freddie's and I remember being terribly disappointed that he wanted to wear this costume,' he said. America remained equally unconvinced, and 'It's a Hard Life' tanked, while reaching number 6 in Britain.

Then again, Mercury's ridiculous costume had been the least of his worries during the shoot. He was having trouble walking, after being involved in a fracas in New York, a Munich bar, which had left him with damaged ligaments in his right knee. 'Some cunt kicked me,' he explained at a press conference. 'It might mean I will have to cut down on some of my more elaborate gorgeous stage moves.'

Mercury had spent some time in plaster, but seemed match fit when the tour opened at Queen's familiar stamping ground, Brussels' Forest National. Fred Mandel had taken a gig with Elton John, and was replaced for the tour by The Boomtown Rats' sometime keyboard player Spike Edney, recruited after 'Crystal' Taylor ran into him in a London nightclub. Edney was flown to Munich to meet the band. It was a baptism by fire. 'Come four o'clock in the morning we were in the Sugar Shack club,' he said. 'By six o'clock in the morning we were back at the hotel, in Roger's suite, where the champagne was flowing . . .'

The Works tour stage set was modelled on Fritz Lang's Metropolis, included Queen's grandest lighting rig yet, a huge catwalk for Freddie to show off on, and two enormous Metropolis-style cogs. Computerised technology being what it was in 1984, the band decided it would be safer for the cogs to be cranked by hand, giving the road crew another job for the night. The Works tour would take in Europe, the UK, Australasia and, controversially, South Africa, but not America. 'That's when the arrogance took over,' ventures Peter Hince. 'An attitude of, "We don't need to tour the States." I know that Gerry Stickells tried very hard to get them to reconsider.'

In a marked contrast to the Hot Space trek, the set drew on Queen's heavier repertoire. After an intro of 'Machines (or Back to Human)' came 'Tear It Up' quickly followed by 'Tie Your Mother Down'. Snippets of now ancient Queen numbers such as 'Liar', 'Great King Rat' and 'Stone Cold Crazy' would also be played as part of a mid-set medley. In Dublin, Mercury forgot the words to 'Hammer to Fall', but on several dates it was his voice rather than his memory that would let him down. Doctors feared a recurrence of nodules on his vocal cords. Mercury was scared that having an operation to remove them would have an adverse effect on his voice.

On top of this, aspects of Freddie's lifestyle had now been made public, after the *Sun* printed a story from a former employee. 'It was Freddie's old driver, who'd been sacked,' sighs Peter Hince. 'It was the strangest thing. Fred could be incredibly tough and ruthless and nasty, but he would just indulge some people, and you'd think, "For fuck's sake, Fred, why?"' The story was split across several editions, timed to coincide with Queen's four-night stand at London's Wembley Arena and Mercury's thirty-eighth birthday. It included the revelation that Freddie was spending £1,000 a week on vodka and cocaine. If the singer was concerned about the story, he masked it well. For the encore, Mercury re-appeared in the wig and false breasts he'd worn for 'I Want to Break Free'. Looking around to see which band member would perhaps least appreciate having his comedy mammaries shoved in their face, he sidled over to John Deacon. The wig-and-boobs routine would become a regular part of the show. Offstage, Freddie carefully deflected questions about claims that he was homosexual. 'It's good to be gay if you're new,' he told *Melody Maker*. 'But if I tried that, people would start yawning: "Oh God! Here's Freddie Mercury, saying he's gay because it's trendy to be gay."'

In Hanover, a fortnight later, the leg injury Mercury had received in a Munich bar came back to haunt him. Halfway through 'Hammer to Fall', his damaged leg gave way on the cat-walk staircase. 'I did a wrong move, fell down, under the spotlights, and they thought it was part of the show,' he said later, 'but I couldn't get up.' Mercury was carried to his piano where he managed two more numbers before the show was cut short. Mercury joked that he was 'now too old for rock 'n' roll'.

In September, having watched Brian May and Roger Taylor struggle to make an impact with their solo projects, Mercury made his debut with the single, 'Love Kills', a Mercury/Moroder composition, written for the *Metropolis* soundtrack. Intriguingly, it was later revealed that May and Taylor and possibly even Deacon had played on the track, leading to speculation that it had started life as a Queen song. But with the song's dancefloor vibe and the chorus' macho but camp backing vocal, the finished article sounded like Mercury unbound, unrestrained, and quite clearly not Queen. 'Love Kills' would buck the trend of Queen solo projects and chart at number 10. Queen's next single, 'Hammer to Fall', released simultaneously, managed number 13. Onstage, Mercury had begun informing audiences that Queen were *not* splitting up. A month later, when the band arrived in South Africa, some wished they had.

On 5 October, Queen played the first of a run of shows in Sun City, a luxury hotel and gambling resort near Johannesburg. Sun City was regarded as a 'whites only Las Vegas' and a totem of the divisive apartheid regime. As far back as 1957, before the emergence of the Anti-Apartheid Movement, the Musicians Union had been instructing its members not to perform in South Africa. Queen thought otherwise. 'We've thought about the morals of it a lot and it's something we've decided to do,' Brian May told a press conference at the start of *The Works* tour. 'This band is not political, we are not out to make any statements, we play to anybody who comes to listen.' Part of Queen's proviso for performing at Sun City would be that they would only play to a mixed audience. A spokesperson for the African National Congress would later insist that 'the people who overwhelmingly attended those concerts were white.'

Queen were booked for a run of shows at Sun City's 6,200-seater Superbowl. Such was the ticket demand that a further 1,000 standing-room-only tickets were quickly released. But before long, Mercury's voice would let him down. During the third show, after struggling through 'Under Pressure', his voice failed completely, and the remainder of the gig was cancelled. A doctor was flown in, Mercury was injected with steroids and the next two shows were cancelled after he was ordered to rest. While Mercury hid away in his hotel suite with Winnie Kirchberger, waiting to complete the remaining dates, Brian May was invited to Soweto to present at the Black African Awards Show. Meanwhile a decision was taken to release a Queen live album through EMI South Africa and donate its royalties to a local school for deaf and blind children. Yet such gestures cut little ice with anti-apartheid groups, who protested that the South African government were making political capital out of Queen's visit, regarding it as some tenuous endorsement of their regime. Back in Britain, Queen met a barrage of hostile press, while their old nemesis *NME* drew a line between the South African visit and what they described as the 'vile, fascist imagery' of the 'Radio Ga Ga' video.

On the one level, Queen's decision to play South Africa could be regarded as another example of their wilfully contrary streak. Even now, there's a suspicion that the visit was partly driven by being told they *shouldn't* play, as well as the band's insistence that they would play music to anyone, anywhere. Brian May would deliver an impassioned speech to the Musicians Union General Committee, insisting that the group were opposed to apartheid but defending Queen's actions. 'The general reaction was, at least, "Thanks for coming, we understand why you did it now,"' he said. 'But they fined us anyway because we'd broken the rules.'

A year later, Bruce Springsteen's point man 'Little' Steven Van Zandt set up the musical collective Artists United Against Apartheid. Their single '(Ain't Gonna Play in No) Sun City', was a protest against those that had played the resort, including Rod Stewart, who followed Queen to Sun City in January 1985. 'I'm sure a lot of people still feel we're fascist pigs because of it,' May admitted to *Q* magazine. 'Sorry, there's nothing I can do about that. We have totally clear consciences.'

Queen saw out the year with a video release for 'We Will Rock You', the concert film shot in Canada on the *Hot Space* tour, and a seasonal single, 'Thank God It's Christmas'. It could have been interpreted as a comment on what had been a difficult year. If so, none but the staunchest Queen followers would go out and buy it. By the time Christmas rolled around, the song had left the Top 20. Instead, Christmas 1984's number 1 song would be Band Aid's 'Do They Know It's Christmas?' Forced to act after seeing the TV news coverage of the Ethiopian famine, The Boomtown Rats' frontman Bob Geldof and Ultravox's Midge Ure had corralled the likes of Boy George, U2's Bono, Phil Collins and Sting into forming a charity supergroup and cutting a record to raise money for family relief.

'We would have loved to have been on the Band Aid record,' insisted Mercury. 'But I only heard about it when we were in Germany.' Inevitably, some muttered that Queen had been deliberately excluded for playing Sun City. Fully aware that Band Aid included the thirty-something Phil Collins and half of the similarly vintage Status Quo, Mercury jumped in with a now familiar joke. 'I don't know if they'd have had me on the record anyway,' he said disingenuously. 'I'm a bit old.'

■   ■   ■

Despite Queen's harrowing experience on the Gluttons for Punishment tour, South America continued to exert a curious pull on the band, and vice versa. 'Under Pressure' had been at number 1 in Argentina in May 1982, when Argentina and Britain had gone to war over stewardship of the Falklands Islands. Immediately, the Argentinian leader General Galtieri banned Queen's music from the country. A year later, the Queen office were back in negotiations with promoters to play more shows on the continent, including Rio's coveted Maracana Stadium. Once again, though, the deal fell through. 'Everything was set up,' explained Roger Taylor. 'But the promoter went broke virtually the day before.'

Somehow, in January 1985, the money transfer was completed and Queen were booked for the headline slot on the opening and closing nights of the ten-day Rock in Rio festival. The show would be staged at 250,000-capacity venue in Barra de Tijuca, purpose-built for around $11 million, funded by a Brazilian advertising mogul. Other headline acts included AC/DC, George Benson and Queen's old sparring partners, Yes and Rod Stewart. But even the acts lower on the bill now read like a Who's Who of eighties rock: Iron Maiden, Whitesnake, Scorpions, Ozzy Osbourne . . . It was estimated that some three million people would attend the festival over the course of its ten days, immediately earning Rock in Rio a place in *The Guinness Book of Records* where it deposed 1973's Watkins Glen Summer Jam, which had seen a mere 600,000 show up to see The Grateful Dead and The Band. As an additional financial sweetener, Brazilian TV station Globo was granted the rights to broadcast the festival, including Queen's performance. Rock in Rio subscribed to Queen's favoured policy of 'bigger, better, more'. They were made for each other.

Booked into the presidential suite of the Copacabana Beach Hotel, where his entourage included both Barbara Valentin and Winnie Kirchberger, Mercury ran on what one tour insider called 'Freddie time'. On the first night Queen didn't arrive onstage until the small hours. Behind the scenes, it was claimed that Brian May had been taken ill with flu, which, according to the *Sun*, led to Queen being helicoptered onto the site 'at the very last minute'. It all added to the melodrama, though Queen hardly needed it. As *Record Mirror*'s Robin Smith observed, Queen's 'operatic grandeur and style drive the lusty Latins wild'. Playing a re-jigged version of *The Works* tour setlist, the show was comfortably loaded with hits. Determined to stay visible in front of over 300,000 people, every band member dressed in white. Taylor rocked up in a Katherine Hamnett T-shirt calling for worldwide nuclear disarmament, Mercury fashioned crotch-hugging tights with a red lightning bolt motif on the thighs, while May's white spandex trousers were offset with an orange sash. The setlist was foolproof: 'Under Pressure', 'Keep Yourself Alive', 'Radio Ga Ga' . . .

Then came 'I Want to Break Free'. Presuming that what had worked in front of an audience in Britain and Europe would work anywhere in the world, Mercury re-appeared to perform the song in a woman's wig, pink jumper and what *People* magazine called 'huge plastic falsies'. As Brian May recently said, 'It was wonderful to have a singer with no compunctions whatsoever. There was nowhere Freddie wouldn't go.' According to *People*, 'a near riot erupted when the crowd of 350,000 began tossing stones, beer cans and other missiles . . .' Interviewed at the time, festival interpreter Maria Caetano explained that 'the song is sacred in South America because we consider it a political message about the evils of dictatorship.' Unknown to Queen, 'Deakey's golden egg' had indeed acquired a deeper message in South America. Video footage from the event disproves the theory of a 'near riot', but there was enough animosity from some of the crowd for Mercury to realise that he'd misjudged the mood. 'It surprised him,' recalls Peter Hince. 'They couldn't work out what was going wrong, so they had this chilling flashback to Mexico.'

The singer reappeared for 'We Will Rock You', arms outstretched, wearing a flag as a cape, displaying the inside lining with the red, white and blue of the Union Jack, before turning to face Roger Taylor and showing the crowd the orange and blue Brazilian emblem on the back. He was forgiven. Interviewed after the event, Mercury, typically, brushed it aside. 'They [Rio] were a wonderful audience, and I love their displays of emotion,' he said. 'They get over-excited sometimes but I can bring the whip down and show them who's in control. I don't know why they got so excited about me dressing as a woman; there are a lot of transvestites here.'

A day later, EMI threw a party for Queen at the nearby Copacabana Palace Hotel, where band members schmoozed with Rod Stewart, Spandau Ballet's Gary Kemp and half of Duran Duran. Supposedly, Mercury and Stewart became embroiled in a game of rock-star one-upmanship by pretending not to notice each other. Others, however, claim that Mercury refused to attend, or put in the briefest of appearances, again fearful of what his friend David Evans described as 'loss of control': it was not his party, it was *for* him, which meant all the old insecurities would come to surface. Meanwhile, a troupe of topless samba dancers were forced to perform with a reduced breast count after some of the dancers were sent home for being too drunk to stand. In a rare display of public tomfoolery, Brian May would be the first to throw himself fully clothed into the hotel swimming pool. Outside the party, besotted fans congregated on the beach, where they spelt out the band's name in the sand using 1,500 candles. May went down to meet them, and, tellingly, spent more time there than he did among the liggers and beautiful people at the EMI bash.

Interviewed in Rio, Mercury, supposedly flanked by models, praised the 'beautiful brown bodies' around him and delivered the now much-quoted line: 'I'm just an old slag who gets up in the morning, scratches his head and wonders who he wants to fuck.' During Queen's stay in Rio, Mercury and his entourage would explore the local gay club scene, though the need for security guards and the hysteria that accompanied any public appearance made the logistics of even leaving the hotel difficult. It was easier, others said, to bring the party to Freddie Mercury. Later, one of Rio's 'taxi' boys, the name given to young male prostitutes in the city, would reveal how he and other males were invited by Paul Prenter to Mercury's hotel suite. There, they were given cocaine and would, it was claimed, each have sex with the singer, who assumed a passive role in the proceedings. The impression given was of a soulless encounter with a moneyed rock star, who had grown bored of having everything and anything on offer, and was merely going through the motions, though Prenter was cast as the instigator. 'Paul's appetite for sex, drugs and alcohol was phenomenal,' cautions Peter Hince. 'And he liked to brag about it, especially when he was drunk: "Oh, I had seven boys today!" He could be a nasty piece of work, especially when he'd been drinking.' Mark Malden once joined Mercury's entourage on a visit to a gay bar in Toronto. 'There was Fred, myself, Dane Clarke and Paul Prenter. It became apparent to me that we were not there for Fred or Dane and certainly not for me. We were there for Paul. It was Paul who directed the limo driver. It was Paul who picked up a man there, not Fred. Paul led things. Paul controlled things. Freddie was very strong when it came to his music, but not as strong in his personal life.'

When Queen returned to Barra de Tijuca to play the last night of the festival, Rio had been subjected to several days of torrential rain, and the site was awash with mud. Filmed by Globo TV, Queen showboated through the same set as a week before. But when it came to 'I Want to Break Free', Mercury had left the wig and plastic breasts back at the hotel. He performed the song stripped to the waist and with a towel draped over his shoulders instead. With more than 600,000 people watching the band across two nights, Queen's ubiquity was assured. In a candid moment, Freddie admitted South America was 'a tremendous market. If you crack it here, the amount of money you can make is tremendous.'

Back in London, John Deacon would spend some of that money on a new Porsche. Driving back from a Phil Collins show at the Royal Albert Hall, Deacon was stopped by the police and breathalysed. He failed the test, was fined £150 and banned from driving for twelve months. Just days later, Brian May guested on DJ Roger Scott's Capital Radio show, playing some of his favourite records. May chose Stevie Wonder's 'Don't Drive Drunk', offering a waggish dedication to 'John, whom some of you may know has had a little problem with his car recently.'

There seemed less to smile about when Queen flew to New Zealand for the first of a nine-date tour, taking in Melbourne and Sydney, Australia. NZTV reporter and music journalist the late Dylan Taite conducted a television interview with all four before the first night at Auckland's Mount Smart Stadium. Mercury did most of the talking, May had his head down and studied his fingernails, Taylor kept his sunglasses on throughout, and all of the band, bar May, cradled a cigarette. Deacon, in particular, struggled to suppress a knowing smirk when Taite raised the subject of money. 'We are all extremely wealthy,' said Mercury. 'But this is a very delicate question and you'd have to ask us individually . . . Wealth brings a lot of problems and we all have different problems. The money we make brings a lot of problems.'

If Mercury's speech sounded just a tad slurred, there was a valid reason: he had been drinking. On the afternoon of the show, Freddie palled up with Spandau Ballet's lead singer Tony Hadley. The New Romantic pop group, at the height of their powers after 1984's platinum-selling *Parade* album, were on an unplanned break after an Australian tour. With nothing else to do, Hadley and Mercury opened a bottle of vodka, finished it, and then cracked open a bottle of vintage port . . . Come showtime, Freddie was flat on his back and needed to be helped into his stage clothes by Joe Fanelli. Once onstage at the 30,000-capacity Mount Smart stadium, Mercury began ad-libbing wildly: 'My voice is fucked,' he informed the crowd, despite having promised New Zealand 'a motherfucker of a good time'. Later, 'Hammer to Fall', Brian May's anthemic party piece, was introduced as 'one for all you heavy metal fans to have a good jerk-off to!' When a similarly inebriated Hadley joined Queen onstage for 'Jailhouse Rock', more chaos ensued. Unable to recall the lyrics, Hadley began singing Little Richard's 'Tutti Frutti' instead. Many in the Queen camp said it was the only time they had seen Mercury drunk before a gig.

The fun and games continued in Sydney, where Queen had sold out four nights at the Entertainment Centre. Drunken hijinks on a hired pleasure cruiser led to one of the road crew jumping overboard for a bet and having to be rescued by the coastguard. As the incident had delayed traffic in and out of Sydney Harbour, Queen were hit with a $5,000 fine. 'There was a lot of slackness around *The Works* tour,' admits Peter Hince. 'It was getting out of control because the money was there and people were abusing it.'

In Sydney, Elton John joined Mercury and Taylor for a night on the tiles. Mercury had told friends that Elton had been especially supportive in Queen's difficult early days and Taylor and Deacon would both play on Elton's 1985 album, *Ice on Fire*, and the following year's *Leather Jackets*. Later, Elton would cite the albums he made in the mid-1980s as some of his poorest, blaming this in part on cocaine. Recounting past wild times in an interview with *Uncut* magazine, Elton admitted: 'Freddie Mercury could out-party me, which is saying something. We'd be up for nights, sitting there at eleven in the morning, still flying high. Queen were supposed to be catching a plane and Freddie would be like, "Oh fuck, another line, dear?" His appetites were unquenchable.'

Then again, Mercury had something to celebrate. On 29 April, Queen's last night in Sydney, Columbia released Freddie's debut solo album, *Mr Bad Guy*. It had taken Mercury the best part of two years to piece together with co-producer Mack. Queen's touring keyboard player Fred Mandel contributed piano on some tracks, while session musicians, including Mary Austin's new boyfriend, bass guitarist Jo Burt, took care of the rest. Breaking one of Queen's cardinal rules, Mercury even used an orchestra on the title track. In the sleeve notes, Freddie thanked 'Brian, John and Roger for not interfering', and included a dedication to all three of his significant others, Mary Austin, Barbara Valentin ('for big tits and mis-conduct') and Winnie ('for board and lodgings'). Most of *Mr Bad Guy* was closer in feel to Queen's *Hot Space* than *The Works*. Freddie, in his gym vest and shades, pulled a brooding pose on the cover. The music inside matched the cover. *Mr Bad Guy* was glossy, flash and completely of the moment. With its dance and funk rhythms, it seemed a lifetime away from the feather-boa-clad pomp metal of *Sheer Heart Attack* or *Queen II*. 'It's very beat oriented,' Mercury told *Record Mirror*. 'It's a very natural album.'

Nevertheless, some of the songs, including 'Man Made Paradise' and 'There Must Be More to Life Than This', had been kicking around Queen sessions since *The Game*. When session player Paul Vincent let fly with a very Queen-like guitar solo on 'Man Made Paradise' it was difficult not to wonder why Mercury hadn't just let Brian May play it instead. Overall, *Mr Bad Guy*'s mood shifted twitchily from the self-aggrandising title track to the heart-on-sleeve closing ballad 'Love Me Like There's No Tomorrow', which had been written especially for Barbara Valentin. Mercury was only too aware of the schizophrenic nature of his writing. 'Most of the songs I write are love ballads and things to do with sadness and torture and pain,' he said. 'But at the same time, it's frivolous and tongue in cheek. That's basically my whole nature.'

A lead-off single, 'I Was Born to Love You', had reached a respectable number 11 in Britain in April. *Mr Bad Guy* debuted in the UK chart at number 6, and managed a fortnight in the Top 10. In America, it flopped at number 159. '*Mr Bad Guy* was just something I wanted to do,' Mercury explained later. 'I wanted to do all the things I wasn't able to do within the band.' With no plans to tour the record and with Mercury conducting few press interviews, it was hardly a shock that it failed to equal Queen's success. While his drug buddy Elton John would painstakingly note down the chart positions of each and every one of his singles and albums and would then pore over the data, Mercury took a more flippant view of the business. As one EMI insider explained: 'If one record didn't work, get another one out. No one song was so special that Freddie ever said, "That's it . . . I'll never do better than that."' Mercury, it seemed, also knew where he worked best. 'I won't be splitting up with Queen,' he insisted, before adding, 'Without the others I'm nothing.'

At the end of *The Works* jaunt, Deacon joined Taylor on the Balearic island of Ibiza, where the drummer had acquired a property and indulged his new passion for powerboat racing; May and his family stayed on in Australia for a holiday, while Mercury returned to Munich and his tangled personal relationships. Aside from the romantic tug of war between Winnie Kirchberger and Barbara Valentin, Freddie had a new love interest. Two years earlier, he had briefly met an Irish hairdresser named Jim Hutton in the South Kensington gay bar Cocobana. In March 1985, the pair had met again in Heaven. Unaware of who Mercury was, Hutton recalled that the singer's opening gambit was, 'How big is your dick?' Jim responded by telling Freddie to drop the 'fake American accent'. The two would begin a relationship that, against expectations, would endure until Mercury's death.

Despite their setbacks in America, at the end of *The Works* tour it was difficult to contemplate where Queen could possibly go next. Rock in Rio felt like the ultimate victory lap. John Deacon said as much: 'When we first started, we were very future-thinking. We wanted to do this or go there. We wanted our albums to be successful here, there and everywhere. But once we'd achieved that and been successful in so many countries in the world, it took away some of the incentive.'

With Deacon's comments in mind, the timing of Bob Geldof's phone call to Queen's business manager Jim Beach couldn't have been better. Queen's next challenge was already in place. Following on from the success of the Band Aid record, Bob Geldof and Midge Ure were now organising a multi-bill charity concert to help raise more funds for African famine relief. As with Band Aid, Geldof was determined to attract as many high-profile names to the bill, and was engaged in begging, persuading, cajoling and emotionally blackmailing as many pampered rock stars as he could. Billed as Live Aid, two shows had been confirmed for 13 July in London's Wembley Stadium and Philadelphia's JFK Stadium, but other simultaneous charity shows would take place in Sydney, Cologne, Moscow and The Hague. Supposedly Geldof made his first approach to The Boomtown Rats' sometime keyboard player Spike Edney. He asked Edney to sound out Queen about the possibility of playing the Wembley show. 'I had the opportunity to ask them while we were in New Zealand,' he said. 'To which they replied, "Why doesn't he ask us himself?" And I had to explain that he was afraid they'd turn him down.'

Edney was almost certain that Queen would refuse, but suggested that Bob Geldof telephone Jim Beach directly. Recalling their conversation in 1990, Geldof said, 'I traced Jim all the way to some tiny little beach, some little seaside resort that he was staying at, and I said, "Look, for Christ's sake, what's *wrong* with them. Jim said, "Oh you know, Freddie's very sensitive." So I said, "Tell the old faggot it's gonna be the biggest thing that ever happened." ' Beach agreed to pitch the idea to Queen. Initially, they turned it down. John Deacon later recalled changing their minds at a post-gig dinner in Japan, while Brian May remembers Geldof approaching Queen directly at a BPI Awards dinner. 'I thought it would be almost impossible for him to put together,' said May. 'But I said that we were interested. Then he rang me and said he needed a commitment.' Queen had planned time off after completing *The Works* shows. 'I didn't think we'd tour again for five years — if at all,' Taylor told Mojo. 'I think there was a chance the band would have broken up at the end of that tour,' says Peter Hince, who also recalls that 'Freddie really needed to be talked into doing Live Aid.'

In the meantime, Columbia Records, eager for a return on their one-off investment, put out another Mercury single. 'Made in Heaven' was a theatrical ballad, for which director David Mallet had created a similarly grandiose promo. Freddie, posing in a diaphanous scarlet cape, held court on top of a 60-feet globe and above a sprawl of writhing half-naked dancers. The video was high camp meets Hieronymus Bosch, but the single stiffed in Britain.

In an unaccustomed act of promotion, Freddie agreed to an interview with BBC Radio 1 DJ Simon Bates. There were two provisos: the meeting had to take place on home turf, at the Queen offices, and Bates was not permitted to ask about Mercury's parents. While the singer's sexuality was almost an open secret in the business, he still kept it private from his mother and father. 'The Bulsaras were a very traditional Parsee family,' explained Mercury's former aide Peter Freestone. 'Freddie instinctively knew the limits to which his family would go in being modern. He was very sensitive to them and never wanted them to be compromised. He also felt the less they knew, the less they could tell.' Although Brian May recalled Mercury announcing before a show, 'Oh, Mother's in the audience tonight, I must throw in some more swear words'. When Mercury's parents came to visit their son at Garden Lodge, boyfriend Jim Hutton would always be briefly introduced to them as his gardener.

After agreeing to a date for the interview, Mercury cancelled, claiming he was too sick. When the meeting finally took place, the DJ was shocked by what he saw when Mercury stuck out his tongue for inspection. 'It looked as if it had a duffel coat on it,' Bates told listeners. 'It was the unhealthiest sight I had ever seen, and it was obvious he was still ill.' Mercury admitted he had been 'overdoing it', but told Bates that juggling his solo album and his commitments to Queen had left him exhausted.

After the first of several vodka and tonics, Mercury became more animated, and was surprisingly candid with some of his answers. He agreed that the 'arrogant, aggressive' persona projected onstage was only one part of his character, but that people became confused and believed that he must be like that at all times. He confessed to be a 'bitch' in business, insisting that it was almost impossible to make it in the music industry by being nice, and sagely observed that audiences had become harder to shock since Queen's early days. 'It takes much more to outrage,' he said, citing Boy George, the cross-dressing lead singer of the nation's pop favourites Culture Club, as a sign of changing attitudes. When asked about his life before Queen, Mercury would only go as far back as Ealing art college. 'So long ago ... during the Boer War,' he joked. There was no mention of India or Zanzibar. Before parting, he told Bates that Live Aid would be an opportunity for Queen to prove themselves without having to rely on a spectacular stage set. For once, Mercury had shown a chink in his armour. Bates came away with the impression that Mercury 'really cared what people thought of him'.

Mindful of the fact that old friends and rivals such as David Bowie, Elton John and The Who had been confirmed for the bill at Live Aid, Queen's competitive streak and hard professionalism kicked in. On 10 July, they booked into North London's Shaw Theatre for three days of painstaking rehearsals. During a break, a BBC interviewer rounded them up for a stilted question-and-answer session. Seeing the four together reprised memories of the New Zealand TV interview from earlier in the year. There was the same nervous cigarette smoking and the same awkward body language. Taylor fidgeted and rubbed his nose, while John Deacon smiled quizzically but said nothing. This time, it fell to May and Mercury to share the ambassadorial role.

When asked if Queen were playing Live Aid because they supported the cause of famine relief or because they couldn't afford to miss out, Freddie answered, 'A bit of both.' Mercury insisted that Live Aid was a good cause and that Queen would have liked to have been on the Band Aid single, but admitted that, as the concert featured 'some of the biggest and best known groups around the world, why not us?' On a purely self-seeking level, there must have been some hope that their participation would repair their reputation after Sun City. More importantly, with the group growing even further apart, it might also give them what Roger Taylor called 'a shot in the arm'.

Asked whether they thought there would be clashes of ego between the bands on the bill, all four started laughing. 'Oh, we will all try and outdo each other, I guess,' said Mercury. What songs are you going to play? asked the interviewer. 'We're still squabbling over that,' grinned the singer. As Taylor explained, 'You have to play things people will know . . . in Turkey.' Step one: Queen drew up a list of songs and then worked out how to run some of them into a medley, abbreviating certain tracks so they could include even more. Step two was to ensure that the entire set didn't exceed their allotted twenty minutes.

'So I went out and bought some electric clocks,' explains Peter Hince. 'We had them wired up and in front of the stage, so we could check to see when we our time was up. Queen were that methodical about it. The attitude was, OK, what are we gonna do? There are no smoke bombs, there's no light show and we're going on in the afternoon. Let's just give people what they want – the hits.'

Four days later, just before midday on 13 July, a pastel-suited Brian May and Roger Taylor, joined by the drummer's tech 'Crystal' Taylor, took their VIP seats at Wembley Stadium, alongside David Bowie, Bob Geldof, George Michael, and Elton John. BBC DJ Richard Skinner's voice boomed out of the PA: 'It's 12 o'clock in London, seven o'clock in Philadelphia, and around the world it's time for Live Aid . . .' Onstage, the Coldstream Guards blasted a royal fanfare as Prince Charles and Princess Diana arrived to take their seats in front of the Queen entourage. Within seconds, bagpipes had given way to guitars as Status Quo cranked up the opening riff to their hit single 'Rockin' All Over the World'. In front of them, a sea of 70,000 people began moving.

Some twenty minutes later, ex-Jam frontman Paul Weller's new group Style Council arrived with their hit 'You're the Best Thing', replacing Status Quo's macho rock with some sophisticated Parisienne café pop. By one o'clock, Bob Geldof had left the BBC's commentary box, where he had been urging TV audiences to pledge their money, and led his own group The Boomtown Rats through two of their hit singles and one new non-hit. There was a pattern emerging. Minutes later, Adam Ant declared 'the world is watching, let's feed it' and then spoiled it all by playing his brand-new single, 'Vive Le Rock'.

But whatever musical own goals were being scored, by one o'clock, the show had raised £40,000. As well as the stadium's captive audience, every television in every house, shop and pub seemed to be tuned into the concert. As the afternoon drew on, the broadcast cut from Spandau Ballet to bluesman B.B. King in Amsterdam to cockney actor Dennis Waterman, star of eighties comedy drama *Minder*, hobnobbing backstage at Wembley and urging viewers to 'give some of your dough'. Onstage, Sting and Phil Collins played musical tag (Collins would follow his set by flying to Philadelphia to perform at the US Live Aid) and Bryan Ferry performed a downbeat set, light on hits, with Pink Floyd's David Gilmour guesting on lead guitar.

Backstage, Brian May would confess to being as nervous at Live Aid as he had ever been in his life. If Queen were ever going to be upstaged by anyone on the day it was going to be by U2. Introduced in Philadelphia by Jack Nicholson as 'a group direct from London whose heart is in Dublin', the Irish rockers opened with their hit 'Sunday Bloody Sunday'. On the day, U2 were regarded as an antidote to the old guard of Dire Straits, Bowie, The Who — and Queen. U2 were the eighties rock band *du jour*, worthy and earnest, but with lead singer Bono also having an old showman's flair for transfixing a crowd. Intriguingly, Queen had turned U2 down a couple of years earlier as a support band, while Peter Freestone later maintained that Mercury couldn't abide the group, particularly Bono's preachiness.

Still, 'Sunday Bloody Sunday' was a masterly opening move, but no sooner had they started their second song, 'Bad', before Bono was hanging over the stage barrier urging a girl in the audience to join him onstage. Frustrated by the security guards, who were unable or unwilling to co-operate, the singer scrambled down into the pit between the barrier and the stage and plucked another young girl from the crowd. Grabbing hold of her, the pair began a slow dance, with every move captured by flashing cameras and the TV crew. A nation was watching. But the impromptu performance cost U2 the rest of their set. By the time Bono made it back onstage, there was no time for 'Pride (In the Name of Love)', their Top 5 hit from the previous summer. U2 left the stage with Bono believing he had scuppered the band's reputation. In truth, his photo-pit waltz had been a welcome distraction after six hours of tightly choreographed performances.

Neither The Beach Boys in Philadelphia nor Dire Straits in Wembley could hope for anything quite so spontaneous. Back in the commentary box, a frazzled Geldof began pleading to the cameras: 'There's not enough money coming in . . . Get on the phone right now! We want to get a million pounds out of this country on the telephone by ten o'clock tonight. Get on the phone!'

An hour before Queen were due on, Freddie Mercury had been limousined backstage, still plagued by the same throat infection he'd been suffering from during the Simon Bates interview. 'Doctors had said he was too ill to perform,' recalled one of the BBC's Live Aid team. 'He wasn't well enough at all, but he absolutely insisted.' Just offstage, comedians Mel Smith and Griff Rhys-Jones, dressed as policeman, waited in the wings to introduce 'the Queen'. Unseen by the crowd, Brian May peered out at a sea of faces. It was the first time in so many years that he had actually seen an audience as Queen hadn't played in daylight for years. But Queen's decision not to insist on a headline slot had paid off. 'By six o'clock, some of the audience had been in there for seven hours,' recalls Peter Hince. 'They needed a lift. They were flagging.'

Having watched the show so far, Queen had just one concern: it wasn't loud enough. 'We didn't have a soundcheck,' Roger Taylor said. 'But we sent our brilliant engineer to check the system.' Out front Queen's soundman Trip Khalaf sneakily set the limiters, with dramatic consequences. 'We were louder than anybody else at Live Aid,' admitted Taylor. 'You've got to overwhelm the crowd in a stadium.'

At 6.40 p.m., Queen walked onstage. Upstairs at Wembley, Bob Geldof put down the phone after receiving a donation of one million pounds from an Arab businessman. Geldof was suddenly aware again of what was happening outside. For the first time that day, he could actually hear a band properly. 'My first thought was, "Who's got the sound together?"' he said, later. His second, on hearing the audience's response to what sounded like a jukebox pumping out hit after hit, was one of shock: 'Who the fuck is that?'

CHAPTER TEN
Sweet Dreams

'When you've achieved everything, what else is there
to achieve?'

Freddie Mercury

'More of the same!'

Roger Taylor

'Thank God that's over!' Having dashed offstage at Wembley, Freddie Mercury, drenched in sweat, downed a large vodka in his trailer. A popular anecdote has it that Elton John ran in, shouting, 'You bastards! You stole the show!' 'I certainly remember Freddie holding court in his portakabin,' said Live Aid publicist Bernard Doherty later. 'Everyone had come straight over to congratulate him — "daaahling, you were wonderful!" — Bowie, Paul McCartney, Linda McCartney taking pictures of the other photographers taking pictures . . .'

While everyone was busy backslapping Queen, Wembley and Philadelphia screened Mick Jagger and David Bowie's video for their new single, 'Dancing in the Street'. It was a high-spirited love-in that almost rivalled Mercury's performance for Olympian levels of campness. Within minutes Bowie was onstage, in the flesh at Wembley, grinding through 'TVC15', a song that would never rouse an audience in quite the same fashion as 'Radio Ga Ga'.

After Bowie came The Pretenders, The Who, and Billy Connolly trooping on to announce that 'this concert is being shown on 95 per cent of the televisions on earth' before introducing Elton John. The

nation was still watching, but in the passing years, Queen's performance seems to have blotted everyone else from memory, including
Brian May and Freddie Mercury's later appearance as a duo.

Backstage, Roger Taylor had been seen with actor John Hurt. At
9.42 p.m., Hurt appeared onstage at Wembley to introduce Mercury
and May's acoustic performance of 'Is This the World We Created?'
The gentle ballad from *The Works* album showed the flip side to
Queen's showboating 'We Are the Champions' or 'We Will Rock
You', but was blighted by sound problems. Minutes later, Paul
McCartney led a mass, ad hoc choir, including Mercury, through
Band Aid's 'Do They Know It's Christmas?', bringing the show to its
conclusion.

The BBC's coverage of the Philadelphia show continued until
gone 4 a.m. Mercury and his entourage had ducked out of the
aftershow party, and, joined by John Hurt, headed back to
Kensington to watch a video of the concert. 'Freddie had a caustic
look at everything that was going on around him,' John Hurt later
told *The Times*. 'He was terrifically competitive, too. I remember
going to watch the tape of Live Aid back at his place and when
Duran Duran came on he said, "Just look at them waddling across
the stage!" He was quite irreverent.' Then again, Mercury had
earned the right to mock the competition. As even the self-critical
Brian May conceded, 'Live Aid proved we didn't need backdrops or
the cover of darkness. I'll remember Live Aid till the day I die.'
Within a fortnight, *The Works* album had re-entered the UK Top 40.
Live Aid was the moment Queen went from being a rock band
with a past to a pop group with a future. It gave them a reason to
carry on.

■ ■ ■

The following day's press claimed that as much as £50 million had
been raised for famine relief. The concerts had also promoted pop
music to the front page of the nation's dailies. 'ROCK'S FINEST
HOUR' declared the *Daily Mail*, which led with a photograph of
Charles and Diana in the Wembley stands, with Roger Taylor peek-
ing from beneath the prince's armpit.

Queen immediately took a six-week break. Mercury and his coterie, including Jim Hutton, took off for Ibiza. Deacon played a session for Elton John (Peter Hince: 'Elton said that Deakey was one of the best bass players he had ever worked with') and Roger Taylor revived his production team with David Richards. Led Zeppelin fan Taylor's latest protégés were a rock band named Virginia Wolf, which now included drummer Jason Bonham, son of Led Zeppelin's John. Their debut album surfaced the following year, but Virginia Wolf never broke through.

In September, Mercury was back in Munich to celebrate his thirty-ninth birthday. He hired Henderson's for the night, paying to redecorate the club to match the theme of the party: a black-and-white drag ball and for many of the 300 guests to be flown to Germany and housed at the Munich Hilton. The bill came to £50,000. After partying until 6 a.m., Mercury and a pack of dancers and drag queens were back at the club again the next day to film scenes for Mercury's next video. 'I find I can survive on two or three hours' sleep a night,' Freddie had told Simon Bates.

'Living On My Own' would be the fourth single from the *Mr Bad Guy* album. It was dance-pop crossover with a nimble piano solo from Fred Mandel and a lyric documenting the highs and lows of Freddie's lifestyle. The video was produced and directed by the Austrian film-makers Rudy Dolezal and Hannes Rossacher, ardent Queen fans who had acquired the nickname of 'The Torpedo Twins'. The promo featured scenes from the party, some of which were supposedly taken by hidden cameras, and the following day's shoot. The end result, with its cross-dressing and bare buttocks, was too much for Columbia and the video was never screened in America. But even in Britain, the single would only go as far as number 50.

Once again, there was little time for Mercury to dwell on such failings. In September, May, Taylor and Mercury regrouped at Musicland in Munich, with Deacon joining them later. By the time he arrived, the other three had written a new song. It was an uncommonly democratic move, and one that would go some way towards stopping Queen's regular arguments over money. The new composition was titled 'One Vision'. Taylor recalled writing lyrics that had been inspired by Martin Luther King, and loaded with anti-establishment sentiments ('one goddam religion' being one line that didn't make the final cut). Reportedly, Mercury and May took the lyrics and began editing and changing. 'One Vision' would end up as a one-size-fits-all call for peace, love and unity, supposedly inspired by the Live Aid experience. The music benefited from the collaborative effort. With its synthesiser fanfare, radio-friendly chorus and heavy metal guitar riff, 'One Vision' found room for every facet of the Queen sound, including some throwaway humour. On the final line, Mercury swapped the words 'one vision' for 'fried chicken'.

In another break from tradition, the group agreed to be filmed for a planned Queen documentary. The Torpedo Twins moved into Musicland and shadowed the band's every move. 'I honestly thought they'd never bloody go away,' complained Taylor. 'The documentary cameras actually ruined the whole thing,' said May. 'I think everyone was so conscious of them being there – everyone sort of played up to the camera.'

Some of the studio footage would be used in the video for 'One Vision', with the whole sequence finding its way into Queen's *The Magic Years* documentary. Whatever doubts May and Taylor had about the fly-on-the-wall cameras, it offers an unaccustomed peek of the band at work. The sight of clunky analogue tape recorders and the fug of cigarette smoke is a flashback to studio life circa 1985. John Deacon had followed Freddie's lead and also begun smoking the year before (Peter Hince: 'a sign of stress maybe'). There is a self-conscious element to the footage (in one scene, Mercury jokes that the film-makers' microphone looks like 'a big fat dick') but once they stop hamming it up, it shows how the four band members interacted.

An animated Freddie is seen fussing over a drum break, complaining that too many harmony vocals will make the song 'sound like the fucking Andrews singers' and ad-libbing risqué lyrics in place of the real thing: 'One dump, one turd, two tits, John Deacon!' The film showed a rare glimpse, also, of Reinhold Mack: silent, stoic, smoking . . .

Queen's plans to take significant time off had already gone awry.

No sooner had they met up at Musicland than they were fielding another soundtrack offer. Video director Russell Mulcahy needed music to accompany his full-length film, *Highlander*, a fantasy action movie starring Sean Connery and French heart-throb Christophe Lambert. Mulcahy had made pop videos for Elton John, Spandau Ballet and the 'waddling' Duran Duran. 'I'd always been a fan of Queen, so I approached them,' he said. 'I cut together a twenty-minute piece, which was excerpts from a number of scenes. They watched it and they said yes.' Immediately, Queen began working up ideas for songs, using points in the *Highlander* plot as jumping-off points for the music. Oddly, 'One Vision' wouldn't be used and instead found its way onto the soundtrack of director Sydney Furie's instantly forgotten action flick, *Iron Eagle*.

While being driven back from watching the clip of *Highlander*, Brian May began humming a melody into a portable tape recorder. It was the beginning of what would become 'Who Wants to Live Forever'. '*Highlander* is about a man who becomes conscious that he's immortal, and he's reluctant to accept that fact,' explained May in 2003. 'But he's told that if he falls in love he's in big trouble, but of course he falls in love anyway. And the girl that he falls in love with eventually grows old and dies in his arms. That opened up a floodgate in me – the death of my marriage, and so forth.'

May's marriage was in trouble, as the guitarist tried to deal with what he had called 'the life-and-death battle' between the group and its 'emotional distractions', and his family life. Equally, John Deacon was battling to balance his professional and private life. Inspired by the same *Highlander* clips, Deacon went away and wrote 'One Year of Love', a ballad on which, later, saxophonist Steve Gregory blew a solo not unlike the one he'd contributed to Wham!'s hit single 'Careless Whisper' a year before. Both songs also featured string players; another bold move for a band once so reluctant to allow other musicians into the studio. Russell Mulcahy's second musical coup, after landing Queen, had been to hire the late Michael Kamen, an arranger and film-score composer who had previously worked on Pink Floyd's *The Wall*. Kamen would conduct the National Philharmonic Orchestra, helping to pile on the drama during 'Who Wants to Live Forever'.

Recording of the next Queen album began in September 1985. Yet two months into the schedule, the band put out 'One Vision' as a stopgap single. It reached number 7 in the UK, but only 61 in America. There were grumbles from some critics that Queen should have donated the royalties from a song supposedly inspired by Live Aid to Geldof's charity. 'I was absolutely devastated when I saw that in the press,' raged Taylor. To add to their woes, the band were also asked to issue a statement to the press confirming that they had no intention of ever playing South Africa again. In truth, behind the scenes, Queen were still donating all royalties from 'Is This the World We Created?', the B-side of 'It's a Hard Life', to Save the Children, but it was apparent that their Sun City faux pas would not be forgotten so easily.

Mercury, as ever, found a way to distance himself from the fuss, turning up at the Royal Albert Hall for Fashion Aid, a catwalk show in aid of Ethiopian famine relief, where he squired actress Jane Seymour across the stage in an Elizabeth and David Emanuel wedding gown. Later, he would cut two tracks, 'Time' and 'In My Defence', for the soundtrack of his friend Dave Clark's West End musical *Time*. In the meantime, CBS allowed themselves a further throw of the dice with another solo Mercury single, 'Love Me Like There's No Tomorrow'. It didn't even make it into the UK Top 50.

Mercury had dedicated 'Love Me Like There's No Tomorrow' to Barbara Valentin, but the end of 1985 would signpost the end of Mercury's relationship with the former actress and model ('One minute we were all over the place together, inseparable, and then out of the blue came this break,' Valentin told writer Lesley-Ann Jones). Mercury would give up the apartment he and Valentin shared in Munich and move back to London and into Garden Lodge, the Kensington retreat he had spent years renovating. While Jim Hutton had often been used to make his Austrian lover Winnie Kirchberger jealous, Mercury had grown closer to the Irish hairdresser. Before long, Jim would be invited to move in with Freddie.

Before her death in February 2002, Valentin suggested that Mercury's decision to leave Munich marked a major turning point in his life. Publicly, the singer still displayed his usual bravado, but privately, Mercury could no longer ignore what was going on around him. In 1981, doctors in New York had first noticed several cases of Kaposi's Sarcoma, a virulent form of cancer, in homosexual men. Almost simultaneously, in New York and Los Angeles, doctors observed an unusually high percentage of gay men contracting the lung infection Pneumocystis Carinii Pneumonia, and failing to respond to conventional treatment. It was the beginning of America's awareness of what would become known as AIDS (Acquired Immune Deficiency Syndrome), a disease caused by the Human Immunodeficiency Virus (HIV) that attacked the body's immune system. One of the ways in which it could be passed between individuals was by unprotected sex. In a climate of suspicion and misinformation, tabloid headlines would dub AIDS 'the gay plague'.

On 3 October 1985, the gay American actor Rock Hudson became the first celebrity to die from AIDS. By the end of 1985, 20,303 cases had been reported to the World Health Organisation. A year earlier Mercury's friend, the American DJ and broadcaster Paul Gambaccini, had run into the singer at London's Heaven nightclub. Gambaccini had already witnessed the impact of AIDS on New York's club scene. When he asked Mercury if he planned to curb his sexual behaviour, Freddie replied: 'Darling, my attitude is I'm doing everything with everyone.' As Gambaccini recalled in a later interview, 'I realised for the first time that Freddie Mercury was going to die.'

Before Mercury left Munich, Barbara Valentin claimed to have noticed a decline in the singer's state of health, including a recurrent and unexplained throat problem. One of the symptoms of an immune deficiency prevalent in AIDS sufferers are extreme cases of candidiasis or oral thrush, bringing to mind DJ Simon Bates's description of the singer's tongue as 'a duffel coat'. Some have speculated that Mercury first took an HIV test in late 1985. Even if he hadn't, others around him had. Peter Hince remembers a scene backstage, when one of Mercury's entourage came into the dressing room, delighted with the negative results of his HIV test. 'The reaction from Freddie and Paul Prenter was very muted,' says Hince, 'which surprised me at the time.'

Still buzzing with the success of Live Aid and 'One Vision', EMI ended 1985 with *Queen: The Complete Works*, an embossed box set which, for £70, included every Queen LP to date, a bonus disc of previously unreleased tracks, and a map of the world, marked with places in which Queen had played or territories conquered.

Queen picked up the album sessions in January 1986, and would spend the next three months between Musicland and Mountain, with extra work at London's Sarm West, Townhouse and Maison Rouge studios. The band members had split themselves between two producers: Mack would work with Mercury and Deacon at Musicland; David Richards would do the same for Taylor and May at Mountain. For Mack, though, this was the opposite of the 'Four Musketeers' approach that had made his first Queen project, *The Game*, such a success. 'Everybody was doing their own thing now, in their own studios,' he sighs.

By now, the original concept behind the album had also changed. 'We did all the music for the film first,' explained Deacon. 'Then, when we came to do the album, we rearranged a lot of the tracks, made them longer, wrote more lyrics and tried to arrange them into fully-fledged songs.' 'There was an extraordinary collaboration between Michael Kamen and the band,' recalled Mulcahy. 'It wasn't just like we finished the film and asked for a song. Queen were very much involved in edit and during the months of post-production.'

The finished Queen album, *A Kind of Magic*, would include nine songs, with alternative versions of six, including the title track, used in the *Highlander* movie. Outtakes from the album would include Roger Taylor's much-regarded 'Heaven for Everyone', a song he would record later with his own side-project The Cross. Michael Kamen and Steve Gregory weren't the only outsiders involved with the record. The new Queen album would also find a home for touring keyboard player Spike Edney, singer-songwriter Joan Armatrading and string arranger Lynton Naiff.

As well as 'One Year of Love', John Deacon had paired up with Mercury and written another soul track, 'Pain is So Close to Pleasure'; a song that Brian May tactfully described as 'very unusual for us'. The guitarist would feel more affinity with Deacon and Mercury's flag-waving 'Friends Will Be Friends'. Meanwhile, at

Mountain, David Richards helped May and Taylor with their material. As well as the heroic 'Who Wants to Live Forever', May came up with 'Gimme the Prize (Kurgan's Theme)', a song named after *Highlander*'s anti-hero, filled with schlock-horror sound effects and an over-the-top guitar solo. Back at Musicland, Mercury would revisit Queen's past life himself with 'Princes of the Universe', a chest-beating rocker of the kind he hadn't written in years.

Representing the Drum Department at Mountain, Roger Taylor would get two of his songs onto the finished album. 'Don't Lose Your Head' (with a backing vocal from Joan Armatrading) was by-numbers synth-rock with a lyric preaching against the perils of driving under the influence, possibly inspired by the Bass Department's encounter with a breathalyser. Far better was Taylor's 'A Kind of Magic'. The song's title had been plucked from a line in the *Highlander* script. A different version of the same track would be used over the film's closing credits, but the album version would end up as one of Queen's purest pop songs. While 'A Kind of Magic' would be solely credited to Taylor, Mercury had a significant part to play. 'Freddie got a bee in his bonnet and said [to Roger], "You go away and I'll make a hit,"' said Brian May in 2010. 'I knew he was going away to LA for a week,' recalled Mercury. 'And I got hold of it and changed it around completely.' As with 'Radio Ga Ga', the singer took the drummer's song, believing that it had greater commercial potential than anyone realised. 'We were knowingly making a pop record, a commercial record,' said Taylor.

Released as a single in March 1986, 'A Kind of Magic' raced to number 3 in the UK, helped by Russell Mulcahy's video (a 'thank you' gesture from the director for Queen's involvement in *Highlander*). Here, a wizardly Freddie Mercury transformed his down-at-heel bandmates into swish rock stars. The song's optimistic lyric sounded immediately familiar to Queen's support band Airrace from the year before. 'Our album had been called *Shaft of Light*,' says guitarist Laurie Mansworth. 'On *The Works* tour, Freddie commented that he liked the name of it. He said that the title would make a great line to use in a song.' Sure enough, in the first verse of 'A Kind of Magic', Mercury could be heard singing about how one shaft of light showed the way. Meanwhile with *Highlander* due to open in America before the UK, Queen opted for 'Princes of the Universe' as their US comeback single, enlisting *Highlander* star Christopher Lambert to appear in the accompanying video. But America looked the other way and the single failed to even break the Top 50.

Further evidence of Capitol's confused relationship with Queen came when Mercury met up with the band's old friend Billy Squier to work on tracks for Squier's next album, *Enough is Enough*. 'Freddie and I collaborated on two songs,' says Squier now. 'We were both on Capitol at the time, and there seemed to be a lot of excitement at the label when they heard we were working together. The head of A&R even flew over to London to express his enthusiasm for our little project.'

Squier and Mercury spent a productive night in Kensington working on the songs 'Lady with a Tenor Sax' and 'Love is the Hero'. 'As dawn broke, Freddie sat down at the piano and threw off a new intro for "Love is the Hero" that totally blew me away,' says Squier. 'Yet, when I delivered the record, the label execs decided they did not want to include it.' The intro comprised a high-camp, high-drama Mercury vocal. 'They mumbled something at the time about it being "confusing for my audience".'

Squier, himself, had already run into trouble with the video he'd made for his 1984 single 'Rock Me Tonite'. Squier performed a solo dance routine, based on a young Tom Cruise's tongue-in-cheek performance in the movie *Risky Business*. Unfortunately, Billy's cavorting hadn't gone down well with his audience. 'It was anathema to those who saw me as a no-frills rock star and guitar slinger,' he admits. 'I've always thought Capitol were concerned about Freddie's image problems, and the fan reaction to "Rock Me Tonite", and feared he might drag me down once and for all. But from my perspective, having one of the biggest stars in the world lending his extraordinary talents to my record seemed like a pretty good idea.'

With a new single in the chart, and the album almost complete, Queen did their customary disappearing act in four different directions. Mercury completed his recordings for Dave Clark's *Time* and showed up for the premiere of the musical at London's

Dominion Theatre, camping it up in the interval by attempting to sell ice creams in the audience. Before long, he was casually tossing tubs of ice cream towards his customers without asking for payment. As one of Mercury's entourage explained: 'Freddie wouldn't have been able to give anyone their change. I don't think he knew what a pound coin looked like.'

Clark had already asked Mercury to appear in *Time*. While claiming to be impressed by David Bowie's recent theatrical performance as the Elephant Man in New York, Mercury was aware of his limitations. 'He declined,' explained Clark. 'He said, "For one thing, my darling, I don't get up until 3 p.m., so I can't do matinées. For another, when I do a show, I sing my butt off for three hours and then I drop dead. So it would be impossible to do eight shows a week."'

In the meantime, Taylor joined David Richards to produce the Queen-influenced rock band Magnum, while John Deacon became one third of a trio called The Immortals, cutting a chirpy pop single 'No Turning Back' for the soundtrack to the First World War flying ace movie *Biggles*. Neither the single nor the film made any impact. Meanwhile, in London, Brian May would have a fortuitous meeting with the woman who would become his second wife, actress Anita Dobson, at the premiere of the Hollywood comedy *Down and Out in Beverley Hills*. At the time Dobson was playing fiery pub landlady Angie Watts in the BBC's hit soap opera *EastEnders*. At the premiere, May and his wife Chrissy squeezed past Anita to reach their seats. Chrissy had coaxed Brian into watching *EastEnders*, and he had become hooked. 'I said [to Anita], "Excuse me, I think you're wonderful,"' May later told *Smash Hits* magazine. "I asked if she'd like to come to our concert at Wembley Stadium . . . and she said, "Er, thank you very much."'

Queen had lined up two Wembley Stadium concerts in June, with other outdoor shows arranged for Dublin's Slane Castle, Newcastle's St James' Park and Manchester's Maine Road. Tickets sold out almost immediately, prompting promoter Harvey Goldsmith to confirm another date in August at Stevenage's Knebworth Park, the scene of Led Zeppelin's final UK concert seven years earlier. The *Magic* tour would also include a run of shows across Scandinavia and Europe, before culminating in Ireland, the UK and Spain.

On 11 May, the band made another appearance at the Montreux Golden Rose Pop Festival, where they mimed to tracks from the new album. Mercury woke up to a copy of the *Daily Mirror* and a photograph of himself performing at the show under the headline 'FLABULOUS FREDDIE'. 'Freddie always took great pride in his trim waist,' recalls EMI's Brian Southall. 'But there was this one picture of him leaning to the side and showing a tiny bit of flab. Of course, the good *Daily Mirror* sub had come up with this headline. Ray Coleman had written the piece, which talked about Queen's excellence and majesty and largesse. But because Ray was the person Queen knew at the *Mirror*, Ray was the one they attacked. Ray got very distressed, and got on to the *Mirror* to explain and made them apologise, so he could be let back into the Queen camp.'

In May, Queen had bedded down at a rehearsal studio in Wembley to prepare for the tour. Though now pushing forty, Mercury could still get away with the cutaway vest and jeans he'd worn at Live Aid. Nevertheless, his friend, the costume designer Diana Moseley was hired to dress the whole band for the tour ('You had to be gentle with Queen,' she recalled. 'You couldn't just rush in and push things. Brian needed a little coaxing.') Among Moseley's creations would be a huge ermine gown and crown, which Mercury intended to wear during the band's final curtain call.

'One Vision', 'Who Wants to Live Forever', 'Friends Will Be Friends' and the title track would introduce the setlist. In came a snippet of the nowarchaic 'In the Lap of the Gods . . . Revisited' and an acoustic rock 'n' roll medley that included 'Tutti Frutti', Ricky Nelson's 'Hello Mary Lou (Goodbye Heart)' – a song Mercury had first played in India with The Hectics – and Lieber and Stoller's '(You're So Square) Baby I Don't Care'.

Mindful of what it took to hold a stadium audience's attention, the *Magic* set was an extravagant construction that included a 64-feet stage flanked by a pair of 40-feet runways. 'We are going to play on the biggest stage ever built at Wembley,' enthused Roger Taylor, whose girlfriend Dominique gave birth to their daughter Rory just days before the tour began. The drummer's parting shot was that Queen's new spectacular would make '*Ben Hur* look like *The Muppets*'. Gerry Stickells and Queen's road crew would now be tasked with managing three separate stages; a process nicknamed 'leapfrogging'. While one stage was being used, the second was being built, and the third was being transported to the next show.

A Kind of Magic, Queen's eleventh's studio album, was released in the UK and US just before the tour opened in Sweden. What the band later called 'The Live Aid Effect' hadn't diminished, and it shifted 100,000 copies in its first week alone, eventually seeing off Genesis' *Invisible Touch* and Simply Red's *Picture Book* to reach number 1 in the UK and Ireland.

Meanwhile, America slipped further away. '*A Kind of Magic* sounds like hard rock with a hollow core,' wrote *Rolling Stone*'s Mark Coleman. The album went as far as number 46, then stopped. Once again, America would be absent from Queen's tour itinerary. On home turf, *The Times* applauded Freddie's 'Diana Ross impersonation' on 'Pain is So Close to Pleasure', but concluded that *A Kind of Magic* was 'as chic as a set of flying ducks on a wall'. 'I'd be a liar to say I'm not hurt by criticism,' admitted Mercury. 'But that's the way of the world. Before, I used to get really mad and start tearing my hair out, but now I don't have any more sleepless nights.'

The album's confused origins made for a somewhat uneven listening experience. Even Mercury sounded bewildered when attempting to explain the record: 'For the first time in Queen's life we actually made a film soundtrack, but we've also made a Queen album, so, we had to try to let people know that it's not just a soundtrack, because we've got other songs as well . . .' To confuse matters still further, the 1985 single 'One Vision' (which had already featured in the *Iron Eagle* soundtrack) reappeared as the album's opening track. Much like *Highlander*'s immortal hero, only the title cut and 'Who Wants to Live Forever' were songs that would survive the album's natural shelf life. Like every Queen record since *Jazz*, *A Kind of Magic* was a so-so album, cleverly loaded with two or three potential hit singles. 'There was some scraping the barrel,' says Mack, drily.

Onstage, Queen made a grand entrance, through billowing clouds of dry ice, straight into 'One Vision' and 'Tie Your Mother Down'. New songs were threaded in between the hits, with 'A Kind of Magic' cueing up 'Under Pressure'. The final part of the show was wisely given over to the same six songs they'd played at Live Aid. Exuding their usual over-confidence, Queen's next single 'Friends Will Be Friends' would later be dropped in as an encore between 'We Will Rock You' and 'We Are the Champions'. 'I can't believe we did that,' murmured Brian May, revisiting the setlist years later.

After the opening night in Stockholm, Diana Moseley took a call from Mercury. The singer's mood could hardly have been helped by the gauntlet of anti-apartheid protesters outside the stadium, but instead he was fussing over the performance and suggesting that it needed 'an extra something'. Mercury asked Diana to bring the newly commissioned ermine gown and crown to France in time for the Paris Hippodrome show a week later. Prior to the gig, Mercury spent an afternoon swishing up and down the corridor of the Royal Monceau Hotel, trying out his new outfit. At the end of the show, as the band scrubbed their way through the final bars of 'We Are the Champions', Mercury promenaded on from the wings, trailing the gown over his shoulders, doffing the crown and waving to the minions below. Billy Squier watched the concert from the wings. 'It was a great feeling,' he says. 'I'd just recorded with Freddie in London, and I was just offstage at the end of his grand piano, watching my friend lay out this huge crowd.' It would be the last time Squier ever saw Freddie Mercury.

The crown and ermine would become Mercury's final flourish for the remainder of the tour. As always, he remained the focus of the show, tirelessly working the enormous stage. 'He's the pivot of what it's all about,' said an earnest Brian May at the time. 'It's all channelled through Freddie, so we look after him.' 'It was just before Fred turned forty,' remembers Peter Hince, 'and he was still smoking, still drinking vodka and still doing other things that were not good for him but still managing to run around for two hours a night.' There were moments when it looked as if the years had started to catch up on the singer. Queen's huge lighting rig could have an illuminating effect on Mercury's slightly thinning hair ('It's a double-crown, dear,' Freddie would protest). Backstage, Mercury was never without a steam inhaler, always aware that the nodes on his vocal cords could flare up at any time. If his health was suffering for any other reason, he told no one.

Among Queen's support acts at the Paris Hippodrome were the UK rock band Marillion. Fronted by larger-than-life Scotsman Derek Dick, aka Fish, Marillion were signed to EMI and had just had a number 1 album with *Misplaced Childhood*. 'I knew Roger Taylor from the London club scene,' says Fish now. 'We were always in the Marquee and I think we went out with a couple of the same girls, but I'd never met the others before.' At the aftershow party in Paris, Fish, to the chagrin of his bandmates, was whisked away to share the 'glamour table' with Queen and Duran Duran's John Taylor and Nick Rhodes. 'Freddie was charming and affable and very funny,' he recalls. 'Brian and I got into a very deep conversation about South African politics. Queen had been absolutely hammered for playing Sun City and I remember being very impressed by Brian's intelligence and passion. To be honest, "Deaks" was a bit weird. Marillion's bass player was off his face and kept coming up and trying to talk to him about what gear he was using. John Deacon kept moving away, and after about three or four times he turned round and just said, "Who the *fuck* are you?" Very funny. There was an apology the next morning.'

In Mannheim, Fish was invited onstage to join Queen for 'Tutti Frutti'. 'I kept thinking, "How the fuck does it go?"' he says. 'Freddie had let me use his radio mic earlier with Marillion, which is an unusual thing for any singer to do, and he'd watched our show from the side of the stage. He welcomed me on for 'Tutti Frutti', and then really put me in my place. Not in a nasty way, but the sheer presence of the man onstage. He owned it. He was the big brother. I didn't stand a chance.'

Four days later, in Berlin, Queen threw in a version of Led Zeppelin's 'Immigrant Song'. Later, they'd dust off Shirley Bassey's 'Big Spender', the song that had so impressed their Trident pay-masters at the Forest Hill gig fourteen years earlier. The Spencer Davis Group's 'Gimme Some Lovin', a tune Fred Bulsara used to pester his college friend to play on the church organ, would also be thrown into the set. These were all flashbacks to Queen's past.

At times, the past must have seemed like a less complicated place than the present. During a break in Holland, May booked a studio to produce a demo for Anita Dobson ('She's a very rock 'n' roll person,' he enthused). Back in England, though, Christine May would soon become pregnant again. On 5 July, Queen's Slane Castle gig in Dublin was marred by bad weather and crowd violence. A local councillor deemed the show as 'a massive rip-off, nihilistic, sensual and anti-social'. Backstage, Mercury supposedly vowed never to play Ireland again.

Offstage, Queen's after-hours activities now included hard-fought Scrabble and Trivial Pursuit championships, but there was no lack of 'nihilistic and sensual' pursuits. 'There'd been a lesbian floorshow in Paris in the early '80s,' recalls one tour insider. 'But in '86, in Germany, Queen had an aftershow party in a brothel. I didn't actually believe it when I was told that all the girls had been pre-paid . . . Obviously only the single members of the entourage attended.' There was also the World Cup. Photographer Denis O'Regan joined Mercury to watch Germany beat Mexico on TV. 'At the end of the match, Freddie jumped up and said, "That's it! I'm going to go out and fuck me a German!" '

'When we first said we wanted to do outdoor shows, promoters weren't confident that Queen would be able to sell enough tickets,' revealed Gerry Stickells. Yet when Harvey Goldsmith had first invited postal applications for tickets for Queen's first show at Wembley Stadium, all 72,000 had sold out within a couple of deliveries. In the end, Queen would perform to 150,000 people across two nights at the stadium on 11 and 12 June. Roger Taylor also fulfilled his promise to fans of performing on the biggest stage ever; so big, in fact, that the band's video screen wouldn't fit between the stage and the stadium roof. As Gerry Stickells explained: 'The architectural plans were awry. The distance to the roof was not what it said on the plans.' After a frantic phone call in which one of the crew suggested, famously, that Stickells 'press the abort button', a crane was hired and the crew, again defying the laws of physics, found a way to make the screen fit.

Queen's first show at Wembley fell on a Friday, and was blighted by torrential rain. The weather held off on the Saturday, where a fifteen-man camera team were in place to shoot the concert for Tyne Tees TV. Backstage, Mick Jagger was among those seen swishing into the VIP enclosure. 'Mick sat on the side of the stage and said he thought it was too big,' recalled Stickells later. In fact, Jagger was assessing the competition. The Rolling Stones would roll out their own *Steel Wheels* extravaganza at Wembley three years later.

'The Live Aid Effect' was now visible in Queen's audience: a balanced split of males and females that also included younger pop fans whose point of entry had been 'Radio Ga Ga' and 'I Want to Break Free'. Queen's chart positions that week said as much: 'Friends Will Be Friends' was in the Top 20, with *A Kind of Magic* still in the Top 5. It was clear, though, that when Queen played 'In the Lap of the Gods . . . Revisited', a song that had once been a corner-stone of their live show, a percentage of the audience had no idea what they were hearing.

'There are fans that I speak to in the street who say, "I like your earlier stuff, but I don't like what you're doing now,"' admitted Mercury. 'But at the same time, there are people who like our new stuff and don't even know what we did five or six years ago.' There was also a more playful element to the show. *A Kind of Magic*'s cover art featured gaudy cartoon images of the band. These had now been turned into helium-filled inflatable models. The blow-up dolls would drift over the audience while they played the title track. Three of the inflatables were captured by the Wembley crowd, while 'Freddie' ended up in a garden miles away in Chelmsford, Essex.

The footage from Wembley would be released later on VHS and DVD. It captured the unprecedented scale of the set, the triumphalism of the band, and, though nobody knew it at the time, what would be Freddie Mercury's last tour. The singer's rascally banter had been a part of Queen's live show for years, but on the *Magic* tour, Mercury seemed more at ease with his role than ever. He would play the prima donna, eyes shut, quivering with supposed emotion one moment, but would just as easily wink at the crowd and send himself up the next. The twitchy smile was a constant, the good-humoured baiting of the audience another. 'After all, it's really only a game,' he said. 'But a serious game.'

Queen celebrated their two-night stand at Wembley with an £80,000 soirée at the Kensington Roof Gardens. Remembered by one of the 500 guests as 'another night of bacchanalian excess', naked waiters and waitresses, their bodies daubed with paint to look like a uniform, joined the usual retinue of drag queens and topless models. The *Sun*'s Page-Three-model-turned-pop-star Samantha Fox, seventies glam-rocker Gary Glitter, and Marillion's Fish joined Mercury onstage to muddle through 'Tutti Frutti' and 'Johnny B. Goode'. The group christened themselves Dicky Hart and The Pacemakers.

While Jim Hutton was told to stay away from the cameras, Mercury would be photographed at the party with Mary Austin. In public, he was still maintaining the façade. The complexity of their relationship became apparent when the *Daily Express* writer David Wigg, one of the few journalists Mercury trusted, wrote a story claiming that Austin has asked Freddie to father a child for her. Mercury, still claiming to be single, had explained that he would prefer to buy another cat.

Jim Hutton was now living with Mercury in the refurbished Garden Lodge. His role would also become confused by the fact that although paid to work as Freddie's gardener, he was also sleeping with the boss. Mercury was aware of the pressure he put any partner under. Stranger still, Mary Austin's job within the Queen organisation made her responsible for paying Hutton's £600 a month wages. 'It's like the old Hollywood stories where all those wonderful actresses just couldn't carry on a relationship because their careers came first,' said Mercury. 'That's the way it is with me. I can't stop the wheel for a while and devote myself to a love affair. The wheel has to keep turning, and that makes it very hard for anyone to live with me and be happy.'

Queen followed their UK stadium dates with a trip to the Continent for outdoor shows in Austria and Communist Hungary. While their old sparring partner Elton John had already played in Budapest, Queen would be the first international rock group to play what EMI trumpeted as 'the first stadium rock gig behind the Iron Curtain'.

The band arrived by hydrofoil on the River Danube, with Roger Taylor sporting a nautical-looking blazer, and Mercury asking how many bedrooms there were in the Hungarian House of Parliament and if it was for sale. Queen were hurried past the fans, newspaper reporters and TV crews gathered on the quay, and straight into the British Embassy, where a reception was being thrown in their honour. For the Hungarian government, having a Western rock band play in Budapest could be spun as an example of improving East–West relations. Queen's motivation was much simpler. 'We like going places where it's a challenge,' said Brian May. 'What happened with Budapest was the same as what happened with South America. Someone comes along and says, "You're huge in X, why don't you go and play there?"' Meanwhile, the president of the 5,000-strong Hungarian wing of the Official Queen Fan Club griped that just 100 of his members had managed to acquire tickets for the gig: 'Queen only want the money now,' he told a reporter from *Sounds*.

For Queen's management, the trip could also be perceived as an olive branch to the press. Several Fleet Street journalists and the writer David Quantick, from *NME*, had been invited. Before long, Quantick found himself in conversation with Mercury, despite being told that the singer would not be granting any interviews. 'I'm not supposed to be talking to you,' Freddie protested, before carrying on regardless and inviting David to join the band for dinner.

'We arrived at something called a "hunter's restaurant",' says Quantick now. 'Freddie told his manager: "Order loads of whatever the best food is. Loads of meat for everyone!" Sat next to Roger Taylor was a terribly chic, if extremely drunk, blonde. Before long, she became the focus of Mercury's attention. 'Freddie leans over,' recalls Quantick. '"Don't start!" cries Roger. "Not again!" Oh yes, again. "How big is your cunt, dear?" asks Freddie. "Can you get it over your head, dear?"' Amid much laughter, particularly from the band's interpreter, and some angry gesturing from the blonde, Mercury backed down – 'Just joking, dear' – and offered his victim a cigarette.

Later, waiting at the baggage carousel at Heathrow Airport, Queen's PR sidled up to Quantick and asked if he'd submit his interview quotes to the band's management for approval. He declined.

On the night, Queen played to 80,000 inside the Neptstadion and an estimated 45,000 ticketless fans who showed up just to listen outside, some of whom had travelled from as far as Odessa and Warsaw. Beforehand, it was announced that the government had announced 'lenient restriction on audience behaviour', although drinking and smoking were not permitted. Mercury and May had spent three days rehearsing an Hungarian folk song, '*Tavaszi Szél Vizet Áraszt*', which they would perform on the night. 'Freddie had the words written on the palm of his hand,' says photographer Denis O'Regan. 'During his performance, he was flicking his fingers and looking down, trying to read the lyrics.' Nevertheless, it was a turning point in the show. 'Before, the audience hadn't known how to react,' said Brian May. 'Then they realised we were serious. The reaction at that point was fucking deafening.' The experience was recorded for *Magic: Queen in Budapest*, an 85-minute documentary and concert film released the following year. Another country conquered, or, to paraphrase Mercury, 'ticked off'.

Less than a week later, Queen flew to Spain for four outdoor shows. Interviewed for a TV arts programme, Mercury let slip appreciation of the Spanish opera singer Montserrat Caballé. Mercury was a huge opera buff, and had seen Caballé perform in Los Angeles and at London's Royal Opera House. His comment would find its way to Caballé, who was away on tour at the time. Just months later, the two would begin working together on Mercury's most ambitious album yet.

The *Magic* tour ended on 9 August in front of 120,0000 at Knebworth Park. By now, the tour statistics had become a story in their own right: 5,000 amps, 8.6 miles of cable, a 20-feet by 30-feet video screen . . . Queen's support acts reflected the headliners' catholic tastes: vogueish pop star Belouis Some (one hit: 'Imagination'), worthy Celtic-rockers Big Country, and Roger Taylor's old drinking buddy Rick Parfitt with Status Quo. Queen arrived backstage in two helicopters, one of which had been decorated with the new album's gaudy artwork.

Onstage, Queen ran like clockwork. Unlike those earlier shows, though, they were playing to a sea of bodies that seemed to go on forever. A stadium audience could be contained. At Knebworth, there were 120,000 human beings disappearing into the distance, beyond the fast-food vans, the drinks tents and as far as the crop of trees on the horizon. Close to the stage, but unseen by the band, a 21-year-old male fan was stabbed to death during a drunken brawl. Tragically, the sheer number of people on site made it impossible for an ambulance to reach him before he bled to death. Up onstage, at the end of 'Radio Ga Ga', John Deacon took off his bass guitar and flung it at his amp.

'John had already smashed his usual bass at another show,' reveals Peter Hince, who was in the wings watching the tantrum. Hince retrieved the instrument, which was unbroken, and re-tuned it. 'John came out to me during the blackout before the encore and started apologising. I said, "It's OK, John, it's OK . . . I've fixed it." He wasn't pissed off at his gear, he wasn't pissed off at me. I don't know what it was. John acted strangely on that tour; he was doing stuff that was out of character.' 'I did have a strange feeling when John threw his bass into the wings,' says Denis O'Regan. 'It had a sense of finality.'

'I am going through a very uncertain phase in my life,' confessed Deacon at the time, blaming his feelings 'on the insecurities of being in the music business and being in a band.' One of Deacon's oldest friends would later explain that 'all the pressure used to make him a bit ill. When he [Deacon] came back off a tour, he couldn't revert to being a normal person.' 'Queen became superstars again on the *Magic* tour,' adds Peter Hince. 'John did appreciate it, but I think he'd had enough a long time before Queen finished: after *Hot Space* probably, before they'd even started *The Works*. Then he had a huge hit single with 'I Want to Break Free', and he felt inspired again. Then there was Live Aid . . . But John tried to play devil's advocate to everybody. He was also slaving away, looking after Queen's business interests with the accountants, and thinking, "Where can it go now?"'

Mercury finished the show draped in his regal gown and crown, declaring 'Goodnight and sweet dreams'; the last words he would ever utter at a Queen concert. Backstage, the aftershow celebrations were soon in full swing, with mud wrestlers, fairground rides, more booze, more drugs, more hangers-on . . . Before long, Freddie was back in a helicopter and on his way to London. Queen's *Magic* tour had played to more than 400,000 people, grossing over £11 million. On the flight home, any victory celebrations were quelled by news of the fatal stabbing.

Years later, Brian May would recall an incident in Spain, just days before Knebworth: 'John and Freddie were having a minor disagreement and Freddie said, "Well, I won't always be here to do this." ' Initially, the guitarist dismissed the comment. In hindsight, it was the first indication that Mercury might give up touring. But he would soon make his intention clear. 'At the end of that tour, Freddie said, "I don't want to do this any more," ' said May. 'It was kind of uncharacteristic, because he was always up for everything and very strong. We thought that maybe it was just a stage he was going through, or maybe there was something wrong. I remember having that thought in my head, but you just push that thought aside.'

'After Knebworth, I had a feeling Queen would never play live again,' says Peter Hince, who had now given up the crew job to continue a new career as a photographer. 'I think he didn't want to become a parody of himself. I think Freddie thought he would still make music and videos but I don't think he wanted to look like a joke.' Despite the success of Wembley and Knebworth, Queen could not be persuaded to take another run at America. 'Gerry Stickells had talked about provisional dates for the *Magic* tour with promoters in the States,' insists Hince. 'He wanted them to do indoor venues in New York, Los Angeles . . . During the tour, Gerry was calling those promoters up and telling them how well it was going in Europe.' Later, in the UK, Queen's next single, 'Who Wants to Live Forever', would make it to number 24. In America, though, Mercury's 'Diana Ross impersonation', 'Pain is So Close to Pleasure', failed to chart.

In September, after celebrating his fortieth birthday, Mercury flew to Japan for a holiday. He returned to find the *News of the World* claiming he had taken a secret AIDS test at a Harley Street clinic. Just days later, the *Sun* splashed with a photograph of Mercury arriving at Heathrow from his '£250,000 shopping trip to Japan' under the headline: 'Do I Look Like I'm Dying Of Aids? Fumes Freddie.' Mercury told the *Sun*'s reporter that he was 'perfectly fit and healthy'. He denied taking the test, but it was impossible for him to continue ignoring what was going on around him. Freddie's ex-boyfriend Tony Bastin, supposedly the inspiration behind the song 'Play the Game', had contracted AIDS and would die in November.

May was now distracting himself from his marital problems by planning another solo album and working with Bad News, the spoof heavy metal band made up of comic actors Rik Mayall, Nigel Planer and Adrian Edmonson. Mercury followed suit. In November, Freddie booked into London's Townhouse Studios to record another single: a version of The Platters' 1956 hit, 'The Great Pretender'. It seemed the perfect song choice. Mercury co-produced the single with Mike Moran, a keyboard player and musical arranger he'd met while working on the *Time* musical. Moran had briefly been a pop star when his song 'Rock Bottom' had been the UK's entry in the 1977 Eurovision Song Contest. Moran would become a close musical collaborator and dear friend.

David Mallet's video for 'The Great Pretender' featured Roger Taylor and Mercury's old friend Peter Straker in drag, with Taylor resembling a particularly raddled Tina Turner. Freddie, meanwhile, recreated some of his most famous video roles, including 'Bohemian Rhapsody' and 'I Want to Break Free'. Clean-shaven and wearing a pink suit, he ended the video descending a huge Hollywood staircase lined with one-hundred life-size cardboard cut-outs of himself.

Watching the performance was Chris Chesney. In 1970, the man still known as Fred Bulsara had briefly joined Chesney's band Sour Milk Sea. Chris had continued to play music, but was now employed in the art department of David Mallet's production company. 'I felt a huge embarrassment about being seen working on Queen's things,' he says. 'I didn't want it to be seen as an admission of failure. I didn't want them to think I'd fucked up. So I tried to stay away.'

Unable to help himself, Chesney snuck onto the set of 'The

Great Pretender'. 'I was in the shadows, trying to be inconspicuous. Freddie was on the great, infinite staircase, and he spotted me: "Chris! How are you?' He came running over and took me off into his dressing room.' It was Chesney's first experience of Freddie Mercury. ' "You want champagne?" He clicked his fingers, and straight away there was champagne. I remember he was knocking back the vodka like it was going out of fashion. Then it was, "Have a line of coke . . . Have a line . . ." But it was nice. It was like rolling the years back. Then he said, "You must play on my solo album. I'll call you!" And, of course, he never called and I felt too awkward to call him.' Chris Chesney never saw Fred Bulsara again.

In December, Queen released another live album, *Live Magic*. Bafflingly, several songs, including 'Bohemian Rhapsody', were edited down to ensure that they fitted on the record. While some followers echoed the Hungarian Queen Fan Club president's complaint ('Queen only want the money now'), they bought it anyway, giving the band a number 3 album in time for Christmas.

■ ■ ■

Considering the speculation now raging about his private life, there was something apt about Freddie Mercury singing 'The Great Pretender'. ' "The Great Pretender" is a great title for what I do because I *am* The Great Pretender,' he said. The public agreed, giving him a Top 5 single in February. In the meantime, Freddie's praise for Montserrat Caballé on Spanish TV had found its way back to the opera star. Queen's Spanish promoter Pino Sagliocci was organising a TV music show, *Ibiza 92*, to celebrate Spain being announced as the host nation for the 1992 Olympic Games. He desperately wanted Freddie Mercury to sing with Montserrat.

Sagliocci brokered a meeting, and in March, Mercury flew to Spain, bringing Mike Moran for moral support, for a lunch date with Caballé at Barcelona's Ritz Hotel. The then 53-year-old soprano was revered throughout her native Spain and throughout the world of opera. Watching her sweep in to the hotel, surrounded by courtiers ('like the Queen of Sheba,' said Moran), Mercury realised that he was no longer the most important person in the room. 'I was nervous,' he admitted. 'I didn't know how to behave or what to say to her.'

Lunch was a slightly stilted affair, but Mercury had come prepared, and played Montserrat a recording of an operatic song he'd co-written with Moran titled 'Exercises in Free Love'. 'This is me pretending to be you,' he told the diva, before offering her the song. To his surprise, she accepted, informing the pair that she would perform their song the following month during her concert at the Covent Garden Opera House. She then tapped a shocked Moran on the shoulder and told him that he would play with her.

Later, after the Covent Garden performance, a deal was struck: Freddie would write a brand-new song for the two of them to perform on Sagliocci's TV special and they would record an album of duets together. 'I thought, "My God!"' said Mercury. '"What am I going to do now?"' A further distinction between the worlds of rock and opera was made when Montserrat informed Freddie that she had just three days available for their album recording session.

Despite the time restraints, Mercury put plans for another solo record on the back burners and began writing with a duets album in mind, collaborating with Mike Moran and, for one song, lyricist Tim Rice. They would eventually compose eight new songs, including 'Barcelona', a piece honouring the Olympic Games' new host city. With English and Spanish lyrics, it gave both the great diva and her untutored rock star partner the chance to shine. Caballé loved it. Yet her schedule was still an issue, and the tapes, on which Freddie improvised her vocals, had to be couriered to the diva for her approval.

When Caballé finally flew to London for a recording session, Mercury became increasingly flustered. 'Freddie's nerves made us more nervous,' says John Brough, Townhouse Studios' in-house engineer. 'Montserrat had only ever been recorded live before. So David Richards and I were like, "We've never recorded an opera singer before. What sort of microphone would she use?" Then we realised she had probably never worn headphones before, so we set up a couple of speakers either side of her.'

Mercury had identified another problem prior to Montserrat's arrival at Townhouse: the state of the women's lavatories. 'Freddie suddenly asked, "Is there a Ladies here? I have only seen the Gents!"' laughs Brough. 'Someone showed him the Ladies, and he decided it was rather drab and asked the studio manager to get it tidied up. He offered to pay, although considering how much money Queen spent at Townhouse, he didn't have to. When Montserrat finally arrived it was fine and everyone relaxed, but before then we were all on edge.' What would become Mercury and Caballé's *Barcelona* album wouldn't be completed until June the following year. By then, Freddie's life would be in turmoil.

In early April, Queen were honoured at the Ivor Novello Awards for their Outstanding Contribution to British Music. But it was the only good news that month. At some point between mid-April and early May 1987 Mercury received the news that he had been dreading. According to Jim Hutton, it was during the Easter holiday that Freddie told him he had undergone a biopsy, with his doctor taking a sample of tissue from his shoulder. Days later, Mercury told him he had tested HIV positive.

Interviewed in 2000, Mary Austin gave a different account. Mary recalled an urgent telephone call from Freddie's GP, concerned that his phone messages to Mercury were being ignored. Mary urged Freddie to get in touch with his doctor. When the GP called again, as Mercury still hadn't responded, Austin, in her own words, 'pursued it, until the GP told me why he needed to speak to Freddie ... My heart fell through my boots.'

As Peter Freestone explained, 'Nobody can say for certain who gave who what', but both he and Queen's photographer Mick Rock have suggested that Mercury was likely to have become infected during his hard-partying times in New York (Freestone: 'In the early eighties, anything went in America"). Once he discovered he was ill, Mercury displayed the same pragmatism that had seen him through every other crisis in his life. He told Jim Hutton that he understood if he wanted to end the relationship (Jim refused). He then informed Queen's business manager Jim Beach of his condition. His staff at Garden Lodge, Joe Fanelli and Peter Freestone, would also be made aware of his illness. But it would be some time before he shared the news with the rest of Queen. In the meantime, everyone was sworn to secrecy.

Yet there was more bad news to come. In 1985, Paul Prenter had been laid off from his job in the Queen office. Mercury agreed to employ Prenter himself, but a year on, the work had dried up and Paul was running out of money. In a further display of what Peter Hince calls 'Freddie's misguided loyalty', Prenter was given the keys to Mercury's flat at Stafford Lodge and, according to Jim Hutton, 'Freddie gave him money so he could go out as much as he wanted over the Christmas holiday.' 'The way I remember it, Prenter had some party at Stafford Terrace and the place got trashed,' continues Hince. 'So Freddie sacked him. Paul started ranting, "I'm gonna do this!" and "I'm gonna do that!" And that is exactly what he did . . .'

The 4 May 1987 edition of the *Sun* ran a lurid front-page headline: 'AIDS KILLS FREDDIE'S TWO LOVERS', showing photographs of the singer with Tony Bastin and an airline steward named John Murphy (though Peter Freestone would later insist that Mercury and Murphy were never actually lovers). The story continued inside the newspaper. Under the headline '4 A.M. PHONE CALL OF TERROR' 'the singer's right-hand man Paul Prenter' revealed that on 29 April, Freddie had telephoned him in the early hours, and told him that he was terrified he was dying of AIDS. Elsewhere, Prenter claimed that Mercury had enjoyed sex with 'hundreds of homosexuals'.

The *Sun*'s exposé would be eked out over the next few days, with Prenter detailing Mercury's cocaine binges with other rock stars; how Michael Jackson had caught him taking the drug, and the truth behind Freddie's falling-out with his friend Kenny Everett (apparently, the DJ enjoyed snorting Mercury's cocaine but never paid for it). The newspaper gained great mileage out of the drug revelations, as years before, Freddie had told the *Evening Standard*, not entirely truthfully, that Queen were 'probably the straightest band around'. The final chapter in Prenter's story ran on 7 May, with the newspaper running numerous photographs from his private collection: Freddie with Winnie Kirchberger, Freddie with 'Vince the Barman' . . . Prenter disclosed that Mercury's ideal male was the actor Burt Reynolds, and outed Jim Hutton as Freddie's live-in lover.

Prenter was rumoured to have pocketed as much as £32,000 from the *Sun*. He later telephoned Garden Lodge to claim that the newspaper had pressured him into selling the story. Mercury refused to take his calls. On 10 May, the *News of the World* ran a short statement, purporting to be from Freddie, in which he denounced Prenter for 'making money out of the dead' and pointing out that 'he [Prenter] did all the things I did . . . and more.'

By the end of May, Mercury had fled to Ibiza for a holiday and to perform at the Ibiza 92 Festival. Pino Sagliocci's wish had come true: Freddie and Montserrat Caballé would perform 'Barcelona' in front of 6,000 invited guests at San Antonio's Ku Club. Also guesting on the show would be movie star Harrison Ford, Argentinian footballer Diego Maradona, Chris Rea, Duran Duran, Spandau Ballet and Marillion. Freddie and his entourage had set up base at Pike's Hotel, an exclusive resort away from prying eyes. In the light of the *Sun*'s recent allegations, and in the presence of his peers and rivals, Mercury knew he was under scrutiny.

Marillion's Fish had spent several late nights and early mornings with the singer on the *Magic* tour ('nights of Stolly and Peruvian,' he admits). 'I went backstage at the Ku Club and it was all so very very different,' he says. 'The mood was very, very sombre. Everything had changed. The wall was up.' Barbara Valentin had flown in from Munich, and knew immediately that her ex-lover was sick. According to an interview with the actress, Mercury needed extra make-up to camouflage the discolouration on his cheek that signified Kaposi's Sarcoma. If so, the disguise worked. Freddie gave every impression of being in the rudest of health when he walked onstage that evening.

Mercury and Caballé were the headline act, both miming but accompanied by Mike Moran, a choir and an orchestra. They cut an unlikely couple: the regal diva dressed in a diaphanous black shawl, and Mercury, in his tuxedo, right leg twitching out of time, just as it did onstage with Queen.

Despite never having heard 'Barcelona' before, the audience gave the pair a standing ovation. In October, the single would give the duo a Top 10 UK hit. The implausible collaboration wasn't lost on Freddie. It was another remarkable chapter in the Fred Bulsara story: after turning himself into a rock star in the 1970s, he had danced with the Royal Ballet, recreated himself again as a pop star in the 1980s, and was now adding opera to his repertoire. 'It's so ridiculous when you think about it,' he pondered. 'Her and me together. But if we have something musically together it doesn't matter what we look like or where we come from.'

David Wigg of the *Daily Express* would join Mercury and friends in Ibiza that summer for Freddie's forty-first birthday. Like others, he had his suspicions, but Freddie would not be drawn, informing those who asked that any signs of ill-health were down to drinking too much ('It's my liver, dear'). His Queen bandmates harboured their own suspicions, but, as Roger Taylor admitted, 'For a long time we tried to tell ourselves it was other things.'

With Queen still on hiatus, *The Magic Years* documentary film would be the only Queen release of 1987. Queen Films proved their business acumen by splitting the documentary across three separate videos, finding a home for old promos, the behind-the-scenes footage of Queen making 'One Vision' and talking-head interviews with A-list fans such as Mick Jagger, Elton John and Paul McCartney.

Away from the band, Brian May's personal life was fast resembling a soap opera. On Christmas Day 1986, over 30 million viewers had watched Anita Dobson's *EastEnders* character Angie Watts served with divorce papers by her onscreen husband. In the real world, May and Dobson continued to deny an affair. But May was now writing and producing an album for Anita. Meanwhile, May's protégés Bad News proved unsuccessful, when their raucous, comedy version of 'Bohemian Rhapsody', produced by Brian, stiffed in the charts. While Deacon sang backing vocals on the single, not all of Queen were so enamoured of this reworking of their greatest hit.

Roger Taylor would spend his summer between studios in England, Switzerland and Italy, cutting tracks for another solo record. Having sung and played every instrument on the record himself, Taylor decided to form a band so he could go out and tour. 'If Phil Collins can fit it all in . . . and acting, I can fit in two bands,' he joked. 'And Queen don't really work much these days.'

With Queen's blessing, Taylor placed two ads in the music press ('Drummer of a top rock band looking for musicians' and 'If you think you're good enough and you want to be a star, call this number'). Taylor was initially cautious about attracting Queen fans rather than genuine players. In the end, he settled on three young unknowns: drummer Josh Macrae, guitarist Clayton Moss and bass guitarist Peter Noone. Spike Edney was brought in to play keyboards, while Taylor handled rhythm guitar and lead vocals. Refusing to use the Roger Taylor brand-name, the band were christened simply The Cross.

Taylor cut a deal with Virgin, and what had begun as his third solo album became The Cross's debut album, *Shove It*. Their first single, 'Cowboys and Indians', was released that September. 'I'm just an accessory,' Taylor told *Sounds*. 'One part of a solid unit.' But the truth was rather different. The Cross were due to appear on the Saturday morning TV show *Number 73*. John Brough was asked to mix the sound. 'Roger announced that he'd travel to the studio in the mini-bus with the band,' says Brough. 'So me and "Crystal" [Chris Taylor] followed behind in Roger's Bentley. When "Crystal" and I arrived at the studio, the concierge asked if we were the band. We had to say, "No, they're behind us in the van" . . . That arrangement lasted a couple of days before Roger was back in the Bentley.' Sadly, The Cross's millionaire general, with his Aston Martin and Ibizan holiday home, was never going to be on the same level as his foot soldiers.

'Cowboys and Indians' flopped, and *Shove It* was released the following February. May, Deacon and Mercury made guest appearances, with Freddie singing lead vocals on 'Heaven For Everyone', a song left over from *A Kind Of Magic*. The album was standard-issue eighties pop-rock, with a hint of one of Taylor's favourite new groups INXS, but only his distinguishing rasp added any character. *Shove It* made it into the Top 50, but further singles offered more diminishing returns. It was another reminder of Queen being more than the sum of its parts. But The Cross offered Taylor something he could no longer get from Queen: the opportunity to play live. He would not give it up so easily.

That year, 1988, was a challenging year for all. In January, Taylor married Dominique Beyrand at Chelsea register office, with Mercury and Mary Austin as his witnesses. Just weeks later, he moved out of the family home and into a new pad with a 25-year-old model named Deborah Leng, whose recent TV ad appearance, biting into a phallic Cadbury's Flake chocolate bar, had caused a stir among *Daily Mail* readers. Naturally, the press were fascinated by the drummer's domestic arrangements; the whirlwind marriage fuelling the suspicion that rock stars did things differently from mere mortals. The wedding had, it seemed, been necessary to secure the financial stability of the couple's two children after their parents split.

Odder still, in the same month John Deacon had a hit single. Almost. The bassist took a walk-on part in the video for the spoof hip hop song 'Stutter Rap' by Morris Minor and The Majors. The group included the comedian and writer Tony Hawks, who'd met Deacon on a Virgin Airlines junket to Miami. 'We hung out together over a long and drunken weekend,' said Hawks. 'John struck me as someone who'd become a rock star by accident.'

No sooner had Taylor set up a new home than he was out on tour with The Cross. After arriving onstage at Newcastle Mayfair, one or two wags in the audience pelted him with Cadbury Flake bars. When the tour reached Germany, Taylor bowed to the promoter's wishes, and posters for the gigs were amended to read: 'Roger Taylor and The Cross'. Yet, as a further reminder of his role as 'one part of the unit', The Cross would only play one Queen song: 'I'm in Love With My Car'.

Life in the day job was no less eventful. In January, Queen met at London's Olympic Studios. An important decision was made: from now on, every new song would be credited collectively to all four members. 'I wish we'd done it earlier,' Brian May told *Q* magazine. 'It's the best decision we ever made. It does mean a sacrifice, letting your baby go, but once you actually do it, you have a group working together on all fronts.' 'It meant that decisions would be made on artistic merit,' added Roger Taylor, 'rather than financial or ego grounds.'

According to May, it was Mercury who had originally suggested separate writer's credits while making Queen's first album. Over twenty years later, though, Freddie was willing to split the money. Similarly, the band took a collective decision to return to their earlier way of working, with all four together in the studio, rather than each working alone with just a synthesiser for company. Queen's next album started out with the working title of *The Invisible Man*, but would become *The Miracle* just weeks before completion. The first song to emerge was a return to what Brian May called 'old-school Queen'. Group credit or not, the mighty riff and mightier guitar solo of 'I Want It All' marked it out as a Brian May creation. The song's petulant lyric was perfect for Freddie Mercury, but the title had apparently come from one of Anita Dobson's popular sayings (May: 'She's a very ambitious girl'). May would later reveal that ideas for the song had been whizzing around his mind while he was digging up weeds in the garden of his second home in Los Angeles.

The Miracle was recorded in fits and starts between Olympic and Townhouse in London and Mountain in Switzerland. Mercury dashed between Queen and the Montserrat Caballé duets album, even fitting in a live appearance when he joined the cast of *Time* to perform four songs at London's Dominion Theatre in April. It was a courageous move in the light of recent press scrutiny, with the show a fundraiser for the newly formed AIDS charity, the Terrence Higgins Trust. But still Mercury refused to discuss his health with the rest of Queen. Interviewed in *Mojo* in 1999, May later said: 'We discovered about Freddie in 1987 or 1988.' Yet speaking to *The Times* in 1992, May claimed that they had only been told 'a few months before [Freddie's] death'. Whatever the truth, the singer was not forthcoming. 'We didn't actually know what was wrong for a very long time,' said Brian. 'We never talked about it, and it was a sort of unwritten law that we didn't because Freddie didn't want to. He just told us that he didn't feel up to doing tours, and that's as far as it went.'

On the one hand, it seems bizarre that Mercury would keep his condition a secret from a group of people he'd spent so much of his adult life with. Yet Mercury had always been an enigma, even to his bandmates. His origins, his childhood and his sexuality had all been areas of his life that he had, at times, kept private. His health issues were the same. 'He obviously wasn't well,' says John Brough, assistant engineer on *The Miracle*. 'But no one spoke about it, and we were expected not to.'

'I personally didn't know that he had AIDS,' said David Richards, who co-produced the final recordings. 'I speculated he had cancer. I think everyone involved pushed aside the fact that it was really that serious. Everyone still had that glimpse of hope that at the end maybe a miracle would happen.'

In June, Brian May's father Harold died. 'The two worst things I ever did in his eyes were: one, give up my academic career to become a pop star and two, live with a woman,' said Brian. After barely speaking to each other for a year, the relationship had thawed, and Harold had supported his son's choice of career. As May pointed out: 'My dad was always trying to stop me going into the rock business but he built my guitar – the thing that propelled me into it.'

The shock of his father's death was compounded by the guitarist's marital problems. The birth of a daughter, Emily, came at the beginning of 1988 but before long, May had left Chrissy and his three children, moving out of the family home and into a house on his own. Although his relationship with Anita Dobson was now public, he claimed that he 'couldn't admit it to myself, and didn't allow myself to be with her.' For May, the end of his marriage and the loss of his father cast a shadow over the Queen album sessions. 'I was in a complete state of mental untogetherness,' he said. 'What I did play I was quite proud of, but my input to the material wasn't as good as it could have been.' Stories about the 'millionaire rocker' and 'Angie' (Dobson was still better known by her *EastEnders* character's name) were soon splashed across the tabloids. May channelled some of his ire into a new song, the stagey mid-paced rocker 'Scandal'. Though not everyone was a fan: 'Not one of our better ones,' said Taylor.

When he wasn't working with the band, May seemed to spend every waking hour playing music with anyone else that asked. Just days after his father's death, he joined Elton John and Eric Clapton at the Royal Albert Hall for The Prince's Trust Gala concert. In the months that followed, he became a guitar-for-hire for the likes of Holly Johnson, Black Sabbath and boyhood hero Lonnie Donegan. 'You need distractions,' he admitted. 'Being busy is one of the great therapies.'

In October, with The Miracle still in progress, Freddie Mercury and Montserrat Caballé released their duets album, *Barcelona*. Even now, there's still something compelling about hearing 'The Fallen Priest' and 'The Golden Boy' in which the self-taught Mercury pits himself against Caballé's mighty soprano, and still manages to get away with it. Reviewing the album for *Q* magazine, David Sinclair made an insightful observation: '*Barcelona* has more to do with *Cats* and *Time* than *Tommy* or *La Traviata*.' The long road to *We Will Rock You: The Musical* began here. *Barcelona* would spend a month in the UK charts, just outside the Top 20.

On the day of the album's release, Mercury and Caballé were the main attraction at La Nit, an open-air concert in Barcelona in front of Spain's King Juan Carlos, to celebrate the arrival of the Olympic torch. Also on the eclectic bill were Jerry Lee Lewis, Dionne Warwick and the ubiquitous Spandau Ballet. It would be Freddie's final live appearance, but, again, the duo chose to mime. Among the press corps gathered to cover the event, there was talk of a 'throat infection' and 'AIDS'. In a post-show interview Mercury protested: 'If my voice was not to come up to scratch I'd be letting her down. I didn't want to take any chances.'

Three weeks before Christmas, The Cross played the Queen Fan Club party at London's Hammersmith Palais. John Deacon and Brian May joined them onstage for a handful of blues tracks. There was no sign of Freddie. At the Barcelona concert, Mercury had been able to maintain the façade. Just. But beneath his immaculate tuxedo, he had a wound on his right calf and a lesion on the ball of his foot, which, due to his depleted immune system, would never properly heal.

Recording for *The Miracle* finally wound up in the New Year. Ten songs were culled from what Roger Taylor called 'a good crop' of thirty tracks, with some extras being held over for the CD and cassette formats of the album and future B-sides. The first single, 'I Want It All', emerged in May and put Queen back in the UK Top 5; its heavy-metal guitar riffs sounding like a gauntlet thrown down to the such fashionably heavy bands as Guns N' Roses and The Cult. The album followed in June, with a sleeve designed by Queen's art guru Richard Gray. Using a forerunner of the design programme that would eventually become Photoshop, the four band members' faces had been morphed into a single image; an unnerving montage of eyes, noses and mouths.

The Miracle went straight to number 1 in Britain, and 24 in the US. Despite Brian May's emotional distractions, he was all over the album. There were no shortage of guitar solos on 'I Want It All' and 'Breakthru', but even on the beach-bar calypso of 'Rain Must Fall', May played like a man trying to blow the song up from the inside. Like Queen's guilty conscience, the troubled guitarist cropped up again and again, salvaging the throwaway opener 'Party', messing up the pop-funk of 'My Baby Does Me' and 'The Invisible Man', and adding extra muscle to the Led Zeppelin-soundalike 'Khashoggi's Ship' (only Queen could write a song inspired by a Saudi playboy and millionaire arms dealer) 'I can remember whole days sitting there blank, I was in such a depression,' May said later. 'I'm surprised how much guitar there is on it.'

For much of the record, Mercury pulled off his customary trick of singing beautifully while giving away very little. Knowing that it's the work of a man on borrowed time, it's easy to read more into the lyrics of the more thoughtful material. May described the title track, with its peace-and-love-to-all sentiment, as 'Freddie's small masterpiece'. On the album's final song, 'Was It All Worth It?', Mercury reflected on a life of money, excess and the eternal quest for perfection. *The Times* would write it off as 'a grotesque stadium-rock equivalent of "My Way",' but other reviews for the album were cautiously complimentary, with *Rolling Stone* praising *The Miracle* for its 'snippets of Queen's former majesty'.

The promotional campaign extended to *Queen for an Hour*, a group interview with BBC Radio 1 DJ Mike Read. Asked why they wouldn't tour, Freddie said he wanted to break the cycle of album, tour, album, tour . . . 'I am the spanner in the works,' he declared.

Following 'I Want It All', four more singles would be lifted from *The Miracle* over the coming months. As well as the new CD format, EMI pushed out 12-inch vinyl, cassette and picture-disc versions of 'Breakthru', 'The Invisible Man', 'Scandal' and 'The Miracle' title track; only the last two failed to crack the Top 20. Yet making promo videos presented a greater challenge than before. In each promo Mercury sported a beard or heavy stubble. 'I couldn't be bothered to shave any more,' Mercury told the press. 'It's as boring as slicing bread.' According to Jim Hutton, in his *Mercury and Me* memoir, it helped conceal the signs of Kaposi's Sarcoma better than layers of make-up. For the 'Breakthru' video, Queen were filmed on a customised steam engine racing through the Cambridgeshire countryside. To all intents and purposes, Mercury looked healthy: flourishing the sawn-off mic stand, soloing on an imaginary guitar and pumping his arms as if nothing had changed.

For 'The Miracle' video, Queen hired stage-school child actors to play themselves, dressing up their mini doppelgängers in versions of their own stage clothes. 'It was a joy to make,' recalled Taylor. 'We were smiling the whole time.' But when the real Queen emerged for the finale, Mercury, in his *Magic* tour yellow jacket, looked visibly older – and frailer – than he had in 1986, as though time had somehow accelerated.

The task of promoting the new album fell to Taylor and May. Talking about the music was easy enough (the party line: Queen were now 'refreshed and rejuvenated'), but at a press conference in Munich, a German reporter asked Taylor outright whether Freddie Mercury had AIDS. 'Freddie is as healthy as ever,' insisted the drummer. 'The reason we're not going to tour is because we can't agree on the process. Everything else is just a stupid rumour.' Whether the drummer already knew the truth or not, Mercury's bandmates were becoming adept at stonewalling questions about his health.

Barely taking a break after finishing *The Miracle*, Mercury, clearly aware of how little time he had left, returned to Montreux, determined to keep working. By the spring of 1989, with *The Miracle* not yet released, Queen began work on a follow-up. 'I think we all thought *The Miracle* was going to be the last one,' said Brian May in 1992. 'There were no guarantees how long Freddie was going to last at that time. So we just knew we had to press on and do what we could.'

According to Jim Hutton, it was in Montreux at this time that Mercury finally told the rest of the group about his condition, with a dramatic display in a restaurant. 'Someone at the table was suffering from a cold, and the conversation got round to the curse of illness,' said Hutton. 'Freddie still looked fairly well, but he rolled up his right trouser leg and raised his leg to the table to let the others see the painful, open wound weeping on the side of his leg: "You think you've got problems," he told them. "Well, look at this." Then, as quickly as he'd mentioned it, Freddie brushed the subject aside.' However, like many anecdotes relating to Mercury's final days, this has been called into question, with one unnamed source insisting the singer would never have broken the news to them in such a public manner.

'At one point he invited us all over for a meeting,' said Roger Taylor in 2000, 'and told us the absolute facts, which we were all starting to realise anyway.' 'As soon as we realised Freddie was ill, we clustered around him like a protective shell,' recalled Brian May. 'But we were lying to everyone, even our own families. Freddie didn't want the world intruding on his struggle. He used to say, "I don't want people buying our records out of fucking sympathy."' Mercury demanded the same of Queen as he did of Jim Hutton and the inner circle at Garden Lodge: business as usual. 'He had to be treated normally,' said Mary Austin. 'If he found you were flagging or becoming too emotional, you would be pushed back in line.'

May had been planning another solo album; Mercury had songs left over from *Barcelona*, and there was still material unused from *The Miracle*. According to Hutton, 'Queen were dazed by Freddie's eagerness to return to the studio', but they agreed, and, for the first few months of 1989, the band worked in two-to-three-week bursts; a schedule partly dictated by their singer's health. When they weren't with Queen, May and Taylor seemed unwilling to rest, guesting on charity covers of Deep Purple's 'Smoke on the Water' and Queen's own 'Who Wants to Live Forever', with Taylor soon moonlighting at Mountain Studios on a second album with The Cross.

No sooner had Queen's anti-tabloid single 'Scandal' dropped out of the chart, than Mercury was back in the news headlines. In November, the *Sunday Mirror* claimed wrongly that Freddie had offered to be a 'father' to Mary Austin's forthcoming child. At the time, Mary was several months pregnant but refusing to name the child's biological father. In the same month, Queen made a public appearance together on a TV special, *Goodbye to the Eighties*, which was scheduled to be broadcast on New Year's Eve. Queen picked up an award from Cilla Black and a youthful Jonathan Ross for Best Band of the Decade. Fans and critics scrutinised Mercury's appearance and every gesture. While he stood back on the podium and let Brian May give an acceptance speech, he did not yet look like a dying man.

At the end of the month, Queen went back to Montreux. Mercury had given up smoking on doctor's orders, and insisted on banning cigarettes from the studio entirely; a popular decision with Brian May, a devout anti-smoker, particularly since the death of his father. In the early 1980s, Mercury had found the chaos and hedonism of Munich preferable to the calm of Montreux; now, however, the slower pace of Swiss life suited him. In his final year, the singer would buy a penthouse flat in Teritet, overlooking Lake Geneva.

Song ideas were pooled, and out of these came Brian May's frustrated love song 'I Can't Live With You' and 'Headlong', an ebullient hard rocker in the style of 'Breakthru'. 'At first I thought about it as a song for my solo album,' he admitted. 'But as soon as I heard Freddie sing it, I said, "That's it." Sometimes it's painful to give the baby away.'

Mercury's contributions were typically diverse: 'Delilah' was a tongue-in-cheek tribute to one of his cats, while the gospel-flavoured 'All God's People' had started life as a piece for the *Barcelona* album. John Brough helped engineer an early take for the song at Townhouse Studios, and saw that, regardless of his failing health, Freddie remained a hard taskmaster.

'It was still a solo track at the time, but Freddie had asked Brian to play a solo on it,' explains Brough. 'Brian did a good solo, but decided he could do better and played it again. Freddie said, "No, I don't like it", and so it went on, and I could see Brian getting more and more tense. After another solo, Freddie said, "Oh, that's rubbish." David Richards, Mike Moran and I were all looking at each other. At the time, it seemed horrific. After another solo, Freddie made some comment like, "Oh, come on! You and that fireplace guitar . . . play it like you mean it!" So Brian let rip with this great solo, and, of course, Freddie had this big grin on his face. He knew what Brian could do, and he was just pushing him.'

A jam between May, Taylor and Deacon in the Montreux casino concert hall became the starting point for what would become the album's title track, 'Innuendo'. Stopping just short of six-and-a-half minutes, 'Innuendo' was a Queen marathon in the tradition of 'Liar' or 'The Prophet's Song'. Mercury sang about crumbling mountains and crashing waves to an opening motif that suggested Led Zeppelin's 'Kashmir' colliding with Ravel's *Bolero*. Steve Howe, guitarist with Yes, visited the studio, and ended up playing acoustic guitar on the song. 'It's a very strange track,' said May later. 'Like a fantasy adventure-land.' The origins of the song's title were rather less mystical. 'It's a word I like to use in Scrabble,' Mercury later revealed. Although the old-school Queen of *Innuendo* was still a year away, EMI's December release of *Queen at the Beeb*, a compilation of their BBC sessions from 1973 onwards, seemed strangely prescient.

Queen Productions declared 1990 to be the band's twentieth anniversary, despite the fact that they had celebrated the tenth only in 1981, and on 18 February, the group were finally given the BPI Award that EMI had long been petitioning for. Queen were rewarded during a ceremony at London's Dominion Theatre. But since their appearance on *Goodbye to the Eighties*, Mercury had gone downhill. Freddie led the band onstage to the sound of 'Killer Queen'. He looked swamped by his baggy suit, his hair thinner and his clean-shaven face haggard beneath a layer of make-up. After May's acceptance speech, and a quick word from Taylor, Mercury leaned hesitantly towards the microphone, quietly said, 'Thank you, goodnight', and disappeared into the wings.

At the anniversary party afterwards, more than three hundred guests crowded the Groucho Club in Soho. Inside, Mercury was photographed with Liza Minnelli, the star of what Queen's first producer John Anthony remembered as Freddie's favourite movie, *Cabaret*. Outside, scenting blood, a press photographer snapped the singer leaving the club looking, frankly, terrible. Joe Fanelli's complaint to the newspaper that Mercury was just 'a little pissed, like everyone else' fell on deaf ears. The speculation about Mercury's health continued.

May found a brief respite from it all, joining his old 1984 band-mates (minus Tim Staffell) at bassist Dave Dilloway's house. 'Brian hadn't changed,' says Dave. 'He was sat there, playing away, while the conversation went on around him. At the time, he must have known Freddie had AIDS.'

Before long, Fanelli would break the news that he had AIDS. Freddie had met Joe almost fifteen years before and they had been lovers, but since the end of their relationship Fanelli had been Mercury's chef. Knowing that Joe would have to leave Garden Lodge after his own death, Mercury brought him a house in Chiswick. It was the first of several magnanimous gestures in what would turn out to be his final year. Jim Hutton would also take the test in secret, only to discover that he, too, was HIV positive. 'I was dazed,' he said later. 'But I didn't tell Freddie. He had enough to worry about.' Before long, and to help Hutton and Peter Freestone administer his medication, Mercury would be fitted with a Hickman line on his chest.

Mercury's bandmates could only wait until their singer was ready to start work again. May began writing the music to the London Riverside Theatre's production of *Macbeth*, and Taylor went back to singing in his own band. In March, The Cross put out their second album, *Mad Bad and Dangerous to Know*. Taylor had found a deal with EMI, and had thrown the songwriting open to his bandmates. The album had a harder sound, with 'Top of the World' like a reworking of Led Zeppelin's 'Whole Lotta Love'. It was a marked improvement on *Shove It*, but the group faced the same problems. 'I've never been able to convince people that it's a group,' Taylor protested. 'Everybody writes, everybody shares the money equally, really it's not the Roger Taylor solo experience.' The album failed to chart, and every interview with The Cross invariably included questions about Queen, Freddie . . .

Come July, Queen had decamped to London's Metropolis Studios, a facility owned by their former engineer Gary Langan. Gary had been there when Queen heard the first playback of 'Bohemian Rhapsody'. In 1985, he had stood at the side of the stage at Live Aid ('When I'm finally popping my clogs, that will be one of the moments I take to my grave'). Langan had heard the rumours, and was shocked by the change in Mercury's appearance. 'The whole thing had taken its toll,' he says. 'We bumped into each other at Metropolis and had a few words, but he was trying to be as private as possible. It wasn't a great thing to see.'

In August, Freddie finally confirmed his sister Kashmira's worst suspicions. "I did suspect he had AIDS,' she later told the *Daily Mirror*. 'But I didn't want to ask a dying man that question so I waited to see if he wanted to tell me.' It was when Kashmira glimpsed the wound on her brother's foot that she realised. 'He chose that moment to say, "Look, my dear, you must know that I am dying."' Just as with his closest friends and his bandmates, Mercury insisted that his sister never mentioned it again. His parents, meanwhile, were never told outright. 'He used to love and respect us so much that he didn't want to hurt us,' explained Jer Bulsara in 2000. 'We knew all along and we didn't want to displease him.'

By now, the singer routinely ran a gauntlet of press photographers just to get from Garden Lodge to Metropolis. Living through the celebrity culture of the twenty-first century, it's easy to forget how unusual it still was then for the press to pursue a pop star to such a degree. Queen's raised profile after Live Aid and the hysteria and misinformation surrounding AIDS proved to be a dangerous combination. However much Mercury insisted on secrecy, it was now impossible for him to conceal the obvious change in his appearance. When a *Sunday Mirror* photographer captured him looking frail, Brian May informed the press that 'Freddie's OK . . . He definitely hasn't got AIDS, but I think his wild rock 'n' roll lifestyle has caught up with him . . .' But May's statement failed to throw anyone off the scent. Just days later, the *News of the World* pictured an emaciated Mercury leaving a London restaurant with his GP, Gordon Atkinson. Before long, Paul Prenter, long banished from the Queen camp, was quoted speculating about his former employer's health in the American press: 'I am desperately afraid that it might be AIDS.'

One afternoon, engineer John Brough found himself summoned to Garden Lodge. 'Every year, the band would record a message for the fan club,' he says. 'Freddie wanted me to record his message. Peter Freestone asked me to come to the house for noon. When I arrived, he apologised and said that Freddie had a meeting that had over-run.' It was one-thirty before Mercury finally arrived, and it was obvious that all was not well. 'He looked very tired and very ill,' says Brough. 'But in himself he was just the same, with the same very dry sense of humour. We went to one of the spare bedrooms. He had the stage mic, the wand, and we recorded a vocal. It was a hot day so the window was open, and every time he went to sing workmen outside started drilling. Freddie was like, "Oh fuck!" Very funny. We did this thing with a synth and a vocal, and then he said he had to have a rest and he'd leave me to do the mix. Afterwards, Peter told me to invoice them, and I said, "Look, forget about it." I was asked to go back a few days later, and when I did, Peter handed me a bag. Inside there was this cardigan from Harrods. It was a thank you from Fred. That was the last time I ever saw him.'

Their singer's health was still an issue as Queen prepared to promote *Innuendo*. In January 1991, they released the epic title track as a single. 'It's a risk because a lot of people say, "It's too long, it's too involved, and we don't want to play it on the radio," ' said Brian May. 'But we had the same feelings about "Bohemian Rhapsody".' 'Innuendo' was a far cry from pop hits such as 'A Kind of Magic'. The introduction sounded like a heavy metal funeral march, the flamenco guitar mid-section like something dropped in from another record. It may have been a challenge to radio pro-grammers, but for Queen fans of a vintage stripe, 'Innuendo' had gratifying echoes of *A Night at the Opera*.

Against expectation, 'Innuendo' gave Queen their first UK number 1 since 'Under Pressure'. The accompanying video used animation and old footage and had the group members re-drawn in the style of artists such as Picasso, Da Vinci and Pollock. In a coincidence reminiscent of Tim Staffell being hired to work on the cover of his ex-bandmate Roger Taylor's first solo album, one of the animators commissioned for 'Innuendo' was Jerry Hibbert, a classmate of Staffell's and Fred Bulsara's at Ealing art college. When Hibbert asked if the video was being animated because his old mate was too sick to appear, he was informed that Freddie was *not* ill.

Nobody in the Queen camp was budging from the party line.

Innuendo, the album, followed in February. Like the single, the artwork also felt like a throwback to Queen's past. Roger Taylor had unearthed a book of illustrations by the nineteenth-century artist Jean Grandville, and suggested using one of the pieces. Grandville's *A Juggler of Universes* would be hand-coloured by Richard Gray and adapted for the *Innuendo* sleeve. While the title track mollified Queen's heavy metal audience, the rest of the album was as diverse as ever. The difference was that *Innuendo* seemed to hang together better than any Queen album since *News of the World*. Brian May, in particular, was a dominant force. 'By *Innuendo*, the others were having emotional problems, and I was a bit more together,' he explained. 'I was able to pitch into the writing a lot more.' As well as his own 'Headlong' and 'I Can't Live With You', May was a notable presence on the feisty heavy metal track 'The Hitman', 'All God's People' and 'Bijou', a showcase for his guitar and Mercury's voice inspired by Jeff Beck.

While every song was credited collectively to Queen, it was often easy to spot the original composers. Mercury's 'Delilah' was pure filler, but so too was Taylor's 'Ride the Wild Wind', which sounded like a companion to *A Kind of Magic*'s 'Don't Lose Your Head'. Mercury, meanwhile, was responsible for *Innuendo*'s best forgotten song, a solemn ballad titled 'Don't Try So Hard'. Missing from *Innuendo* was any of the funk influence that John Deacon had previously bought to Queen. The bassist had recently purchased a holiday apartment in the French ski resort of Biarritz, and the appeal of the slopes outweighed that of Metropolis studio, resulting in Deacon being absent from some sessions.

Innuendo also came with three more obvious singles; songs that would, though no one could have known it at the time, plot the last days of Mercury's life. 'I'm Going Slightly Mad' was an offbeat pop song, built around some arch wordplay. 'These Are the Days of Our Lives' had a wistful lyric from Roger Taylor, which sounded, unavoidably, like Queen reflecting on their time together. Brian May's 'The Show Must Go On' was another melodramatic piece in the style of 'Who Wants to Live Forever'. 'I sat down with Freddie and we decided what the theme should be and wrote the first verse,' May told *Guitar World* magazine. 'It's a long story, that song, but I always felt it would be important because we were dealing with things that were hard to talk about at the time, but in the world of music you could do it.' Painfully aware that his friend was dying, May wanted to change what he believed would be the song's working title, but Mercury, business-like as ever, insisted that he didn't. 'The last thing he wanted was to draw attention to any kind of weakness or frailty,' said Taylor. 'He didn't want pity.'

In the press, *Innuendo* drew the same measured praise and criticism as *The Miracle*. 'It recognises few frontiers of style, let alone taste,' wrote *The Times*, before giving a thumbs-up to 'These Are the Days of Our Lives', and its 'shamelessly soppy paean to the passing of youth'. *Q* magazine flew a cautious flag for *Innuendo*, while nailing a side of Queen that others often missed: 'Clearly they take their work seriously, but taking themselves seriously is another matter entirely.'

The album matched the single with another number 1 chart placing in Britain. In the US, though, it stalled at number 30. While American sales had been lagging behind for most of the last ten years, the band's circumstances had now changed. Jim Beach had spent much of 1990 negotiating Queen out of their US deal with Capitol. In November, the band had signed a new American deal with Hollywood Records, a label affiliated to Walt Disney. Hollywood's label president Peter Paterno had bought Queen out of their Capitol contract for a rumoured $10 million.

The sweetener for the label was that Queen owned their back catalogue. In 1990, with money to be made from consumers wanting to replace their vinyl records with state-of-the-art CDs, Hollywood planned to digitally remaster and re-release Queen's previous albums. Still, several music business insiders couldn't fathom why Hollywood had paid so much for a band that hadn't had actually had a Top 20 US album since 1982, raising the question of whether Hollywood Records knew something about Queen's future that others didn't.

The new label's launch party for *Innuendo* took place in February on the *Queen Mary* cruise ship, at California's Long Beach. Guests were plied with free drink and treated to an extravagant firework display, but only two of the band bothered to attend. Even Queen's old friends were confused. 'Mack and I were invited to the party on the *Queen Mary*,' remembers Fred Mandel. 'We went down there and only Roger and Brian showed up. We thought that was strange as the band usually came together. Mack and I had started to speculate. Freddie looked thinner in the videos and things weren't adding up. I tried to call Freddie, heard nothing, and so I called John but he was close-lipped about it.'

Deacon and Mercury's absences were excused with vague talk of 'family commitments'. Once again, it had fallen to the original Smile/Queen duo to press the media flesh and bullshit their way out of trouble. *Billboard* magazine's Dave DiMartino was among those who interviewed May and Taylor during their Los Angeles trip. 'They were dutifully undertaking that most undignified of tasks,' said DiMartino, 'talking about commerce rather than art.' Throughout the trip, the pair praised their new label ('Hollywood has everything to prove,' said Taylor, 'and that's what we felt we needed'), and the new album (Taylor: 'In some ways it does remind me of *A Night at the Opera*') and addressed the controversy sparked by rapper Vanilla Ice's recent hit, 'Ice Ice Baby', which had sampled the bassline from 'Under Pressure' (May: 'He should have asked for permission but he didn't').

Asked about why Queen hadn't played live for five years, they were forced to trot out the usual excuses. 'Freddie finds it hard physically and mentally to be on tour,' volunteered May. 'He hates the idea of being an older rocker onstage,' added the drummer. In an interview for Canadian TV, May looked positively rueful when asked whether Queen would ever play live again. 'It would be my fondest dream to go out on tour,' he sighed, looking like a man with the weight of the world on his shoulders.

In March, Queen released 'I'm Going Slightly Mad' as a single in the UK. For the video, a fancy-dressed Queen shared the set with an extra in a gorilla suit and a waddle of penguins. In his shaggy wig, white gloves and deliberately ill-fitting suit, Mercury resembled a Chaplin-esque silent movie star, but also, sadly, a consumptive nineteenth-century poet. The layers of white panstick on his face only accentuated how gaunt he now was; beneath his costume he wore an extra layer of clothing to pad out his skeletal fame. 'He looked pretty ill at that point,' conceded Taylor.

Queen's press office fed the tabloids a quirky news story about one of the penguins urinating on the video set's sofa while Freddie was sitting on it. 'A little bit of Queen madness is wanted right now,' claimed an upbeat Mercury. 'So don't bother to question our sanity.' But regrettably, the singer's appearance became a greater talking point than the song, which stayed outside the Top 20.

Just as he'd done after *The Miracle*, Mercury had followed *Innuendo* with an instruction to his bandmates that he wanted to keep working. Montreux was a private jet ride away and offered an escape from the constant press intrusion in London. At Mountain Studios, he worked as and when he felt physically able. 'Freddie just said, "I want to go on working, business as usual, until I fucking drop,"' recalled Brian May. '"That's what I want. And I'd like you to support me, and I don't want any discussion about this."' The initial plan was to record some B-sides. Before long, though, the band realised there was enough material for another studio album. Business-like as ever, Mercury was determined that Queen should get as much music out of him while they still could.

Working two or three days a week, the band recorded a batch of new tracks, including 'You Don't Fool Me', 'A Winter's Tale' (the last song Mercury ever wrote) and 'Mother Love'. The 22 May recording session for 'Mother Love' is widely believed to be Freddie's last recorded vocal. In the studio, he pushed himself harder to sing the song's difficult middle-eight, insisting that it demanded a higher vocal. 'Freddie got to some point, and said, "No, no, no . . . this isn't good enough! I have to go higher here. I have to get more power in,"' recalled May. After downing a couple of vodkas, said May, 'he stands up and goes for it.' Mercury achieved the performance he wanted. 'Even when he couldn't even stand without propping himself up, he was just giving us his all.'

'He wanted to make music till the last second,' said David Richards. "It was a difficult situation for all of us, but especially for Freddie, but he really wanted this project to be finished, even though he knew that the album would be released after his death.'

A fortnight before, Queen had released the blustery 'Headlong' as their new single. It made it to number 14 in the UK charts. But the whole band, even the puckish Taylor, looked noticably older in the song's video. Mercury was wasting away beneath his baggy sweatshirt, but threw his usual shapes, grinning toothily into the camera, as if trying to convince the world that it was still business as usual.

On 31 May, just over a week after the last Mountain session, Mercury made what would turn out to be his final appearance in front of the camera. Hollywood Records had earmarked 'These Are the Days of Our Lives' for a US single release. With Brian May in Los Angeles still promoting *Innuendo*, Taylor, Deacon and Mercury repaired to London's Limehouse Studios to make a video for the song (May would be edited in later). The unhealed lesion on the ball of Mercury's foot now made walking so painful for him that he was forced to remain static for the majority of the shoot. Though shot in black and white, it was all but impossible to mask Freddie's physical decline. In the video's final frame, he whispered the song's melodramatic line 'I still love you' into the camera, like one of his favourite showboating Hollywood heroines. Few that saw the video could be in any doubt that they were watching a very sick man.

In August, Paul Prenter died of an AIDS-related illness. His demise was a bleak reminder of how little time Freddie now had left. Jim Hutton took a second HIV test, but the results were the same. This time, he chose to tell Mercury. The singer marked his forty-fifth birthday with a quiet dinner party at Garden Lodge. His social circle had grown smaller, as the singer closed ranks. Old party companions Barbara Valentin and Peter Straker had been excluded, as if they were too much of a reminder of the lifestyle he could no longer enjoy. Others, too, would find their requests to visit turned down ('I'm not looking too good today, dear'). Instead, Mercury relied on a handful of trusted friends and employees: the clique at Garden Lodge, Mike Moran, Dave Clark, his chauffeur Terry Giddings and the ever-present Mary Austin. Shortly after his birthday, he drew up a will, appointing Queen's business manager, Jim Beach, as one of his executors.

In October, EMI swung into action, releasing *Queen's Greatest Hits*

II, and two video compilations, *Greatest Flix II* and *Box of Flix*. In the light of such a rigorous release campaign, there was something apt about the title of Queen's new single, 'The Show Must Go On'. Mercury was too ill to make a video, forcing the band to rely on a montage of older clips. But the song's sentiment spoke volumes in the light of their current situation. It was typical Freddie Mercury: the most melodramatic of swansongs.

In early November, the singer took the most important decision of his life, and announced that he no longer wished to take his AIDS medication. He had effectively chosen to die. Interviewed in 2000, Mary Austin believed that 'he'd given himself a limit. I think, personally, that when he couldn't record any more or have the energy to do so, it would be the end.' The press were now keeping a permanent vigil outside the house. As Peter Freestone complained, 'Freddie became a prisoner within the walls of Garden Lodge.' When Montserrat Caballé asked to visit, Mercury refused, claiming he didn't want her to be harassed.

His parents, his sister and her family, and most of his bandmates visited Mercury during what would turn out to be the last week of his life. According to Jim Hutton, Taylor and May both made separate calls to the house. Pulling up outside the house, on one occasion, the Queen drummer was blinded by the photographers' flashguns and crashed into the back of a stationary police car. For the ever-anxious May, there was another issue on his mind. The guitarist had finally finished his solo album, and was planning to release a single from it in a week's time. Knowing that Freddie could die at any moment, May was worried that the release would look as if it was cashing in. May asked Jim Beach to broach the subject. The singer's reply proved that his gallows humour was as sharp as ever: 'Freddie said: "If I pop off while it's happening, it'll give you an extra bit of publicity."'

On Thursday, 21 November, Mercury asked Peter Freestone to call Jim Beach. The following morning, Beach arrived at Garden Lodge for a meeting with Freddie that lasted over five hours. According to Freestone, 'Freddie and he [Beach] had decided that it was time to release a statement with regards to Freddie's AIDS status.' The news came as a shock to those at Garden Lodge as they had, at Mercury's behest, consistently lied to their friends and families about Freddie's health. Writing in his own memoir, Jim Hutton suggested that Mercury had been pushed into making the statement, but agreed to it when he realised that it would scupper any planned newspaper scoop after his death. 'He didn't want to be usurped, having not announced it,' explained Roger Taylor. 'It was absolutely right to do it at the time that it was done.'

'The last three weeks of his life, when he was in his house, were made a total misery,' said Brian May. 'The press was outside his house twenty-four hours a day. So he was literally kind of hounded toward his death. And I think if he'd made his announcement earlier that he had AIDS, all of that would have happened much earlier.'

While the AIDS hysteria of the early 1980s had now subsided, in 1991 there was still a huge stigma attached to what many still believed to be a uniquely 'gay disease'. Mercury was acutely aware of this, and of the impact the news of his illness could have had on his bandmates, their wives, girlfriends and children. As one of Mercury's old friends explained, 'Freddie was terrified of what the public's reaction would have been towards them.' Like so many aspects of his life, Mercury chose to remain silent until the last possible moment.

Queen's PR, Roxy Meade, released Mercury's official statement at midnight on Friday: 'Following the enormous conjecture in the press over the last two weeks, I wish to confirm: I have been tested HIV positive and have AIDS. I felt it correct to keep this information private to date in order to protect the privacy of those around me. However, the time has now come for my friends and fans around the world to know the truth. I hope everyone will join with me, my doctors and all those worldwide in my fight against this terrible disease.'

On the morning of Sunday, 25 November, the *News of the World* gave its front page over to the story: 'FREDDIE: I'VE GOT AIDS – QUEEN STAR'S ANGUISH'. Freddie Mercury had scored his little victory over the press, but only just. At around 6.48 p.m. the day before, the rock star born Farrokh Bulsara passed away.

CHAPTER ELEVEN

A Ferrari in the Garage

'We don't want to become old, rich and useless.'

Roger Taylor

Freddie Mercury died barely two miles from where his hero Jimi Hendrix's body had been found twenty-one years earlier. Back then, Mercury and Roger Taylor had closed their stall at Kensington Market in Hendrix's honour. In 1970, it would have seemed inconceivable that Mercury's own death would eclipse that of Hendrix, but on the morning after his demise, the *Sun*'s front page was a photograph of the singer, a Union Jack flag fanned out across his shoulders, with the headline 'FREDDIE IS DEAD'. Tabloids, broadsheets, television and radio reports alike treated the story with a mix of gravitas and prurient fascination. It was a very twenty-first-century affair, a portent of the celebrity culture to come.

Despite almost fifty journalists and photographers camped outside Garden Lodge, the news of Mercury's death was not made public straight away. On Sunday evening, his doctor Gordon Atkinson had told his friends that the singer's death was imminent, but that he was likely to survive for another few days. Just minutes after Atkinson left, Mercury died. Joe Fanelli ran from the house to flag down Atkinson's car, unintentionally alerting the press.

On the certificate, signed by Atkinson, the cause of death would be given as 'Bronchopneumonia b. AIDS'. Peter Freestone had filled in the rest of the document. Tellingly, he wrote the singer's name as 'Frederick Mercury otherwise Frederick Bulsara'. There was no mention of his real birth name, Farrokh.

In his own account of that night, it was also Freestone who broke the news via telephone to Mary Austin, Mercury's parents and Jim Beach, who had flown to Los Angeles a day earlier. Another decision was taken: a statement announcing Freddie's death would be released by the Queen office, but not until midnight. Freestone's father was a funeral director in nearby Ladbroke Grove, and arranged to collect the body. The police were told what had happened, and a temporary roadblock was set up to delay the press for a few vital minutes while the undertaker's van made its getaway.

With his family and closest friends already informed, Mercury's bandmates were told. 'I was numb the first night after it happened,' said Brian May later. 'We all met and talked. Then the next day I fell to pieces completely; couldn't do anything; crying.' Sure enough, Mercury's droll quip to the guitarist that his death would be good for business came to pass. EMI held off for a few days before releasing Brian May's new single 'Driven By You', a song that had first soundtracked a TV ad for Ford cars. It went to number 6.

At the agreed time, Queen released their statement to the press: 'We have lost the greatest and most beloved member of our family. We feel overwhelming grief that he has gone, sadness that he should be cut down at the height of his creativity, but above all, great pride in the courageous way that he lived and died . . . As soon as we are able we would like to celebrate his life in the style to which he was accustomed.'

Peter Hince was now a photographer, and had taken pictures of Mercury for his solo albums. Unaware that Freddie had AIDS, Hince had been considering sending the singer a jokey card ('Hurry up and get better, you old bastard . . . or something like that') on the night he died. He'd last seen Mercury at Queen's twentieth anniversary celebrations. 'Freddie was two people,' he says. 'You could only get so close to him, and he never let his emotions overtake him. When I worked with him, it would get through to me from other people, "Oh, he's so happy with you, he'd never go on tour without you." But he'd never tell me that to my face. But when he died it was a huge part of my life gone.'

For those that had known Mercury when he was still Fred

Bulsara, it was a curious experience. 'There was always that feeling,' says one old friend. 'Should you have made the phone call? Should you have tried to stay in touch? But life gets in the way, and his life was so different from ours. You don't want to be the hanger-on. There were times when I saw him on TV and wondered if he was the same person I had known all those years ago.'

In one of his usual glib exchanges with the press, Mercury had said that after his death he 'wanted to be buried with all my treasures, like Tutankhamen'. In reality, Mercury told his friends that he wanted to be cremated. The singer had abandoned his Zoroastrian faith, along with his birth name and so much of his past, but in keeping with Parsee tradition and with his parents' wishes, a service was arranged as quickly as possible for 10 a.m. on Wednesday, 27 November in West London Crematorium, Kensal Green.

The day before the funeral, the *Daily Mirror* ran a front-page story from Dave Clark, under the headline 'FREDDIE: THE LAST MOMENTS'. Inside, Clark was pictured in the doorway of Garden Lodge, surrounded by bouquets of flowers from grieving fans. The story claimed – untruthfully, said others – that the singer's bedroom had been fitted with an oxygen tent and that round-the-clock nurses had been hired to ease his suffering. Alongside Clark's story was another from Mary Austin, the woman who, said the *Mirror*, 'regarded herself as Freddie's wife'. Mary revealed the singer's physical decline during his final hours: 'He couldn't even speak, and his sight faded fast . . .' She also explained that she had been the one that had broken the news of his death to Mercury's parents. Aspects of both stories rankled with some, not least Jim Hutton. Yet there would be more disagreements and contradictions to come.

The complex nature of both Mercury's private life and Queen's relationship with the press was highlighted on the day of the funeral. Queen may have complained that the press had hounded Mercury in the final weeks of his life, but the Queen office had still arranged for the celebrity photographer Richard Young to take pictures before and after the service at Garden Lodge; a decision that irked Hutton ('Our last private moments were taken from us'). Young was one of the few photographers the band trusted, though Brian May complained after he had sold a photo of May with Anita Dobson at one of Mercury's private parties.

Instead of Hutton, Mary Austin requested that Dave Clark share the first funeral car with her. Hutton, Freestone and Fanelli would be relegated to another vehicle. Barbara Valentin, the only other significant woman in Mercury's life in recent years, had been told not to attend, and stayed in Munich at the apartment she and Mercury had bought together.

Around forty-five guests made up of Mercury's bandmates, family and friends, including Elton John, gathered for the service. Outside, the grounds of the crematorium were covered with a carpet of wreaths and bouquets from Queen fans. Inside, two Parsee priests, chanting prayers in Avestan, an ancient language used in Zoroastrian scriptures, conducted the twenty-minute service. As one newspaper pointed out, under Parsee law, a dead body would 'traditionally be left to be picked clean by vultures'. Less dramatically, Mercury's coffin was carried into the crematorium to the sound of Aretha Franklin. He exited to a recording of Montserrat Caballé performing 'D'Amor Sull'Ali Rosee' from Verdi's *Il Trovatore*. 'I've lived a full life and if I'm dead tomorrow, I don't give a damn,' Mercury had once told an interviewer. 'I've lived. I really have done it all.'

The day after the funeral, the *Daily Mirror*'s firebrand critic Joe Haines wrote a column denouncing Mercury as 'a man bent – the apt word in the circumstances – on abnormal sexual pleasures, corrupt, corrupting and a drug taker', before concluding that 'his private life is a revolting tale of depravity, lust and downright wickedness . . . For his kind, AIDS is a form of suicide.'

Queen had optimistically hoped that Mercury's death would help raise understanding of the illness. But there was still too much of a stigma, too much fear, for that to happen so easily. In the days that followed, Brian May took great exception to the press's claim that AIDS was exclusively 'a gay disease'. 'They were saying things like, "Fred got AIDS because he was promiscuous, the rest of us needn't worry,"' he complained. 'To print this stuff is going to make a few kids think, "I'm OK", and the next day they'll be HIV positive.'

May's frustration was behind his decision to be interviewed in the week after the funeral. May and Roger Taylor appeared on the breakfast show TV-AM, fielding questions from presenter Mike Morris and looking as if they were still struggling to make sense of what had happened. 'We get very angry about how he is represented in the tabloid press,' protested May. 'He wasn't wildly promiscuous or consumed by drugs.' Their task of convincing the world was made more difficult by Freddie's own fabulous bon mots ('I'm just an old slag who wakes up in the morning, scratches his head and wonders who he wants to fuck'), many of which were gleefully reproduced in the newspapers. Mercury had worked so hard at creating his persona that many in the outside world struggled to equate the larger-than-life presence they saw onstage with the 'shy, kind, gentle person' May was trying to describe.

May and Taylor were adamant that Mercury wanted the world to know he had AIDS to raise awareness; both took the time to condemn the homophobia in much of the press coverage. But it was also obvious how much pressure Mercury's earlier need for secrecy had placed on his bandmates. 'Freddie made a decision very early on in his life that he was going to do things his way,' said May. 'We respected he would handle his own life. But we were gagged by that, and so you find yourself not being able to talk about that to friends . . .' 'You give the impression none of you really knew him,' ventured Mike Morris. Taylor's answer summed up the Queen mindset: 'He was a mystery . . . but we feel absolutely honour-bound to stick up for him.' To his credit, May also made clear that Mercury had been in 'a stable, loving relationship . . . and had three guys who were very caring who were with him until the very end. But nobody mentions that.' It was a rare public acknowledgement of his friends and carers at Garden Lodge.

The interview offered one moment of dark comedy, when the cameras panned back to reveal the show's other guest, TV magician Paul Daniels. 'Were you a fan of Queen and Freddie Mercury, Paul?' asked Morris' co-host Kathryn Holloway rather earnestly. 'Er . . . no,' he shrugged, before launching into a rambling explanation of how most pop music had passed him by.

As well as righting the wrongs of the press, May and Taylor had also appeared on GM-TV to promote 'Bohemian Rhapsody'. Queen's most famous single had been re-released with all proceeds to be donated to the Terrence Higgins Trust. It would reach number 1, raising £1 million for the AIDS charity. Before long, ten of Queen's studio albums would also be back in the UK Top 100.

In America, there was now speculation that Hollywood Records had known about Mercury's condition before signing Queen. Interviewed by Bruce Haring for his 1996 book, *Off the Record: Ruthless Days and Reckless Nights Inside the Music Industry*, Hollywood's then label president Peter Paterno admitted that he had been aware of the rumours about Mercury's health but insisted that Jim Beach had never told him outright that Freddie was sick. 'He [Beach] said that Mercury would not tour. He made that absolutely clear that Queen would not tour,' said Paterno. 'Honestly, I felt the catalogue was good. So you sit there and go, "Okay. It's something I believe in musically, and there's two possibilities: either he isn't sick, in which case maybe I can convince them to tour, which means I will sell some records; or he's really sick and he may die." I was willing to take the risk one way or another.'

Hollywood had begun reissuing Queen's back catalogue on CD in February 1991, believing that that they needed to sell 2.7 million Queen albums to break even on their $10 million deal. By the time of Mercury's death, they were on target with 1.1 million units sold. As Paterno told Bruce Haring: 'When he died, sales accelerated to the point where it became clear that within three years we were going to get our money back.'

Christmas 1991 brought a victory, albeit a hollow one, with 'Bohemian Rhapsody' and *Queen's Greatest Hits II* both at number 1. Before long, the single's B-side – the wistful 'These Are the Days of Our Lives' – was being played on the radio more than its A-side. It seemed more appropriate than the endless 'Bismillahs!' and 'Galileos!' 'It was a very strange time for us,' recalled Taylor. 'We hardly noticed what the record was doing.'

For Freddie Mercury's former friends and employees, the end of the year brought the realisation that everything in their lives had now changed. Hutton, Fanelli and Freestone were remembered in Mercury's will and received a tax-free sum of £500,000 each, and

Mercury's driver Terry Giddings was given £100,000. Mercury had already bought Fanelli a house and Hutton a plot of land in Ireland. The gardener's relationship with the singer had lasted for over five years, but Hutton had always known that almost everything else would be left to Mary Austin.

In the end, Mary inherited Garden Lodge and a fifty per cent share of Mercury's estate (valued at approximately £10 million) and his future income. The remainder of his estate was split evenly between his parents and his sister. Initially, Hutton had been told it was Mercury's wish that the three friends stay on at Garden Lodge for as long as they wanted. However, Mercury, it seems, neglected to write this into his will. With Mary inheriting the house, Hutton and the others were asked to leave.

Peter Freestone would train as a nurse, before moving, for a time, into the hotel industry, and since becoming a regular at Queen fan club conventions. Seven years after Mercury's death, he published a book, *Freddie Mercury: An Intimate Memoir*, about his time working for the singer. Joe Fanelli returned to the United States, but died of AIDS in 1992. The disease would strike down many of Mercury's other friends, ex-lovers and associates. Jim Hutton moved back to Ireland and published his own book, *Mercury and Me*, in 1994. It included a highly dramatic account of his ex-lover's dying days, and was not uncritical of Mary Austin, Dave Clark, Jim Beach and others within the inner circle. To the end, Hutton insisted that Mercury had never consented to news of his disease being made public. Ultimately, Jim's experience seemed to underline the impossible nature of Freddie's relationships. Hutton was the man with whom Mercury had shared the last years of his life, but he could still never compete with his lover's ex-girlfriend from years earlier. Although he had tested HIV positive in 1990, advances in AIDS medication allowed Hutton to enjoy the years denied to Mercury and Fanelli. He died of lung cancer on New Year's Day 2010.

Mary Austin moved into her palatial new home with her two young sons and then partner, the interior designer Piers Cameron, in 1992. But the relationship she'd had with Mercury, who was also a godfather to her eldest son, overshadowed her relationship with Cameron, and the couple split. For five years, she left Mercury's bedroom at Garden Lodge untouched. 'I lost somebody who I thought was my eternal love,' Austin told writer David Wigg. 'When Freddie died I felt we'd had a marriage. We'd lived our vows. We'd done it for better for worse, for richer for poorer. In sickness and in health. You could never have let go of Freddie unless he died. Even then it was difficult.'

For the rest of Queen, Mercury was a similarly tough act to follow. During their GM-TV interview, May and Taylor had spoken of 'some kind of event' to honour the singer. In February, they made an official announcement at the BRITs, where they had just picked up an award for 'These Are the Days of Our Lives'. The Freddie Mercury Tribute: A Concert for AIDS Awareness would be staged at Wembley Stadium on 20 April. The remaining members of Queen would perform, with a changing cast of guest musicians and vocalists. All 72,000 tickets for the event sold out in just six hours.

By March, rehearsals were underway in Shepherd's Bush. The Queen trio were joined by keyboard player Spike Edney and, on the day, extra players, including Mike Moran and Black Sabbath's Tony Iommi. In a curious role reversal, May, Taylor and Deacon now found themselves cast as a collective 'Bob Geldof', recruiting guest singers for the show, just as Geldof had recruited Queen for Live Aid. Before long, Live Aid veterans Elton John, David Bowie, Roger Daltrey and Robert Plant had committed to the show, as did Geldof himself.

Mercury's early vocal heroes and rivals would also be joined by younger musicians that had grown up on his music, including the hard rock bands Def Leppard, Metallica, Extreme and Guns N' Roses. As the weeks passed, the line-up would grow to include George Michael, Seal, Lisa Stansfield, Annie Lennox, Liza Minnelli . . . The artistes were free to choose their own Queen songs, but as Taylor pointed out, 'We thought it appropriate that nobody should do "Another One Bites the Dust" because . . . that was rather unfortunate phrasing there.' In another parallel with Live Aid, the concert would be televised live around the world to seventy-six countries. With the remainder of Queen still grieving their loss, the gig offered something else: a distraction. 'I threw all my energy and all my persuasive, telephonic powers into helping to organise the show,' admitted May. 'So that was good for about three months and it kept my mind off what on earth I was going to do.'

'Freddie would have said, "Darling, Wembley Stadium? Are you sure it's big enough?"' joked Roger Taylor. On the day, the stadium was filled to its furthest tier with the old, the young, the Queen faithful, the curious observer, and those who, in the years since Live Aid, had flocked to the stadium for every major music act from Madonna to Queen to Springsteen.

Queen's survivors strode out on stage to rapturous applause. 'We are here today to celebrate the life and work and dreams of one Freddie Mercury,' announced Brian May. With the hair, the sunglasses and the drummer's dandyish frock coat, the old Smile duo looked every inch the rock stars-about-town. In contrast, John Deacon resembled a former rock star already embracing his retirement – his hair cut short, his clothes unassuming, his voice, when he finally spoke, quiet and understated.

The show's opening act was Metallica, rattling through three hits from their recent *Black Album*. A number 1 seller on both sides of the Atlantic, it was a heavy metal record that had sold to those outside the core constituency. Metallica were an Anglophile rock band who knew their way around Queen albums such as *Sheer Heart Attack*. But they were also on their way to become one of the biggest rock bands in the world. It's doubtful whether Mercury was ever a fan, but Metallica were a huge draw for TV.

The first Queen song of the day came from the second band on the bill, Extreme. Like Metallica, the Boston group had also crossed over to a pop audience. Their music owed a giant debt to Queen's, reflected in a medley that included 'Keep Yourself Alive' and 'Bicycle Race'. Lead singer Gary Charone bravely began the performance with a snippet from 'Mustapha', Mercury's half-Arabic vocal extravaganza from the *Jazz* album.

Brian May would be the first of Queen to break cover, dashing onstage to join Def Leppard for a faithful version of 'Now I'm Here'. Later, blurring the lines between parody and what U2's Bono once called 'the brainless swamp of big-label rock music', spoof band

Spinal Tap's arrival brought some welcome humour to pro-ceedings. The band said they had been asked to 'cut their set short by twenty-five songs to one . . .' Their quip that 'Freddie would have wanted it this way' was an uncomfortable reminder of some of the well-meant, if glib platitudes heard since the singer's death.

During the interval, video footage of Mercury in action was screened on either side of the stage, prompting hysterical applause. But it was the show's second half that contained its most memorable moments, as guest vocalists stepped up to join Queen. It was curious to see Robert Plant trying, and failing, to master 'Innuendo'. The Led Zeppelin singer was gracious in defeat. 'I went to Morocco one Easter and I had the lyrics taped to the dashboard of my car trying to memorise them,' he said later. 'Freddie had said they'd written it as a tribute to Zeppelin, but I couldn't get my head around the words. I ended up with a huge lyric sheet taped to the stage . . . I think they cut my performance out of the video.' They did. Then again, as Plant declared earlier, 'Freddie sang all of these songs better than we're going to sing them.'

Plant wasn't alone. There was enough goodwill from an audience caught up in the excitement of the day to carry even the shakier performers through. But it was a sign of how idiosyncratic Mercury's music was that several oldtimers came unstuck. Peter Hince had returned to the Queen camp to work at the tribute concert. 'It emphasised how great Freddie was as a singer,' he says now. 'Roger Daltrey and Lisa Stansfield did a good job.' Stansfield would memorably appear onstage in hair curlers, pushing a vacuum cleaner for 'I Want to Break Free'. 'But so many people were not worthy . . . Paul Young was appalling.' Young at least had the chance to witness, first hand, thousands of pairs of hands clapping in unison to 'Radio Ga Ga'. 'Freddie was so demanding of himself,' adds John Brough. 'He'd come in sing and do backing vocals, and it could take three hours, but that was the norm. It was only when other people were doing the tribute concert that I saw how difficult it really was.'

With emotions running high, it was inevitable that someone would take everything, including themselves, too seriously. David Bowie did not disappoint. Bowie was joined by Annie Lennox for

'Under Pressure', and Mott The Hoople's Ian Hunter and Mick Ronson for 'All the Young Dudes', before finishing with his own hit, 'Heroes?' It was a sterling performance. Before leaving the stage, the singer began a rambling soliloquy about 'our great friend Freddie Mercury . . . and your friends, our friends . . . members of your families . . . that have been toppled by this relentless disease.'

Amid all the musical hubris, it was a reminder of the life-and-death issue that had prompted the concert. But then, as Bowie later explained, 'I felt as if I was being transported by the situation.' After his speech, he dropped to one knee and begun reciting the Lord's Prayer. Bowie later proudly claimed that members of Spinal Tap watching had been rendered 'speechless with disbelief'. The subsequent footage certainly captured the look of disbelief on Roger Taylor's face. Gracious as ever, Brian May would only comment: 'I remember thinking it would have been nice if he'd warned me about that.'

Just as Queen had stolen Live Aid, the tribute show would have its own outright winner. Mercury had taken time to praise George Michael during his last ever radio interview. Since the end of his pop duo Wham!, Michael had carved out a reputation as a serious songwriter and solo performer. On the night, his performance of 'Somebody to Love', aided in no small part by the London Community Gospel Choir, came close to matching Mercury's for verve, energy and pure showmanship. 'George Michael was the best,' agreed May. 'There's a certain note in his voice when he did "Somebody to Love" that was pure Freddie.'

'Freddie loved the George Michael track "Faith",' recalls John Brough. 'I remember talking to George about that after the tribute concert, and he said that "Somebody to Love" was the most difficult song he had ever sung in his life. He said, "It's ridiculous. One minute it's up here, one minute it's down there . . ."' 'I was living out a childhood fantasy,' said Michael later. 'It was the proudest moment of my career, but mixed with real sadness.' At that time, George had still not discussed his homosexuality in public. A year after the tribute concert, his then-secret boyfriend would die of an AIDS-related illness.

Elizabeth Taylor had, supposedly, been among those rattling

their jewellery in the VIP seats at Queen's last show in Los Angeles. The Hollywood legend, now sixty years old, ramped up the celebrity count no end when she arrived onstage at Wembley, 'not to sing' as she assured the crowd, but to offer advice. 'Use a condom!' she implored them. 'The world needs you to live.' It was a heartfelt sentiment, but even to an audience in which many, no doubt staunchly heterosexual males had been moved to tears by Freddie Mercury's memory, Taylor's speech was a step too far. Traditional British cynicism, buoyed perhaps by the thousands of pints of lager sold during the day, took over, and the audience's catcalls and laughter were clearly audible amid the applause.

For some in the Freddie Mercury camp, Guns N' Roses' lead singer Axl Rose was the concert's unwanted guest. Guns N' Roses thrived on their reputation as latter-day hellraisers in the Stones/Led Zeppelin tradition. But their singer had been accused of racism and homophobia after their song 'One in a Million' mentioned 'immigrants' and 'faggots'. Axl Rose's presence on the bill was deemed controversial. It was a shock, then, to see him walk out onstage alongside Elton John to perform 'Bohemian Rhapsody'.

'I'm a big fan of Axl,' insisted Brian May. 'He's a mouthpiece for honest feelings which he shares with all sorts of other people. The fact that he speaks honestly about being scared of gays is actually very valuable, and the fact that he came out when he did our concert and said, "I'm doing this because I feel for Freddie and because I feel that this issue involves everybody."'

In Axl Rose, Elton had also achieved the seemingly impossible and found a rock star with a temperament to match his own. Earlier in the day, he had been unceremoniously turned away from Rose's dressing room, while complaining loudly 'But I've got to do a duet with him in two hours!' On the night, the pair acquitted themselves well; Rose's midriff-revealing T-shirt and leather skirt suggesting he was perhaps more in touch with his feminine side than some might have thought. While Rose scampered across the stage like an over-enthusiastic puppy, Elton played the role of the elder statesman, even putting an arm around him during the song's closing verse.

Yet even Rose's leather skirt couldn't match the grand finale for high camp. That prize fell to the concert's final act Liza Minnelli, coincidentally now signed to Hollywood Records, who turned 'We Are the Champions' into a showstopping Broadway show tune, now featuring a ramshackle choir of hirsute rockers, both young and old. While Minnelli emoted outfront, Roger Daltrey, Axl Rose, various members of Extreme, Metallica and the German heavy metal band Scorpions (who hadn't played but showed up anyway) appeared behind her, arms around each other's shoulders: a giant, swaying backdrop of fringed leather, polka-dot shirt-tails and split ends. It was an image that captured the very essence of Freddie Mercury and Queen: that strange place where spit-and-sawdust heavy rock met musical theatre. As *The Times*' critic later wrote: 'Liza Minnelli proved in her brilliant finale rendition that Freddie was a cabaret diva in trousers.'

Yet *The Times* also posed the question: 'What would the man himself have made of it?' There was no sign of Mercury's beloved Aretha Franklin, but then she'd also turned down a request to play Live Aid, as had Michael Jackson. Montserrat Caballé, the opera singer who had made such a musical impact on Mercury's final days, had also been unable to attend. Peter Hince maintains that some of those present instead were there for their own aims. 'I'm sure some of them were thinking, "I can get my career back on course,"' he sighs. 'It was almost like Celebrity Big Brother.'

Yet, as Roger Taylor explained, the show had been meant as a 'dual-purpose event'. It had achieved its aims: celebrating Mercury's life and music, and raising awareness of the disease that had killed him. Profits from the Wembley concert and its later video release would be donated to the Mercury Phoenix Trust, the AIDS charity established the year before, which listed May, Taylor, Jim Beach and Mary Austin as its trustees.

Staging the Wembley concert had preoccupied Queen's remaining members for months. The question they faced now was: what next? John Deacon dropped out of view and returned to family life; his wife Veronica was now pregnant with the couple's fifth child. (A son, Luke, was born in December that year.) For May and Taylor, giving up would not be so easy.

In April, Queen had bagged an Ivor Novello award for 'These Are the Days of Our Lives', but May had also been awarded his own Novello for 'Driven By You'. *Back to the Light*, his first solo album since 1983, was now close to completion. In the meantime, Taylor had finally called time on The Cross. Their final album, 1991's *Blue Rock*, had been pieced together while the drummer was working on Queen's final sessions, and he had taken a back seat, even allowing his bandmates to take many of the lead vocals. But *Blue Rock* had only been released in Europe, not in the UK. Taylor had also started a family with Debbie Leng, who had given birth to their son, Rufus Tiger, in March 1991. May summed up their shared situation: 'Apart from the grief of losing someone so close, suddenly your whole way of life is destroyed. All that you have tried to build up for the last twenty years is gone.' Elton John went one better: 'For May, Deacon and Taylor, it must be like keeping a fabulous Ferrari in the garage and not being able to drive.'

Meanwhile, there were reminders everywhere. In May that year, the US teen-comedy film *Wayne's World* gave Queen's profile its biggest boost yet in the US. The movie, a spin-off from a regular sketch on NBC's comedy show *Saturday Night Live*, charted the misadventures of a pair of suburban teenage rock fans, Wayne Campbell and Garth Algar. In one momentous scene, the duo and two of their friends drove through their neighbourhood with 'Bohemian Rhapsody' playing on the car's cassette deck. The foursome's karaoke vocals and headbanging routine became a huge hit.

Wayne Campbell had been played by the comedian and writer Mike Myers who had lived in London in the 1980s. He knew Queen's music, and had contacted Brian May about using 'Bohemian Rhapsody'. 'Mike Myers phoned me up and sent me a copy and said, "You make sure Freddie hears it,"' said May in 2010. 'Freddie was already not well by that time but I took it round to him and he loved it.' The singer had also hoped that the song's performance in the movie might give Queen the break they needed in the US. As he told May at the same time: 'I suppose I have to fucking die before we ever get big in America again.'

In the end, it was *Wayne's World*, more than Freddie's death, which revived Queen's American fortunes. 'Bohemian Rhapsody' was re-released in the US and went to number 2 (the proceeds donated to the Magic Johnson AIDS Trust, named after the HIV-positive basketball player). Another compilation, *Classic Queen*, followed the single to number 4. Meanwhile, in England, Montserrat Caballé, backed by the European Chamber Opera, gave a charity performance of Mercury's favourite opera, *Il Trovatore*, at London's Whitehall. Mercury and Caballé's 'Barcelona' single was re-released to celebrate the city's hosting of the 1992 Olympics, giving the duo a Top 5 hit.

In September, Brian May released *Back to the Light*. 'I wanted to make this record on my own, with nobody else to argue with, just to see what happened,' he explained. May's last solo release, *Star Fleet Project*, had been an exercise in guitar virtuosity; the songs on this one were more contemplative. One track, 'Nothing But Blue', was about Mercury, and had been completed the night before his death; another, 'I'm Scared', found May reeling off a list of extraordinary fears and insecurities. The album went Top 20 in Britain, while the first single, an earnest ballad titled 'Too Much Love Will Kill You', which May had premiered at the tribute concert, became a Top 5 hit. With a South American tour, supporting Joe Cocker, in the offing, May now faced the challenge of fronting his own live band.

May's touring party included Spike Edney, bassist Neil Murray, guitarist Mike Caswell (later replaced by Jamie Moses) and showman drummer Cozy Powell, with May as lead guitarist and lead vocalist. 'I'll never be Freddie – he was the ultimate stadium rock singer,' he explained. 'A few years ago, I don't think I would have even tried to front a band. It would have been too intimidating. My role now is to be me.' May fought through his nerves and proved an able frontman. The tour's penultimate gig found them opening at Buenos Aires' Vélez Sársfield, where Queen had headlined their historic Argentinean show in 1981.

In death, though, as in life, it seemed as if Freddie Mercury would have the last word. With May on tour, EMI released *The Freddie Mercury Album*, a compilation of remixed solo tracks. The album and a remix of 'Living On My Own' would put the late singer back into the UK Top 5 singles and albums charts. Another live album, *Queen at Wembley Stadium*, went to number 2. With a VHS release for the Freddie Mercury Tribute concert also out in time for Christmas, and a brief Smile reunion at London's Marquee club, 1992 became one of Queen's busiest years yet.

May's need to keep working found him back on the road the following February. The Brian May Band had been booked for a US tour, but some theatre shows were badly attended. Drafted as a support act to Guns N' Roses, May found himself playing bigger venues, but at the mercy of the headliners' volatile lead singer. After a contretemps with their sound engineer in Birmingham, Alabama, Axl Rose flounced off and refused to finish the gig. The next few dates were immediately cancelled.

When the tour resumed, The Brian May Band would often arrive onstage to rows of empty seats, as fans, slurping on soft drinks and chewing hot dogs, drifted in and out. In March, they played the Boston Winter Gardens; a venue in a city that Queen had once owned. 'For the first time in twenty years, I'm going out in front of people who really need to be shown what I do,' said May. 'It's a question of being very patient, which is very, very different from what I'm used to.' Brian was insistent that he didn't want the gigs to be a 're-hash of a Queen show'. But he faced the same problem encountered by the likes of Robert Plant and Mick Jagger before him: how to escape the shadow of his former band. As the *Boston Globe* reported: 'Although some of the new material has a nice kick to it, it was the Queen classics, "Hammer to Fall" and "Now I'm Here", that fared best.'

In May, the band returned to headline throughout Europe and the UK, including two nights at London's Brixton Academy, which would be recorded for a live album. Barely pausing for breath, May led them back to North America in October for another headline tour. Between shows, he graciously fielded questions from the press about Freddie Mercury, while revealing more about his personal life than he'd ever done before: how the end of Queen as a touring band, the death of his father and the break-up of his first marriage had left him 'very unhinged'. If playing live was, as he put it, 'a great therapy', there were still drawbacks. The Brian May Band were not

Queen, and The Danforth Music Hall in downtown Toronto was not the same as the city's Maple Leaf Gardens, where Queen had once headlined two nights. Smaller audiences, smaller venues, even smaller dressing rooms . . . It was a sobering experience.

More than a year after his death, the posthumous Freddie Mercury/Queen industry rolled on. *The Five Live* EP, featuring George Michael and Queen's version of 'Somebody to Love', raced to number 1; Mercury's childhood stamp collection, once pored over by his first English friends at Isleworth Polytechnic, was sold at Sotheby's auction house for £8,000, while India heralded Freddie as 'The First Asian Pop Star'; a role he had, frankly, never acknowledged in his lifetime.

There was still one other unresolved issue. There was enough material in the vaults for Mercury's bandmates to consider releasing another Queen album. A prescient Roger Taylor referred to the dormant Queen album as 'the difficult child'. Interviewed on Virgin Radio in June 1993, Brian May told the DJ Richard Skinner that 'there is a bit of material, but probably not enough for a whole album', admitting that the whole issue of another Queen record was 'something we don't find it easy to agree about at the moment'. Not for the first time, May would insist that 'there cannot be a Queen without Freddie'.

However, in September, with May away on tour, Taylor and John Deacon had played together at a charity gig at West Sussex's Cowdray Park. In the New Year, the pair booked a studio and began sifting through Queen's leftover songs. At some point they began adding drums and bass to the material. At which point, Brian May stepped in. 'The remaining new material is very precious stuff,' he said in spring 1994. 'The most important consideration is that this final collection must be worthy of the name Queen, so I've been delving very deep.' Later, May would admit: 'I took the tapes off them [Deacon and Taylor], felt that they'd done it wrong, and spent months putting it all back together.' It was a process that would carry on until the early part of the following year. But May had relented: there *would* be another Queen album.

In May 1994, BBC radio listeners voted 'Bohemian Rhapsody' number 1 in their All-Time Top 100 Songs. In the same month,

Roger Taylor released a new solo single. The track, 'Nazis 1994', was unlikely to make even the staunchest fans' All-Time Top 100 Songs. 'I thought at my stage in life I might as well write about something I believed, that meant something,' he explained, adding, 'You can't write pop songs all your life.'

'Nazis 1994' was an attack on Holocaust deniers and the recent rise of far right politics. However good its intentions, it was hamstrung by some extremely poor lyrics, and open to mis-interpretation. Asked what he thought of the song, Brian May was guarded. 'You have to be clear what signals you put out,' he said. 'If you say a word like "Nazis", people's ideas are triggered. You can't make subtle statements like that in our market. It's a pity because Roger's message was the opposite from how it was perceived.'

In September, Taylor followed the single with another solo album, *Happiness?*, recorded in his newly built home studio, Cosford Mill. Taylor's concerns ranged from fascism, to the starving poor, to personal alienation. Like Brian May's 'Nothing But Blue', one song, 'Old Friends', was inspired by Mercury, while 'Dear Mr Murdoch' was a tirade against the media mogul Rupert Murdoch, whose newspaper the *Sun* had been among Mercury's most ardent pursuers. Sales were encouraging, and *Happiness?* shifted more copies than any of The Cross albums, persuading Taylor to go out on what would be his first solo tour, playing Europe, the UK and Queen's old stronghold Japan. Songs from the new record would be mixed with 'A Kind of Magic', 'Radio Ga Ga', 'I Want to Break Free', 'We Will Rock You' . . . And it was that back catalogue which always drew the biggest applause of the night.

In the summer of 1995, after months of speculation, Queen announced their plans to release another album. 'It has not been easy,' confessed John Deacon. 'As Roger, Brian and myself see things differently, and coming to an agreement between us takes time.' Queen immediately invited members of their fan club to suggest titles for the album. Roger Taylor's friends from Cornwall, Pat and Sue Johnstone, had started Queen's fan club in 1973. Since 1982, the club had been run by Jacky Smith (née Gunn), who had co-authored with Queen expert Jim Jenkins, the group's semi-official biography, *Queen: As It Began*.

In the end, the album would be titled *Made in Heaven*, after one of its songs. But the title also seemed like a mawkish acknowledgement of the circumstances in which it had been made. *Made in Heaven* would run to thirteen complete songs, with one track, 'Yeah', lasting just four seconds. 'It was like doing a jigsaw puzzle,' May told *Q* magazine. 'But I wouldn't have put my seal of approval on it if I hadn't thought it was up to standard.' The jigsaw had been assembled from more than a decade's worth of material by a crack production team of Queen, David Richards, Justin-Shirley Smith and Joshua J. Macrae. The oldest song, 'It's a Beautiful Day', was a relic from 1980's *The Game*; the newest, 'Mother Love', had been from Mercury's final recording session, and was an incredibly assured vocal performance from what had been a dying man. The song's closing seconds were said to include sped-up snippets of every Queen song ever recorded

Ultimately, it was Mercury who saved the day. Even the weakest material was salvaged by that voice. The Mercury-sung versions of Roger Taylor's 'Heaven for Everyone' and May's recent hit single, 'Too Much Love Will Kill You' knocked both originals into a cocked hat. The rest of the album was a tribute to his bandmates' and producers' diligence. Somehow, they had laboriously stitched it all together to make a coherent record. 'It was a huge job,' admitted Brian May. 'Two years of my life finding a way of developing the songs, but at the same time using the limited input we had from Freddie. Sometimes there was just a complete first-take vocal, while other times there were no more than three or four lines.' May also admitted: 'It took a couple of weeks to get over the sound of Freddie. The worst thing were the little spoken ad-libs between the takes.' The album included a final, hidden track: an instrumental, near-ambient piece of music that lasted for over twenty-two minutes on the CD version, and ended with Mercury's voice uttering the single word 'Fab'. The front cover artwork showed a silhouette of sculptor Irena Sedlecka's statue of the singer, which was officially unveiled at Lake Geneva the following year. In the absence of conventional promo videos, Queen had also commissioned directors from the British Film Institute to produce short films to accompany each track.

Released on 6 November 1995, *Made in Heaven* emerged just weeks before The Beatles' posthumous single, 'Free as a Bird'; a John Lennon demo that had been completed by his bandmates and producer Jeff Lynne. Queen would enjoy less of the goodwill extended to The Beatles in what *The Times* called 'the battle of the bands with dead singers'. Of the music papers, *NME* was the most visceral in its criticism: '*Made in Heaven* is vulgar, creepy, sickly and in dubious taste.' It was the circumstances of its creation, the sleight of hand and what *NME* called 'the multi-tracking like mad' that made some reviewers uncomfortable. 'The immediate question must be: what manner of tasteless, barrel-scraping are the surviving members of Queen involved in now?' asked *Q* magazine, before praising *Made in Heaven* as 'a better album than *Innuendo*.'

There was, however, something almost relentless about Queen's latest campaign. Barely a week after the posthumous collection came another box set, *Ultimate Queen*, presented in a wall-mounted case for those fans with especially deep pockets and questionable judgement in home furnishings. On top of this came the Queen video documentary *Champions of the World*, a Channel 4 documentary about Queen, and a BBC Radio 1 special. Showing great foresight, though largely unreported at the time, Queen also launched their own website in November.

Whatever doubt critics and fans may have had about *Made in Heaven*, the evidence suggested that, to quote Spinal Tap at the Mercury tribute concert, 'Freddie would have wanted it.' Interviewed in German *Rolling Stone*, co-producer David Richards insisted, 'If he [Freddie] wouldn't have wanted this album so badly, he wouldn't have recorded so many songs. The fact that Freddie wanted this album finished gave us strength.' Brian May followed the same partyline. But with some reservations. 'The last album is one of the most ridiculously painful experiences creatively I have ever had,' he told Radio 1. 'But I'm sure the quality's good, partly because we did have those arguments. Whether it's healthy for life or not is another matter.'

Made in Heaven didn't disappoint the band or EMI. Another number 1 hit, it also yielded five Top 20 UK singles, although one, 'Let Me Live' (conjured out of a snippet of Mercury from 1983), was banned from the BBC Radio 1 playlist on the grounds that Queen were too old for the station's new young demographic. In America, though, *Made in Heaven* only just registered in the Top 60. Brian May's parting shot from 1995 suggested that he planned to move on in his life and career, without Queen: 'Having had twenty years of this very volatile democracy, I don't feel I need it in my life any more.' This would prove easier said than done.

■ ■ ■

Without Queen to distract them, the surviving members went back to real life. For John Deacon, it was an easy transition. His brood now included a sixth child, Cameron, born during the *Made in Heaven* sessions. Asked what he did with himself these days, the lapsed bass player said, 'I am mainly involved with looking after the children at home.' Roger Taylor also had a new addition, a daughter named Tiger Lily, born in 1994, but, before long, he was writing songs for another solo album.

Brian May filled his time with guest spots, tracks for children's movie soundtracks, charity gigs and records, Jimi Hendrix, Shadows and Mott The Hoople tribute albums . . . It was Mott The Hoople's ex-keyboard player Morgan Fisher that approached May for the tribute disc. 'R.E.M. and Aerosmith were supposedly up for it,' he chuckles. 'But I was living in Japan and I had no lawyer, no management . . . So it ended up becoming a Japanese Mott The Hoople tribute album with Japanese bands. By then, Brian had already done "All the Way from Memphis". I had to write and say, "Look, I'm sorry, the project's off, I have to do a Japanese one." To his great credit, he came back and said, "Put my song on anyway. I can be your guest foreigner."'

Fisher had toured Europe with Queen in the early 1980s, before being told his services were no longer required. May's involvement with the tribute album was a rapprochement of sorts. Yet when Fisher crossed paths with Roger Taylor at rehearsals for a tribute concert to Mott's late guitarist Mick Ronson, 'there was not much spoken between us.' Then again, as May once put it, 'I've always been too much of a nice guy, I'm such a pleaser. Freddie was never like that. A kid could be waiting outside for five hours, and Freddie would be like, "Oh, fuck off, darling, I need my rest." I'm the nice guy who sits there signing everything that's put in front of me.'

Though nobody knew it at the time, there was also a pattern emerging to some of May's outside work. In October 1991, a month before Mercury's death, Brian had played at the Guitar Legends concert in Seville. For the show's finale, May had joined vocalist Paul Rodgers on a version of Free's 'All Right Now'. Two years on, May had played on Rodgers' album, *Muddy Water Blues: A Tribute to Muddy Waters*. In February 1994, May joined him during his gig at London's Kentish Town Forum, and again that summer at Rodgers' show in Montreux. But it would be some time before both parties chose to make the arrangement more permanent.

In January 1997, the Queen trio made their first public performance together since the Mercury tribute concert. Deacon, May and Taylor joined Elton John to close the opening-night performance of a new ballet, *Le Presbytère (A Ballet For Life)*, partly inspired by Mercury and his fight against AIDS. The quartet would perform 'The Show Must Go On' in Paris at the Théâtre National de Chaillot. Brian May would scoop another Ivor Novello award that year for 'Too Much Love Will Kill You', while the more May-centric end of the Queen songbook was revisited for the *Queen Rocks* compilation album. 'We wanted to remind people that we were always a rock band,' he explained. 'Personally, I'd rather people just bought *Queen II*.' Nevertheless, Deacon, May and Taylor joined forces to record a new song for the compilation. The ballad, 'No One But You (Only The Good Die Young)' was the album's one moment of restraint.

Back at his Allerton Hill home studio, May was completing a new solo album. *Another World* was released in June 1998. It had begun life as a covers record, but ended up containing a mix of original material (including songs originally written for TV and the Gwyneth Paltrow movie, *Sliding Doors*) alongside Mott The Hoople's 'All The Way From Memphis' and Jimi Hendrix's 'One Rainy Wish'. There were special guests, including Jeff Beck, Ian Hunter and Taylor Hawkins, the Queen-worshipping drummer with US rock band Foo Fighters. Just two months before release,

May was holidaying in Africa when he learned that Cozy Powell had been killed in a car accident. It was a dreadful blow. 'I get very depressed quite often,' he admitted, 'and Cozy could always lift you out of it.' He remixed one song, 'The Business', as a tribute to Powell, waspishly telling Q magazine, 'I'm sure that somebody somewhere will complain that I'm trading off his memory.'

With Powell's replacement, Kiss drummer Eric Singer, The Brian May Band went out on the road for the rest of the year, playing the UK, Europe, Russia, Japan and Australia. *Another World* made it into the UK Top 30, selling to ardent Queen fans and guitar aficionados. 'Truthfully, I'd love somebody to come up to me and say, "I love your new record . . . it's new and it's different," ' said May, 'rather than, "How do you do that guitar effect on *A Night at the Opera*?" '

Just two months after May's *Another World*, Roger Taylor returned to the fray. Never shy about making his views known, Taylor had just donated £10,000 to the campaign by Manchester United Supporters Association to stop broadcasting giants BSkyB from taking over their football team. BSkyB was owned by media giant Rupert Murdoch, whom Taylor had savaged in his song 'Dear Mr Murdoch'. Meanwhile, his new album, *Electric Fire*, found him sticking the boot into lazy journalists, greedy lawyers and wife-beaters. The music vaulted from hard rock to pop to ballads to a cover of John Lennon's 'Working Class Hero'; some of it let down by what one music magazine described as 'our host's baffling lyrical conceits'.

Electric Fire was promoted with a concert from the drummer's home studio, re-named The Cyberbarn, and broadcast across the internet. It received a record number of 595,000 online views. In March, the following year, Taylor returned to play a brief UK tour, joined onstage in Wolverhampton by Brian May for 'Under Pressure'. But the album still stalled outside the Top 50. As Taylor pointed out: 'Mick Jagger is one of the biggest stars and he can't sell a solo record.'

Another World's sleeve note had included a dedication to Brian May's personal assistant Julie Glover for 'management, therapy and day care'. Julie had been a mainstay of Queen Productions before working exclusively for the guitarist. It was she who broke the news to May that Freddie Mercury had died. In August 1999, the *Sunday Mirror* ran a story claiming that Brian had been having an affair with Julie ('his glamorous Girl Friday') behind his partner Anita Dobson's back. All parties remained silent over the story, but Glover quit her job soon after.

Before long, another newspaper wrote that May had booked himself into the Cottonwood Clinic in Tucson, Arizona, a retreat describing itself as 'the premiere holistic behavioural health and addiction treatment centre'. The reason: his so-called 'addiction to lover Anita Dobson'. Again, neither May nor Dobson would comment. But in recent interviews May had talked candidly about his emotional problems. 'I was always screwed up about sex,' he told *Mojo*'s David Thomas. 'I got married at totally the wrong time. In the midst of all this, I'm trying to be a husband and a good father to my kids. So that really excluded me from being wildly promiscuous. But emotionally I became utterly out of control, needy for that one-to-one reinforcement, feelings of love and discovery, and that's what I became addicted to.'

It was also odd, if illuminating, to read the guitarist pouring his heart out to a celebrity magazine. 'I've had serious battles with depression,' he told *OK*'s Martin Townsend. 'It sounds stupid, because people think, "Poor little rich bastard." But it doesn't make any difference what your situation is.' Asked about his on-off relationship with Anita Dobson, May volunteered the titbit: 'I didn't think I could ever be with someone that didn't like Led Zeppelin! And the stuff she likes I got dragged into by my heels . . . the whole world of musical theatre made me physically ill . . . and still occasionally does.' Like his earlier statement that 'there cannot be a Queen without Freddie', May's comment about musical theatre would come back to haunt him. Interviewed some years later, May quietly acknowledged the Cottonwood Clinic for helping him out of the depression 'so deep that I had to admit powerlessness, and ask for help'. In November 2000, after spending several months apart, May married Anita Dobson at a private ceremony in Richmond register office.

Away from his troubled private life, the guitarist seemed to spend his free time playing live with anyone that asked:

Motörhead, Foo Fighters, Spike Edney's rock ensemble, the SAS Band . . . EMI managed to squeeze out another Top 5 album with *Queen's Greatest Hits III*, while Roger Taylor enraged 'some crusty old duffers', when his image appeared behind Freddie Mercury's on one of the Royal Mail's Millennium stamps. As one prominent philatelist pointed out: 'The Royal Mail has broken the strict rule that no living person other than a member of the Royal Family may appear on a postage stamp.' Others complained that Mercury, 'a hedonistic gay man', was on a stamp in the first place.

In spring 2000, the Queen duo came back to work together, ruffling feathers by performing 'We Will Rock You' with the all-singing, all-dancing pop group 5ive at the BRIT Awards. Some fans griped about their heroes demeaning themselves by performing with a boy band. Yet the look on both musicians' faces when the stage curtains parted, the dry ice plumed and they crashed into the song's mid-section suggested May and Taylor missed the thrill of playing live.

A single version of 'We Will Rock You' by 5ive and Queen became a number 1 hit that summer, again raising the question of whether Queen would consider working with another singer. Less than a year later, 5ive had gone to boy-band heaven, and Queen turned their attention to Robbie Williams, the refugee singer from Take That, and then riding high with his own solo career.

Williams had been asked to record 'We Are the Champions' for the soundtrack to a romantic action movie, *A Knight's Tale*. 'Robbie said it would be nice to do it with Queen,' explained May. 'So, at two days' notice, we went into the studio and did it — live! We did four takes. Rob sang live and he came up with the goods. It's a controversial thing to do . . . because a lot of Queen fans were like, "Why are they consorting with that person from Take That?" Shock, horror!'

The collaboration was in keeping with the long Queen tradition of doing the unexpected, and upsetting people along the way, including, it seemed, John Deacon. In April 2001, Deacon informed the *Sun*: 'I didn't want to be involved with it, and I'm glad. I've heard what they did and it's rubbish. It's one of the greatest songs ever written, but I think they've ruined it. I don't want to be nasty but let's just say Robbie Williams is no Freddie Mercury. Freddie can never be replaced – and certainly not by him.' Tellingly, Deacon had also been absent a month earlier when Queen were inducted into the Rock & Roll Hall of Fame in New York.

Yet despite stories that Williams had been offered the job of singing with Queen, the trail suddenly went cold. Interviewed in 2005, May said: 'We sat around and downed a fair amount of wine and talked about it, and thought, "Yeah, perhaps we can do this." But it never came to fruition, and I don't know why.' 'We talked about maybe touring America with Robbie,' elaborated Taylor. 'And we were quite serious about it, but circumstances didn't come together. He is very young, much younger than us anyway . . . In retrospect, though, it wouldn't have been a good idea.' It was impossible not to wonder whether John Deacon's public condemnation had contributed to a change of heart.

While Queen wouldn't yet tour with a new singer, they had already found another way to ensure their music's longevity. In March 2001, Brian May had told London's Capital Gold radio station, 'We're doing a musical, and Ben Elton has written us a fantastic script.' The idea for the musical, *We Will Rock You*, dated back to 1996, when May and Taylor had met Hollywood actor Robert De Niro at the Venice Film Festival. De Niro had his own production company, Tribeca, and was intrigued by the idea of a Queen musical. As May explained, it had taken so long for the idea to come to fruition as 'there were so many storylines along the way'. After much deliberation, the initial plan for an autobiographical story was rejected (May: 'too embarrassing'). By which time Ben Elton had been brought on board.

A former comedian, turned novelist and director and one of the writers behind the period comedy *Blackadder*, Elton pitched an original story – 'The Matrix meets Arthurian legend' – that would 'capture the spirit of Queen's music'. Elton's tale was set 300 years in the future, where Earth is now Planet Mall, and ruled by the Globalsoft Corporation, who have banned musical instruments and suppress any individuality, freedom of expression and – of course – rock music. In a nutshell: the ensuing struggle between the musical freedom fighters and 'the man' was sufficient, just, for a trawl through the Queen back catalogue.

We Will Rock You opened at London's Dominion Theatre on 14 May 2002. It was an immediate, unprecedented success, but received a critical savaging on a par with, if not greater, than any meted out to Queen in over thirty years. Much of the critics' ire was directed at what the *Daily Mirror* called 'Ben Elton's risible story'. But audiences thought otherwise. In August 2003, the show had opened in Melbourne before touring the rest of Australia; in November it opened in Madrid . . . By the end of 2005, *We Will Rock You* was playing in Las Vegas, Moscow and Cologne, and had become the longest-running musical in the history of the Dominion Theatre. In 2010 it was still box-office gold, with a sequel planned for the near future.

May and Taylor had suspended whatever their misgivings had been about musical theatre to promote the show, often joining the cast onstage for 'Bohemian Rhapsody'. Gung-ho in the face of criticism ('They're just bitter old journalists'), the pair also insisted that 'Freddie would have loved it.' Ben Elton's story may have been, as the *Daily Mail* put it, 'totally vacuous', but it was hard to imagine Mercury not wanting his music performed in London's West End night after night in front of a new audience, many of whom had never seen Queen play live. For many who had witnessed Queen in their prime, *We Will Rock You* would always be a far tougher sell.

From their involvement with the musical to their solo albums to the duo's collaborations with young pop stars, the evidence suggested that neither May nor Taylor were prepared to go quietly. In June 2002, the duo performed with guests at the Queen's Jubilee Concert at Buckingham Palace. The show began with May playing the National Anthem on the roof of the royal household. 'It was a symbol – for my generation,' he said, 'because when I started off it would have been unthinkable for somebody playing that loud thing, on top of the Queen's Palace.' It was also a sign that May and Taylor were musicians in need of a regular gig.

■ ■ ■

In early 1969, Fred Bulsara had joined his fellow students at Ealing art college's annual rag ball. Held in the local town hall, a gothic building on Ealing Broadway, the musical entertainment was being provided by Free, a blues-rock quartet, fronted by gravel-voiced singer Paul Rodgers. After the gig, Bulsara, hankering after a musical career of his own, hung around, plying the band with questions. Thirty-five years later, Paul Rodgers would succeed the late Fred Bulsara to become Queen's new lead singer. The announcement was made in December 2004. Said Brian May: 'The Queen phoenix is rising from the ashes.'

Three months earlier, Rodgers had joined May onstage in London for the Fender Stratocaster's 50th Anniversary Gig. 'I made the first move,' said the guitarist. 'We talked after the show, and Paul's lady, Cynthia [Kereluk, also his manager] was there and she just stood between us and her eyes went back and forth and she said, "There's something happening here, isn't there?" And we both looked at each other and said, "Well, yes."' When Kereluk suggested that all they now needed was a drummer, May fired back unhesitangly, 'Well, I do know a drummer . . .' Within days, May had sent Roger Taylor a video of the gig. Two months later, Rodgers sang with May and Taylor at London's Hackney Empire for a television performance celebrating Queen's induction in to the UK Rock 'n' Roll Hall of Fame. 'We did "All Right Now" and Brian asked me to play "We Will Rock You" and "We Are the Champions",' recalled Rodgers. 'We knew we were on to something when we rehearsed those three songs and the TV crew gave us a standing ovation.'

According to Rodgers, what began as 'three dates in London' turned into a European tour. Carefully billed as Queen + Paul Rodgers (and given the acronym Q+PR), the trio were joined by old hand Spike Edney, The Brian May Band's guitarist Jamie Moses and bassist Danny Miranda, an American who'd spent the past nine years with heavy rockers Blue Öyster Cult.

Edney was one of the few veterans from past Queen campaigns. The 'Drum', 'Bass' and 'Guitar Departments' that ate, slept and drank side by side with their employers in the 1970s and 1980s had all quit for civilian life: Gerry Stickells had retired, Roger Taylor's

Man Friday, Chris 'Crystal' Taylor was now a landscape gardener, Peter 'Ratty' Hince a photographer ... 'I thought it was interesting that none of the old guard were on the Paul Rodgers tour,' says Hince. 'Queen were a good band to work for in that you were always doing something exciting, they did things that other bands could only dream of, and they were fun to be with. But were they a generous band to work for? No. Were they appreciative? Most of the time, no. Though to give Brian his credit, I think he appreciated us. Brian always had a conscience.'

Queen + Paul Rodgers made their debut on 19 March 2005 in Capetown, at the second concert for Nelson Mandela's 4664 AIDS awareness charity. They opened with 'Tie Your Mother Down', followed by 'Can't Get Enough' from Rodgers' post-Free group Bad Company, before flitting between Queen, Free and Bad Company numbers, closing with the hits, Free's 'All Right Now', 'We Will Rock You' and 'We Are the Champions'. There were the inevitable first-night nerves and fluffed lyrics, but it boded well for the first date in Europe. Just over a week later, Q+PR rolled into London's Brixton Academy, bravely playing in front of an audience largely made up of Queen fan club members.

May and Taylor were a natural fit for the Free and Bad Company songs. Free's 'Tons of Sobs' had been a regular on the turntable at Taylor's flat in Sinclair Gardens. Bad Company's first album had also soundtracked Queen's debut US tour ('Freddie loved Paul Rodgers' voice,' said Brian May, 'but he used to have a go at me in the studio when I tried to have him sing bluesy stuff. He'd say, "Brian, you're trying to make me fucking sound like Paul Rodgers, and I can't do it!" '). The real challenge, though, lay with Rodgers.

The son of a Middlesbrough docker, and steeped in soul and blues, Paul's fervent vocal style had been an inspiration to a generation of rock singers. At fifty-six, he was the right age, with a background and ego that would allow him to go head to head with his new bandmates. 'We couldn't have hired a young unknown, however good, and expected this to work,' said May. 'With Paul, we can find some newness and some way of reinterpreting the past.' But Paul Rodgers wasn't Freddie Mercury. As Taylor pointed out, 'You're a mug not to use your brand name,' but for all its commercial weight, the Queen brand name also came with some heavy emotional baggage.

Taylor had hired a personal trainer to get fit for the tour. Rodgers was already one step ahead. A martial arts black belt, he had long swapped the excesses of his youth for yoga and the gym, and had also acquired a mysteriously youthful hairline compared to a few years before. Paul could twirl a mic stand with the best of them, but as he forewarned Q magazine: 'You'll see dynamism and movement up onstage, but not flamboyance. There'll be no cape – and probably a lack of tights.' Vocally, he made light work of 'Tie Your Mother Down'. But it was peculiar hearing 'Fat Bottomed Girls' and 'I Want to Break Free' without Mercury's camp nuances. Onstage, Queen's late singer would materialise on a video screen performing the intro to 'Bohemian Rhapsody', with Rodgers only taking over the lead vocal during the song's second half. The ghost of Freddie Mercury was everywhere.

After Brixton, the tour moved to the Continent, taking in France, Spain, Germany, Belgium . . . In Italy, Pope John Paul II suffered a heart attack on the day of the first show, throwing it into jeopardy. (It was the second time the Pope had jinxed a Queen tour.) Three days later in Firenze, Rodgers had to sit out most of the gig with a throat infection.

In every interview, May and Taylor would pledge their love of Free and Bad Company, and insist that Freddie would have been happy with his replacement. Fans, critics and old friends were divided. 'Brian loves playing and loves an audience, Roger likes being a pop star and Paul Rodgers was a sensational singer in Free and Bad Company,' offers Peter Hince. 'It was very polished and well orchestrated, but it was a bit Las Vegas.' 'A lot of people will be very angry but I think they may be missing the point,' said Brian. 'Freddie himself would rather enjoy ticking people off – he'd probably say, "Go for it."' However, May revealed he had written to Mercury's mother, asking for her blessing, which she'd given. Taylor explained that John Deacon had been invited to participate, but had declined. 'He has decided to hide away – and I respect that,' he said. 'I think he was a little more fragile and not as well equipped to deal with the rough and tumble of everyday existence. He prefers not to undergo the stress of it all.'

For Rodgers, though, not an interview went by without some question about his predecessor. 'There is no question in my mind of replacing Freddie Mercury,' he said, pointing out that he didn't expect 'Brian May to be [Free's] Paul Kossoff.' But then Rodgers had faced a similar problem in the 1980s, when he'd joined former Led Zeppelin guitarist Jimmy Page's band, The Firm, and been asked what it was like to be 'the new Robert Plant'. Talking about Queen, Rodgers said he remembered passing the band on the stairs of his management offices; Bad Company's manager Peter Grant had been interested in managing Queen. Elsewhere, he applauded Mercury's decision to stop taking his medication ('That takes some guts') and praised Queen's music ('They're almost up there with The Beatles'). But Rodgers was also quick to point out that he had a solo career to go back to.

Stepping away from the machine would take time. The Q+PR European tour was followed by eight UK arena dates. In July, a show at London's Hyde Park, where the group were to be joined by flamboyant UK rockers and Queen fans The Darkness, was postponed by a week after fears of a terrorist attack. Brian May revealed that John Deacon had been due to attend the gig, though only as an observer. 'John gave us his eternal blessing,' said Taylor. 'But you could say John kept his mystery . . . Though I don't know where he's keeping it right now.' Taylor's waggish aside could have referred to Deacon's recent run-in with the press. In January, the *Mail on Sunday* revealed the bassist's affair with a 25-year-old dancer he'd met in a London strip club. 'He suffered from depression after Freddie died,' suggested one old friend, 'and I'm not sure he ever got over it.' Naturally, Deacon refused to comment.

If Paul Rodgers had intended to return to his solo career, then he was forced to shelve any plans for the remainder of 2005. In October, Q+PR played three sold-out US dates, including the Hollywood Bowl. It was their first American tour under the Queen brand name since 1982. Billy Squier, their friend and support act on that last tour, was in the audience. 'Paul Rodgers is one of the all time great rock 'n' roll singers, and he brought it all to the stage . . . but ultimately they fell short of the mark. It was kind of a no-win situation, because no one can replace Freddie, and Freddie was just too big a part of Queen to be replaced.'

Meanwhile, EMI's old MD Bob Mercer was struck by how little had changed, despite Mercury's absence. Mercer had squired some of Queen around New Orleans during a night of Hallowe'en madness in 1978. But Queen always minded their manners. 'They used to call me "Mr Mercer" for God knows what reason,' he laughs. 'Years and years after I'd worked with them, I went to see them at the Hollywood Bowl with Paul Rodgers, and I bumped into Brian May in the elevator in the Chateau Marmont hotel . . . and what's the first thing he says? "Oh, hello, Mr Mercer."'

Encouraged by the sold-out shows, Q+PR returned to America for a further twenty-three dates the following spring. But not every date sold well, especially in some southern states where Queen's popularity had never been high. A Q+PR live album and DVD, *Return of the Champions*, put them in UK Top 20 but would do little in the US. Yet, despite these setbacks, there still seemed to be a genuine rapport between the players. The tour ended on a high. 'The last show we did was in Vancouver,' said Rodgers. 'Normally by the end, everybody is ready to go home, but we weren't. We'd just played what we all felt was the best gig on the tour. We were gobsmackingly together. We all turned around and said, "We have got to do something else." The next logical step was to go into the studio.'

■ ■ ■

'We couldn't become our own tribute band,' insists Roger Taylor. 'I don't want us to be thought of as a golden oldies act.' It is summer 2008 and Queen's drummer has taken a trip back to Queen's good old bad old days: wincing at a mention of his first solo album, *Fun in Space*, praising *The Game* and chuckling about high times in New Orleans and Munich. Now, though, he is ready to talk about Queen's future. 'If we were going to keep doing this,' he adds. 'We had to have some brand-new stuff to play.' On 5 September 2008, Queen + Paul Rodgers released the 'new stuff'. *The Cosmos Rocks* was the first album of new studio material to appear under the Queen name since *Innuendo*. In the great tradition of Queen albums, it had not come together easily.

No sooner had Rodgers stepped off the road with Queen than he had gone back out to play his own shows. Meanwhile, Brian May completed *Bang! The Complete History of the Universe*, a book written with astro-physicist Chris Lintott and astronomer Sir Patrick Moore ('Wow! A rock star who knows something about real stars,' gushed one review). At Moore's encouragement, May then went back to Imperial College, spending nine months conducting extra research to complete the PhD thesis he had abandoned thirty-three years earlier.

'I kept all my notes,' he told *The Times*, 'and was able to find them in my loft and start working on them again.' May would receive his PhD the following summer, firmly cementing his reputation as the world's most highly educated rock star. 'I am utterly amazed that Brian was able to do go back and do that,' says his old schoolfriend Dave Dilloway. 'To survive with your brain unscrambled after all those years in the rock industry is remarkable. He did try and explain radio velocities and cosmic dust to me over dinner, but I said, "I'm sorry, Brian, I have no idea what you're talking about ..."'

By summer of 2007, though, May, Taylor and Rodgers cleared their schedules to start work at Taylor's home studio. The most obvious difference between *The Cosmos Rocks* and every other Queen album was the absence of John Deacon. Had he been asked? 'If you call him, you don't always get an answer,' said Taylor. 'He's turned into a recluse.' 'Deakey doesn't speak to anyone, except Queen's accountant,' elaborated one unnamed source. 'He just wants to spend time with his family and play golf.' Instead, it fell to May and Rodgers to play bass.

On April 2008, Queen + Paul Rodgers broke cover to appear on *Al Murray's Happy Hour*, a TV chat show hosted by comedian Murray in the guise of his alter ego, the Pub Landlord. Queen purists winced at the sight of the trio in Murray's 'Green Room', where May told the host they 'were going to play something completely new'. They chose their next single, 'C-lebrity', which was still four months away from release. The song had a dizzying heavy metal riff and sounded just like a cross between Free and early Queen, but the lyrics – griping about the hollow concept of celebrity in the twenty-first century – suggested Queen were shooting at fish in a barrel. Viewers breathed a collective sigh of relief when the band got stuck into 'All Right Now', even with the Pub Landlord on shouty backing vocals.

'C-lebrity' was released as a single in August. 'It's to do with celebrity culture,' explained Taylor, who'd written the lyrics, 'the desperation to get your face on the telly.' In a world awash with rubbish reality TV shows, Taylor had a valid point. But his comment in *Classic Rock* magazine that 'It annoys me that there are so many famous, useless people,' sounded a little churlish. 'C-lebrity' made it to number 33, before disappearing. With the singles market now in terminal decline, this was no great shock. There was still the album to come . . .

Asked about the making of *The Cosmos Rocks*, Rodgers saluted his bandmates, while offering an outsider's view of Queen's working practices. 'Brian is a revelation when it comes to harmonies,' he said. 'He'd tell us he had an idea for a harmony, troop us into the studio, and there it is. It's like he'd been carrying the whole thing fully formed in his head.' Taylor, meanwhile, was reassuringly bullish: 'We know some people will moan, "Oh, Freddie's not on it!" Of course he's not, you dickhead. If they want to know why we're bothering to do this, it's because we're still alive.' May, on the other hand, was his usual cautious self, telling *Mojo* that while making the album 'there had been some arguments, where we all had to go off and have a think.'

The Cosmos Rocks turned out to be a strangely inoffensive rock album. 'Say It's Not True' had been played on the Q+PR tour, and a live version had already released as a free download in 2007. It was the kind of pomp-and-circumstance ballad on which Queen's reputation had been built. 'Surf's Up (School's Out)' sounded like a vintage Roger Taylor rocker, but, despite being better than the hackneyed opening track, 'Cosmos Rockin', was buried away at the back end of the album. There was another welcome flashback to the past with the 'boom-boom cha!' of 'We Will Rock You' reprised on 'Still Burnin'.

Rodgers had already been playing two of the songs on his solo tour. 'Warboys (A Prayer For Peace)' and the Bad Company copycat ballad 'Voodoo'. They sounded like Paul Rodgers songs with Brian May playing guitar and Roger Taylor on drums. What they didn't sound like was Queen. Once again, the name was the sticking point. Even Rodgers seemed to think so: 'I was as wary of calling it Queen as anyone else. At first I thought we would use May, Taylor, Rodgers, like Crosby, Stills & Nash . . .' The trouble was, Queen albums had always dealt in the unexpected – white funk, gospel, disco, ragtime jazz – however much that may have upset some fans and certain band members. *The Cosmos Rocks* lacked the unexpected. Taylor's statement that we're 'doing this because we're still alive' was heartfelt and honest. But both he and May were unavoidably in competition with their own past.

'The worst thing on earth would be for it [*The Cosmos Rocks*] to come out with a whimper,' said Taylor. Yet that was exactly what happened. The album spent a fortnight on the UK charts, peaking at number 5, before slipping away. It was a similar story in Europe where it made the Top 10 in Germany, Holland and France (even reaching number 2 in Estonia) before disappearing. In America, it scraped to number 47, a better showing, at least, than *Made in Heaven*. But this was not the comeback of all comebacks.

In the press, reviews ranged from *Mojo*'s prudent thumbs-up ('Without Freddie's decorative flourishes, the onus is on straight-shooting heavy rock') to the *Guardian* decrying *The Cosmos Rocks* as terrible, but not as terrible as the musical, *We Will Rock You*. But EMI were also guilty of a very poor campaign. At the time, like much of the record industry, the company was in a state of flux. EMI had been bought by private equity firm, Terra Firma, in 2007; a move that had prompted Paul McCartney to leave the label in protest. A year later, Tony Wadsworth, EMI's chief executive of twenty-five years followed suit. Queen's new record seemed to get lost along the way. 'I think the record company did an absolutely shockingly bad job on our album,' grumbled Taylor later.

There would be no follow-up single to 'C-lebrity' and no more TV appearances. Instead, the band did what they did best, and went back on the road. Queen + Paul Rodgers would spend three months on tour, playing arenas across Europe. Tracks from *The Cosmos Rocks* were thrown in alongside the standards. Rodgers gamely told the press that 'Killer Queen' was one of the few Queen songs they couldn't do 'as the harmonies are so spot on'. Some wished he'd added 'Another One Bites the Dust' to that list. Rodgers struggled manfully with the song, but it just didn't suit him. Others noticed that he kept forgetting the words to 'Radio Ga Ga'. Yet with a setlist that now featured Free's 'Wishing Well' and Bad Company's 'Seagull' alongside 'Hammer to Fall', 'Crazy Little Thing Called Love', 'Love Of My Life', 'Bohemian Rhapsody' . . . it was a crowd-pleasing greatest hits set, even if Queen + Paul Rodgers had become what they'd always feared: their own tribute band.

In November, the tour headed to the southern hemisphere for five shows in Chile, Buenos Aries, São Paulo and Rio de Janeiro. On 8 March 1981, Queen had played their first South American show at Buenos Aires' Vélez Sársfield. May had played there since with his own group, but this was Queen. The shows were a triumph, but at a press conference on Argentinian TV, it seemed that the questions were only directed at returning heroes Brian May and Roger Taylor, not Paul Rodgers. 'Paul would be Freddie's choice to sing with us,' Brian May told one TV reporter. 'He would be laughing . . . I think he is laughing.' 'Freddie had a great time here,' added Taylor with a knowing grin. 'He'd be very pleased to see us here now . . .' 'He was great with the one-liners, Freddie . . .' chipped in May. With their new singer standing just feet away, both men looked and sounded wistfully nostalgic for their absent friend.

Mercury once said, 'We'll just carry on until one of us drops dead, or is just replaced. I think if I suddenly left, they'd have the mechanism to replace me.' Laughing, he'd added, 'Not so easy to replace me, huh?' Perhaps not. With the end of the tour in South America, the rumours began that Queen + Paul Rodgers were no more. 'I don't know where anyone got that idea,' protested Brian May, writing on his website. 'We just need a rest.' In April 2009, though, Rodgers informed *Billboard* that his tenure with Queen was over. It was, he insisted, an amicable split. The singer had now signed up for another reunion, with Bad Company. 'It was never meant to be a permanent arrangement,' he said. 'I think we made a huge success of it actually.'

Before the Q+PR tour, Brian May had admitted: 'Part of me is saying, "Why not stay at home and enjoy the life you've created?"' But this is what I do, and who knows how much longer we'll be able to do it?' Back at home, though, May had a new non-musical project to be getting on with. His next book, *A Village Lost and Found*, was due for publication. Co-written with art conservator Elena Vidal, it explored the work of nineteenth-century photographer T.R. Williams, a specialist in stereoscopic images. The guitarist had, it transpired, spent years trying to identify the village that featured in many of Williams's pictures. It was a painstaking labour of love. While the press marvelled at this rock star's most un-rock-starry pastime, to those that knew May's working methods it made complete and perfect sense. As their old engineer Gary Langan recalled, 'I can tell tales of Brian May spending a week on a guitar solo.'

Away from Queen and his scientific research, the vegetarian May was also busy campaigning against fox hunting and badger culling, firing off angry broadsides to a wide array of a wide array of journalists and MPs, and expounding his views on his website, where the comments often made for a compulsive, if on occasions bemusing read ('I'm not an extremist . . . but I've decided my guitar straps won't be leather any more').

November 2009 saw the appearance of *Queen's Absolute Greatest*: the hits, repackaged yet again, complete with a second disc on which May and Taylor ruminated about the songs. They proved themselves to be witty, self-deprecating commentators, the ice in their glasses chinking in the background, as they shared fond memories of Freddie Mercury and the many misadventures they'd had along the way.

Contrary as ever, the duo seemed to forget the subject of their last single, 'C-lebrity', to appear on both the reality TV music show, *The X-Factor*, and its US counterpart, *American Idol*. 'I've not always been positive about shows like this,' countered May. 'But there is no doubt that it offers a door to some real genuine talent along the way.' On *American Idol*, they performed 'We Are the Champions' with the show's finalists. But it was Adam Lambert, the eventual runner-up, who truly impressed them. 'He's the most phenomenal singer,' said Taylor, 'and we would like to do something with him.' There was speculation that the 27-year-old Lambert would become Queen's next singer, though nothing has come of it. In the meantime, May and Taylor threw themselves into tirelessly promoting *We Will Rock You*, as the jukebox musical opened in new territories around the world. In summer 2010, Queen left EMI Records after thirty-nine years. With 300 million album sales worldwide, and their back catalogue again up for grabs, all the signs pointed towards a high-profile and highly lucrative fortieth anniversary in 2011.

■ ■ ■

In the spring of 1964, Farrokh Bulsara and his family had arrived from Zanzibar in the West London suburb of Feltham. Almost thirty-five years later, in the winter of 2009, Queen fans, inquisitive locals, Freddie Mercury's mother, Jer Bulsara and Brian May gathered in Feltham's anonymous shopping centre to watch the unveiling of a memorial to Freddie Mercury.

There was so something both incongruous yet strangely fitting about the tribute. The square plaque, depicting a red, white and gold star, set into the ground inside the unprepossessing mall, may have honoured one of the most famous rock stars that had ever lived, but it was also a reminder of the unremarkable, thoroughly suburban world from which he'd come. The plaque acknowledged the four years Farrokh Bulsara had spent in Feltham, after which he'd fled the coop for a nomadic lifestyle, moving between houses and flats in London, leaving Farrokh and even Fred Bulsara Behind, and becoming, to the world at large, 'FREDDIE MERCURY, MUSICIAN, SINGER AND SONGWRITER.'

'Freddie, you pursued your dream,' said Brian May at the ceremony. Through Mercury, May and the rest of Queen had also been able to pursue theirs. Yet while many of their heroes and contemporaries could never survive the loss of such a crucial band member, Queen's resolve to carry on marks them out as astonishingly and uniquely resilient.

'We'll never stand still,' said Roger Taylor recently. 'Queen is still alive in Brian and myself. We will do the best we can.' Whether performing with fellow rock stars, talent-show hopefuls, the cast of their own worldwide musical or commissioning actor Sacha Baron Cohen to star as Freddie Mercury in a forthcoming Queen biopic, the intrepid duo shows little sign of stopping. As long as there is someone willing to take the wheel, the juggernaut that is Queen in the twenty-first Century will continue to roll.

Acknowledgements

Very special thanks to my wife Claire and son Matthew for too many lost weekends; the ever-patient Graham Coster and all at Aurum Press, particulary Lucy Smith for picture research; my agent Rupert Heath and friends and co-conspirators, including Phil Alexander, Martin Aston, Dave Brolan, Dave Everley, Pat Gilbert, Mark Hodkinson, Dave Ling, Kris Needs and Peter Makowski.

This book draws on my own interviews with Brian May and Roger Taylor conducted between 1998 and 2008 for *Q* and *Mojo* magazines. Also my own interviews with and contributions from: John Anthony, Mark Ashton, Judy Astley, Louis Austin, Mike Bersin, Douglas Bogie, Mick Bolton, Caroline Boucher, John Brough, Rick Cassman, Tony Catignani, Chris Chesney, Patrick Connolly, Geoff Daniel, Dave Dilloway, Rik Evans, Brian Fanning, Fish, Morgan Fisher, Nigel Foster, John Garnham, Christian Gastaldello, Alan Hill, Peter Hince, Paul Humberstone, Ian Hunter, Gary Langan, Geoffrey Latter, Renos Lavithis, Reinhold Mack, Aubrey Malden, Mark Malden, Fred Mandel, Alan Mair, Laurie Mansworth, Bob Mercer (RIP), Barry Mitchell, Adrian Morrish, Keith Mulholland, Bruce Murray, Jack Nelson, Martin Nelson, Gary Numan, Chris O'Donnell, Denis O'Regan, Jeff 'Dicken' Pain, Ray Pearl, Rick Penrose, Glen Phimister, Mick Rock, Paul Rodgers, Steven Rosen, Subash Shah, Norman Sheffield, Brian Southall, Ken Scott, Chris Smith, Billy Squier, Ray Staff, Chris Stevenson, John Taylor, Ken Testi, Richard Thompson, Andy Turner, Kingsley Ward, Susan Whitall, Terry Yeadon and Richard Young. Many thanks to everyone that spared the time to talk to me. Extra special thanks to: Adrian Morrish, Dave Dilloway, Peter Hince and Mark Malden (author of the currently unpublished book, *Freddie Mercury: From the Inside Out*) for going the extra distance on my behalf.

Numerous magazine articles and interviews proved invaluable during the writing of this book, including many published in *Q, Mojo, Classic Rock, Uncut, Record Collector, New Musical Express, Melody Maker, Sounds, Disc & Music Echo, Creem* and *Rolling Stone*. For the best online resource for Queen information, go to: www.queenonline.com, www.queenzone.com, www.queenconcerts.com, www.queenarchive.com, www.queen cuttings. com, www.brianmay.com and Rupert White's impeccable blog, queenincornwall. Thanks to all webmasters for their help.

Select Bibliography

Queen & Freddie Mercury books

Evans, David and David Minns. *This Is the Real Life ... Freddie Mercury: His Friends And Colleagues Pay Tribute* (Britannia, 1992)

Freestone, Peter and David Evans. *Freddie Mercury: An Intimate Memoir by the Man Who Knew Him Best* (Omnibus, 2001)

Gunn, Jacky and Jim Jenkins. *Queen: As It Began* (BAC Publishing, 1992)

Hodkinson, Mark. *Queen the Early Years* (Omnibus, 1995)

Hutton, Jim. *Mercury And Me* (Bloomsbury, 1994)

Jackson, Laura. *Brian May: The Definitive Biography* (Piatkus, 1998)

Jones, Lesley-Ann. *Freddie Mercury: The Definitive Biography* (Coronet, 1998)

Purvis, Georg. *Queen: The Complete Works* (Reynolds & Hearn, 2007)

Rock, Mick. *Classic Queen* (Omnibus, 2007)

Sutcliffe, Phil. *Queen: The Ultimate Illustrated History of the Crown Kings of Rock* (Voyageur, 2009)

Background

Buckley, David. *Strange Fascination: David Bowie – The Definitive Story* (Virgin, 2005)

Buckley, David. *The Thrill of It All: The Story of Bryan Ferry and Roxy Music* (Andre Deutsch, 2004)

Elton, Ben. *We Will Rock You* (Carlton 2004)

Gorman, Paul. *The Look – Adventures in Pop and Rock Fashion* (Sanctuary 2001)

Haring, Bruce. *Off the Record: Ruthless Days and Reckless Nights inside the Music Industry* (Carol Publishing, 1996)

Kent, Nick. *Apathy for the Devil* (Faber, 2010)

Lydon, John and Keith & Kent Zimmerman. *Rotten: No Irish, No Blacks, No Dogs* (Picador, 2008)

McDermott, John and Eddie Kramer. *Hendrix: Setting the Record Straight* (Little, Brown, 1993)

Norman, Philip. *Sir Elton – The Definitive Biography of Elton John* (Pan, 2002)

Rock, Mick. *Glam: An Eyewitness Account* (Omnibus, 2005)

Van der Vat, Dan and Michelle Whitby. *Eel Pie Island* (Francis Lincoln, 2009)

Index